The Constitution and Governance in Cameroon

This book provides a systematic analysis of the major structural and institutional governance mechanisms in Cameroon, critically analysing the constitutional and legislative texts on Cameroon's semi-presidential system, the electoral system, the legislature, the judiciary, the Constitutional Council and the National Commission on Human Rights and Freedoms.

The author offers an assessment of the practical application of the laws regulating constitutional institutions and how they impact on governance. To lay the groundwork for the analysis, the book examines the historical, constitutional and political context of governance in Cameroon, from independence and reunification in 1960–1961, through the adoption of the 1996 Constitution, to more recent events including the current Anglophone crisis. Offering novel insights on new institutions such as the Senate and the Constitutional Council and their contribution to the democratic advancement of Cameroon, the book also provides the first critical assessment of the legislative provisions carving out a special autonomy status for the two Anglophone regions of Cameroon and considers how far these provisions go to resolve the Anglophone Problem.

This book will be of interest to scholars of public law, legal history and African politics.

Laura-Stella E. Enonchong is a Senior Lecturer at De Montfort University, UK.

Routledge Studies on Law in Africa

Series Editor: Makau W. Mutua

The Constitution and Governance in Cameroon
Laura-Stella E. Enonchong

The Constitution and Governance in Cameroon

Laura-Stella E. Enonchong

Routledge
Taylor & Francis Group
LONDON AND NEW YORK

First published 2021
by Routledge
2 Park Square, Milton Park, Abingdon, Oxon OX14 4RN

and by Routledge
605 Third Avenue, New York, NY 10017

First issued in paperback 2022

Routledge is an imprint of the Taylor & Francis Group, an informa business

Publisher's Note
The publisher has gone to great lengths to ensure the quality of this reprint but points out that some imperfections in the original copies may be apparent.

British Library Cataloguing-in-Publication Data
A catalogue record for this book is available from the British Library.

Library of Congress Cataloging-in-Publication Data
A catalog record has been requested for this book

ISBN: 978-1-138-49310-0 (hbk)
ISBN: 978-0-3676-2732-4 (pbk)
ISBN: 978-1-351-02886-8 (ebk)

DOI: 10.4324/9781351028868

Typeset in Baskerville
by MPS Limited, Dehradun

For Mumsy Etombi

Contents

List of Abbreviations

AAC	All Anglophone Conference
ARCAM	Assemblée Représentative du Cameroun
ALCAM	Assemblée Législative du Cameroun
CACSC	Cameroon Anglophone Civil Society Consortium
CAM	Cameroon Anglophone Movement
CCLR	Cameroon Common Law Report
CDU	Cameroon Democratic Union
CHRC	Cameroon Human Rights Commission
CMC	Cameroon Music Corporation
CNU	Cameroon National Union
CONAC	National Anti-Corruption Commission
CPDM	Cameroon People's Democratic Movement
CWU	Cameroon Welfare Union
DSC	Divisional Supervisory Commissions
EI	L'exception D'inconstitutionnalité
ELECAM	Elections Cameroon
ENAM	National School of Administration and Magistracy
ERRC	Electoral Register Revision Commission
FWCM	Free West Cameroon Movement
GCE	General Certificate of Education
HJC	Higher Judicial Council
HRC	United Nations Human Rights Committee
ICCPR	International Covenant on Civil and Political Rights
ICJ	International Court of Justice
JEUCAFRA	Jeunesse Camerounaise Francaise
JOO	Judicial Organisation Ordinance
KNC	Kamerun National Congress
KNDP	Kamerun National Democratic Party
LPC	Local Polling Commissions
MRC	Movement for the Renaissance of Cameroon
MP	Member of Parliament
NCFCV	National Commission for the Final Counting of Votes
NCHRF	National Commission on Human Rights and Freedom

NEO	National Elections Observatory
NLC	Nigerian Legislative Council
NUDP	National Union for Democracy and Progress
OHADA	Organisation for the Harmonisation of Business Law in Africa
OMJ	Decree Organising the Ministry of Justice
PIC	Public Independent Conciliator
PM	Prime Minister
QPC	Question Prioritaire de Constitutionnalité
RA	Regional Assembly
REC	Regional Executive Council
SCACUF	Southern Cameroons Ambazonia Consortium United Front
SCAPO	Southern Cameroons Peoples Organisation
SCNC	Southern Cameroons National Council
SCYL	Southern Cameroons Youth League
SDF	Social Democratic Front
SDO	Senior Divisional Officer
SOM	Statute of the Magistracy
TCCM	Technical Committee on Constitutional Matters
UC	Union Camerounaişe
UPC	Union des Populations du Cameroun
UNHCR	United Nations High Commissioner for Refugees
VCIDC	Voter Card Issuance and Distribution Commission

Table of Cases

African Commission on Human and Peoples' Rights

Civil Liberties Organization v Nigeria ACHPR Communication No. 129/94 (1995)

Katangese Peoples' Congress v Zaire, Comunication No. 75/92, 1HRL 174(ACHPR 1995)

Kevin Mgwanga Gunme and 13 Ors v Cameroon, Communication No. 266/2003 ACHPR (05/2009), Ex.CL/529(XV) Annex 4

Botswana

Letsweletse Motshidiemang v Attorney General [2019] MAHGB000591-16(High Court of Botswana at Gaborone)

Cameroon

Akiangan Fombin Sebastian v Foto Joseph & Others, Suit No. HCK/3/96 of 6 January 2000 (unreported)

Albert Chidi v The People, Suit No. LM/98/M/2002 (unreported)

Benjamin Itoe v Joseph Ncho, Suite No. BCA/1/81 of 13 July 1981 (unreported)

Bonu Innocent v Bakongo Simon (1997) 1 CCLR 142

Cameroon Music Corporation (CMC) v Ministry of Culture, Judgment No. 192/2011/CS/CA of 7 September 2011 (unreported)

D. S. Oyebowale v Company Commander of Gendarmerie for Fako. Suit No. HCF/0040/HB/09 (unreported)

Eglise Presbytérienne du Cameroun, Ordonnace No. 02/CS/CA of 26 October 1994 (unreported)

Eitel Mouelle Kouala v République Fédéral du Cameroun, Arrêt No. 178/CFJ/CAY of 29 March 1972

Etengeneng J. T. v The Governor of South West Province (1998) 1CCLR 9

James v Tchoussongou (2001) 1 CCLR 730

Jesco Manga Williams v Chantier Naval (2005) 2 CCLR 99

Kouang Guillaume v État du Cameroun, Jugement No. 53/CS/CA of 26 June 1980 (unreported)

Kouang Guillaum v État du Cameroun, Judgment No. 66 ADD/CS/CA of 31 May 1979 (unreported)

Mbarga Symphorien v Etat du Cameroun, Judgment No. 29/CS/CA of 3 May 1990

Michel Zouhair Fadoul v Omaïs Kassim et Société Omaïs Selecta Sarl, Arrêt No. 21/Civ/CS/CJ of 15 July 2010 (ohadata J-12-242)

Mvogo Jean-Marie v État du Cameroun, Judgment No. 1203/CS/CA/1999–2000 (unreported)

Namondo Makake v Bernard O. Bilai Suit No: HCF/164/IR/04-05 (unreported)

Nji Ignatius v The People, HCF/22M/03-04 (unreported)

Nve Ndongo v Ngaba Victor, Decision of the Full Bench of the Federal Supreme Court No. 10 of 17 October

Senior Divisional Officer (SDO) Oku v *Shey Ndifon & Oku Rural Radio Association*, Suit No. HCB/05M/2003–2004 (unreported)

Social Democratic Front (SDF) v État du Cameroun, Ordonance No. 01/OSE/CCA/CS/2009 (unreported)

Société Forestière de la Sanaga v État du Cameroun, Arrêt No. 5/CFJ/AP of 15 March 1967 (unreported)

The People v Nya Henry & 4 Others (2005) 1CCLR, 61

Wakai & 172 Others v The People, 1997, 1CCLR, 127

Walter Numvi, Che Nji & Kongnso Lawrence v The People, Suit No. CANWR/MA/3C/2015, SLR 6[2017] 10

Woundjou Samuel v Ministère Public & Kamdem Emillienne, Arrêt No. 102 of 20 November 2014 (unreported)

Cameroon – Constitutional Council

Decision No. 02/SCCL/G/SG/CC of 12 February 2019

Decision No. 01/SCCL/G/SG/CC of 10 January 2019

Decision No. 30/CE/CC/2018 of 18 October 2018

Decision No. 028/G/SRCER/CC/2018 of 17 October 2018

Decision No. 28/CE/CC/2018 of 16 October 2018

Decision No. 024/CE/CC/2018 of 16 October 2018

Decision No. 001/G/SCT/CC/2018 of 30 July 2018

Decision No. 09/CE/CC/2018 of 3 April 2018

Decision No. 008/CE/CC/2018 of 3 April 2018

Court of Justice of the European Union

Case C-509/18 PF (Prosecutor General of Lithuania)

Case C-508/18 OG (Public Prosecutor's office of Lübeck)

Case C-82/19 PPU PI (Public Prosecutor's office of Zwickau)

European Court of Human Rights

A v United Kingdom (35373/97) (2003) 36 E.H.R.R. 51

France

Decision 2013-156 PDR of 4 July 2013

Decision CC No. 44–71 (1971)

Syndicat Général des Ingénieurs-conseils & *Administration des Douanes v Société des Cafés Jacques Vabre*, Judgment of 24 May 1975, CC (chamber mixte), 1975, D.S. Jur, (Fr) 497

CE Ass. 20 October 1989, Nicolo, Rec. Lebon, 190

India

Kesavanda Baharati v State of Kerala (1973) 4. S.C.C. 225

Nigeria

Gunme & Ors v Attorney General of the Federal Republic of Nigeria. Suit No. FHC/ABJ/CS/30/2002

Sisiku Ayuk Tabe & 11 Ors v The National Security Adviser & Anor (Suit No./FHC/ABJ/CS/85/2018)

Wilfred Tassang & 50 Ors v The National Security Adviser & Anor (Suit No./FHC/ABJ/CS/147/2018)

United Kingdom

M v Home Office & another [1994] 1AC377

United Nations Human Rights Committee

Toonen v Australia, Communication No. 488/192 U.N.Doc. (CPR/C/50/D) 488/1992 (1994)

Young v Australia Communication No. 94/2000 U.N.Doc. (CCPR/C/78/D/941/2000)

United States of America

Hamdan v Rumsfeld, 126 S. Ct 2749, 2798 (2006)

Zambia

Chiluba v Attorney General, 2003 [ZMSC] 4

Table of Legislation

Benin

Constitution of the Republic of Benin 1990

Law No. 91-009 of 4 March 1991 relating to the Constitutional Court as amended by Law N0. 91-009 of 31 May 2001

Botswana

Constitution of the Republic of Botswana 1966 (as amended in 2006)

Cameroon

British Cameroons Ordinance No. 5 of 1924

Cameroons under British Administration Order-in-Council N° 1621, 1923

Constitution of *La République du Cameroun* 1960

Constitution of Cameroon (Federal) 1961

Constitution of Cameroon (Unitary) 1972

Constitution of Cameroon 1996 (as amended)

Decree No. 2019/3179/PM of 2 September 2019 to Grant the Status of Economic Disaster Areas to the Far-North, North-West and South-West Regions

Decree No. 2018/5190/PM of 22 June 2018 appointing officials at the Ministry of Basic Education

Decree No. 2018/242 of 12 April 2018 relating to the Appointment of Senators

Decree No. 2017/013 of 23 January 2017 on the creation of the National Commission for Bilingualism and Multiculturalism

Decree No. 2016/072 of 15 February 2016 relating to certain aspects of the Social Security System Managed by the National Social Insurance Fund

Decree No. 2013/149 of 8 May 2013 Relating to the Appointment of Senators

Decree No. 2012/119 of 15 March 2012 to set up Administrative Courts

Decree No. 2011/412 of 9 December 2011 relating to the Organisation of the Presidency of the Republic

Decree No. 2011/408 of 9 December 2011 to Organise the Government

Decree No. 2010/384 of 23 December 2010 on the creation, organisation and functioning of the National Civic Service Agency for Participation in Development

Decree No. 2008/463 of 30 December 2008 appointing Electoral Commission members
Decree No. 2007/003 of 13 July 2007 establishing the National Civic Service for Participation in Development
Decree No. 2006/088 of 11 March 2006 relating to the Creation, Organisation and Functioning of the National Anti-Corruption Commission
Decree No. 2005/122 of 15 April 2005 Organising the Ministry of Justice
Decree No. 95/048 of 8 March 1995 on the Status of the Magistracy
Decree No. 90/1459 of 8 November 1990 to set up the National Commission on Human Rights and Freedoms
Decree No. 72/270 of 2 June Promulgating the Constitution of the United Republic of Cameroon
Law No. 2019/024 of 24 December 2019 to Institute the General Code of Regional and Local Authorities
Law No. 2019/019 of 24 December 2019 on the Promotion of Official Languages in Cameroon
Law No. 2019/014 of 19 July 2019 relating to the Establishment, Organisation and Functioning of the Cameroon Human Rights Commission
Law No. 2019/005 of 25 April 2019 to amend some provisions of Law No. 2012/001 of 19 April relating to the Electoral Code
Law No. 2018/012 of 11 July 2018 Relating to the Fiscal Regime of the State and other Public Entities
Law No. 2018/011 of 11 July 2018 to Lay Down the Cameroon Code of Transparency and Good Governance in Public Finance Management
Law No. 2017/14 of 12 July 2017 to amend and supplement some provisions of Law No. 2006/16 of 29 December 2006 to lay down the Organisation and Functioning of the Supreme Court.
Law No. 2017/012 of 12 July 2017 to lay down the Code of Military Justice
Law No. 2016/011 of 27 October 2016 to amend and supplement certain provisions of Law No. 2013/006 of 10 June 2013 on the Standing Orders of the Senate
Law No. 2016/007 of 12 July 2016 relating to the Penal Code
Law No. 2014/028 of 14 December 2014 on the Repression of Acts of Terrorism
Law No. 2014/016 of 9 September 2014 to amend and supplement certain provisions of Law No. 73/1 of 8 June 1973 on the Standing Orders of the National Assembly
Law No. 2013/006 of 10 June 2013 on the Standing Orders of the Senate
Law No. 2012/001 of 19 April 2012, relating to the Electoral Code (Electoral Code)
Law No. 2011/28 of 14 December 2011 relating to the creation of the Special Criminal Court
Law No. 2009/011 of 10 July 2009 on the Financial Regime of Regional and Local Authorities

Law No. 2008/001 of 14 April 2008 to amend and supplement some provisions of Law No. 96/6 of 18 January 1996 to amend the Constitution of 2 June 1972
Law No. 2007/001 of 19 April 2007 to institute a Judge in Charge of Litigation Related to the Execution of Judgments and Lay Down Conditions for the Enforcement in Cameroon of Foreign Court Decisions, Public Acts and Arbitral Awards
Law No. 2006/022 of 29 December 2006 on the Organisation and Functioning of Administrative Courts
Law No. 2006/017 of 29 December 2006, to Lay Down the Organisation, Duties and Functioning of Regional Audit Courts
Law No. 2006/016 of 29 December 2006 on the organisation of the Supreme Court
Law No. 2006/015 of 29 December 2006 on the organisation of the Judiciary
Law No. 2006/011 of 29 December 2006 on the organisation of the Electoral Commission
Law No. 2006/001 of 25 April 2006 relating to the Declaration of Assets and Property
Law No. 2004/019 of 22 July 2004 to lay down Rules Applicable to Regions
Law No. 2004/018 of 22 July 2004 to lay down Rules Applicable to Councils
Law No. 2004/017 of 22 July 2004 on the Orientation of Decentralisation
Law No. 2004/005 of 21 April 2004 relating to the Status of Constitutional Council Membership
Law No. 2004/004 of 21 April 2004 on the Organisation and Functioning of the Constitutional Council
Law No. 2000/016 of 19 December 2000 to set up a National Elections Observatory
Law No. 96/12 of 5 August 1996 on the Framework Law on Environmental Management
Law No. 90/60 of 19 December 1990 to set up and organise the State Security Court
Law No. 90/056 of 19 December 2019 on Political Parties
Law No. 90/055 of 19 December 1990 on Public Meetings and Processions
Law No. 90/54 of 19 December 1990 on the Maintenance of Law and Order
Law No. 90/053 of 19 December 1990 on Freedom of Association
Law No. 90/052 of 19 December 1990 on the Freedom of Social Communication
Law No. 90/47 of 19 December 1990 relating to the State of Emergency
Law No. 84/1 of 4 February 1984 to amend and supplement some provisions of the 1972 Constitution
Law No. 82/14 of 26 November 1982 relating to the Higher Judicial Council
Law No. 73/1 of 8 June 1973 on the Standing Orders of the National Assembly
Law No. 67/LF/1of 12 June 1967 Introducing the Cameroonian Penal Code
Loi Cadres 1956

Ordinance No. 2018/002 of 4 June 2018 to Amend and Complete Certain Provisions of Law No. 2017/021 of 20 December 2017 relating to the 2018 Finance Law of the Republic of Cameroon
Ordinance No. 72/12 of 26 August 1972 Relating to the Immunity of Members of the National Assembly
Southern Cameroons High Court Law 1955

Democratic Republic of Congo

Constitution of the Democratic Republic of Congo 2005
Law No. 08/013 of 2008 on the Congolese *Conseil Supérior de la Magistrature*

France

Constitution of the Fifth French Republic 1958
Loi Organique No. 2009-1523 of 10 December 2009 on the application of art 61-1 of the French Constitution
Loi Organique No. 2010-830 of 22 July 2010 on the application of article 65 of the French Constitution

Ghana

Constitution of the Republic of Ghana 1992

Kenya

Constitution of Kenya 2010

Nigeria

Constitution of the Federal Republic of Nigeria 1999

South Africa

Constitution of the Republic of South Africa 1996

Tanzania

Acts of Union of Tanganyika and Zanzibar, 25 April 1964, Act No. 22 of 1964 (Cap. 557 of the Laws)
The United Republic (Declaration of Name) Act of 1964, Act No. 61 of 1964 (Cap.578 of the Laws)

International Treaties and Agreements

Convention against Torture and Other Cruel, Inhuman or Degrading Treatment or Punishment (adopted 10 December 1984, entered into force 26 June 1987) 1465 UNTS 85 (CAT)
International Covenant on Civil and Political Rights 1966 (adopted 16 December 1966, entered into force 23 March 1976) 999 UNTS 171 (ICCPR)
Treaty of Versailles 1919
United Nations Charter (adopted 26 June1945, entered into force 24 October 1945) 1 UNTS XVI
Universal Declaration of Human Rights (adopted 10 December 1948 UNGA Res 217 A(III) (UDHR)

Regional Instruments

African Charter on Human and Peoples' Rights (adopted 27 June 1981, entered into force 21 October 1986) (1982) 21 ILM 58 (African Charter)
European Convention for the Protection of Human Rights and Fundamental Freedoms 4 November 1950, ETS 5; 213 UNTS 221
Treaty on the Harmonisation of Business Law in Africa, 17 October 1993

Other Regional and International Instruments

Principles relating to the status of National Human Rights Institutions (Paris Principles) (adopted 20 December 1993) UNGA Res 48/134

Others

Mandate and Trusteeship Agreements for Cameroon

British Mandate for the Cameroons as confirmed and defined by the Council of the League of Nations London, 20 July 1922

French Mandate for Cameroon as confirmed and defined by the Council of the League of Nations London, 20 July 1922

Trusteeship Agreement for the Territory of the Cameroons under British Administration (UNGA Approved on 13 December 1946) 118 UNTS 135

Trusteeship Agreement for the Territory of the Cameroons under French Administration (UNGA Approved on 13 December 1946) 119 UNTS 135

UN General Assembly Resolutions on Cameroon

UN General Assembly Resolution 2013(XXVI) of 31 May 1960

UN General Assembly Resolution 1352(XIV), 16 October 1959

UN General Assembly Resolution 1350(XIII), 13 March 1959

UN General Assembly Resolution 1349(XIII), 13 March 1959

Preface

This book provides a systematic analysis of the governance system of Cameroon within the framework of the Constitution. It scrutinises the institutional structures established by the Constitution and other legislative instruments and assesses the ways in which they shape and construct contemporary governance in Cameroon. The analysis is deployed through a historical exploration of constitutional developments and the contemporary contextual application of the Constitution. The book examines the operational dynamics of key institutions such as the executive, the legislature, the judiciary, the National Electoral Commission, the Constitutional Council and the National Commission on Human Rights and Freedoms. It explores the extent to which these institutions have been designed to address or influence contemporary governance challenges. It further provides an in-depth original analysis of more recent features in the governance landscape such as the Senate, the upper legislative chamber that has only been in existence since 2013 and the even more recent Constitutional Council established in 2018. Both institutions were provided for in the 1996 Constitution and their role was deemed vital to the democratisation process underpinning the adoption of that Constitution. The book analyses and assesses the influence of these institutions on the constitutional and democratic governance of Cameroon.

One prominent feature that permeates discourse on constitutional governance in post-colonial states is the recognition of minority identities. Cameroon has grappled with that issue in relation to the recognition of the English-speaking minorities – the Anglophone problem. The book provides a comprehensive analysis of that problem tracing its historical origins from the immediate post-independence constitutional history of Cameroon to more contemporary legislative developments. It explores alternative narratives geared at resolving the Anglophone problem within the framework of the Constitution. It further provides an original in-depth analysis of the recent 2019 legislative provisions establishing a special autonomy status for the minority English-speaking North-West and South-West Regions.

The book draws on comparative approaches to constitutional governance in common law and civil law-oriented jurisdictions in Africa and Europe to highlight the fundamental idiosyncrasies in the understanding and the application of constitutional concepts in Cameroon. The book will be a valuable resource for scholars of public law, legal history and African politics.

The publication of this book would not have been possible without the assistance of the editorial team at Routledge. I would like to thank, in particular, Leanne Hinves, Henry Strang, Alison Macfarlane and Neema Sangmo Lama. Many colleagues, friends and family supported me throughout this project. I am particularly grateful to my Head of School at De Montfort University, Mr Tim Hillier, for his encouragement when I first mentioned the prospects of writing this book and for his support throughout, especially in facilitating a funded research trip to Cameroon, which was vital in completing many chapters of this book. Special thanks also go to my 'roomie' and dear friend Dr Oludara Akanmidu and Dr Irene Antonopoulos, Dr Simisola Akintoye and Dr Ohio Omiunu for their support and encouragement. I owe a debt of gratitude to Professor Andrew Williams who encouraged me to write this book and always provided his help and advice. I am also grateful to family friends who have supported me in different ways, notably Mrs Beryl Shortland, Mr Robert and Mrs Marian Matthews, Mrs Benic Sarr and Mrs Renée Nfor.

My family also deserves special thanks, particularly mumsy Kate Tumenta for holding the fort in Cameroon allowing me the psychological space to pursue this project, my sister and star cheerleader Mrs Marion Titanji for cheering me on to the finish line and my sister-in-law Dora Wotany for facilitating my research during my trip to Cameroon. I am immensely grateful to my husband Nelson and our children, Ebangha, Ngowo and Egbe Jr for providing me with the love and enthusiasm required to undertake a project of this nature. Immense gratitude also goes to mum, Etombi Tabe, for her strength and tenacity in enduring life with much grace even in the midst of adversity. It is to her that this book is dedicated.

Introduction

In the last three decades, law, politics and governance in Cameroon have been characterised by change and continuity. The decade of the 1990s was a pivotal moment in the democratic governance and political advancement of Cameroon, marking a period of constitutional, legislative, political and institutional change. These developments were purportedly intended, among other things, to introduce a paradigm shift from a colonial heritage of autocracy to a contextualised, progressive system of democratic governance. The climax of these developments was the promulgation of the 1996 Constitution. That Constitution marked a watershed in the constitutional and political history of Cameroon as it introduced features of a modern constitutional system. It made provision for a purportedly more balanced separation of powers system between the executive, the legislature and the judiciary. In that respect, a semi-presidential executive system was consolidated to mitigate the overconcentration of powers in the President, a feature of the old dispensation. The implication was that executive power was shared between the President and the Prime Minister (PM). Concerning the legislature, a Senate was introduced as the upper house of parliament to enhance democracy and popular representation. In relation to the judiciary, its historically subordinate status was elevated from an 'authority' to a 'power', on par with the executive and the legislature. Another significant innovation was the creation of a constitutional jurisdiction, which is increasingly perceived as an essential feature in enhancing constitutional justice in a modern constitutional state. Further legislative instruments made provision for a national electoral commission, to remove the organisation of national elections from the hands of the executive to a separate, purportedly independent institution. In relation to the protection of human rights and fundamental freedoms, a national human rights institution was created to enhance their protection and promotion. In the light of these developments, Cameroon seemed poised to become a modern constitutional state.

However, that has not materialised. The country faces myriads of governance challenges epitomised by a failed democratic transition, structural and institutional weaknesses, a persistently poor human rights record, poverty and underdevelopment. More recently, events in Cameroon's two Anglophone regions have brought to the fore some of the consequences of a failed democratic transition. Cameroon has been embroiled in a violent conflict between armed separatists in the Anglophone regions and security forces.

A major explanation for the failure to develop a modern constitutional state is the survival of an authoritarian philosophy, underpinned by a Jacobin constitutional framework. That has conditioned the trajectory of governance in the direction of a stymied constitutional advancement and persistent, periodic digression from democratic ideals. The developments in the 1990s did not transform the structure of law and governance, as the structural and institutional innovations were instead infused with old authoritarian tenets, creating internal inconsistencies between change and continuity. The disjuncture between the establishment of new and purportedly progressive institutional structures and the persistence of authoritarian political ideals has prevented the development of a more democratic and accountable governance system.

This book aims to provide a systematic analysis of the challenges in attaining constitutional and democratic governance in Cameroon. It offers a critical assessment of the major structural and institutional governance mechanisms. This book critically examines constitutional and legislative texts on the executive, the legislature, the judiciary, the National Electoral Commission (ELECAM), the Constitutional Council (CC) and the National Commission on Human Rights and Freedoms (NCHRF). It assesses the practical application of the relevant laws regulating these institutions and how they impact on governance. Thus, it critically examines executive power within the framework of semi-presidentialism. It examines the fundamental role of ELECAM and related electoral commissions in providing a democratic electoral space. This analysis provides a crucial background to understanding some of the dynamics that shape the functioning of the legislature. The book also provides an in-depth examination of the legislature (the National Assembly and the Senate) and its contemporary role in developing legislation and exercising oversight of the government. It is the first work to assess the Senate since it was established in 2013. Judicial power is analysed in the light of its elevated status and the extent to which it is effective in exercising oversight of the government and safeguarding human rights. The role of the Council in enhancing constitutional justice and democracy is analysed. The analysis is original and provides novel insights into the practical functioning of the Council.

In relation to the crisis in the Anglophone regions, the analysis includes an assessment of the current and proposed governance mechanisms to manage it. A number of crucial legislative developments occurred at the end of December 2019 which have major implications for governance and the Anglophones' quest for self-determination (the Anglophone problem). Notably, the granting of special autonomy status to the two Anglophone regions. This book provides the first in-depth and critical analysis of the new legislative texts carving out a special autonomy status for the two Anglophone regions and the extent to which they provide lasting solutions to the Anglophone problem.

With respect to the protection of human rights, a critical analysis of the scope of the relevant constitutional provisions is carried out. This analysis brings to light normative human rights issues which are peculiar to Cameroon. Some of these issues, such as individual duties and 'claw-back' clauses, are reflected in the African Charter on Human and Peoples' Rights. These normative issues are important to the extent that they have an impact on the scope of human rights in Cameroon. An original assessment of the NCHRF is also provided, applying best international standards espoused in the Paris Principle on national human rights institutions.

This book adopts a three-dimensional research methodology. First, a doctrinal method is applied in the critical analysis of the constitutional and legislative texts. In doing so, a wide range of sources have been applied. These include decisions of the courts relating to these texts, decisions of the newly established Council, available literature and primary sources such as records of parliamentary proceedings and government publications. Second, a contextual method is applied to place the analysis in the context of the historical, constitutional and political evolution of the country. This includes a historical account of the decolonisation process from 1960 to 1961. The analysis further traces the roots of the over centralised governance system and the roots of the Anglophone problem. It explains the political context of the adoption of the 1961, 1972 and 1996 Constitutions. It also explains the operation of the current constitutional and legislative provisions in the face of the current political crisis in the country. Third, the book applies a comparative analysis to highlight variations in institutional design and procedural mechanisms and how these operate in different countries and contexts. This provides a basis for considering alternative approaches to law reform and institutional design in Cameroon, taking into account the circumstances under which the reforms have potential to achieve the desired objectives. The analysis is captured in seven main chapters as synopsised here.

Chapter 1 lays the foundation for understanding the constitutional framework and the political culture underpinning governance in Cameroon. It provides a historical account of constitutional and political developments beginning with a very brief outline of German colonialism and proceeds to an account of the British and French colonial administration. In view of the importance of the colonial history to contemporary governance, attention is paid to the decolonisation process. This chapter analyses the contentious issue of the reunification of the former British Southern Cameroons and former French Republic of Cameroon in 1961. The process of the reunification of Cameroon is contrasted with Tanzania, which is a union of the former Republic of Tanganyika and Zanzibar. That comparative analysis brings to light some of the insurmountable difficulties faced by the politicians of Southern Cameroons in negotiating satisfactory terms for reunification. The chapter also discusses the development and demise of federalism in Cameroon. That is another important dimension of Cameroon's constitutional and political history as it is considered a catalyst for the Anglophone Problem. The chapter concludes with an examination of the process through which the 1996 Constitution was drafted and adopted by parliament. That Constitution was described as the document laying the foundation for modern constitutionalism.[1] However, as will become apparent in subsequent chapters, that assertion is simply a myth.

Chapter 2 examines executive power, which lies at the heart of governance in contemporary Cameroon and to a large extent shapes the outlook of institutions and political processes. Executive power in the Constitution operates in the framework of semi-presidentialism. Thus, the concept of semi-presidentialism provides the theoretical background against which executive power is analysed. The chapter provides innovative insights into the weaknesses of semi-presidentialism, as applied in Cameroon. As will be discussed, semi-presidentialism in principle has the advantage of providing an additional separation of executive power between the President and the PM, to mitigate the risk of overconcentration of powers in the President. An assessment of the powers of the President and the PM shows that the Constitution defines the contours of the PM's powers so narrowly as to erode the advantages of semi-presidentialism. The power imbalance between the President and PM has resulted in a de facto highly presidential system. The chapter reflects on what this portends for governance in Cameroon. The chapter also examines executive accountability and finds significant weaknesses in the accountability mechanisms, particularly with respect to the accountability of the President. The chapter draws on comparative examples in Africa and Europe to consider how some of these weaknesses can be addressed.

Chapter 3 explores the electoral system and the legislature. In view of the centrality of the electoral system to democracy and governance, the chapter first embarks on an examination of the role of the National Electoral Commission and various sub-commissions and institutions that occupy the electoral landscape. The chapter finds considerable weaknesses in the electoral system and asserts that these weaknesses contribute to undermine democracy in Cameroon.

The analysis of the electoral system provides the background for examination of various features of the legislature (composed of two houses – the National Assembly and Senate). Specifically, the chapter discusses the process of election of MPs and Senators and the appointment of Senators. It demonstrates how the weaknesses identified earlier in the electoral system operate in practice to grant incumbency advantages to the ruling political party, Cameroon People's Democratic Movement (CPDM). Using statistical data on the representation of political parties in parliament since 1992, the chapter highlights how incumbency advantages have contributed to the continuous domination of the CPDM.

The chapter also critically analyses the scope of the powers of the National Assembly, with reference to the Constitution and the National Assembly's standing orders. It examines its legislative powers and its powers to exercise oversight of the executive. It finds that the National Assembly is endowed with an array of powers to perform its constitutional functions. However, some of the powers are severely circumscribed. In other instances, the National Assembly is undermined by constitutional and legislative provisions which provide scope for presidential interference. These weaknesses are compounded by the fact that the CPDM retains an overwhelming and largely disciplined majority in parliament. The chapter concludes that those factors make it difficult for the National Assembly to legislate effectively or to exercise effective oversight of the executive.

The chapter further offers an original and critical analysis of bicameralism introduced in the 1996 Cameroon. This is done through an examination of the upper house of parliament (Senate) which is a recent feature in the political/legislative landscape. Although provision was made for a Senate in the 1996 Constitution, it was not until 2013 that the first Senators were appointed and elected. The institution has therefore only been in operation for seven years. The chapter examines the extent to which the Senate complements the role of the National Assembly and whether it expands popular representation, to lend greater significance to the principle of popular sovereignty[2] espoused in the Constitution. It finds that Senate replicates the institutional deficiencies of the National Assembly and perpetuates the predominance of the ruling party. The chapter reflects on these issues and the effects of bicameralism, which ironically symbolise change and continuity – a new institution perpetuating a political culture of neopatrimonialism and presidential absolutism.

The judiciary is discussed in Chapter 4. The judiciary is a very important institution, not least for its function in promoting accountable governance and safeguarding human rights. It is perhaps in recognition of its pivotal role that the Constitution elevated the judiciary's status from an 'authority' to a 'power'. Chapter 4 thus explores the constitutional and political implications of that elevated status. In particular, it critically assesses the effectiveness of the judiciary in promoting accountable governance and safeguarding human rights. The chapter first discusses the structure and jurisdiction of the courts. It then examines the structure of the judiciary and its relationship to the executive. The chapter finds that the judiciary is excessively dependent on the executive. First, it relies on the President who, according to the Constitution, is the guarantor of judicial independence. Second, the career of judges (including appointments, promotion and discipline) is largely dependent on the executive through mechanisms which are neither transparent nor objective. Third, the judiciary is financially dependent on the executive and accountable to it. These factors cumulatively result in the absence of judicial independence. The chapter uses case law to demonstrate how the absence of judicial independence undermines the ability of the courts to exercise effective oversight of the government and to protect human rights. In the light of the weaknesses identified in the judiciary the chapter applies comparative insights from other jurisdictions such as France, Botswana, Ghana, South Africa and Uganda to highlight how some of the weaknesses can be overcome.

The chapter also provides an in-depth examination of the complex relationship between judges, prosecutors and the executive. It aims to demonstrate the peculiarity of the system in Cameroon which is based on the French judicial system. It argues that the relationship is inimical to judicial independence conceptually and as a matter of its practical operation in Cameroon. The chapter further examines the scope of the judiciary's powers in administrative review, highlighting the controversial principle of *actes de gouvernement*' which exempts a category of executive acts from judicial scrutiny. The relevant category of acts are important as they may have significant consequences on individual rights and effective governance. The chapter argues that, due to their significance, their exemption from review may constitute a major weakness in the checks and balances system.

Chapter 5 offers the first detailed analysis of the practical functioning of the Constitutional Council and its contributions to Cameroon's democratic advancement. As mentioned earlier, this institution is another product of the democratic wind of change, introduced into the political landscape by the 1996 Constitution. Its mission is to uphold the supremacy of the Constitution, promote democracy and constitutional justice. It was not until 2018 that the Council was established and effectively went into operation. Chapter 5 thus provides an original analysis of its functioning, with reference to constitutional and legislative provisions, its internal mechanisms and its developing case law.

The chapter examines the method of appointment of Council members and compares their status to that of constitutional judges in other jurisdictions. It finds that the Council members lack independence, due significantly to their method of appointment which depends to a large extent on the President. The chapter further examines the jurisdiction of the Council. In particular, it examines its jurisdiction in constitutional review, regulating the functioning of state institutions and regions and in ensuring the regularity of presidential and parliamentary elections. The analysis reveals a number of significant weaknesses. The chapter considers how some of these weaknesses can be addressed.

In Chapter 6, the very divisive issue of the Anglophone struggle for self-determination is examined. The origins of that problem were discussed in Chapter 1. Chapter 6 extends that analysis by providing a detailed examination of the disparate options that have been advanced as ideal governance alternatives to accord the Anglophones meaningful self-determination. First, it examines the government's preferred option of decentralisation. It analyses the constitutional origins of that option and assesses its strengths and weaknesses. In light of the important legislative developments that occurred in December 2019, this chapter provides a critical assessment of the main legislative provisions setting out the special status arrangements. It first analyses the political context and the procedural mechanisms preceding the promulgation of the relevant legislation. It then analyses the specific normative provisions. It assesses the extent to which they provide satisfactory responses to the Anglophone demands for respect of their minority status and a measure of autonomy. The chapter proceeds to offer an alternative approach to carving out meaningful special autonomy status, drawing from comparative arrangements in the Åland Island, Hong Kong, Aceh and Papua.

Two other contending options are examined in detail – federalism and secession. The chapter analyses the historical, legal and functional arguments advanced for adopting a federal system of governance. It assesses the strengths and weaknesses of these arguments and considers the potentials for federalism to provide viable solutions to the Anglophone problem. Secession is also examined in detail. This option has gained renewed significance more recently and accounts for the current armed struggle between separatists and security forces.

The chapter reviews some of the legal arguments that have been advanced in support of secession. It analyses relevant domestic and international law and argues that domestic law provides no legal route for secession. International law, on the other hand, provides extremely limited scope for a legal mechanism through which secession can be achieved. The chapter also considers the prospects for achieving secession through armed struggle. Drawing from the experience of violent self-determination conflicts in Eritrea and South Sudan, the chapter contends that armed struggle is likely to be protracted, costly and the outcome is highly indeterminate.

Chapter 7 provides an overview of the protection of fundamental human rights and freedoms (human rights). It examines the normative basis for the protection of human rights, principally focusing on the constitutional provisions embodied in the pre-amble and discusses some basic concepts emanating from it. The rest of the chapter focuses on implementation mechanisms, mainly the NCHRF and the Department for Human Rights in the Ministry of Justice. It offers an original analysis of the NCHRF with reference to the Paris Principles on human rights institutions and assesses the extent to which the NCHRF complies with international standards. It contends that some of the legislative provisions relating to the NCHRF and its operational mechanisms fall short of the Paris Principles. The chapter further highlights the strides made in enhancing human rights and the main weaknesses that contribute to undermine the role of the NCHRF and the Department for Human Rights. The chapter complements discussions on aspects relating to the protection of human rights by the judiciary in Chapter 4 and the Council in Chapter 5.

The book concludes with an outlook for the future trajectory of governance in Cameroon. In particular, it briefly considers the potentials for a more democratic and accountable governance system, engineered by a popularly adopted Constitution.

Notes

1 Augustin K Kouomegni, 'Minister of Communication's Introductory Note to the 1996 Constitutional Amendment' in *Fundamental Legal Texts* (vol 1, National Printing Press 1996).

2 Constitution of Cameroon 1996, art 2.

1 A history of the constitution and governance in Cameroon

Introduction

This chapter will explore the chequered constitutional history of Cameroon which provides a useful foundation for understanding its contemporary constitutional, political and governance institutions and cultures. It provides a simplified account of the emergence of the French and British constitutional systems, beginning with the period of colonial administration to independence and immediate post-independence. Additionally, the chapter discusses the events and political machinations which explain to an extent, the predominance of the French civilian tradition in Cameroon's constitutional system, an aspect fundamental to its governance.

Part I. Background

The Germans were the first European powers to establish colonial administration in Cameroon from 1884 to the outbreak of the First World War in 1914. Following their defeat in the War, an Anglo-French *Condominium* was set up from 1914 to 1916 and the Germans were eventually expelled from Cameroon in February 1916.[1] Cameroon was subsequently divided unequally between France and Britain with Britain gaining control of two disconnected sections of the territory which later became known as Northern and Southern Cameroons. In contrast, France gained approximately 90% of the remaining territory, which became known as French Cameroon. In June 1919, the Treaty of Versailles established a mandates system to place conquered colonies under international administration.[2] Cameroon was brought under that system and from 1922 it was administered by France and Britain as a mandated territory of the League of Nations until 1945 when the mandates were replaced by trusteeship agreements under the auspices of the United Nations.[3] France and Britain proceeded to administer their territories according to their respective policies from that point until independence was granted in 1960 and 1961, respectively. That explains how Cameroon became endowed with two dissimilar and often conflicting constitutional traditions that have frequently marred governance and peaceful coexistence of the disparate communities in Cameroon.

Part II. Colonial governance and administration

France and Britain adopted a civil law or common law system in their respective sections of the territory. The basis for that transplantation was initially Article 9 of the League of Nations Mandate Agreement with France[4] and Britain[5] which gave these colonial powers authority to pursue administration and legislation in accordance with their laws contingent on modifications to accommodate local conditions. Subsequently, that provision was replaced by article 4 of the Trusteeship Agreement with France and Article 5 of the Trusteeship Agreement with Britain when Cameroon became a Trust Territory of the United Nations. Article 5(a) relating to Britain provided that Britain shall have 'full powers of legislation, administration and jurisdiction in the Territory' to be administered in accordance with its laws subject to modifications necessitated by local conditions and subject to the United Nations Charter and the present Trusteeship Agreement.[6] Article 4(1) of the Agreement relating to France was similarly worded except that it did not require French law to be modified to accommodate local conditions.[7] The developments in both the French and British territories are considered separately later.

A. The civil law and governance in French Cameroon

Unlike other French colonies in Africa which were administered through the administrative structures of French West Africa or French Equatorial Africa, French Cameroon maintained a distinct and separate administrative system. Nevertheless, a decree of 1924 made applicable in Cameroon, laws and decrees promulgated in French Equatorial Africa prior to 1 January 1924,[8] which consisted of legislation transplanted from metropolitan France. The rest of the colonial era witnessed further enactment of decrees specifically applicable to French Cameroon, complemented by the application of legislation already enforced in France.[9] Customary law was preserved although its influence was considerably diminished and applied only insofar as it was not repugnant to public policy (*ordre public*) and its jurisdiction was limited to the indigenous populations that had not acquired French citizenship.[10]

The French colonial administrative landscape consisted of a high commissioner at the helm and supported by regional and district administrators and an advisory body known as the *Conseil d'Administration.*[11] By 1925 in a bid to incorporate indigenous populations into the administrative network, a *Conseil de Notables* composed of local chiefs was created in each district.[12] That institution was firmly controlled by the French authorities who proceeded to alter the chieftaincy system by creating artificial chiefs amenable to colonial influences.[13] The administrative system was complemented by a judicial system (consisting of courts with jurisdiction over persons of French origin and indigenes). The judiciary was considered an administrative body under the French Ministry of Justice and the Ministry of State in Charge of relations with Associate States.[14] Their administration at the territorial level was overseen by the *Conseil Supérieur de la Magistrature* (CSM) and the high commissioner was responsible for the judicial tenure.[15]

In terms of political participation, a key policy of the French administration known as the *indégenat,* which was repressive in nature, prevented the participation of indigenes in political activity.[16] The administration did not permit the formation of political associations until the 1930s when it approved the formation of *Union Camerounaise* (UC) and *Jeunesse Camerounaise Francaise* (JEUCAFRA) in 1937 and 1938, respectively.[17] However, two watersheds transformed the legal and political situation.

The first was the Brazzaville Conference in 1944 held at the instance of General de Gaulle to improve Franco-African relations.[18] Resolutions passed at the Conference saw inter alia, the abolition of the *indégenat* across French colonial Africa.[19] A further consequence was the creation of a representative assembly for French Cameroon, *Assemblée Représentative du Cameroun* (ARCAM). The institution remained accountable to the French *Conseil d'Etat* which had to veto all its decisions.[20] Trade unions were legalised in 1944 and from then on political associations proliferated.[21] Nevertheless, political activity was restricted and the administration did not hesitate to crack down on those organisations that propagated nationalist views.[22] One of such associations which came into frequent conflicts with the administration was the *Union des Populations du Cameroun* (UPC) which advocated for complete independence for French Cameroon and reunification with Southern (British) Cameroons.[23] The administration reacted by issuing emergency decrees which curtailed the activities of the UPC and its members were frequently arrested, detained and tortured.[24] Following prolonged violent altercation with the administration, the UPC was banned and some of its members sought refuge in Southern Cameroons.[25]

The second watershed was in June 1956 when the French Assembly passed the *Loi Cadres* revolutionising colonial administration in French Africa. One of its major objectives was to provide an institutional framework for eventually according autonomy to the territories. In French Cameroon, the ARCAM was dissolved and a new assembly, the *Assemblée Législative du Cameroun* (ALCAM), was constituted following elections in December 1956. ALCAM was accorded more powers over territorial affairs although France retained authority over such aspects as defence, civil liberties and education.[26] Moreover, provision was made for internal self-government. Following the legislative elections in December 1956, Andre Marie Mbida was appointed the first Prime Minister of French Cameroon in 1957. Meanwhile, the exiled UPC continued to instigate opposition and violence from behind the scenes.[27] Mbida's regime soon fell into disrepute with the indigenous population due to its brutal response to the UPC and his reluctance to endorse a programme for eventual independence.[28] Owing to immense unpopularity, Mbida lost confidence in the Assembly and in anticipation of impending impeachment proceedings, resigned from office in February 1958. This paved the way for Vice Prime Minister Amadou Ahidjo to be appointed to succeed him as Prime Minister.[29] The independence of French Cameroon and eventual reunification with British Cameroons became a key objective.

B. The common law and governance in British Cameroons

The British Cameroons had a different colonial experience to its French counterpart. It was administered as part of the neighbouring British colony of Nigeria.[30] That arrangement was prompted by financial and geographical reasons[31] and endorsed by article 9 of the Mandate Agreement which provided inter alia that Britain could constitute the territory (Cameroons) into an administrative union or federation with its adjacent territories. Thus, the territory was divided into Northern Cameroons and Southern Cameroons. As per the British Cameroons Order-in-Council of 26 June 1923, Northern Cameroons was administered as part of Northern Nigeria, whereas Southern Cameroons was administered as part of the southern provinces of Nigeria and subsequently as part of the Eastern Province of Nigeria.[32]

As with the civil law in French Cameroon, some aspects of the British common law system were transplanted into British Cameroons. The laws applicable in Southern Cameroons consisted of the common law, doctrines of equity and the statutes of general application which were in force in England on 01 January 1900.[33] In addition, in 1924 the Nigerian Legal System was extended to Southern Cameroons as a result of which some of its statutes and ordinances became applicable.[34] Similar to the French approach, customary law was retained to the extent that it passed the repugnancy test.[35]

As elsewhere in British colonial Africa, the system of administration applicable in Southern Cameroons was indirect rule. This system was characterised by the use of traditional authority (chiefs and *fons*)[36] as instruments through which the local British administrators implemented their policies.[37] At the helm of the territorial administration of Southern Cameroons, there was the Governor General of Nigeria who was responsible for governance, administration of justice, revenue and maintenance of law and order.[38] The territory was divided into administrative divisions headed by a Resident, below whom were Divisional Officers and District Officers. The administration was represented at the local levels by chiefs or *fons*.[39] The native authorities had responsibility for the efficient running of the administration in their jurisdiction, particularly with respect to the maintenance of law and order, collection of taxes and the provision of elementary health and education facilities.[40]

In terms of political activity, the colonial administration was not adverse to the creation of political organisations, although Nigeria appeared more politically advanced than Southern Cameroons.[41] Its status as part of Nigeria meant that Britain's administrative focus was largely on Nigeria. Until 1940, Southern Cameroons had no representative in the Nigerian Legislative Council (NLC) which catered for Nigeria and the Cameroons.[42] In 1939, a trade union organisation, the Cameroon Welfare Union (CWU) successfully petitioned the colonial authorities demanding Southern Cameroons representation in the NLC.[43] Consequently, in 1942 Chief Manga Williams and the senior colonial administrative authority in Southern Cameroons were appointed as the territory's representatives in the NLC.[44] Subsequently in 1946 when Southern Cameroons became a trust territory of the United Nations, a new constitution, the Richards Constitution, was drafted for Nigeria and the Cameroons. The Constitution divided Nigeria into three regions, incorporating Southern Cameroons administratively into the Eastern Region with increased representation in the Eastern Regional House of Assembly.[45] However, it did not prevent financial and administrative subordination of Southern Cameroons coupled with its lack of representation in the Central Legislative Council in Lagos. These grievances prompted Southern Cameroon's politicians to continue to press for autonomous status.[46] In 1951, a new constitution, the Macpherson Constitution made provision for increased representation at the regional level as well as representation at the centre. This included an increase in the representation in the Eastern House of Assembly, the Executive Council, the Eastern House of Representatives and the Council of Ministers. Despite these developments, Southern Cameroons persisted in seeking autonomous regional status. In 1953, the Eastern Regional House of Assembly was engulfed by political and constitutional crisis[47] which precipitated the collapse of the McPherson Constitution. This also provided the opportunity for Southern Cameroonian politicians to make more decisive demands for regional status. In that respect, a conference was held in London in 1953 during which the Colonial Secretary intimated that if elections which were scheduled later that year reflected a desire for regional status, then it would be likely that an autonomous region would be created for Southern Cameroons. The pro-regionalists, led by Dr EML Endeley's Kamerun National Congress (KNC) eventually emerged victorious in the elections and a further constitutional conference was held in Lagos in 1954 during which specific arrangements were made for reorganising the governance structure in Southern Cameroons. These arrangements were given effect in the Lyttleton Constitution of 1954 under which the Southern Cameroons was granted quasi-federal status with a Legislative Assembly and an Executive Council.[48] Endeley became Leader of Government Business, although Southern Cameroons continued to be linked to the Nigerian Federal Legislature and administration.

Further constitutional developments occurred following yet another constitutional conference in London in 1957, held to discuss the revision of the Nigerian Constitution. It was agreed that, the 'quasi-federal status' of Southern Cameroon would be dropped, there would be an expansion of the legislative assembly, a House of Chiefs would be created as an upper legislative chamber and a ministerial government would be established in Southern Cameroons. At the request of Southern Cameroons, the Colonial Secretary undertook to request a transitional period of continued trusteeship for Southern Cameroons when Nigeria became independent in 1960. At a further constitutional conference in London in 1958, delegates, including the colonial secretary agreed that, the Southern Cameroons government which would come into effect after elections scheduled for 1959, would be vested with the duty to request Her Majesty's government for separate regional status. The 1959 elections were subsequently won by the Kamerun National Democratic Party (KNDP) and the leader, John Ngu Foncha, emerged as premier. The agreements from the 1958 constitutional conference were thus given effect through the Southern Cameroons (Constitution) Order-in-Council 1960. The existing powers and functions of the Southern Cameroons' government were not altered by the new Constitution. However, the powers and functions exercised by the Governor General and the Government of the Federation of Nigeria were transferred to the commissioner of Southern Cameroons.

C. The decolonisation process

I. French Cameroon

After the resignation of Prime Minister Mbida, the new Prime Minister Ahidjo immediately began to work closely with the French government towards the independence of French Cameroon. Although no overt statements had been made by France to that effect, it inherently supported Ahidjo's plans for independence and reunification, and the granting of some concessions to the UPC.[49] On 19 October 1958, Xavier Torre the new high commissioner officially affirmed France's willingness to grant independence on 1 January 1960. The ALCAM proceeded immediately on 24 October 1958 to adopt a resolution expressing Cameroon's desire to become independent. France submitted that resolution to the Fourth Committee of the UN on 28 October 1958, but before that could be debated, objections were raised by an exiled wing of the UPC. They complained that ALCAM was not representative and that the Ahidjo government was illegitimate, repressive and a puppet of France. On account of these factors, they asserted that Ahidjo's demands for independence should be rejected. The UN debates were suspended pending a report by a UN visiting Mission to Cameroon on November 1958, aimed at ascertaining the wishes of the people of Cameroon.

The UPC rebellion continued to plague the Ahidjo government and as a measure to mitigate the hostilities, the French government promulgated an amnesty law on 17 February 1959. By the end of December 1958, the government had succeeded in quelling the rebellion, particularly following the death of Um Nyobe, an iconic leader of the movement. On 1 January 1959, French Cameroon was granted autonomy by virtue of a statute which also made provision for independence on 1 January 1960.[50] Additionally, effective control of the government of Cameroon was to be transferred from the high commissioner to the government of Cameroon, although the former would retain a superior position in the administrative hierarchy. These changes were hailed by the government and the ALCAM.

The UN General Assembly resumed on 20 February 1959 after receiving the report of the UN Visiting Mission. The report spoke in favour of the Ahidjo government, commending the progress it had made towards preparing for independence. It rejected the UPC's claims that ALCAM was not representative, recommending that no new elections were required prior to independence, against the wishes of the UPC. The UN was equally satisfied with statements and assurances from the governments of Cameroon and France indicating that civil and political freedoms were protected in Cameroon, the Amnesty Law was widely implemented and the exiled UPC leaders were invited to return to Cameroon.[51] Partly for those reasons, the UN passed resolution 1349(XIII) affirming the declaration of independence of French Cameroon on 01 January 1960, concurrently terminating the Trusteeship Agreement.[52]

That outcome further antagonised the UPC prompting a resumption of violence which the Ahidjo government (aided by French troops) met with severe repression.[53] On 30 October 1959, ALCAM granted special legislative powers to the government to rule by ordinances and decrees. Ahidjo proceeded to declare a state of emergency in various parts of the country and created ad hoc tribunals to summarily try dissidents for terrorism.[54] The special legislative powers included powers to draft a new constitution.[55] The draft eventually produced was closely modelled on the Constitution of the fifth French Republic and its institutions. Ahidjo's draft constitution met with disapproval from the opposition, a situation which was exacerbated by the hostility and violence from the UPC uprising. Notwithstanding these upheavals, Ahidjo led French Cameroon to independence on 1 January 1960. The draft constitution was approved in a referendum in February 1960 and became the first constitution of the independent Republic of Cameroon The Republic.

II. Southern Cameroons

Meanwhile, politics in Southern Cameroons was quite animated, not least by the fact that the colonial administration announced the imminent independence of Nigeria for 1 October 1960. Inevitably, the future of Southern Cameroons had to be determined, given that it still formed part of the wider Federation of Nigeria. The question hinged on the manner in which Southern Cameroons would gain independence. In 1949, the reunification of both Northern and Southern Cameroons had been considered by the latter's politicians as a potential option for the future of both territories. That option was eventually abandoned, partly because the Northern part had followed a different colonial trajectory and although backwards and underdeveloped politically and economically, appeared content to continue its existence within the Federation of Nigeria.[56] The UN visiting Mission to Territories in West Africa in 1958 was convinced that a realistic approach to the future of the Cameroons under British administration was to treat them as distinct entities due to the different courses their history and development had taken and the significant differences in their administrative systems, their political attitudes and loyalties.[57] It recommended that the questions to be put to the people in respect of their future aspirations should be determined by the UN General Assembly, the Colonial Government in consultation, and as far as possible, in agreement with the political parties in the Southern Cameroons.[58] That would be a colossal endeavour given that the leaders of Southern Cameroons remained undecided on the issue.[59] While the Premier's KNDP was in favour of continued trusteeship until such a time as

Southern Cameroons would be ready for independence (and possibly re-unification with the Republic of Cameroon), Endeley's KNC in alliance with the Kamerun People's Party pressed for integration with Nigeria or unification with the Republic of Cameroon.[60]

In March 1959, the UN General Assembly adopted Resolution 1350(XIII) which recommended that the British colonial authority, in pursuance of Article 76(b) of the UN Charter,[61] and in consultation with a UN Plebiscite Commissioner should take steps to organise two separate plebiscites in Northern and Southern Cameroons to be supervised by the UN.[62] It recommended further that the colonial authority should seek to organise the plebiscite between December 1959 and April 1960.[63] In view of the intransigence of the political leaders of Southern Cameroons, the UN General Assembly hoped that the leaders would endeavour to reach an agreement on the question to be put to the electorate in the plebiscite before the next General Assembly.[64] The latter call was not heeded even after a Plebiscite Conference was held in Mamfe in August 1959. Following the failure to reach a consensus, the Premier and the Leader of the Opposition issued a joint statement to the UN General Assembly to the effect that it would be wiser to defer consultation with the people and suggested 1962 as an alternative date for the plebiscite.[65] In October 1959, the UN adopted Resolution 1352(XIV) by which it decided that the date for the plebiscite would be no later than March 1960[66] in effect, ignoring the request of the Southern Cameroons politicians. The two questions for electorates to decide at the plebiscite where recommended to be as follows:

> (a) Do you wish to achieve independence by joining the independent Federation of Nigeria?
>
> (b) Do you wish to achieve independence by joining the independent Republic of the Cameroons?[67]

The publication of the plebiscite questions sparked protests and opposition from the Southern Cameroons politicians who felt betrayed. Although consensus had not been attained at the Mamfe Conference, it became clearer that re-unification was the least favourite option among the delegates and had indeed been dropped. Instead, they favoured secession from Nigeria and independence as the second question.[68] It is not clear how or why the UN arrived at the two plebiscite questions given that the Premier at the time was fervently in favour of a further period of trusteeship. Moreover, there seemed to have been some support for the independence of Southern Cameroons as a separate entity.[69] It was obvious that the UN had very little or no support for an independent Southern Cameroons and would reject any such request.[70] Moreover, following the publication of the UN commissioned Philipson Financial Report, it became conclusive that independence as a separate entity was an impractical option.[71] The report noted first and ironically that, the option of an independent sovereign state had very negligible public support and should be disregarded.[72] Second, it revealed not only the colonial government's neglect of Southern Cameroons, but more importantly it stated clearly that the territory was financial weak and unstable and unable to survive independently in the modern economy.[73] Those findings partly influenced a shift in the position of the Colonial Secretary who at the 1957 Constitutional Conference had intimated that he would request a period of continued trusteeship for Southern Cameroons after Nigeria gained independence.[74] He had even given consideration to the fact that all possible alternatives would be explored including integration of Northern and Southern Cameroons to form a single entity.[75]

It is significant to note that the Report recommended a continued period of trusteeship to afford Southern Cameroons the time it needed to develop and test its financial strengths. It recommended that such a period should not be too long or indeterminate but not too brief to prevent reasonable long term planning.[76] This should have strengthened the position of the Premier who continued to press for a period of trusteeship, but the UN seemed adamant on pursuing the two alternatives contained in Resolution 1352(XIV). That situation was not made easier by the fact that the leaders in Southern Cameroons appeared to have inconsistent interpretations of the second alternative. While it was clear what achieving independence by joining Nigeria entailed, the position was not clear with respect to joining the Republic of Cameroon. The opposition leaders understood the latter option to imply that independence and reunification would happen sooner, whereas the Premier thought that there would be a further period of trusteeship, should the plebiscite result in a decision to join the Republic of Cameroon. The political leaders were eager to pursue the independence option further and also seek clarification as to the purport of the second question, particularly because Resolution 2013(XXVI) of 31 May 1960 requested that the two alternatives in the plebiscite be explained fully to the electorate prior to the event.[77] A conference was held in London in November 1960 with the Colonial Secretary, the Premier and other leaders of the Southern Cameroons, including the opposition. The Colonial Secretary and the opposition agreed that a consistent interpretation of the second question would rule out any period of continued trusteeship.[78] However, the Premier still insisted on that point. It was unanimously agreed that prior to meeting President Ahidjo of the Republic of Cameroon (to pursue reunification discussions), the UN should be approached to provide an authoritative interpretation.[79]

It may be worth pausing at this point to consider why the UN seemed fervidly opposed to continued trusteeship, despite support for it from the Premier and buttressed by the Philipson Report. Moreover, given the uncertainties involved in joining the Republic of Cameroon and the reluctance to embrace Nigeria, it would seem propitious to afford the territory some time to arrive at a well informed and considered decision. The UN was very keen for measures to be taken by the colonial authorities to ensure the separation of Southern Cameroons from Nigeria no later than 1 October 1960 and reiterated that request unremittingly.[80] At the London Conference, the Colonial Secretary made clear that the UN was unlikely to support a period of continued trusteeship especially in the light of the fact that the questions had already been published. Besides the financial viability problems of the Southern Cameroons, a major concern was that continued trusteeship would require an amendment of the Trusteeship Agreement to permit its separate administration. The latter process would involve the consent of Great Britain as the Administering Colonial Authority and an agreement of a two-third majority of the General Assembly. It was uncertain that success was feasible. Moreover, the period of continued trusteeship was not fixed and no specific plans were being offered by the Premier as to what would happen at the end of the trusteeship. In addition, the African Bloc at the UN, led by Ghana's Kwame Nkrumah, a renowned Pan-Africanist, fiercely opposed the creation of micro-states and instead entreated Southern Cameroons to unite with Ahidjo's Cameroon.[81] While these are plausible explanations to account for the reluctance of the UN, were they sufficient to prevent considering that option? Was the UN simply reluctant to make that request to Great Britain or was the latter unwilling to continue its administration of Cameroon for financial reasons? Be that as it may, the answers to these questions remain a moot point. It is irrefutable that, the failure to give serious consideration to that alternative has had significant implications for the historical and contemporary development of Cameroon. Southern Cameroonians were forced to choose between two alternatives, neither of which they zealously embraced. They were thus denied the opportunity to exercise their right to self-determination in a way that they desired.

Prior to approaching the UN to clarify the interpretation of the second option as per the decision of the London Conference, the Premier met for the fourth time with President Ahidjo in December 1960.[82] These meetings had been encouraged by the UN as a way of accelerating discussions between the two leaders to ascertain the terms on which they proposed to reunite, should the plebiscite decision sway in that direction.[83] Following the December 1960 meeting, the Premier and President Ahidjo issued a joint statement effectively, endorsing the interpretation of the Colonial Secretary at the London Conference and declaring that it was no longer necessary to approach the UN for an interpretation and the options could be explained to the electorate. That was given effect through Southern Cameroons Notice No. 36 by which the interpretations and explanations of the questions were printed and widely disseminated in the Southern Cameroons in January 1961.[84]

On 11 February 1961, the Southern Cameroons electorates voted overwhelmingly to join the Republic of Cameroon by a majority of 233,571 (70.49% of the votes) as against 97.741 (29.5%) in favour of joining Nigeria.[85] Meanwhile, in a separate plebiscite held in Northern Cameroons, the electorates voted in favour of joining Nigeria by a majority of 146,296 (59.97%) votes as against 97,659 (40.03%) votes in favour of joining the Republic of Cameroon.[86] These results were endorsed by the UN in its Resolution 1608(XV)[87] in which it decided to terminate the Trusteeship Agreement for both Northern and Southern Cameroons, respectively, from 1 June 1960 and 1 October 1961, upon Northern Cameroons joining Nigeria as a separate province of the Northern Region and Southern Cameroons joining the independent Republic of Cameroon.[88]

Part III. Post-independence constitutional developments

A. Federalism and the coexistence of French and British constitutional traditions

Prior to reunification of the two Cameroonian territories in October 1961, it was expected that their representatives would address the issue of a constitution governing the entire union.[89] This was a complex task given that both territories had over forty years of divergent colonial experiences and it was important to achieve internal coherence without excessive disruption of existing subsystems. The formula agreed at the London Conference provided inter alia that specific arrangements for the governance framework between Southern Cameroons and the Republic of Cameroon would be worked out at a conference consisting of representative delegations of equal status from both entities.[90] Significantly, it also required the participation of the United Nations and the United Kingdom.[91] That formula was endorsed by the representatives of the governing party of Southern Cameroons led by Foncha, the Premier and that of the government of the Republic of Cameroon led by Ahidjo at their meeting in December 1960.

In July 1961, a constitutional conference was held in Foumban with the aim of drafting a constitution – or at least so it seemed to the Southern Cameroons delegation.[92] Although some discussions on the issue had taken place between Premier Foncha and President Ahidjo, where the former expressed the desire for a loose federation, the specific details would be ironed out in a number of constitutional conferences following their experience of constitutional conferences with Nigeria. The Foumban Conference was thought to be one of such platforms where those details would be ironed out. At the conference, the proposals from the delegation representing the Southern Cameroons reflected a desire to adhere to their British colonial heritage.[93] According to Frank Stark, Foncha was concerned with the cultural autonomy of Southern Cameroons and was apprehensive of French domination, a fact which was reflected in his speech at Foumban.[94] His delegation advocated for a loose federation, a ceremonial executive head of state with limited powers and the requirement to act with the consent of his ministers (who in turn would be responsible to parliament), the vesting of considerable legislative powers to state legislatures on the understanding that some of those powers would be transferred to the central government after a transitional period. Other proposals included specifically entrenched provisions for constitutional amendments, specific provisions for the protection of fundamental rights, especially minority rights, vesting ordinary courts with jurisdiction to review the constitutionality of laws, retention of the House of Chiefs and the separate legal systems.[95] This was in fact the results of an agreement among the Southern Cameroons delegation at a conference in Bamenda in June 1961 on the understanding that it would form the basis for imminent negotiations with the Republic of Cameroon. However, their counterparts from the Republic had different ideas regarding the federation. With the exception of the last two proposals, the others were rejected by President Ahidjo who sought to consolidate his existing centralised executive powers.[96] Ahidjo rejected the proposals for a loose federation on the basis that it would make the government unstable.[97] It is also alleged that, he was influenced by the innate fear of secession of the Southern Cameroons.[98]

Ahidjo's success in suppressing the Southern Cameroons proposals has been attributed to a number of factors.[99] First, he did not conceal the fact that both Southern Cameroons and the Republic were entering into the negotiations as unequal powers.[100] On the one hand, The Republic was an independent sovereign state ten times the geographical size of its counterpart, whereas Southern Cameroons was a territory with no independent international status.[101] Second, Ahidjo's delegation came prepared with a draft constitution, whereas the Southern Cameroons delegation only had outlines and disagreed among its delegates as to their objectives and underlying concepts in relation to the federation.[102] Third, the Southern Cameroons delegation had little time to produce its own proposals on the basis of what had been presented by the Ahidjo delegation.[103] The position of Southern Cameroons was further undermined by the fact that neither the British colonial authority nor representatives of the UN were present at this discussion. An uneasy compromise was reached between Southern Cameroons and the Republic. It would seem that the Southern Cameroons delegations capitulated mainly because they were under the illusion that further discussions would be held with a view to drafting a definitive document.[104] That never occurred.

The Foumban conference was followed by a meeting of the governing delegation of the Southern Cameroons led by Premier Foncha and President Ahidjo in Yaoundé in August 1961. The meeting culminated in the adoption of the Federal Constitution of 1961 by the National Assembly of the Republic of Cameroon (which became the East Cameroon Parliament). The Southern Cameroons House of Assembly did not adopt the Constitution, raising a fundamental question regarding its legitimacy.[105] Moreover, there was no act or treaty of union – no legal instrument effecting the union between Southern Cameroons and the Republic and defining the terms of that union. This can be contrasted with the process through which the United Republic of Tanzania came into existence. Tanzania is the product of a union between former Tanganyika which gained independence on 9 December 1962 and Zanzibar which gained independence on 10 December 1963. The union was effected by means of the Acts of Union of 1964,[106] section 4 of which specifically provided that the two entities shall be united into one sovereign republic by the name of the United Republic of Tanganyika and Zanzibar. The name was later changed to the United Republic of Tanzania with the approval of both entities.[107] The process of union was the culmination of Articles of Union agreed by the parliaments of both Tanganyika and Zanzibar.[108] Similarly, the United Kingdom of Great Britain was established by the Acts of Union of 1 May 1707 passed by the English and Scottish parliaments. In Cameroon, as already noted, there was no act of union and the Federal Constitution was adopted by the parliament of the

Republic of Cameroon, to the exclusion of the Southern Cameroons House of Assembly. This process raised significant constitutional questions on the legitimacy of the union and the resulting Constitution due to the absence of an act of union and the fact that the Constitution was not endorsed by the elected representatives of West Cameroon.

The Federal Constitution created a Federal Republic consisting of two federated states of East and West Cameroon representing respectively the former Republic of Cameroon and Southern Cameroons.[109] It is significant to note that the 1961 Constitution was not a newly drafted Constitution. It was an amended version of the 1960 Constitution of The Republic of Cameroon with adaptations to accommodate the Federation.[110] The domination of West Cameroon was evident in article 59 which provided that 'La Constitution ainsi révisée sera publiée en français et en anglais, le texte français faisant fois'.[111] This was clearly indicative of the status of the Anglophone minority and the English language within the newly federated republic.[112] The British colonial legacy was only preserved to the extent that the Constitution provided for the recognition and continued application of legislation formerly enforced in the two territories, provided they were not inconsistent with the provisions of the Federal Constitution.[113] However, at the federal level, the institutions that dominated were those introduced by the 1960 Constitution of the Republic with its very centralised Gaullist framework, which concentrated powers in the executive and accorded restricted powers to the legislature and the judiciary.

Despite the federal nature of the state, Ahidjo by decree created six administrative regions, with West Cameroon as one of the regions.[114] One of the most controversial issue regarding this arrangement was that federal inspectors were appointed to represent the federal government in all aspects of civil life and in judicial matters and to supervise the enforcement of federal laws and regulations, to maintain order according to the laws and regulations in force with the assistance of the forces of law and order. In West Cameroon, the federal inspector was a francophone and considered himself equal to the Prime Minister.[115] This inevitably led to conflict of powers between the Prime Minister and the federal inspector. This arrangement effectively curtailed the powers of the Prime Minister and vested them in the inspector who was accountable to President Ahidjo.[116] This was a further method by which Ahidjo sort to undermine the federal character of the country and to entrench his centralised authority.

Economically, West Cameroon also entered the union in a very disadvantaged position. Due to years of neglect by the British colonial administration, West Cameroon was far less developed than East Cameroon. Substantial income generated from the export of cash crops such as rubber, banana, palm oil and tea dropped considerably with the introduction of the Franc CFA as federal currency and also following West Cameroon losing preferential trading within the Commonwealth.[117] Its economic subordination was further exacerbated by the arrangements for revenue sharing which was at a considerable disadvantage to West Cameroon.[118] All revenue from the federated states went to the central government before eventually being returned in the form of subsidies usually insufficient to meet local needs. The revenue sharing arrangements and general lack of financial autonomy served to increase the subordination of West Cameroon.[119]

Contrary to some theories of federalism which often attribute it to a constitutional arrangement between *independent* political entities,[120] the Cameroonian federation was not the result of constitutional arrangements or bargains between independent states. In fact, as noted earlier, the union emerged from an agreement between an independent state and another entity still in the process of determining its international status. In the case of Zanzibar and Tanganyika, perhaps the ability to negotiate a mutually agreed formula for their union, hinged significantly on the fact that they were both independent entities. Interestingly, Zanzibar had only been independent for a brief period of four months before the union became effective. Perhaps a brief period of independence for Southern Cameroons (which Foncha unsuccessfully fought for) might have made all the difference. Nevertheless, at the time off entering into the union, West Cameroon, then Southern Cameroons was still a UN Trust Territory in the process of determining the nature of its rupture from colonial domination. That inevitably had an impact on the bargaining power of its representatives and the extent to which they were able to leverage president Ahidjo for protection of their minority status. As Stark notes with respect to the position of Southern Cameroons, '[n]ot only would its small size and population stand against equality in such a relationship, but the two parts of the federation ... would be unequal in terms of sovereignty at the beginning of the relationship'.[121] There was nevertheless a need to determine the basis of a union of the two entities.

Thus, the formation of federalism in Cameroon can be explained by the need to 'bring together' two distinct entities with different cultures and historical experiences within a harmonious union without dissolving these cultural cleavages. That was the principal concern of the Anglophones on account of their minority status. In fact, following discussions between cabinet representatives from the two territories on 25 November 1959, the Southern Cameroonians are reported to have indicated that, unification 'might take the form of a loose federation with the aim of preserving the individuality of the Southern Cameroons state'.[122] This desire for the recognition of diversity was reflected in a speech by president Ahidjo who acknowledged that Southern Cameroonians joining the union had different linguistic, administrative and political cultures and a distinct *modus vivendi.*[123] He reiterated that it was therefore not for the majority to impose their customs and practices. It has been argued however that, the lack of balance within the federation at its inception is indicative of a hidden agenda to subsume the cultural heritage of West Cameroon. Ahidjo himself hinted at a long term objective 'to move as far as possible towards real homogeneity'.[124] There was never a genuine intention of the Ahidjo government to integrate West Cameroon on an equal basis with East Cameroon, instead, as described by Joseph Ebune, there was a 'Falsehood of Federalism in West Cameroon' due to the asymmetrical nature of the federal arrangements.[125]

B. The Glorious Revolution of May Twentieth and the demise of the Westminster model

After the adoption of the Federal Constitution, there was an indication from the Ahidjo leadership of the intention to consider the creation of a unified party in Cameroon.[126] That vision was subsequently strengthened by continuing political instability occasioned principally by the opposition UPC party attempting to challenge Ahidjo's authoritarian regime. Moreover, single party dictatorships were becoming rife across sub-Saharan Africa, justified by the need to reinforce national unity and to promote the 'African Tradition'.[127] In Cameroon, the arrest of some UPC members in 1962 gave a firm indication that the future of political opposition was bleak.[128] Moreover, the administration created artificial obstacles to the participation of the opposition in daily political activities. Registration offices were closed to opposition candidates wishing to register their candidacy for local elections.[129] On other occasions, party meetings or rallies were dispersed by security officers.[130] Constrained by these difficulties, some members of the UPC and other opposition parties deserted to join the ruling party, the UC.[131] By 1965, all political parties in East Cameroon had been integrated into the UC.[132]

Meanwhile, the West Cameroonian political parties were embroiled in political wrangling, aware of where power actually resided in the Federation, they tried in their different respects to gain Ahidjo's favour.[133] Ahidjo used these differences to highlight the need to reach a consensus by forming a unified party. In June 1966, the West Cameroonian politicians were to heed Ahidjo's firm demand for the dissolution of political parties in that state.[134] In August 1966, the regime succeeded in bringing all political parties at the federal level under one umbrella organisation dubbed the Cameroon National Union (CNU) thereby ensuring the demise of political pluralism in Cameroon.[135] Ahidjo's rationale for the formation of a single dominant party was the underdeveloped nature of the country and he was careful to emphasise that the measure was only temporary.[136] However, that as it later emerged was a move to ensure the centralisation of political parties in order to pave the way for a unitary state.[137]

In May 1972, Ahidjo surprised the Federal Assembly with his intention to hold a popular referendum aimed at abolishing the Federation.[138] He argued that federalism was too costly and incompatible with the development of a young country like Cameroon and it promoted regionalism. A referendum was organised on 20 May 1972 to determine the fate of the federation. Following an overwhelming vote in favour of a unitary system, the federation was abolished. By organising the referendum, Ahidjo ignored the saving provision in article 47(1) of the Constitution which provided that 'Any proposal for the revision of the present constitution which impairs the unity and integrity of the federation shall be inadmissible'. This provision was inserted to assure West Cameroonian authorities that the Federation, the basis of the union, will not be altered.[139] In fact, article 47(3) further provided a mechanism for any alteration of the federation, should it become imperative. The provision required that a revision should be approved by a simple majority of the federal assembly provided that the majority included a majority of the representatives in the assembly of the *two federated states*. It therefore implied that a referendum was not contemplated as a means of dissolving the federation. It has been asserted that the choice of a referendum was Ahidjo's means to ensure that the proposal was not rejected by the West Cameroon Assembly and given the dictatorial nature of his regime, the public was likely to vote in favour of a unitary state.[140] It may also be the case that the people were presented with no choice but to vote in favour of a unitary state as the referendum question was framed in the language of economic progress, stability and development. A vote against a unitary state may have been interpreted as a refusal to support the country's development.

A unitary Constitution was thus adopted in June 1972.[141] That Constitution divided Cameroon administratively into provinces with the name of the country changed from the Federal Republic to the United Republic of Cameroon.[142] The word 'United' was very significant, as it acknowledged the fact that the country was composed of a union of two distinct entities. Besides the abolition of state institutions, the 1972 Constitution preserved much of the underlying centralised themes of the Federal Constitution and its Gaullist institutions. In particular, it increased the centralised authority of the president, abolished the position of the vice president, the West Cameroon House of Assembly and inevitably its House of Chiefs and subordinated the judiciary to the executive. The 1972 referendum, or what became known as the 'Glorious Revolution of May Twentieth',[143] brought an end to the last vestiges of the Westminster colonial legacy in Cameroon.

Although the federal system was not entirely favourable to West Cameroon, sentiments of subordination did not emerge immediately or at least were not overtly expressed. The repressive nature of the Ahidjo regime did not provide the space for that to happen. However, the 1972 referendum and the abolition of the federal form of the state represented for Anglophones a betrayal of the basis of the union in 1961.[144] It served to further alienate an already aggrieved people and paved the way for Anglophones to openly challenge their perceived marginalisation. That move became a catalyst for what is known as the 'Anglophone problem'.

C. The return to multi-party democracy

With the suppression of multi-party politics in Cameroon, Ahidjo's CNU remained at the centre of politics. However, in 1982, reportedly for health reasons he unexpectedly resigned from power automatically conferring presidential power on the then Prime Minister Paul Biya.[145] The first congress of the ruling CNU held under the Biya administration took place in Bamenda in 1985 and saw a change in the name of the CNU to the Cameroon People's Democratic Movement (CPDM). President Biya perpetuated the authoritarian regime established under his predecessor strengthened even further after April 1984 following an abortive coup d'état orchestrated by supporters of Ahidjo.[146] Biya's presidency was a pivotal point for the strengthening of Anglophone nationalism. Following a constitutional amendment in February 1984, the name of the country was changed from the United Republic of Cameroon to the Republic of Cameroon and the second star which had represented West Cameroon was eliminated from the national flag.[147] According to the government, the amendments were prompted by the desire to consolidate national unity and democracy, to give 'de jure and de facto recognition to Cameroon's fundamental option of national unity' and to adopt a less ambiguous and more prestigious name which 'stresses the one and indivisible nature of the nation'.[148]

Despite the government's explanations, the amendments had an alternative significance for the Anglophones. First, it eliminated any illusions that Cameroon was a result of two separate entities that had come together in a union, further betraying the basis for the 1961 agreement. Second, the new name was the original name adopted by French Cameroon when it gained independence from France in 1960. Reverting to that name, was a denial of the existence of the former West Cameroon as a distinct entity.[149] There was a sustained attempt by the Biya government to standardise the education systems and in particular to transform the Cameroon General Certificate of Education Examination (GCE), a relic of British colonialism, to be in line with the French Baccalaureate. This was fiercely resisted by the Anglophones who sort to retain their distinct education system. Following periods of violent altercations and repression of the Anglophone protesters by security forces, the government finally succumbed to pressure by creating the GCE Board which gave independent management of the exams to Anglophone educators. Unlike the Ahidjo government which had a semblance of regional balance in political and administrative appointments, the Biya government embarked on the appointment of predominantly Francophones to key government positions and also overtly favouring members of his ethnic group.[150] Biya's ideal of a unitary state was at variance with the recognition of the Anglophone minority and helped to provide a conducive environment for the nurturing of Anglophone sentiments of marginalisation. In 1985, the prominent Anglophone lawyer and paramount chief Gorji Dinka was arrested and tried for treason when he advocated for secession of the Anglophone regions to form the Ambazonia Republic.[151]

The regime remained repressive and intolerant to opposition and criticism. Nevertheless, the political environment witnessed gradual changes through increasing domestic demands for political liberalisation.[152] This course was championed by the Anglophone minority that witnessed sustained marginalisation in socio-economic development and insufficient representation in public administration.[153] The wave of political change sweeping through sub-Saharan Africa in the late 1980s and early 1990s helped to fuel political and legal developments in Cameroon.[154] The regime resisted calls for democratisation and responded to such demands with repression.[155] In February 1990, a group of Anglophone elites organised meetings to discuss the declining economic and political conditions in Cameroon and the possibility of forming a political party.[156] They were arrested, tried and convicted for holding clandestine meetings, for promoting secession and for insulting the President.[157] This sparked further tension as it became clear that the regime was not ready for a democratic transition.[158] The government argued that the country was not ready for multiparty democracy as it would promote ethnic division and instability.[159] The government's response only increased the political tension and in May 1990 the opposition party Social Democratic Front (SDF) was formed.[160] During its official launching, security forces responded with repressive force killing six participants, mainly children.[161] The opposition responded by forming a coalition which organised nation-wide civil disobedience campaigns to paralyse governmental institutions.[162] The Anglophone movement received a further boost when former vice President Foncha, one of the main architects of the federation and vice chair of the ruling CPDM party tendered his resignation, lamenting the treatment of Anglophones.[163]

The government attempted to ease the political tensions by making some reforms through the enactment of what became known as the Liberty Laws, some of which authorised political participation in Cameroon.[164] A consequence was the proliferation of opposition parties, pressure groups, civil society organisations and independent press organisations.[165] Some of these included the Southern Cameroons Peoples Organisation (SCAPO), Free West Cameroon Movement (FWCM), the Ambazonia Movement and the Cameroon Anglophone Movement which became very instrumental in Anglophone nationalism in 1993 and 1994. The new liberty laws, however, operated within the framework of the 1972 unitary Constitution which was hostile to genuine democratic advancement.[166] The opposition continued to request a sovereign national conference which the President had rejected as having no purpose in Cameroon.[167] However, in October 1991, a Tripartite Conference was organised by the government to bring together representative of the opposition, the ruling CPDM and government officials in an attempt to resolve the political crisis.[168] It resulted in the Yaoundé Declaration which was essentially a concession to which the opposition agreed to end the civil disobedience campaigns while the government acceded to making democratic and constitutional reforms.[169] The government failed to keep its side of the agreement particularly by failing to provide for an independent electoral system prior to presidential election in 1992. The incumbent President Biya won the elections which were reportedly marred by gross irregularities and electoral rigging.[170] In response, supporters of the SDF whose candidate was alleged to have been the actual winner staged massive demonstrations in the North-West region.[171] A state of emergency was declared in that region and resulted in massive violations of human rights by security forces.[172] The leader of the SDF was placed under house arrest.[173]

Although the government continued to resist genuine democratic reforms, international donors such as the International Monetary Fund and the World Bank pressured repressive regimes such as that of Cameroon to increase the pace of democratic reforms.[174] The government subsequently gave into those demands, and to demands for a constitutional review. The President appointed eleven members to a Technical Committee on Constitutional Matters (TCCM), initially established during the Tripartite Conference.[175] The TCCM was composed of seven Francophones and four Anglophones and chaired by Joseph Owona, then Secretary General at the presidency and member of the central committee of the ruling CPDM.[176] It set to work on a constitutional *revision* contrary to the terms of the Yaoundé Declaration which had agreed on the drafting of a new constitution.[177] Meanwhile, an All Anglophone Conference (AAC I) was convened in April 1993 to adopt a common Anglophone stance and to make proposals to the TCCM.[178] The standing committee established by the AAC I submitted a draft constitution to the TCCM, proposing among other things, recognition of the principles of liberal democracy, respect for human rights and fundamental freedoms, a return to federalism, reinstatement of the House of Chiefs, a presidential system with more stringent features of separation of powers, checks and balances, judicial independence and judicial review reminiscent of the Southern Cameroons Constitution.[179] A number of opposition parties, including the SDF, National Union for Democracy and Progress (NUDP) and Cameroon Democratic Union (CDU) also submitted proposals echoing those of the AAC. The SDF and NUDP went further to propose the establishment of a bicameral legislature comprising a House of Assembly and Senate, and that all presidential appointments be confirmed by Senate.[180]

However, the TCCM did not meet to discuss the proposals and amidst pressure from the government, it rejected those proposals prompting the resignation of its Anglophone members.[181] This purported rejection of the Anglophone initiative prompted the Cameroon Anglophone Movement (CAM) which was affiliated to the AAC to declare the so called 'zero option' which implied that the only option was an outright secession of the Anglophone regions. This proposal gained support in the second AAC (AAC II) held in 1994. The AAC II resulted in the Bamenda Declaration which among other things agreed on secession if the government failed to engage in meaningful constitutional negotiations or persisted in its refusal to do so.[182] The Anglophone Council was to become a constituent assembly should independence be declared for Anglophone Cameroon. The Anglophone Council, the elected governing body of the AAC was subsequently transformed into the Southern Cameroons National Council (SCNC) with its youth wing, the Southern Cameroons Youth League (SCY). The SCNC has since been at the forefront of the demand for independence and secession of Anglophone Cameroon.

In November 1994, a new TCCM was appointed with different terms of reference, vis, to study a presidential proposal for the revision of the Constitution.[183] The proposals were then submitted to parliament in the November 1995 parliamentary session,[184] and subsequently enacted as the 1996 Constitution.[185] That Constitution completely ignored the proposals of the AAC and preserved much of the underlying centralised theme of the 1972 Constitution. The 1996 Constitution is the current Constitution of Cameroon and although not an entirely new document, the amendments are substantial and perhaps account for why it was described as ushering in a new era for the separation of powers, democratic governance and human rights.[186] It is purported to harness political liberalism introduced through the liberty laws, even though genuine political participation is yet to be really achieved.

Conclusion

Contemporary Cameroon is undoubtedly haunted by its chequered history. There is useful debate to be had in respect of the factors that could account for the many legal, political and governance issues bedevilling its development. As mentioned previously, the very nature of its colonial administration speaks volumes as to the genuine intentions of the colonial masters to equip their sections of the territory for eventual self-determination. In the case of British Southern Cameroons in particular, its attachment to Nigeria, though not unreasonable, necessarily implied its development was sacrificed for administrative convenience. However, an argument could be made that a substantial focus on its development would have potentially put that section of the territory in a resilient position, more equipped to take on the challenges of a modern society. Be that as it may, Cameroon's animated colonial history accounts significantly, for its constitutional and political development, or the lack thereof and its multifarious governance problems discussed in subsequent chapters. However, the 1996 Constitution should arguably be a defining point for the liberalisation of Cameroon given that it introduces essential elements of a constitutional democracy. Yet, the country continues to face considerable governance challenges which have hampered its development and contributed to a stalled democratic process.

Notes

1 Neville Rubin, *Cameroon: An African Federation* (Pall Mall 1971) 42. See also Emmanuel Chiabi, *The Making of Modern Cameroon: A History of Substate Nationalism and Disparate Union, 1914–1961* (University Press of America 1997) 9–10; Victor J Ngoh, *Southern Cameroons, 1922–1961: A Constitutional History* (Ashgate 2001) 1–2. See also Laura-Stella Enonchong, 'The Problem of Systemic Violation of Civil and Political Rights in Cameroon: Towards a Contextualised Conception of Constitutionalism' (PhD Thesis, University of Warwick 2013) 59–60.

2 Yale Law School, 'The Avalon Project. Documents in Law, History and Diplomacy: The Versailles Treaty, 28 June 1919' http://avalon.law.yale.edu/imt/partxv.asp (accessed 31 October 2012). See also Rubin (n 1) 42; Ngoh, *Southern Cameroons* (n 1) 2.

3 Cameroon under French Trusteeship Agreement as Approved by the General Assembly of the United Nations, and Cameroon under United Kingdom Trusteeship Agreement as Approved by the General Assembly of the United Nations, reproduced in Rubin (n 1) 203–213, Appendices III and IV, respectively. See also Ngoh, *Southern Cameroons* (n 1) 2.

4 Mandate for the Administration of Part of the Former German Territory of the Cameroons Conferred upon the Government of the French Republic, Confirmed and Defined by the Council of the League of Nations. London, 20 July 1922. Reproduced in Rubin (n 1) Appendix 1, 196–198.

5 British Mandate for the Cameroons, 20 July 1922. Reproduced in Rubin (n 1) Appendix II, 199–203.
6 Trusteeship Agreement for the Territory of the Cameroons under British Administration (UNGA Approved on 13 December 1946) 118 UNTS 135.
7 Trusteeship Agreement for the Territory of the Cameroons under French Administration (UNGA Approved on 13 December 1946) 119 UNTS 135.
8 Decree of 22 May 1924, art 10 cited in Jeswald W Salacuse, *Legal Systems of Africa Series: French Speaking Africa (Africa South of the Sahara)* (vol 1, The Michie Company 1969) 29.
9 Salacuse, *Legal Systems of Africa Series* (n 8) 31; Enonchong, 'The Problem of Systemic Violation' (n 1) 60–65.
10 *Afrique Équatoriale Française:* Decree of 16 August 1912, art 36.
11 Rubin (n 1) 50; David Gardinier, *Cameroon: United Nations Challenge to French Policy* (Oxford University Press 1963) 15; Victor T Le Vine, *The Cameroons: From Mandate to Independence* (University of California Press 1964) 94.
12 Le Vine, *The Cameroons: From Mandate* (n 11) 92–94.
13 Rubin (n 1) 50.
14 Carlson Anyangwe, *The Cameroonian Judicial System* (CEPER 1987) 102–103.
15 ibid 102–103, 112.
16 It has been described as 'the most resented facet' of French discriminatory policies in French Cameroon. See Rubin (n 1) 51.
17 Le Vine, *The Cameroons: From Mandate* (n 11) 117.
18 Edward Mortimer, *France and the Africans: 1944–1960* (Faber and Faber Ltd 1961) 49; Robert Collins, *African History: Western African History* (Markus Wiener Publishers 1997) 117–120. See also Rubin (n 1) 52–53.
19 French Government Decree of 8 December 1945 and 20 February 1946. See Le Vine, *The Cameroons: From Mandate* (n 11) 110.
20 Rubin (n 1) 54.
21 ibid 61. See also Le Vine, *The Cameroons: From Mandate* (n 11) 142–144.
22 Richard Joseph, *Radical Nationalism in Cameroon: Social Origins of the UPC Rebellion* (Oxford University Press 1977) 32.
23 Willard Johnson, *The Cameroon Federation: Political Integration in a Fragmentary Society* (Princeton University Press 1970) 136–140; Rubin (n 1) 63–64.
24 Le Vine, *The Cameroons: From Mandate* (n 11) 156.
25 ibid 153–160. See also Rubin (n 1) 66–69; Johnson (n 23) 128.
26 Rubin (n 1) 55; Le Vine, *The Cameroons: From Mandate* (n 11) 156.
27 Le Vine, *The Cameroons: From Mandate* (n 11) 163–166.
28 Rubin (n 1) 55; Le Vine, *The Cameroons: From Mandate* (n 11) 157, 162–166.
29 Le Vine, *The Cameroons: From Mandate* (n 11) 166; Martin Atangana, *The End of French Rule in Cameroon* (University Press of America 2010).
30 Cameroons under British Administration Order-in-Council No. 1621, 1923, art 3.
31 Ngoh, *Southern Cameroons* (n 1) 4–5; Enonchong, 'The Problem of Systemic Violation' (n 1) 66–72.
32 Mufor Atanga, *The Anglophone Cameroon Predicament* (Langaa RPCIG 2011) 42.
33 Southern Cameroons High Court Law 1955 (hereafter, SCHCL), s 11.
34 British Cameroons Ordinance No. 5 of 1924; Rubin (n 1) 73. See Anthony N Allott, *Judicial and Legal Systems in Africa* (Butterworths 1962) 76–78.
35 SCHCL 1955, s 27(1). The caveat to the application of customary law was that it was not repugnant to natural justice, equity and good conscience, nor incompatible with any law being enforced. Today, customary law has a very limited application.
36 'Fon' is the terminology used to describe traditional leaders (chiefs) in the North-West Region of Cameroon. See Enonchong, 'The Problem of Systemic Violation' (n 1) 68.
37 Ngoh, *Southern Cameroons* (n 1) 6.
38 Nigeria Protectorate Order-in-Council 1922, art 4. See also Anyangwe (n 14) 57.

39 Ngoh, *Southern Cameroons* (n 1) 7. See also Bongfen Chem-Langhee, 'The Origins of the Southern Cameroons House of Chiefs' (1983) 16(4) *The International Journal of African Historical Studies* 653, 655–656.
40 Ngoh, *Southern Cameroons* (n 1).
41 Nicholas Ofiaja, *Stability and Instability in Politics: The Case of Nigeria and Cameroon* (Vantage Press 1979) 50, 53; Le Vine, *The Cameroons: From Mandate* (n 11) 199.
42 Ngoh, *Southern Cameroons* (n 1) 10; Enonchong, 'The Problem of Systemic Violation' (n 1) 71–72.
43 Ngoh, *Southern Cameroons* (n 1) 12.
44 ibid.
45 Atanga, *The Anglophone Cameroon Predicament* (n 32) 42; Charles Fombad, *Constitutional Law in Cameroon* (Wolters Kluwer 2012) 25.
46 Ngoh, *Southern Cameroons* (n 1) 61.
47 Eastern Region, Nigeria (Commission of Inquiry) HC Deb, 24 July 1956, vol 557, cc215-21.
48 The Lyttleton Constitution of 1954. See also Nigerian Constitution, HL Deb 10 February 1954, vol 185, cols 795–797; Ngoh, *Southern Cameroons* (n 1) 87–88.
49 Atangana, *The End of French Rule in Cameroon* (n 29) 85.
50 See French Government Order No. 58-1357 of 31 December 1958. It went into effect on 1 January 1959.
51 UN General Assembly Resolution 1349(XIII), 13 March 1959, paras 2–6.
52 UN General Assembly Resolution 1349(XIII), 13 March 1959, para 10(1).
53 Atangana (n 29) 98.
54 ibid.
55 By virtue of Law No. 59-56 of 31 October 1959; Atangana (n 29) 101.
56 Eme Awa, *Federal Government in Nigeria* (University of California Press 1964) 58.
57 United Nations Trusteeship Council, 'Report of the United Nations Commissioner for the Supervision of the Plebiscites in the Southern and Northern Parts of the Cameroons under United Kingdom Administration' (3 April 1961) UN Doc. T/1556, 9. Hereafter, Plebiscite Report.
58 Plebiscite Report, 11.
59 Southern Cameroons: Constitution, HC Deb 11 June 1959, vol 606, cols 1153, 1154. See also Piet Konings and Francis Nyamnjoh, *Negotiating an Anglophone Identity: A Study of the Politics of Recognition* (BRILL 2003) 22–36; Ngoh, *Southern Cameroons* (n 1) 122–132.
60 Plebiscite Report, 14. See also Konings and Nyamnjoh (n 59) 22–36; Ngoh, *Southern Cameroons* (n 1) 122–132.
67 ibid, para 2.
61 According to which one of the purposes of the trusteeship system was 'to promote the political, economic, social, and educational advancement of the inhabitants of the trust territories, and their progressive development towards self-government or independence as may be appropriate to the particular circumstances of each territory and its peoples and the freely expressed wishes of the peoples concerned, and as may be provided by the terms of each trusteeship agreement'.
62 UN General Assembly Resolution 1350(XIII), 13 March 1959, para 1.
63 ibid, para 3.
64 UN General Assembly Resolution 1350(XIII), 13 March 1959, para 5.
65 See Foncha, John [Premier of the Southern Cameroons] and Dr EML Endeley. Agreed Statement. UN Doc A/C.4/414, GAOR, 14th Session, 199, Annexes, Agenda Item 41.
66 UN General Assembly Resolution 1352(XIV), 16 October 1959, para 5.
68 Nicodemus Awasom, 'The Reunification Question in Cameroon History: Was the Bride an Enthusiastic or a Reluctant One?' (2000) 47(2) *Africa Today* 90, 109–111.
69 Awasom, 'The Reunification Question' (n 68) 109–111; Atanga (n 32) 46–47.

70 Atanga (n 32) 47.
71 Sydney Philipson, *Financial and Administrative Consequences to the Southern Cameroons of Separation from the Federation of Nigeria, 1959* (Government Printer 1959) 8–10; Plebiscite Report, 32.
72 Philipson Report (n 71) para 3(d).
73 ibid, paras 12 and 49(1).
74 Southern Cameroons: Constitution, HC Deb 11 June 1959 vol, 606, cols 1153, 1154. See also *Ngoh, Southern Cameroons* (n 1) 34, 83–84; Johnson (n 23) 100, 104–107.
75 United Kingdom and Nigeria (Ministerial Discussions), HC Deb 19 May 1960, vol 623, cols 1494–1498.
76 Philipson Report (n 71) para 49(1).
77 Future of the Trust Territory of the Cameroons under United Kingdom Administration, Resolution 2013(XXVI) of 31 May 1960, para 3.
78 Plebiscite Report, 39.
79 Plebiscite Report, 40. See also Southern Cameroons: Future, HC Deb 09 April 1959, vol 603, cols 32-3W; United Kingdom and Nigeria (Ministerial Discussions), HC Deb 19 May 1960, vol 623, cols 1494–1498.
80 See, for instance, Resolution 1352(XIV) para 4, Resolution 1608(XV) of 21 April 1961 paras 4(b) and 5.
81 Awasom, 'The Reunification Question' (n 68) 109; Atanga (n 32) 46–47.
82 Plebiscite Report, 39–44.
83 ibid.
84 Southern Cameroons Gazette No. 4, vol 7 of January 1961. The UN appointed Plebiscite Commissioner noted that although the electorate understood that the two options were to join Nigeria or the Republic of Cameroon, it was uncertain whether they understood the actual implications of the two options. Plebiscite Report, 44.
85 Plebiscite Report, 140.
86 Plebiscite Report, 246.
87 Resolution 1608(XV), para 2(a)(b).
88 Resolution 1608(XV), para 4(a)(b).
89 HC Deb, 1 August 1961, vol 645, cols 1332–1351.
90 Plebiscite Report, 146.
91 ibid.
92 Johnson (n 23) 183; Ngoh, *Southern Cameroons* (n 1) 156–163.
93 Rubin (n 1) 11–114; Johnson (n 23) 171–172.
94 Frank Stark, 'Federalism in Cameroon: The Shadow and the Reality' (1976) 3(10) *Canadian Journal of African Studies* 423, 431–434.
95 Rubin (n 1).
96 ibid. See also Ngoh, *Southern Cameroons* (n 1) 159–164.
97 Ngoh, *Southern Cameroons* (n 1) 160.
98 ibid.
99 ibid 159–164; Stark, 'Federalism in Cameroon' (n 94) 427. See also Rubin (n 1) 113–114; Johnson (n 23) 184.
100 ibid.
101 Though Southern Cameroons had been separated from Nigeria, it still remained a trust territory of the UN. See Ahmadou Ahidjo, *Contribution to National Construction* (Presence Afriçaine 1964) 23. See also Ngoh, *Southern Cameroons* (n 1) 160; Ndiva Kofele-Kale, 'Ethnicity, Regionalism and Political Power: A Post-mortem of Ahidjo's Cameroon' in M ichael Schatzerberg and William Zartman (eds) *The Political Economy of Cameroon* (Praeger 1986) 63.
102 Ngoh, *Southern Cameroons* (n 1) 163; Rubin (n 1) 114; Namata N Mbile, *Cameroon Political Story: Memories of an Authentic Eyewitness* (Presprint 1999) 165–195.

103 Prior to the Foumban encounter, Ahidjo had sent his proposals to Premier Foncha in order for his delegates to familiarise themselves with the Republic's proposal and produce their counter proposals. It is alleged that Foncha concealed this document from his delegates and as a result they were only presented with it on the first day of the Foumban Conference. See Rubin (n 1) 114; Ngoh, *Southern Cameroons* (n 1) 163; Mbile (n 102) 165–195.
104 Atanga (n 32) 50–60.
105 The legitimacy of that constitution has defined some of the arguments relating to the Anglophone problem in Cameroon. This issue will be discussed in Chapter 6.
106 Acts of Union of Tanganyika and Zanzibar, 25 April 1964, Act No. 22 of 1964 (Cap. 557 of the Laws).
107 This was done on 29 October 1964 through the United Republic (Declaration of Name) Act of 1964, Act No. 61 of 1964 (Cap. 578 of the Laws).
108 Markku Suksi, *Substate Governance Through Territorial Autonomy: A Comparative Study in Constitutional Law of Powers, Procedures and Institutions* (Springer 2011) 188–210.
109 Federal Constitution, 1961 (hereafter, Fed. Const.) art 1. According to the British Under-Secretary for Colonies, a federation was the best possible option to promote unity while preserving the separate identity of the two territories. See HC Deb, 1 August 1961, vol 645, cols 1332–1351.
110 Article 59 of the Federal Constitution made that clear by providing that 'Les présent dispositions, qui portent révision de la Constitution de la République adoptée le 21 Février 1960 par le peuple camerounais …'.
111 Translated as 'The revised constitution shall be published in French and in English, the French version being authentic' (official translation).
112 The issue of the possible subordination of the Southern Cameroons was significantly discussed in the UK. House of Commons where some members of Parliament raised concerns about reports from the Republic of Cameroon indicating a certain perception that Southern Cameroons would be colonised by them. In fact, Honourable Mr Thompson (Dundee, East) repeated a phrase 'Le premier Octobre on va saisir le Cameroun du Sud' which had become a familiar slogan in the Republic. (On 1 October, we will take control of Southern Cameroons – author's translation). HC Deb, 1 August 1961, vol 645, cols 1332–1351.
113 Fed. Const, art 46.
114 Decree No. 61-DF-15 of 20 December 1961.
115 Stark, 'Federalism in Cameroon' (n 94) 432.
116 ibid.
117 Jacques Benjamin, *Les Camerounais Occidentaux. La Minorite´ Dans un Etat Bicommunautaire* (Montreal University Press 1972) 197.
118 ibid
119 Stark, 'Federalism in Cameroon' (n 94) 432.
120 Daniel Weinstock, 'Towards a Normative Theory of Federalism' (2001) 53(167) *International Social Science Journal* 75.
121 Stark (n 94) 427.
122 Stark (n 94) 428.
123 Benjamin, *'Les Camerounais Occidentaux'* (n 117) xvi.
124 Benjamin, *'Les Camerounais Occidentaux'* (n 117) xvi; Stark (n 94) 434, 437. This long-term objective was affirmed recently by President Paul Biya at the November 2019 Paris Peace Summit. See Amos Fofung, 'Cameroon: From Biya, A Mea Culpa on the Anglophone Crisis in Paris' (*Pan African Vision*, 14 November 2019) https://panafricanvisions.com/2019/11/cameroon-from-biya-a-mea-culpa-on-the-anglophone-crisis-in-paris/ accessed 30 November 2019.

125 Joseph Ebune, 'The Dilemma of the Federal System in West Cameroon, 1961–1972' (2016) 7(2) *Journal of Scientific Research and Studies* 133, 135. See generally Stark (n 94).
126 Rubin (n 1) 143–144; Jean Francois Bayart, 'The Birth of the Ahidjo Regime' in Richard Joseph (ed) *Gaullist Africa: Cameroon under Ahmadou Ahidjo* (Fourth Dimension Publishers 1978) 60–61.
127 Johnson (n 23) 280; Rubin (n 1) 144.
128 Johnson (n 23) 254. See also Bayart, 'The Birth of the Ahidjo Regime' (n 126) 62.
129 Johnson (n 23) 254–255.
130 Bayart, 'The Birth of the Ahidjo Regime' (n 126) 61. See also Gardinier (n 11) 125 esp. note 15.
131 Le Vine, *The Cameroons: From Mandate* (n 11) 221–224; Johnson (n 23) 254–255; Bayart, 'The Birth of the Ahidjo Regime' (n 126) 62.
132 ibid.
133 Johnson (n 23) 257–258.
134 Johnson (n 23) 284–285; Rubin (n 1) 152; Bayart, 'The Neutralisation of Anglophone Cameroon' in Richard Joseph (ed) *Gaullist Africa: Cameroon under Ahmadou Ahidjo* (Fourth Dimension Publishers 1978) 87.
135 Johnson (n 23) 285; Rubin (n 1) 153; Bayart, 'The Neutralisation of Anglophone Cameroon' (n 134) 87.
136 Bayart, 'The Birth of the Ahidjo Regime' (n 126) 61.
137 Johnson (n 23) 280.
138 Bayart, 'The Structure of Political Power' in Richard Joseph (ed) *Gaullist Africa: Cameroon under Ahmadou Ahidjo* (Fourth Dimension Publishers 1978) 89; Atanga (n 32) 76.
139 Piet Konings, 'The Anglophone Struggle for Federalism in Cameroon' in Lidija Basta and Jibrin Ibrahim (eds) *Federalism and Decentralisation in Africa: The Multicultural Challenge* (Institute of Federalism 1999) 303.
140 Konings, 'The Anglophone Struggle for Federalism' (n 139) 303.
141 Decree No. 72/270 of 2 June Promulgating the Constitution of the United Republic of Cameroon, 1972 Constitution (Unitary Constitution).
142 Unitary Constitution, art 1. In 1984, this appellation was changed to the Republic of Cameroon. See art 1 as amended by Law No. 84/1 of 4 February 1984.
143 Stark (n 94) 423.
144 This is discussed further in Chapter 6.
145 Victor Ngoh, 'Biya and the Transition to Democracy' in John Mbaku and Joseph Takougang (eds) *The Leadership Challenge in Africa: Cameroon under Paul Biya* (Africa World Press Inc. 2004) 427.
146 Charles Fombad and Jonie Fonyam, 'The Social Democratic Front, the Opposition and Political Transition in Cameroon' in Mbaku and Takougang (eds) *The Leadership Challenge in Africa: Cameroon under Paul Biya* (Africa World Press Inc. 2004) 462; Piet Konings, *The Politics of Neoliberal Reforms in Africa: State and Civil Society in Cameroon* (Langaa Research/African Studies Centre 2011) 30.
147 Unitary Constitution, art 1. As amended by Law No. 84/1 of 4 February 1984.
148 El Hadj Hayatou, 'Secretary General of the National Assembly's Explanatory Note on the February 1984 Amendment of the Constitution of Cameroon' (1985) 1(143) *Inter-Parliamentary Union Bulletin* 4.
149 Konings, 'Anglophone Struggle' (n 139) 306.
150 ibid.
151 ibid.
152 Ngoh, 'Biya and the Transition to Democracy' (n 145) 434–437; Konings, *The Politics of Neoliberal Reforms* (n 146) 35–36.
153 ibid. See also Konings, 'The Anglophone Struggle' (n 139) 305–307.

154 Konings, *The Politics of Neoliberal Reforms* (n 146) 35–37.
155 Ngoh, 'Biya and the Transition to Democracy' (n 145) 434; Fombad and Fonyam 'The Social Democratic Front' (n 146) 462; Konings, 'The Anglophone Struggle' (n 139) 306.
156 Ngoh, 'Biya and the Transition to Democracy' (n 145) 433; Fombad and Fonyam (n 146) 462.
157 ibid. See also Joseph Takougang and Milton Krieger, *An African State and Society in the 1990s: Cameroon's Political Crossroads* (Westview Press 1998) 105.
158 ibid.
159 Ngoh, 'Biya and the Transition to Democracy' (n 145) 434.
160 ibid 435–436; Fombad and Fonyam (n 146) 463; Konings, The Anglophone Struggle' (n 139) 307; Takougang and Krieger, *An African State and Society* (n 157) 107.
161 ibid.
162 Ngoh, 'Biya and the Transition to Democracy' (n 145) 437.
163 Konings, 'The Anglophone Struggle' (n 139) 307.
164 Law No. 90/052 on the Freedom of Social Communication (FSC); Law No. 90/053 on Freedom of Association; Law No. 90/055 on Public Meetings, Processions and Parades; Law No. 90/056 on Political Parties, all promulgated on 19 December 1990.
165 Ngoh, 'Biya and the Transition to Democracy' (n 145) 437; Fombad and Fonyam (n 146) 464–465; Konings, 'The Anglophone Struggle' (n 139) 308.
166 Ngoh, 'Biya and the Transition to Democracy' (n 145) 437.
167 Konings, *The Politics of Neoliberal Reforms in Africa* (n 146) 39–40.
168 Ngoh, 'Biya and the Transition to Democracy' (n 145) 440.
169 ibid.
170 Ngoh, 'Biya and the Transition to Democracy' (n 145) 441–442; Fombad and Fonyam (n 146) 470; Konings, 'The Anglophone Struggle' (n 139) 308.
171 ibid.
172 ibid.
173 ibid.
174 Ngoh, 'Biya and the Transition to Democracy' (n 145) 432; Konings, *The Politics of Neoliberal Reforms* (n 146) 356–357.
175 Ngoh, 'Biya and the Transition to Democracy' (n 145) 442.
176 Ngoh, 'Biya and the Transition to Democracy' (n 145) 442; Takougang and Krieger (n 157) 183.
177 ibid.
178 Konings, 'The Anglophone Struggle' (n 139) 310–311.
179 ibid 311– 315.
180 Takougang and Krieger (n 157) 184–189.
181 Konings, 'The Anglophone Struggle' (n 139) 316; Takougang and Krieger (n 157) 183.
182 Konings, 'The Anglophone Struggle' (n 139) 316.
183 Konings, 'The Anglophone Struggle' (n 139) 316; Takougang and Krieger (n 157) 183, 190.
184 Takougang and Krieger (n 157) 190.
185 Law No. 96/06 of 18 January 1996 to amend the Constitution of 2 June 1972.
186 Augustin K Kouomegni, 'Minister of Communication's Introductory Note to the 1996 Constitutional Amendment' *Fundamental Legal Texts* (vol 1, National Printing Press 1996). Except otherwise indicated, all references to the Constitution, henceforth, relate to the 1996 Constitution.

References

Ahidjo A, *Contribution to National Construction* (Presence Afriçaine 1964).
Allott A, *Judicial and Legal Systems in Africa* (Butterworths 1962).

Anyangwe C, *The Cameroonian Judicial System* (CEPER 1987).
Atanga M, *The Anglophone Cameroon Predicament* (Langaa RPCIG 2011).
Atangana M, *The End of French Rule in Cameroon* (University Press of America 2010).
Awa E, *Federal Government in Nigeria* (University of California Press 1964).
Awasom NF, 'The Reunification Question in Cameroon History: Was the Bride an Enthusiastic or a Reluctant One?' (2000) *47*(2) *Africa Today* 90.
Bayart JF, 'The Birth of the Ahidjo Regime' in Richard Joseph (ed) *Gaullist Africa: Cameroon under Ahmadou Ahidjo* (Fourth Dimension Publishers 1978).
Bayart JF 'The Neutralisation of Anglophone Cameroon' in Richard Joseph (ed) *Gaullist Africa: Cameroon under Ahmadou Ahidjo* (Fourth Dimension Publishers 1978).
Bayart JF 'The Structure of Political Power' in Richard Joseph (ed) *Gaullist Africa: Cameroon under Ahmadou Ahidjo* (Fourth Dimension Publishers 1978).
Benjamin J, *Les Camerounais Occidentaux. La Minorite' Dans un Etat Bicommunautaire* (Montreal University Press 1972).
Chem-Langhee B, 'The Origins of the Southern Cameroons House of Chiefs' (1983) *16*(4) *The International Journal of African Historical Studies* 653.
Chiabi E, *The Making of Modern Cameroon: A History of Substate Nationalism and Disparate Union, 1914-1961* (University Press of America 1997).
Collins R, *African History: Western African History* (Markus Wiener Publishers 1997).
Ebune J, 'The Dilemma of the Federal System in West Cameroon, 1961–1972' (2016) *7*(2) *Journal of Scientific Research and Studies* 133.
Enonchong L, *'The Problem of Systemic Violation of Civil and Political Rights in Cameroon: Towards a Contextualised Conception of Constitutionalism'* (PhD Thesis, University of Warwick 2013).
Fofung A, 'Cameroon: From Biya, A Mea Culpa on the Anglophone Crisis in Paris' (*Pan African Vision*, 14 November 2019) https://panafricanvisions.com/2019/11/cameroon-from-biya-a-mea-culpa-on-the-anglophone-crisis-in-paris/ accessed 30November2019.
Fombad C, *Constitutional Law in Cameroon* (Wolters Kluwer 2012).
Fombad C and Fonyam J, 'The Social Democratic Front, the Opposition and Political Transition in Cameroon' in John Mbaku and Joseph Takougang (eds) *The Leadership Challenge in Africa: Cameroon under Paul Biya* (Africa World Press Inc. 2004).
Gardinier D, *Cameroon: United Nations Challenge to French Policy* (Oxford University Press 1963).
Hadj HE, 'Secretary General of the National Assembly's Explanatory Note on the February 1984 Amendment of the Constitution of Cameroon' (1985) *1*(143) *Inter-Parliamentary Union Bulletin* 4.
Johnson W, *The Cameroon Federation: Political Integration in a Fragmentary Society* (Princeton University Press 1970).
Joseph R, *Radical Nationalism in Cameroon: Social Origins of the UPC Rebellion* (Oxford University Press 1977).
Kofele-Kale N, 'Ethnicity, Regionalism and Political Power: A Post-Mortem of Ahidjo's Cameroon' in Michael Schatzerberg and William Zartman (eds) *The Political Economy of Cameroon* (Praeger 1986).
Konings P, 'The Anglophone Struggle for Federalism in Cameroon' in Lidija Basta and Jibrin Ibrahim (eds) *Federalism and Decentralisation in Africa: The Multicultural Challenge* (Institute of Federalism 1999).
Konings P, *The Politics of Neoliberal Reforms in Africa: State and Civil Society in Cameroon* (Langaa Research/African Studies Centre 2011).

Konings P and Nyamnjoh F, *Negotiating an Anglophone Identity: A Study of the Politics of Recognition* (BRILL 2003).

Kouomegni AK, 'Minister of Communication's Introductory Note to the 1996 Constitutional Amendment' *Fundamental Legal Texts* (vol 1, National Printing Press 1996).

Le Vine VT, *The Cameroons: From Mandate to Independence* (University of California Press 1964).

Mbile NN, *Cameroon Political Story: Memories of an Authentic Eyewitness* (Presprint 1999).

Mortimer E, *France and the Africans: 1944–1960* (Faber and Faber Ltd 1961).

Ngoh VJ, *Southern Cameroons, 1922–1961: A Constitutional History* (Ashgate 2001).

Ngoh VJ 'Biya and the Transition to Democracy' in John Mbaku and Joseph Takougang (eds) *The Leadership Challenge in Africa: Cameroon under Paul Biya* (Africa World Press Inc. 2004).

Ofiaja N, *Stability and Instability in Politics: The Case of Nigeria and Cameroon* (Vantage Press 1979).

Philipson S, *Financial and Administrative Consequences to the Southern Cameroons of Separation from the Federation of Nigeria, 1959* (Government Printer 1959).

Rubin N, *Cameroon: An African Federation* (Pall Mall 1971).

Salacuse JW, *Legal Systems of Africa Series: French Speaking Africa (Africa South of the Sahara)* (vol 1, The Michie Company 1969).

Stark F, 'Federalism in Cameroon: The Shadow and the Reality' (1976) *3*(10) *Canadian Journal of African Studies* 423.

Suksi M, *Substate Governance Through Territorial Autonomy: A Comparative Study in Constitutional Law of Powers, Procedures and Institutions* (Springer 2011).

Takougang J and Krieger M, *An African State and Society in the 1990s: Cameroon's Political Crossroads* (Westview Press 1998)

Trusteeship Agreement for the Territory of the Cameroons under British Administration (UNGA Approved on 13 December 1946) 118 UNTS 135.

Trusteeship Agreement for the Territory of the Cameroons under French Administration (UNGA Approved on 13 December 1946) 119 UNTS 135.

United Nations Trusteeship Council, *'Report of the United Nations Commissioner for the Supervision of the Plebiscites in the Southern and Northern Parts of the Cameroons under United Kingdom Administration'* (3 April 1961) UN Doc. T/1556.

Foncha, John [Premier of the Southern Cameroons] and Dr EML Endeley. Agreed Statement. UN Doc A/C.4/414, GAOR, 14th Session, 199, Annexes, Agenda Item 41.

Weinstock D, 'Towards a Normative Theory of Federalism' (2001) *53*(167) *International Social Science Journal* 75.

Yale Law School, 'The Avalon Project. Documents in Law, History and Diplomacy: The Versailles Treaty, 28 June 1919' http://avalon.law.yale.edu/imt/partxv.asp (accessed 31 October 2012).

2 Executive power in the context of semi-presidentialism

Introduction

It is worth noting that, under the 1996 Constitution, executive power operates in the context of semi-presidentialism, which is meant to reduce the over-concentration of executive authority in one institution. This was perhaps necessary as both the Federal Constitution of 1961 and the Unitary Constitution of 1972 granted wide powers to the President with insufficient restraint mechanisms, giving rise to a form of presidential absolutism. The 1996 Constitution purported to reverse that position by creating a more equitable balance of powers between executive, legislative and judicial power and also by entrenching additional separation of executive power between the President and the PM.

This chapter explores various roles constitutionally assigned to the executive and how different institutions act individually and collectively as the executive arm of state. In particular, it examines the powers of the President, the PM and the role of the government. It also examines the accountability structures and identifies emerging trends and weaknesses in the system. It further analyses the extent to which power has been effectively distributed between the President and the PM to determine whether executive power-sharing under the 1996 Constitution is more apparent than real.

Part I. Semi-presidentialism and the structure of the executive

A. Structure of the executive

The Constitution deals primarily with executive power in Part II, whereas executive and legislative relations are dealt with in Part IV. The executive branch is made up of the President, who is Head of State, the PM who is head of government, and the government. Their relationship is hierarchical with the President at the apex of that hierarchy, followed by the PM who is appointed by the President. The government has over thirty ministries each of which is headed by a minister, a minister delegate or a minister of state appointed by the President. Other members of government may include secretaries of state. In order to understand better the nature of executive power sharing in Cameroon, the concept of semi-presidentialism is explained in the subsequent section.

B. Semi-presidentialism and executive power

What is semi-presidentialism and why should we be interested in it? 'Semi-presidentialism' is a term for a political system that combines a presidential system (for instance, the USA) with a parliamentary system (for instance, the UK). According to Maurice Duverger, who first coined the term, the distinguishing features of semi-presidential systems are a popularly elected president vested with 'quite considerable powers' and a cabinet led by a PM who is responsible to the legislature.[1] Although Duverger failed to describe what constitutes 'quite considerable powers', recent scholarship has identified three distinctive powers as falling within that category. They include power to dismiss the PM and the cabinet, presidential veto power and power to dissolve the legislature.[2]

One of the main benefits of semi-presidentialism is that it can be described as an additional separation of powers because of the division of executive power between the president and PM.[3] An advantage of that additional separation is the potential of mitigating the over concentration of powers in a single executive head possibly affording the opportunity for a more equitable balance of power between the executive and other governmental authorities. However, not all semi-presidential regimes exhibit a factual additional separation of powers. That is particularly the case with highly presidential semi-presidential regimes.[4] This sub-type is characterised by a very powerful president and a ceremonial PM, a variant which exhibits an over-concentration of executive powers in a president similar to some purely presidential systems.[5] In addition, highly presidential sub-types face the problem of dual accountability of the PM[6] who can be dismissed by the president and also censured by parliament. However, the president is neither accountable to the PM nor parliament and in fact can make use of his special powers to dissolve parliament.[7]

Cameroon's semi-presidential system reflects the highly presidential sub-type. As will be demonstrated later, the President is vested with considerable powers over the government, the civil service, the judiciary,[8] the legislature and authority to regulate the state of emergency. The exercise of those powers has also been facilitated in practice by the fact that the President's party retains an overwhelming and largely disciplined majority in parliament.[9] In view of those circumstances, it may perhaps be more accurate to describe the regime as presidential.

Part II. The President

A. Election

The conditions for the election of the President of the Republic are laid down in the Constitution and the Electoral Code.[10] The President is elected for a period of seven years by universal suffrage and is eligible for re-election indefinitely.[11] He is elected in a single round by the majority of the votes cast,[12] irrespective of the margins.[13] In terms of eligibility, candidates for the position must fulfil a number of conditions. They must be Cameroonians by birth, they must enjoy their civic and political rights and must have attained the age of 35 by the date of election.[14] There is an additional residency requirement that a candidate must have resided in Cameroon for an uninterrupted period of a minimum of twelve months and mandatorily registered onto an electoral register.[15] The law permits candidates to be nominated by a political party or to run independently,[16] perhaps indicating that the office is open to any eligible Cameroonian. However, the obstacles inherent in independent nominations are insurmountable in the context of Cameroon. A potential independent candidate can only be nominated on the condition of obtaining 300 signatures from 'dignitaries' from all administrative regions, with thirty signatures from each of the ten regions of Cameroon.[17] One of the problems with that requirement is the practicality of obtaining the required signatures, due to the nature of the 'dignitaries' to be solicited for that purpose. The relevant dignitaries include Members of Parliament (MP) or Trades Chambers, Regional Councillors, Municipal Councillors or First-Class Chiefs.[18] MPs are usually representatives of political parties and are unlikely to support an independent candidate in preference for their own candidate, except perhaps in the unlikely event that no candidate from their party is running for the office of the president. Moreover, an independent candidate may find it difficult to obtain signatures from First-Class Chiefs or representative from Trade Chambers due to the fact that these group of people often are presidential appointees and hold office at the pleasure of the President. Therefore, it is unlikely that they would support an independent candidate if that action would jeopardise their position. As a result, a potential candidate has a better chance of being nominated by a political party.

The law provides curiously that:

> All persons who, by their own doing, have placed themselves in a situation of dependence on or connivance with a foreign person, organisation or power or foreign State shall not be eligible.[19]

It is not clear what this provision is intended to address, particularly given its vagueness. For instance, what would be considered 'a situation of dependence' or what constitutes 'connivance' and for what purpose? It appears to be a potent weapon in the hands of the state, to deal with potential challenge to the incumbent government in terms of a candidate who either enjoys international support or appears to do so. They may be accused of 'connivance'. Similarly, the head of a domestic civil society organisation who receives aid from international partners or foreign governments may be accused of placing themselves 'in a situation of dependence' if they decided to run for office.

The laws regulating presidential elections appear to make it open for eligible candidates to be put forward. In spite of that, the history of elections in Cameroon makes the openness questionable as the incumbent government applies its incumbency advantages to the detriment of other candidates. For instance, the current provisions of article 6(2) was introduced through a controversial constitutional amendment in 2008, amending the original article 6(2) that had imposed a term limit of two terms. Given the upheavals in the 1990s and the demand to strengthen democracy in Cameroon, the term limit provision was one of the provisions that assuaged the political tension at the time. In fact, the provision was first introduced in the draft constitution prepared by the Tripartite Conference. Its amendment was seen as a betrayal of the democratisation process.[20] It was expected that the incumbent President Biya, who has been in office since 1982, would eventually leave power at the end of his two terms. His proposal to remove term limits sparked political disturbances across the country. The government in characteristic style responded with repression,[21] while the compliant legislature dominated by the ruling party intractably adopted the controversial amendment. According to Paul Ayah who at the time was MP for the ruling Cameroon People's Democratic Movement (CPDM), a number of his colleagues, like himself were unimpressed by this amendment but dared not oppose it.[22] In fact, he alleged that, on the day of the parliamentary vote, there were more security officers in parliament than there were MPs and that situation was sufficiently intimidating.[23] Partly due to the perks springing from incumbency advantages, presidential elections in particular are often deemed predictable.[24] The most recent presidential election held in October 2018 was no different. President Biya who was expected to retain power won the election by a landslide majority of 71%. While the results were widely contested due primarily to gross electoral irregularities, the results were confirmed and proclaimed by the Constitutional Council. Maurice Kamto, the candidate for the Movement for the Renaissance of Cameroon (MRC) who is widely believed to have won the election proclaimed himself winner and organised several campaigns throughout Cameroon.[25] This was not well received by the authorities. He was arrested with numerous supporters and spent nine months in jail. The backlash which often follows presidential elections are symptomatic of the fact that, while the rules on eligibility allow multiple presidential candidates to run for office, the political landscape does not provide scope for organising credible elections.

B. Competencies and powers

The Constitution grants the President considerable powers generally and powers over specific aspects of governance, unambiguously affirming his supremacy. Thus, generally the President represents the state in all acts of public life[26]; defines national policy[27]; ensures respect for the Constitution[28]; and 'through his arbitration' ensures the proper functioning of public authorities[29]; promulgates laws[30]; guarantees the independence, territorial integrity and continuity of the polity[31]; and ensures the internal and external security of the state.[32] Those powers create a paternalistic image of the President, reinforcing a perception that his authority is imperative for the survival of the country. The following subsections will demonstrate the pervasiveness of presidential powers and how these have been firmly established by the Constitution.

I. Appointment of the PM, the cabinet and other state officials

The President is vested with powers to appoint the PM and 'on the proposal of the latter, appoint the other members of government'.[33] In practice, however, ministerial appointments are made concurrently with the appointment of a PM.[34] In which case, it is possible to infer that he is not always consulted in the selection of his Cabinet. The Constitution provides further that their duties shall be defined by the President who can also terminate their appointment.[35] That position gives a prima facie case of Cabinet's accountability to the President rather than the PM who is head of government.

With respect to other military and civil service responsibilities, the president's influence is significant in that he is head of the armed forces[36] and is responsible for setting up and organising administrative services,[37] and appointments to civil, military and para-public institutions.[38] These powers, in addition to those discussed in the previous subsection, place the state almost entirely in the hands of the President.[39] The excessive dependence of state and para-public institutions is one of the problems associated with inefficient governance in Cameroon. As decision-making powers depend significantly on the President, considerable delays occur where he is unable to act. In the specific context of the current regime, there is a reported problem of inertia which has been attributed to the frequent absence of President Biya, particularly resulting from prolonged private visits abroad.[40] These absences have meant that key decisions which need to be taken are put on hold for the length of time that the President is absent, causing delays in the implementation of government policies and the making of expeditious decisions when emergencies arise.[41]

The power of appointment to civil, military and para-public institutions also provides a formidable basis for a patronage system for the reward of key figures that support the regime.[42] Due partly to the underdeveloped nature of the economy, spurred by scarcity of resources, there is competition for resources and key positions in the government and public services.[43] The select few officials appointed to various positions are keen to remain in them to secure their political, economic and social status.[44] Individually or collectively, some have expanded their support networks by granting favours to members of the public in order to elicit popular support for the regime.[45] An example here is the former Anglophone PM Peter Musonge who was appointed in 1996. In a speech delivered to an audience in Buea,[46] capital of the South-West region, he called on the Anglophone community to unanimously support President Biya as a mark of appreciation for appointing an Anglophone to that office and also to receive further favours from the government.[47] The Governor of that region at the time

(Peter Oben) endorsed South-westerners and 'immigrants' to support the CPDM party for similar reasons.[48] In addition to the benefits of patronage, there is also the fear of reprisal.

Appointments are generally viewed with cynicism by the public – as a reward for loyal supporters of the government and failure to uphold that support may result in dismissal, in view of the fact that the President often has the sole power of appointment and removal from office. Thus, appointments may be used to elicit and secure support for the President. Prior to the controversial 1992 presidential election, the Minster of Territorial Administration at the time summoned all regional governors, tasking them with the duty to ensure that President Biya won at least 60% of the votes in each region.[49] A failure to attain the threshold would result in sanctions for the governors as it would be deemed a betrayal of the President.[50] These allegations were confirmed by the National Democratic Institute. An excerpt of their report is worth reproducing.

> The NDI has received direct testimony to the effect that, prior to the election, high level government officials were told that their performance would be rated on the number of votes President Biya garnered in their respective areas. They were given a goal of 60% and told that this figure should be achieved by whatever means was necessary.[51]

It is unsurprising, therefore, that the results suffered from a serious lack of credibility as a result of reported electoral malpractices.[52]

II. Legislative powers

Although Parliament is the primary legislative organ, its areas of competence have been specifically delineated and some legislative authority has been accorded to the President. This approach follows typically that of France where the President is vested with some legislative and regulatory powers. In Cameroon, the President is authorised to exercise statutory authority[53] and to issue rules and regulations in the areas which do not fall under parliament's competence.[54] Moreover, parliament may empower the President to legislate by way of ordinance for a limited period and for given purposes, in those areas which are reserved for parliament.[55] Ordinances promulgated under that provision enter into force on the day of their publication and remain applicable as long as parliament has not refused to ratify them.[56]

A significant problem with the legislative powers of the President is their extensive scope as there is no indication of what the 'given purposes' may be and every aspect that does not come within parliament's competence is the responsibility of the President. Arguably, the Constitution cannot contemplate all the possible circumstances under which delegated legislation may be necessary. Yet in the particular context of Cameroon where the President formulates government policy, has a disciplined parliamentary majority and substantial control of its party, it is unlikely that without specific criteria guiding the delegation of legislative powers, they may not be used to promote unpopular policies like those that have potential to inhibit democracy and the exercise of human rights.[57] Although delegation of legislative power is not unusual, exercise of such powers should be circumscribed by the provision of clear limits on their exercise.[58] In Germany for instance, the legislature is required to provide clear guidelines for the content of regulations.[59] Caroline Morris and Ryan Malone assert that the ability of the executive to utilise delegated powers to implement its policy preferences without parliamentary oversight is particularly inimical to the exercise of human rights.[60] This is partly due to the fact that the government may seek to maintain its hold on power and if that objective can be achieved through policy facilitated by delegation, then individual liberties which conflict with those policies may be undermined as a result of their implementation.[61]

In the case of Cameroon, both the residual and delegated powers of the President serve to further alter the balance of power to the latter's advantage. It further reinforces the perception of an authoritarian President, given the enormity of its powers even within the legislative or regulatory sphere thereby undermining the benefits of semi-presidentialism.

III. Dissolution powers

The position of the executive is further strengthened by presidential powers to dissolve the legislature. The Constitution provides that:

> The President of the Republic may, if necessary and after consultation with the Government, the Bureaux of the National Assembly and the Senate, dissolve the National Assembly …[62]

There are at least three problems that can be identified with that provision with regard to checks and balances.[63] First, dissolution powers are not circumscribed. The President merely *consults* the relevant institutions rather than acquire their assent. It is doubtful that any objection on their part would be complied with.[64] Dissolution can be a latent weapon to control a legislature that would otherwise exercise effective oversight of the executive.[65] That was the case in Niger in 2009 when President Mamadou Tanja dissolved parliament following a failed attempt to amend constitutional provisions which prevented him from running for a third term.[66] In light of the fact that that dissolution powers can have drastic effects when used, it is important that some form of checks and balances are put in place to regulate their use.[67] In Namibian, for instance, the provision vesting the president with dissolution power is more specific than the Cameroonian provision and limits the discretion of the President. He may dissolve parliament 'on the advice of Cabinet if the Government is unable to govern effectively'.[68] Moreover, it creates a form of constraint which may diminish incentives to resort to its use. If parliament were to be dissolved, the President will equally be subjected to re-election at the same time that a new parliament is elected.[69] This may prove detrimental where he has lost popularity and the threat of losing elections may inhibit any aspiration to dissolve parliament for unconstitutional reasons.

The second aspect which makes the Cameroonian position problematic is the vagueness of the Constitution as to the circumstances that should trigger dissolution. Responsibility to determine the circumstances has been left entirely with the President. This provides scope for arbitrary use by the President as any circumstance which he deems 'necessary' can provide the basis for the use of dissolution powers. Moreover, it provides scope for the President to deflect criticisms onto the legislature for unpopular laws. Although such laws would most probably have been initiated by the executive and in particular the President, the intricacies of parliamentary processes are not common knowledge to the public. If the public were to demonstrate opposition to unpopular laws, the President could seize the opportunity to deflect criticism onto parliament and use that as a pretext to dissolve it.

The third problem associated with that provision is that a decision to dissolve parliament is unlikely to be subject to judicial review.[70] Such a decision falls within the spectrum of activities known as 'acts of the government'. 'Acts of the government' originates from the French doctrine of *actes de gouvernement* according to which a category of acts undertaken by the executive cannot be reviewed by any court.[71] This leaves parliament in a considerably weakened position where it can be dissolved at the whim of the President without any form of oversight. Arguably, due to the current disciplined parliamentary majority, it may not be in the interest of the President to use that power. However, its availability can have a pre-emptive effect on parliamentary initiative.[72]

IV. Power to extend or abridge the parliamentary term

Besides power to dissolve the National Assembly, the President can similarly alter the parliamentary term by abridgement or extension. The Constitution provides that:

> In case of serious crisis, the President of the Republic may, after consultation with the President of the Constitutional Council and Bureau of the National Assembly, decide by a law, to extend or abridge its term of office.[73]

Where parliament is extended or abridged as per article 15(4), the election of a new assembly shall take place between forty and sixty days following the expiry of the extended or abridged period.

Unlike the dissolution power discussed previously, the present constitutional provision makes an abridgment or extension contingent upon the occurrence of a serious crisis. Although 'serious crisis' may be sufficiently vague to afford a perilously broad interpretation, it certainly differs from the dissolution power which depends on 'a matter of necessity' to be determined by the President. Moreover, an abridgment or extension is to be decided by a law passed by parliament. Thus, if properly implemented, there is some prospect in assuming that a parliamentary term would be extended or abridged in order to address a serious crisis which could undermine effective governance or be otherwise perilous to the entire nation. Abridging the parliamentary term may be necessary in this inherited French constitutional model where there is always a possibility of an uneasy coalition arising from the different presidential and parliamentary terms.[74] Although abridging parliament may be incompatible with some basic tenets of representative democracy, it may well be necessary as has been the case in France, for the President to use that power to regain his parliamentary majority.[75]

Nevertheless, the provision on abridgment and extension must be interpreted with caution as the absence of a clear definition of 'serious crisis'[76] may provide scope for ambiguities which could be used by the President to unjustifiably extend or abridge the parliamentary term to his advantage. Although an act of parliament is required to validate the process, as discussed earlier, this is not particularly reassuring due to the characteristic loyalty of the current majority in parliament. It is unlikely that parliament will take a firm stance against any potential executive pretence of the existence of a serious crisis.

In fact, in practice, the power has been used not under the circumstances contemplated, but rather to conceal poor governance and to foster the executive's cavalier attitude towards the general governance of the country, the electorate and the Constitution. For instance, the parliamentary term was extended three times between August 2012 and July 2013.[77] The executive's rationale for this move was to allow the government to prepare a new electoral roll and to introduce a biometric electoral card system.[78] Although that in itself is commendable in terms of enhancing the transparency of the electoral process, the government was well aware of the fact that the parliamentary term was to elapse on 21 August 2012 and should have taken the necessary steps to prepare for elections. As has become characteristic of the governance system, the government waited till the last minute to begin serious preparations to reorganise the electoral system despite persistent calls from the opposition and the international community.[79] Parliament was initially extended for six months. During deliberations for the initial extension, some members of the parliamentary opposition noted that the six-month period was insufficient to fully reorganise the electoral system and to prepare for elections.[80] While the government was adamant, the opposition was vindicated as the government later tabled two further bills with the effect that the parliamentary term was extended twice following the initial six months. Such inconsistency from the executive created uncertainty and partially undermined the effective deployment of parliamentary functions.

Besides the apparent incompetence of the government to organise in time for elections, there were also doubts as to the constitutionality of the two further extensions in light of the constitutional requirement that elections should be conducted between forty and sixty days following an extension. More recently, the parliamentary term which was meant to end in 2018 was extended twice. Initially, according to the bill adopted by the National Assembly, the mandate was extended for a year until 29 October 2019.[81]

In July 2019, the National Assembly adopted another bill extending the term further to end on 29 December 2019. The next elections were scheduled to take place on 9 February 2020.[82] The government justified the extensions by referring to the logistical difficulty of managing presidential, legislative, and municipal elections concurrently which were all scheduled to take place in 2018.[83] In view of the constitutional term of the respective institutions, the election dates should not have come as a surprise and the government should have taken measures well in advance to ensure constitutional term limits were adhered to. In addition, it is not clear why parliamentary elections were not held in 2019 as per the first extension. Thus, while the power to extend or abridge the parliamentary term can be useful to resolve serious crises, it may also be abused for self-serving purposes or as in the circumstances described previously, to conceal the government's ineptitude.

V. Emergency powers

The Constitution confers powers on the President to declare by decree, a state of emergency where circumstances so warrant and to declare a state of siege in the event of a serious threat to the nation's territorial integrity or to its existence, its independence or institutions.[84] With regard to the state of siege, the Constitution appears to reflect the severity contemplated by international law as it permits a declaration when the nation's territorial integrity, existence and independence are under serious threat. The emergency regime is elaborated in a regulatory instrument which deals with its scope. It defines a state of emergency as:

> [A]n occurrence which, by its nature and gravity, is considered a national disaster, or a series of disturbances undermining public order or the security of the state, or a foreign invasion.[85]

On the face of it, the provision appears to contemplate circumstances which may transcend ordinary disasters or public disturbances, to the extent that they affect the security of the state. However, besides 'foreign invasion', a missing element which is a fundamental consideration is that of a 'threat to the life of a nation' which is overshadowed by the lesser conditions provided. Perhaps the more significant issue though, is that in both cases (state of emergency and siege), the determination of the circumstances under contemplation is in the subjective opinion of the President who is under no obligation to consult any other institution. He is simply required to inform the nation of his decision.[86] This is, indeed, a threat to constitutionalism as the President is empowered to act without regard to the other institutions that would otherwise provide objective appreciation of the perceived circumstances. In the absence of parliamentary oversight and more stringent conditions to determine emergency situations, it is probable that emergency powers could be invoked for purely political reasons to suit the personal whim of the President.[87] The situation is even more precarious in the light of the fact that he is vested with powers to 'take any measures as he may deem necessary'.[88] Again, it is subjective and the President has no obligation to consult any institution with regard to measures undertaken or measures contemplated to ensure they are strictly necessary in the circumstance.[89]

The situation is further exacerbated by the fact that the emergency law vests administrative and security officers with wide powers which are susceptible to abuse. Section 5(6) permits the detention of persons without charge for seven days by the Prefect, fifteen days by the Governor and two months (renewable once) by the Minister of Territorial Administration. These are lengthy periods for which the law provides little safeguards by way of justifying their necessity. A victim may be subjected to detention for up to, or longer than four months, even beyond the subsistence of the emergency. The law imposes a time limit of three months for a state of emergency to last although it can be renewed once for an additional period of three months.[90]

In the absence of legislative oversight, the only alternative is judicial review. As will be discussed in detail in Chapter 4, the mechanisms for judicial review are ineffective. Worthy of note here is that ordinary citizens whose rights are likely to be affected by the emergency regulation do not have access to constitutional review to challenge the constitutionality of laws.[91] Moreover, under the doctrine of *actes de gouvernement*, it is unlikely that a presidential decree promulgating a state of emergency would be subject to review. With regard to review of administrative acts, previously, there were physical, economic and procedural difficulties associated with access to the Supreme Court which, until March 2012, had exclusive jurisdiction in that respect. But more fundamentally, the judiciary lacks independence and therefore unlikely to provide sufficient restraint on authorities exercising power under an emergency regime.[92]

Although since the 1996 constitutional amendments, emergency powers have not been used. As opposed to the Ahidjo regime which thrived under a perpetual state of emergency, the Biya regime has declared a state of emergency twice only (in 1984 to deal with the *coup d'etat* and in 1992 following the declaration of results of the presidential elections of that year).[93] The infamous case of *Wakai v The People*[94] which originated from the 1992 declaration of presidential election results demonstrated the practical weaknesses in the system, particularly in the light of the massive violations of human rights by administrative authorities and the difficulties faced by the courts in effectively securing justice for the victims.[95]

Although emergency powers have not been used under the 1996 Constitution, the regime is structured in such a way that it appears to be the proverbial 'loaded weapon ready for the hand of any authority that can bring forward a plausible claim of an urgent need'.[96] It falls far short of international standards especially as formulated in the International Covenant on Civil and Political Rights[97] (which Cameroon has ratified) and requires reform to ensure at least that there are stringent oversight mechanisms in place.

VI. National defence and the military

The national defence of the country is the responsibility of the President.[98] In that respect, he is the head of the armed forces[99] and vested with powers to appoint to military posts.[100] The institution that oversees national defence is the Ministry of Defence which ironically is not an independent institution. It is institutionally attached to the Presidency of the Republic and headed by a Minister Delegate in Charge of Defence.[101] The duties of the Minister include studying and implementation of the defence policy, coordination and control of the forces of law and order and the organisation and operation of the military tribunal.[102] The minister is responsible to the President and receives instructions from him.

The institutional dependence of the Ministry of Defence on the President is another mechanism by which presidential power is consolidated in Cameroon. The current arrangements are an attempt to keep a close eye on the military to pre-empt attempts at subversion, which has been rife in Africa where unconstitutional change of government was achieved through military coups. In Cameroon more particularly, after the abortive coup in 1984, the Ministry was brought under the aegis of the Presidency of the Republic and the President keeps very tight control of it.[103]

The military and security officers are a key fabric in the governance network as they have played an indispensable role in reinforcing an authoritarian regime.[104] In the last few decades, the Biya regime has increasingly come under criticism, providing a pretext for resort to repressive force in order to maintain power.[105] Following the failed *coup* attempt in 1984, the President has consistently appointed senior members of the military from his ethnic group to secure loyalty to the regime.[106] The military and security forces are said to be treated more favourably than the rest of the civil service. In the 1990s, for instance, when the salaries of public servants were gradually reduced by approximately 50% as part of measures taken under the Structural Adjustment Programme,[107] the police and armed forces remained unaffected and continued to be endowed with various fringe benefits as reward for their loyalty.[108] According to the *Bertelsmann Stiftung*, the military is constantly monitored by the presidency to detect signs of discontent.[109] Security forces have been repeatedly deployed to crack down on opposition and other civilian groups as a means of preventing any perceived threat to the regime. During the fateful 2008 riots, security forces did not hesitate to violently crack down on protesters opposing the increasing cost of living and proposed amendments to the Constitution to eliminate presidential term limits. More recently, the Rapid Intervention Unit (well known by its French acronym, BIR) which has gained notoriety due to its use of brute force have been constantly deployed to the North-West and South-West regions to 'maintain public order' in the crisis stricken areas. Despite reports of egregious human rights abuses and other atrocities committed by the BIR, the government has not condemned them. Instead, they continue to be deployed to these areas. In view of the challenge to the regime posed by the events in the North-West and South-West, the deployment of repressive forces to 'maintain public order' seemed inevitable.

VII. Foreign affairs

As with most aspects of the Cameroonian governance system, the President is overall responsible for Cameroon's external relations.[110] Thus, as head of state, he represents Cameroon abroad, accredits ambassadors and envoys extraordinary to foreign powers, while ambassadors and envoys extraordinary of foreign powers are accredited to him.[111] His influence in foreign affairs is further gleaned from his responsibility to conclude international treaties and agreements, although he may require authorisation from parliament where the subject of the agreement or treaty falls within the legislative competence of parliament.[112]

C. Accountability

An essential feature of a good governance system is accountability. In Cameroon, this point becomes particularly relevant in view of the vast array of presidential powers discussed earlier. Taking into account the wide scope of the powers, a robust system of checks and balances is necessary to enhance their effective exercise and, in particular, to pre-empt potential abuse. In the light of the government's assertion that the Constitution ushers in an era of checks and balances, how far does the Constitution reflect the need to limit presidential powers? The following subsections attempt to respond to that question by examining the constitutional provisions on immunity and impeachment.

I. Immunity from prosecution

Immunity from prosecution is an important principle of public law and may be supported by the supposition that it can promote the consistent functioning of public power and continuity of the state.[113] It is supposedly for the benefit of the public that immunity is granted to public officials such as presidents to enable the discharge of their duties without unnecessary distractions or impediments emanating from law suits.[114] While that may be the case, there is also the necessity to consider presidential accountability. Presidential immunity provisions are a common feature of various regime types, be they presidential or semi-presidential[115] and even in parliamentary systems some senior executive officials and parliamentarians enjoy a certain level of immunity. Yet, it should not be the case that immunity provisions are drafted to ensure absolute immunity from prosecution. That does not augur well for accountability and indeed goes against a basic tenet of the rule of law – that no one is above the law.[116]

In Cameroon, prior to 2008, there was no constitutional provision ostensibly dealing with presidential immunity.[117] Therefore, in *theory* it may have been possible for prosecution to be initiated in domestic courts. That position was altered in 2008 following a constitutional amendment.[118] Article 53(3) of the Constitution provides that:

> Acts committed by the President of the Republic in pursuance of Articles 5, 8, 9 and 10 above shall be covered by immunity and he shall not be accountable for them after the exercise of his functions.[119]

There are at least two major aspects of this provision which can be deemed inconsistent with the need for accountability.

First, there is uncertainty as to the scope of the President's immunity. The provision simply states that the relevant acts are covered by immunity. It is not clear that these acts are limited to criminal or civil or both. Given that the amendment followed a string of amendments that had the effect of further consolidating the presidency of the incumbent,[120] the inference can be drawn that article 53(3) intended to cover both civil and criminal acts in which the President may be implicated in pursuance of his constitutional duties.

Second, presidential immunity covers the period after the expiration of his term of office. This is a case of absolute immunity which has the potential to turn an already authoritarian regime into outright dictatorship. In the absence of any form of accountability during and after the expiration of his term, the President is left with free reign to use his powers excessively.

The Cameroonian position seems to reflect that of France where traditionally the head of state is reputed to be inviolable.[121] Yet in France, the President can be prosecuted after the expiration of his tenure.[122] That position has been reaffirmed by the French *Conseil Constitutionnel*[123] and the *Cour de Cassassion*,[124] respectively, which ruled that a serving president could not (except for high treason) be charged, prosecuted or forced to testify in court proceedings for the duration of his term. But that it did not preclude any criminal proceedings against him once his term expired.[125]

In the African context, as is the case in Cameroon, presidential immunity appears to be gaining prominence as an inducement for long-term presidents to relinquish power.[126] Some members of the parliamentary opposition in Cameroon seemed to have been influenced by that argument and did not object to the government's proposal to introduce an immunity clause in the Constitution on that basis.[127] They, however, acknowledged that immunity functions well in a situation of checks and balances and therefore did not constitute a recipe for constitutional dictatorship.[128] That is, however, not the situation in Cameroon.

II. Impeachment

Impeachment can provide a useful means of enforcing accountability, if well conceived. Its very existence and the probability of its use can act as a source of pressure to induce a president to respect the rule of law.[129] In Cameroon, the current provision on impeachment is an amended version of article 53 (amended in 2008) which vested the Court of Impeachment with jurisdiction to try the

President for high treason. It provided further that the organisation, composition, conditions of reference and the applicable procedure before that Court shall be laid down by a subsequent legislation. That legislation is still being awaited.

The new article 53 provides that:

> The Court of Impeachment shall have jurisdiction, in respect of acts committed in the exercise of their functions to try:
>
> -The President of the Republic for high treason; ...[130]
>
> The President of the Republic shall be indicted only by the National Assembly and the Senate deciding through an identical vote by open ballot and by a four fifth majority of their members.[131]

The Constitution is silent on the meaning of high treason and there is no jurisprudence from which an interpretation can be deduced. Although it may be unrealistic to require an exhaustive list of circumstances constituting high treason, it is important that as a mechanism for accountability, particularly of a President who exercises such broad powers, there should be some carefully defined guidelines.[132] Lack of clarity can provide scope for subjective interpretations to enhance the personal objectives of the interpreters.[133]

Further, the procedure contemplated by subsection (2) requires the National Assembly and Senate to indict the President through an identical vote of a four-fifth majority of each House. That is a difficult majority to achieve in any democracy and particularly in Cameroon where currently the ruling party commands an overwhelming and disciplined majority. The parliamentary opposition unsuccessfully objected to that amendment when the bill was presented in parliament arguing that it averted any possibility of impeaching the President.[134]

Moreover, the votes are required to be in open ballot implying that there is no confidentiality. For such an extreme mechanism which can precipitate regime change, dispensing with confidentiality potentially compromises the process as MPs particularly from the ruling party are likely to be reluctant to expose themselves as the 'renegades' of their party. Considering the patronage networks that exist within these institutions, concurring to a motion to impeach the President can expose an MP to possible loss of favours from the system and even more drastic consequences. The requirement of 'transparency' in the voting system is perhaps deliberate and intended to compromise the impeachment process by deterring any prospective vote in favour of the President's impeachment. Opposition MPs specifically requested an amendment to the government bill with respect to the open ballot, to be replaced with secret ballots. They argued that it had the potential to influence the independence of MPs.[135]

The inadequacy of the impeachment system is compounded by the fact that the Court of Impeachment is yet to be established since it first appeared in the 1972 Constitution and was re-enacted in the 1996 Constitution. Article 53(4) states that the organisation, composition and the conditions under which matters shall be referred to, as well as the procedure applicable before the Court shall be laid down by law. When this law will be enacted is a matter of speculation.

Part III. The PM and the government

After various phases of abolition, the position of PM was reinstated in 1991 following a constitutional amendment.[136] As noted earlier, the PM is the head of government and is appointed by the President.

A. *Powers of the PM*

Although the office of the PM was consolidated under the 1996 Constitution and seen as an additional separation of powers, it should be noted that it is a largely ceremonial position. As head of government, he is responsible for directing government action[137] and despite being vested with some executive responsibilities, his powers are largely dependent on the President.

I. Formation of government

As the PM is the head of government, it would be expected that he has the authority to form his government. However, presidential influence is also clearly entrenched here. Thus, the President appoints the other members of government, on the proposal of the PM.[138] In practice however, ministerial appointments are sometimes made concurrently with the appointment of a PM.[139] In which case, it is possible to infer that he is not always consulted in the selection of his cabinet. Although he may appoint to civil posts, his powers are subject to presidential prerogatives with respect to appointments.[140] He is nevertheless responsible for directing all the government services required for the accomplishment of his duties,[141] although here again this is dependent on delegation of powers by the President.[142]

II. Policy implementation

As head of government, the PM is responsible for implementing government policy as defined by the President of the Republic.[143] This is a rather strange formulation as the PM who is head of government, has no say in defining national policy.[144] This is another aspect which demonstrates the predominance of the President, in a supposedly semi-presidential system. Additionally, the Council of Ministers which discusses the implementation of government policy is convened and presided by the President.[145] It has been argued that the formulation which regards the PM as head of government belies the vacuity of that institution because the President has been constitutionally established as the actual head of government and the nerve-centre of national politics.[146] The PM 'implements' policies defined by the President rather than defining the policy as the head of government in conjunction with the cabinet.

III. Regulatory powers

The PM can exercise statutory authority[147] in the form of decrees and orders.[148] In terms of hierarchy of domestic norms, statutory instruments issued by the PM assume a subordinate position to acts of parliament and are subject to the principle of legality. The regulatory authority of the PM is primarily used to ensure the application of acts of parliament or presidential decrees, in the context of the PM's responsibility for law enforcement.[149] The PM can also issue circulars which are binding on the individuals or state officials concerned. For instance in 2018, following reports received from the presidency regarding the financial accountability of state officials undertaking official state business abroad, the PM issued a circular compelling compliance with specific conditions and procedures.[150]

B. Structure and role of government

The structure of the government is represented as follows[151]:

- The PM, head of government
- Vice Prime Ministers, where applicable
- Ministers of state, where applicable
- Ministers
- Ministers in Charge of Missions
- Ministers without portfolio, where applicable
- Ministers delegate
- Secretaries of state

There is a hierarchical relationship between the members of government, with the PM at the apex and the secretaries of state at the lower end.[152] Despite that relationship, curiously, the Ministers in Charge of Missions and Ministers without portfolio are directly responsible to the President, while Ministers Delegate are responsible to the President, the PM or Ministers when required to discharge specific and permanent duties.[153] The number of ministries in Cameroon is in a state of flux as the President continuously restructures the government by dividing the functions of individual ministries into several different ministries. An example is the former Ministry of Education which has undergone various permutations and currently, there are four separate ministries dealing with education.[154] More recently, the former Ministry of Territorial Administration and Decentralisation has morphed into two separate ministries.[155] These reorganisations are undertaken by the President, often without credible explanation as to the purpose. It is widely believed that the strategy is necessary to maintain the patronage network of the regime as it subsists partly on the basis of rewarding its supporters.[156] Irrespective of the questionable arrangements, the government has a role to play in directing the nation, for instance, through policy implementation.

C. Accountability

The government is accountable to the President and parliament.[157] The President can terminate the functions of the PM and Ministers.[158]

Parliament controls government action through oral and written questions.[159] In theory, government can also be held accountable through a motion of censure or a vote of no confidence,[160] after which the PM would be expected to tender the resignation of the government to the President.[161] In terms of achieving a balance and separation of powers, those arrangements are problematic for at least two reasons.

First, although the PM is head of government, policy is dictated by the President but it will be the PM and the Cabinet that would be censured if parliament were to call into question the confidence of the government. The dual accountability of the PM makes that institution practically of little significance in terms of separation of powers. Considering that the PM and Cabinet are subservient to the President, it is in their interest to ensure that government policy (as defined by the President) is fully implemented. That position allows the President to deflect criticism and censure onto the PM and the Cabinet. Such a situation has been evident during the Anglophone crisis which has resulted in many deaths and displacement of populations in the North-West and South-West regions.[162] The crisis began in October 2016 and one year later had transformed into an armed conflict between the military and armed groups fighting for secession of those regions. It was the President's decision to address the crisis by using a military solution which has proved to be unsuccessful.[163] Despite several calls for dialogue, there was no response from the regime until September 2019 when the President announced that a major national dialogue would be organised between 30 September and 4 October 2019. The dialogue was fraught with a number of conceptual, organisational and political inadequacies. Although it was the President's policy objective, it was implemented by the PM and his Cabinet. Due to the inadequacies mentioned previously, the PM and the relevant cabinet ministers received wide criticisms.

The formulation that allows the President to determine government policy also allows the latter to act unilaterally even in circumstances where consultation would be the most appropriate approach. For instance, in October 2019 on the occasion of the Sixth Replenishment Conference of the Global Fund to Fight AIDS, Tuberculosis and Malaria hosted in France,[164] President Biya pledged an amount of 3 billion CFA to support the Fund.[165] While Cameroon's contribution is commendable as its populations suffer from these diseases, it is curious to note that the pledge was made unilaterally by the President. In a well-functioning democracy, a decision of that magnitude should ideally be discussed among the relevant government institutions in the context of the most appropriate government policy and a proposal put before parliament to ensure accountability and also that a decision is arrived at democratically and in consideration of the existing budgetary allocations. According to Joseph Kankeu, the subordination of the PM and the government has been entrenched by the Constitution which has merely developed the prime ministry as an institution with an instrumental role rather than one that develops and implements government policies.[166] Kankeu and Solomon Bilong assert that the PM's role is that of concretising and implementing unpopular policy preferences of the President.[167] In which case, it might be more accurate to speak of the executive as composed of the President who is both head of state and head of government.

Second, the provision on motions of censure and vote of no confidence as measures to achieve government's accountability is not effective in practice. The PM can be subsequently reappointed by the President even after a motion of censure leads to his resignation.[168] This implies that parliamentary oversight is rather ineffective if it can be overridden by the reappointment of the PM. More particularly, under the current government, it is unlikely that a motion of censure has a chance to succeed as the ruling CPDM controls a highly disciplined majority in parliament that is unlikely to censure the government. According to Paul Ayah,[169] in practice, the constraints have made it impossible for parliament to hold the government to account.[170] He argues that CPDM parliamentarians are reluctant to vote against their party as that may constitute grounds for disciplinary action.[171]

Another factor which may explain the reluctance of CPDM members to vote against party initiatives (even if they disagree with such initiatives) is the patronage advantage that comes with belonging to the ruling party.[172] The CPDM party affords the best opportunity for patronage and according to the *Bertelsmann Stiftung* candidate selection is based on 100% loyalty to presidential policy.[173]

Besides the ineffective accountability through parliament, members of government can be criminally liable for acts committed in the exercise of their functions, for conspiracy against the security of the state.[174] In which case, they would be tried by the Court of Impeachment described earlier.[175]

D. Accountability through good governance and anti-corruption strategies

One of the most endemic problems that continue to undermine governance in Cameroon is corruption. Cameroon has frequently been at the top of the International Corruption index and corruption is said to pervade key institutions like the police and the judiciary.[176] Due partly to pressure from international donors, the government has adopted some measures to enhance good governance and to gradually eliminate corruption. How far these initiatives have been successful remains uncertain. Nevertheless, it would appear that under the initiative of President Biya, corruption which for many years appeared to be a norm in society, is beginning to invoke the ire of the law and the society in general. In this section, the discussion will focus on the National Anti-Corruption Commission (CONAC) and the law on the declaration of assets. Although judicial institutions are involved in the accountability mechanism, they are discussed separately in Chapter 4.

I. Declaration of assets

The starting point for transparency and good governance in the management of public finance in Cameroon is article 66 of the Constitution which makes it mandatory for senior executive officials such as the President, the PM, Ministers and other members of government to declare their assets and properties at the beginning and at the end of their tenure of office. The constitutional provision has been supplemented by a law on the declaration of assets which replicates the list of officials under a duty to declare their assets.[177]

The law establishes a Commission responsible for receiving, exploring and preserving declarations.[178] One of its strengths in enhancing accountability is its powers to raise questions and even report to the appropriate prosecuting and investigating authorities, questionable ownership of property where its origin cannot be accounted for[179] or where an official's means are not commensurate with the properties or assets declared.[180] Where the origin cannot be clearly established especially with regard to earnings, the state may confiscate all or part of the property in question.[181] Worthy of note is the fact that, officials are obliged to declare properties or assets for which the registered owners are spouses or minor children, regardless of the location of the property (whether within Cameroon or abroad).[182] This is commendable in that, it limits the potential for state officials to syphon state funds into private accounts of family members. The sanctions for failure to comply with the requirement of declaration include dismissal and suspension from office.[183]

The Law on the Declaration of Assets provides a foundation for building transparency and accountability in governance and the financial affairs of executive officials. This has become increasingly necessary in view of the widespread misuse of public funds by state officials vested with the responsibility to manage these funds on behalf of tax payers. Despite the aforementioned analysis, the potentials of the law are undermined by the lack of implementation.[184] This is due largely to the fact that, like most aspects of governance in Cameroon as seen previously, it is dependent on the President of the Republic. For instance, the President is responsible for appointing directly or indirectly, five of the Commission's nine members[185] and the progress reports are to be forwarded to the President.[186] The law is not clear on what action should be taken by the President once the report has been received. This is rather ironical as the President is one of the officials mandated to declare his assets. It makes the issue of independence of the institution questionable. In addition, the law provides that the President 'shall, as and when necessary, define the conditions of implementation of this law' by decree.[187] This therefore makes implementation subject to the will of the President.

II. The CONAC

The CONAC was established by presidential decree in March 2006 and went into operation a year later.[188] The role of that institution is to contribute to the fight against corruption through, inter alia, the monitoring and evaluation of the effective implementation of the government's anti-corruption programme.[189] In that respect, it is vested with powers to investigate complaints and denunciation of acts of corruption, to oversee the execution of public projects, to evaluate the conditions for the award of public contracts, to identify the causes of corruption and to propose to the competent authorities, solutions to eliminate corruption in all public and para-public institutions.[190] With respect to its investigative powers, CONAC can request the production of documents from any state or para-public institution. The institutions are obliged to cooperate, failure of which may attract sanctions and a specific report to the President of the Republic.[191] Despite that provision, CONAC still faces instances of lack of cooperation from state institutions, an aspect which undermines its efficiency.[192]

The investigations of CONAC may lead to criminal proceedings during which CONAC may be represented in court.[193] This is perhaps the greatest means by which CONAC can contribute to the accountability of state officials. However, prosecution is not automatic as a finding of facts relating to allegations of corruption must be reported to the President of the Republic.[194] It may also appeal to the Minister of Justice who in turn informs the relevant employer of the suspect in any investigation.[195] The implication is that CONAC has no powers to independently initiate judicial action. It must rely on the President or the Minister of Justice. This is quite limiting as CONAC has no means of guaranteeing completion of its work by ensuring that where necessary, investigations result in prosecution. It has been argued that CONAC can be a more effective institution if vested with powers to independently initiate judicial proceedings.[196]

According to the decree establishing CONAC, it is an independent body,[197] yet it is highly dependent on the President of the Republic. For instance, key officials of CONAC such as its president, vice president and members of the coordination committee are appointed by the President of the Republic.[198] Moreover, its annual programme must be approved by the President,[199] the institution reports to him[200] and submits its annual reports to him (although these are made public).[201]

The subservience of CONAC has been identified as a major weakness of the institution and is considered as a means by which the presidency attains complete control of the institution.[202] For instance, despite its successes in facilitating the prosecution of high-level bureaucrats and former ministers accused of embezzlement through the Operation Sparrow Hawk anti-corruption programme, this is often perceived as a political tool to stifle opponents of the regime or ambitious bureaucrats.[203] Therefore, as an accountability mechanism, CONAC's influence or effectiveness is considerably limited.

Conclusion

The consolidation of semi-presidentialism in the 1996 Constitution appears not to have made a practical difference to an equitable separation of executive power between the PM and the President. Rather, as the chapter has demonstrated, any evolution of executive power has served to strengthen presidential power even more and to weaken accountability mechanisms. Thus, the President continues to wield considerable powers and dominate executive authority, while accountability mechanisms are bedevilled with significant inadequacies. In fact, every relevant accountability institution or mechanism is dependent on the President. It would appear that a system of personal rule or what has been recently described as 'Biyaïsme' has developed to the extent that all aspects of political, social and economic life are under 'presidential siege'.[204] According to Jean Claude Kamdem, the head of state is not simply the head of the executive, he is 'the power'.[205]

It follows that the transition to democracy and constitutional governance in the 1990s played very little in practice to alter presidential absolutism. This was inevitable in light of the fact that, as was seen in Chapter 1, the authoritarian 1972 Constitution had merely undergone cosmetic changes. More powers have been accorded to the President. Every aspect of governance depends on that institution and in view of the current fact of the President's frequent physical absences from the country, decision-making has inevitably stalled. Cameroon's variant of semi-presidentialism has therefore failed to accrue the benefits of that system and accounts for some of the governance challenges faced by the country. Until those institutional and normative weaknesses identified previously are addressed, it is likely that the challenges will continue to overburden the country.

Notes

1 Maurice Duverger, 'A New Political System Model: Semi-Presidential Government' (1980) 8 *European Journal of Political Research* 166. See also Laura-Stella Enonchong, 'The Problem of Systemic Violation of Civil and Political Rights in Cameroon: Towards a Contextualised Conception of Constitutionalism' (PhD Thesis, University of Warwick 2013) 104–105.
2 Martin Shugart, 'Semi-Presidential Systems: Dual Executive and Mixed Authority Patterns' (2005) 3 *French Politics* 323, 340–342.
3 Cindy Skach, 'The "Newest" Separation of Powers: Semipresidentialism' (2007) 5(1) *International Journal of Constitutional Law* 93, 96.
4 Martin Shugart and John Carey refer to it as 'president-parliamentarism'. Martin Shugart and John Carey, *Presidents and Assemblies: Constitutional Design and Electoral Dynamics* (Cambridge University Press 1992) 23. Various subtypes of this regime have been identified. They include highly presidential, balanced semi-presidential regimes and semi-presidential regimes with a ceremonial president. See generally, Robert Elgie, 'A Fresh Look at Semi-Presidentialism: Variations on a Theme' (2005) 16(3) *Journal of Democracy* 98, 202–203; Enonchong, 'The Problem of Systemic Violation' (n 1) 105.
5 Elgie, 'A Fresh Look at Semi-Presidentialism' (n 4) 202–203.
6 Francesco Cavatorta and Robert Elgie, 'The Impact of Semi-Presidentialism on Governance in the Palestinian Authority' (2010) 63(1) *Parliamentary Affairs* 22, 29–30; Skach, 'The "Newest" Separation of Powers' (n 3) 97–98.
7 Cavatorta and Elgie, 'The Impact of Semi-Presidentialism' (n 6) 29–30; Enonchong, 'The Problem of Systemic Violation' (n 1) 105.
8 The judiciary is examined in Chapter 4.

9 As of January 2020, the ruling CPDM occupied 153 of the 180 seats in Parliament.
10 Law No. 2012/001 of 19 April 2012, relating to the Electoral Code (Electoral Code).
11 Constitution, art 6(2); Electoral Code, s 116(1)(2).
12 Constitution, art 6(1); Electoral Code, s 116(3).
13 Charles Fombad, *Constitutional Law in Cameroon* (Wolters Kluwer 2012) 111–112.
14 Constitution, art 6(5); Electoral Code, s 117(1)(2).
15 Electoral Code, s 117(2).
16 Electoral Code, s 121(1)(2).
17 Electoral Code, s 121(2).
18 Electoral Code, s 121(2).
19 Electoral Code, s 118(1).
20 Jean Calvin Aba'a Oyono, 'L'insécurité Juridique en Matière Constitutionnelle: Questionnement Sélectif sur l'articulation et la Pratique Constitutionnelles au Cameroun' in Maurice Kamto, Stephane Doumbe-Bille and Brusil Metou (eds) *Regards Sur le Droit Public en Afrique* (L'Harmattan 2016) 49.
21 Amnesty International, 'Impunity Underpins Persistent Abuse' (29 January 2009) www.amnesty.org/en/library/info/AFR17/001/2009 accessed 15 May 2012; United Nations Human Rights Committee (HRC), 'Concluding Observations of the Human Rights Committee: Cameroon' (CCPR/C/CMR/CO/4, 4 August 2010) 5, para 18 www2.ohchr.org/english/bodies/hrc/docs/CCPR.C.CMR.CO.4.doc accessed 13 December 2010.
22 Aba'a Oyono, 'L'insécurité Juridique en Matière Constitutionnelle' (n 20) 49.
23 ibid.
24 See generally, Michael Yanou, 'Democracy in Cameroon: A Socio-Legal Appraisal' (2013) 46(3) *Law and Politics in Africa, Asia and Latin America* 303; Nantang Jua, 'Problematising a Transition: The Power Elite, the State and Transition Politics in Cameroon' in Julius Ihonvbere and John Mbaku (eds) *Political Liberalisation and Democratisation in Africa: Lessons from Country Experiences* (Praeger Publishers 2003) 97–98.
25 Moki Kindzeka, 'Cameroon's Biya Declared Election Winner' (*Voice of America News*, 22 October 2018) https://www.voanews.com/africa/cameroons-biya-declared-election-winner accessed 14 January 2019.
26 Constitution, art 8(1).
27 ibid art 5(2) para 1.
28 ibid art 5(2) para 2.
29 ibid art 5(2) para 3.
30 ibid arts 8(5) and 31.
31 ibid art 5(2) para 4.
32 ibid art 8(3).
33 Constitution, art 10(1).
34 For instance, the former PM, Yang Philemon, was appointed in June 2009 on the same day as the Ministers for Defence, Sports, Women's Affairs, Transport, Communication, Post and Telecommunications and Basic Education. Georges Dougueli, 'Paul Biya Remanie Son Gouvernement: Valse des Ministres à Yaoundé' (30 June 2009) www.JeuneAfrique.com/Article/ARTJAWEB20090630235233/-RDPC-Paul-Biya… accessed 12 November 2012.
35 Constitution, art 10(1).
36 Constitution, art 8(2).
37 ibid art 8(9).
38 ibid art 8(10).
39 Jean Tobie Hond, 'De L'affirmation du Caractère Parlementaire du Régime Politique Camerounaise au Regard de la Constitution du 18 Janvier 1996' in Maurice Kamto, Stephane Doumbe-Bille and Brusil Metou (eds) *Regards Sur le Droit Public en Afrique* (L'Harmattan 2016) 65–78.

40 See, for instance, BBC News, 'Paul Biya: Cameroon's Absentee President' (5 October 2018) https://www.bbc.co.uk/news/world-africa-43469758 accessed 29 November 2019; Emmanuel Freudenthal, Frank William and Gaelle Tjat, 'Paul Biya, Cameroon's Roaming President' (Organised Crime and Corruption Reporting Project, 18 February 2018) https://www.occrp.org/en/investigations/7653-paul-biya-cameroon-s-roaming-president accessed 29 November 2019; Cyril Bensimon, 'Au Cameroun, Paul Biya, trente-cinq ans de pouvoir et d'absences' (*Le Monde Afrique*, 6 October 2018) https://www.lemonde.fr/afrique/article/2018/10/06/au-cameroun-le-systeme-biya-promis-encore-a-de-beaux-jours_5365622_3212.html accessed 29 November 2019.

41 For instance, the President was absent during a fatal train derailment in Eseka in October 2016 and when armed conflicts broke out in the Anglophone Regions. Freudenthal et al, 'Paul Biya, Cameroon's Roaming President' (n 40).

42 Jean-François Bayart, *The State in Africa: the Politics of the Belly* (Longman 1993) 19; Joseph Takougang and Milton Krieger, *African State and Society in the 1990s: Cameroon's Political Crossroads* (Westview Press 1998).

43 Takougang and Krieger (n 42) 52, 99; Susan Dicklitch, 'Failed Democratic Transition in Cameroon: A Human Rights Explanation' (2002) 24(1) *Human Rights Quarterly* 152, 164–166; Ketil Hansen, 'The Politics of Personal Relations: Beyond Neopatrimonial Practices in Northern Cameroon' (2003) 73(2) *Africa: Journal of the International African Institute* 202; Oben Mbuagbor and Robert Akoko, 'Roll Back: Democratisation and Social Fragmentation in Cameroon' (2004) 13(1) *Nordic Journal of African Studies* 1, 3–5.

44 Hansen, 'The Politics of Personal Relations' (n 43) 212–218; Mbuagbor and Akoko, 'Roll Back' (n 43) 3–5.

45 ibid.

46 Buea is a historically significant town because it was the capital of the former West Cameroon.

47 Peter Geschiere, *The Perils of Belonging: Autochthony, Citizenship and Exclusion in Africa and Europe* (University of Chicago Press 2009) 47.

48 ibid 63.

49 Jua, 'Problematising a Transition' (n 24) 95.

50 ibid.

51 National Democratic Institute, 'Interim Report: International Delegation to the Presidential Elections in Cameroon' (28 October 1992) 93 www.ndi.org/files/0822_cm_interim_102892.pdf accessed 5 January 2012.

52 ibid 95.

53 Constitution, art 8(8).

54 Constitution, art 27.

55 Constitution, art 28(1).

56 Constitution, art 28 (2)(3).

57 That was the situation when the parliament of the former French Cameroon authorised President Ahidjo to rule by ordinances and decrees as discussed in Chapter 1.

58 In South Africa, for instance, delegated power may be struck down by the Constitutional Court if there are no clear standards or guidelines regulating their exercise. Ziyad Motala and Cyril Ramaphosa, *Constitutional Law: Analysis and Cases* (Oxford University Press 2002) 210–211. See also Enonchong, 'The Problem of Systemic Violation' (n 1) 120–122.

59 Judicial Qualifications case, BVerfGe 52, cited in Motala and Ramaphosa, *Constitutional Law* (n 58) 211.

60 Caroline Morris and Ryan Malone, 'Regulations Review in the New Zealand Parliament' (2004) 2 *Macquarie Law Journal* www.austlii.edu.au/au/journals/MQLJ/2004/2.html accessed 12 June 2012.

61 ibid.
62 Constitution art 8(12).
63 Enonchong, 'The Problem of Systemic Violation' (n 1) 127–128.
64 Joseph Kankeu, *Droit Constitutionnel* (Tome 1, 1st edn, Presses Universitaires de Dschang 2003) 171.
65 Kankeu, *Droit Constitutionnel* (n 64) 171.
66 BBC News, 'Niger Leader Dissolves Parliament' http://news.bbc.co.uk/1/hi/world/africa/8067831.stm (UK, 26 May 2009) accessed 29 June 2011.
67 Shugart, 'Semi-Presidential Systems' (n 2) 341.
68 Constitution of the Republic of Namibia, arts 32(3), 57(1).
69 Constitution of Namibia, art 57(2). See also Shugart, 'Semi-Presidential Systems' (n 2) 341.
70 There is no jurisprudence on dissolution power in Cameroon and therefore no certain way of determining what the courts' attitude would be if it were faced with such a matter. The jurisprudence of the French *Conseild'Etat* on the doctrine of *actes de gouvernement* may be useful precedence.
71 Law No. 2006/022 of 29 December 2006 relating to the Organisation and Functioning of Administrative Courts, art 4; *Kouang Guillame Charles*, Jugement No. 53/CS-CA of 26 June 1990.
72 Since 1990, parliament has been dissolved once. In 1992, it was prematurely dissolved to bring forward legislative elections due to take place in 1993. This move was widely believed to be a strategy by the President to minimise the opposition's potential to mobilise in time for the elections. See Inter-Parliamentary Union, 'Cameroon (National Assembly)' (27 August 2007) www.ipu.org/parline-e/reports/Ctr/parlementaire/2053_F.htm accessed 2 February 2012; Enonchong, 'The Problem of Systemic Violation' (n 1) 128.
73 Constitution, art 15(4).
74 Fombad, *Constitutional Law in Cameroon* (n 13) 126.
75 ibid.
76 ibid.
77 See, for instance, Inter-Parliamentary Union, 'Cameroon-National Assembly: Information about the Parliamentary Chamber' (6 November 2013) www.ipu.org/parline-e/reports/2053.htm accessed 29 April 2014; Commonwealth Secretariat, 'Report of the Commonwealth Expert Team: Cameroon Legislative and Municipal Elections, 30 September 2013', 4 https://read.thecommonwealth-ilibrary.org/commonwealth/governance/cameroon-legislative-and-municipal-elections-30-september-2013_9781848599079-en#page3 accessed 29 April 2014.
78 ibid.
79 ibid 3.
80 Emmanuel Kendemeh, 'Cameroon: Parliament - Extending MP's Term of Office Examined' (28 March, 2012) http://allafrica.com/stories/201203281240.html accessed 30 April 2014. See also Valentine Mulango, 'Cameroon: MPs Speedily Adopt Bill Extending Mandate Again' (Yaoundé, 4 May 2013) http://Cameroon-info.net/reactions/@,45736,7 accessed 30 April 2013.
81 Inter-parliamentary Union, 'Cameroon National Assembly' https://data.ipu.org/node/31/elections?chamber_id=13357 accessed 5 November 2019.
82 Decree No. 2019/612 of 10 November 2019 to convene the electorate for the election of Members of Parliament and Municipal Councilors.
83 Freedom House, 'Freedom in the World 2019: Cameroon Country Report' https://freedomhouse.org/report/freedom-world/2019/cameroon accessed 1 February 2020.
84 Constitution, art 9(1)(2).
85 Law No. 90/47 of 19 December 1990 on the State of Emergency, art 1.
86 Constitution, art 9(2).

87 Charles Fombad, 'Cameroon's Emergency Powers: Recipe for (Un)Constitutional Dictatorship' (2004) 48(1) *Journal of African Law* 62, 89.
88 Constitution, art 9(2).
89 Enonchong, 'The Problem of Systemic Violation' (n 1) 136–137.
90 Emergency Legislation, ss 2, 3(a).
91 Discussed further in Chapter 4.
92 See the position in South Africa where the regime is stringently regulated, complying with international standards. Constitution of South Africa, art 37.
93 Fombad, 'Cameroon's Emergency Powers' (n 87).
94 *Wakai & 172 Others v the People*, 1997, 1CCLR, 127.
95 The case is discussed further in Chapter 4.
96 Oren Gross, 'Constitutions and Emergency Regimes' in Tom Ginsburg and Rosalind Dickson (eds) *Comparative Constitutional Law* (Edward Elgar Publishing 2011) 348.
97 ICCPR, art 4(1); Human Rights Committee, 'General Comment 29: States of Emergency (Article 4)' UN Doc. CCPR/C521/Rev.1/Add.11 (2001).
98 Constitution, art 8(3).
99 Constitution, art 8(2).
100 Constitution, art 8(10).
101 Decree No. 2011/412 of 9 December 2011 on the Organisation of the Presidency of the Republic, art 1 and Decree No. 2011/408 of 9 December 2011 to Organise the Government, art 8(1).
102 Decree No. 2011/408, art 8(1).
103 US Department of State, 'Cameroon Executive Summary' (31 March 2018) 6 https://www.state.gov/documents/organization/186385.pdf accessed 12 June 2018.
104 Takougang and Krieger, *African State and Society* (n 42) 71; Enonchong, 'The Problem of Systemic Violation' (n 1) 113–114.
105 Victor Le Vine, 'Leadership and Regime Changes in Perspective' in Michael Schatzberg and William Zartman, *The Political Economy of Cameroon* (Praeger 1985) 20–49.
106 Takougang and Krieger (n 42) 71; Dicklitch, 'Failed Democratic Transition in Cameroon' (n 43) 164.
107 Geschiere, *The Perils of Belonging* (n 47) 48; Bertelsmann Stiftung, 'Bertelsmann Transformation Index 2012 – Cameroon Country Report' (Gütersloh: Betlelsmann Stiftung, 2012) 6 www.bti-project.de/fileadmin/lnhalte/reports/2012/pdf accessed 20 July 2012.
108 Geschiere, *The Perils of Belonging* (n 47) 48.
109 Bertelsmann Stiftung, 'Bertelsmann Transformation Index 2012' (n 107) 6.
110 Constitution, art 8(1).
111 Constitution, art 8(4).
112 Constitution, art 43.
113 Enonchong, 'The Problem of Systemic Violation' (n 1) 140–150.
114 ibid.
115 See, for instance, French Constitution, art 68; Nigerian Constitution, s 308; Zambian Constitution, art 43(3); Namibian Constitution, art 31(3); Constitution of Pakistan, s 248(2).
116 In advanced democracies, it is repeatedly emphasized that none, including executive officials, is above the law. For instance, in *Hamdan v Rumsfeld*, 126S. Ct 2749, 2798 (2006) the US Supreme Court emphasised that the executive is bound to act in accordance with the law. See also *M v Home Office & Another* [1994] 1AC377. That recognition is not exclusive to advanced democracies as exemplified by Zambia where parliament has the discretion to lift presidential immunity (Zambian Const. art 43(3). This was confirmed in *Chiluba v Attorney General*, 2003 [ZMSC] 4, where the Court held that parliament acted legally in lifting former President Chiluba's immunity. Enonchong, 'The Problem of Systemic Violation' (n 1) 140 eps note 221.

117 Enonchong, 'The Problem of Systemic Violation' (n 1) 140–142.

118 Law No. 2008/001 of 14 April 2008 to amend and supplement some provisions of Law No. 96/6 of 18 January 1996 to amend the Constitution of 2 June 1972.

119 Presidential powers and duties under articles 8, 9 and 10 are those dealt with in the preceding sections. Other powers not discussed in this chapter include art 8(6) referring matters to the Constitutional Council; art 8(7) exercising the right of clemency after consultation with the Higher Judicial Council.

120 Presidential term limits were also eliminated and a new impeachment regime instituted (discussed later).

121 Marcel Monin, *Textes et Documents Constitutionnels Depuis 1958: Analyse et Commentaires* (Armand Colin 2001) 328.

122 French Constitution, art 68.

123 In Décision No. 98-408 DC of 22 January 1999, Cour Pénal International.

124 Arrêt du Octobre 2001 (Assemblée plénière, Breisacher).

125 Loius Favoreu, Richard Ghevontian, Guy Scaffoni and Otto Pfersmann, *Droits Constitutionnel* (Éditions Dalloz 2008) 660–662.

126 Charles Fombad and Nat Inegbedion, 'Presidential Term Limits and Their Impact on Constitutionalism in Africa' in Charles Fombad and Christina Murray (eds) *Fostering Constitutionalism in Africa* (Pretoria University Law Press 2010) 23–24. Tom Ginsburg, James Melton and Zachary Elkins have inferred that granting immunity from prosecution may be an incentive to persuade 'overstayers' to quit but also note the potential controversy with issues of accountability. Tom Ginsburg, James Melton and Zachary Elkins, 'On the Evasion of Executive Term Limits' (2011) 52 *William and Mary Law Review* 1807, 1865.

127 That was the explanation proffered by Adamu Mbah Ndam of the SDF who introduced the oppositions counter proposals. See Report No. 007/AN/8 on Bill No. 819/PJL/AN (March 2008); Kini Nsom, 'SDF Backs Biya's Presidential Immunity' (Buea, 11 April 2008) www.postnewsline.com/2008/04/sdf-backs-biyas.html#tp accessed 15 May 2012.

128 ibid.

129 Although recent events relating to attempts to impeach President Donald Trump of the USA may necessitate a reassessment of that contention.

130 Constitution, art 53(1).

131 ibid art 53(2).

132 John Hatchard argues with respect to the African context that it is important that there are carefully defined standards. John Hatchard, 'Presidential Removal: Unzipping the Constitutional Provisions' (2000) 44(1) *Journal of African Law* 1, 2–3.

133 Richard Posner, *An Affair of State: The Investigation, Impeachment, and Trial of President Clinton* (Harvard University Press 1999) 174, 111–113.

134 SDF Proposed Amendment to Bill No. 819/PLJ/AN, No. 06 (art 53(2)).

135 SDF Proposed Amendment to Bill No. 819/PLJ/AN, No. 06 (art 53(2)).

136 Kankeu, *Droit Constitutionnel* (n 64) 168.

137 Constitution, art 12(1).

138 Constitution, art 10(1).

139 Dougueli (n 34).

140 Constitution, art 12(3); Hond, 'De L'affirmation du Caractère Parlementaire' (n 39) 78.

141 Constitution, art 12(4).

142 Hond, 'De L'affirmation du Caractère Parlementaire' (n 39) 78.

143 Constitution, art 11; Decree No. 2011/408, art 1(3).

144 Cf the position in France where the PM is in charge of defining national policy – French Constitution, art 20.

145 Constitution, art 10(1).

146 Hond, 'De L'affirmation du Caractère Parlementaire' (n 39) 74.
147 Constitution, art 12(3).
148 For instance, Decree No. 2019/3179/PM of 2 September 2019 to Grant the Status of Economic Disaster Areas to the Far-North, North-West and South-West Regions and Decree No. 2018/5190/PM of 22 June 2018 appointing officials at the Ministry of Basic Education.
149 Constitution, art 12(2).
150 Circular No. 002/PM of 26 February 2018 on Missions Abroad for Board Chairs, Administrators, Directors General and Deputy Directors General of State-Owned Companies and Establishments.
151 Decree No. 2011/408 of 9 December 2011 to Organise the Government, art 1(2).
152 Decree No. 2011/408, art 3.
153 Decree No. 2011/408, art 3(1)(2)(3).
154 Decree No. 2011/408, art 1, Ministry of Basic Education, Ministry of Secondary Education, Ministry of Higher Education, and the Ministry of Youth and Civic Education.
155 Decree No. 2018/191 of 2 March 2018, supplementing provisions of Decree No. 2011/408, art 1.
156 For instance, the appointment of Paul Atanga Nji as Minister of Territorial Administration and Nalova Lyonga as Minister of Secondary Education have been perceived in some sectors as reward for overtly denying the existence of the 'Anglophone Problem'. See Ajaga Nji, *Understanding the Politics of Jesus* (Friesen Press 2018) 343; Journal du Cameroun, 'Anglophones Split over Atanga Nji's Ministerial Appointment' (6 March 2018) https://www.journalducameroun.com/en/anglophones-split-atanga-njis-ministerial-appointment/ accessed 29 April 2019.
157 Constitution, arts 11, 34, 35.
158 Constitution, art 10(1).
159 ibid art 35(1).
160 ibid art 34.
161 ibid art 34(5).
162 The crisis is discussed in Chapter 6.
163 In a traditional New Year message to the nation, the President indicated that 'Security Forces will be instructed to neutralize' armed separatist groups if they failed to lay down their arms. See Head of State's New Year Message to the Nation (31 December 2018) https://www.prc.cm/en/multimedia/documents/6986-message-de-se-paul-biya-a-la-nation-31-12-2018-en accessed 14 April 2019.
164 Details of the conference are available at https://www.globalfundsixthreplenishment.org/en/.
165 Journal du Cameroun, 'Cameroon: Paul Biya Pledges FCFA 3 Billion for HIV, TB, Malaria Global Fund' (10 October 2019) https://www.journalducameroun.com/en/cameroon-government-contributes-3billion-to-fund-hiv-tb-malaria-prevention/ accessed 29 October 2019.
166 Kankeu, *Droit Constitutionnel* (n 64) 168–169. See also Solomon Bilong, 'La Structure du Pouvoir de L'Etat au Cameroun: Une Analyse Socio-Juridique' (Morocco: African Training and Research Centre in Administration for Development, 2001) 6–8 http://unpan1.un.org/introduc/groups/public/documents/cafrad...pdf accessed 16 July 2012.
167 ibid.
168 Constitution, art 34(6).
169 Paul Ayah was formerly a CPDM parliamentarian who defected to join the opposition. Prior to becoming a politician, he was a judge in the Court of Appeal.
170 Paul Ayah, 'A Cameroonian Case Study: Executive Presidency versus Parliamentary Executive' (2004) 85(4) *The Parliamentarian: Journal of the Parliaments of the Commonwealth* 318.
171 ibid.

172 Jürg M Gabriel, 'Cameroon's Neopatrimonial Dilemma' (1999) 7 *Journal of Contemporary African Studies* 187; Dicklitch, 'Failed Democratic Transition in Cameroon' (n 43) 152.
173 Bertelsmann Stiftung, 'Bertelsmann Transformation Index 2012' (n 107); National Democratic Institute, 'Interim Report' (n 51) 93.
174 Constitution, art 53(1).
175 See page 17.
176 Transparency International, 'Overview of Corruption and Anti-Corruption', 4 https://knowledgehub.transparency.org/helpdesk/cameroon-overview-of-corruption-and-anti-corruption accessed 12 June 2019.
177 Law No. 2006/001 of 25 April 2006 relating to the Declaration of Assets and Property (Law on the Declaration of Assets) s 1. It should be noted that the law also puts legislative and judicial officials and those responsible for state corporations under the same obligation.
178 Law on the Declaration of Assets, s 6, Assets and Property Declaration Reception Commission.
179 Law on the Declaration of Assets, s 9(1).
180 Law on the Declaration of Assets, s 13(1).
181 Law on the Declaration of Assets, s 13(1).
182 Law on the Declaration of Assets, s 3(2).
183 Law on the Declaration of Assets, s 15.
184 Ngambouk Vitalis Pemunta, 'An Evaluation of European Union Development Aid to the Democratisation Project in Cameroon' (2020) 16(1) *Democracy and Security* 1, 17.
185 Law on the Declaration of Assets, s 7(1).
186 ibid s 14(1).
187 ibid s 17.
188 Decree No. 2006/088 of March 2006 relating to the Creation, Organisation and Functioning of the National Anti-Corruption Commission (CONAC Law).
189 CONAC Law, s 2(1) (2).
190 CONAC Law, s 2(2).
191 CONAC Law, ss 20, 21.
192 CONAC reported that during the preparation of its 2016 report, eleven ministries and agencies refused to supply them with information. See Business Anti-Corruption Portal, 'Cameroon Corruption Report' (*Cameroon Intelligence Report*, December 2016) https://www.ganintegrity.com/portal/country-profiles/cameroon/ accessed 12 June 2019.
193 CONAC Law, s 22(1).
194 CONAC Law, s 22(2).
195 CONAC Law, s 22(3).
196 Azize Mbohou, 'Lutte contre la corruption: faut-il plus de pouvoir à la conac?' (Cameroon Tribune 14 January 2019) https://www.cameroon-tribune.cm/article.html/23561/fr.html/lutte-contre-la-corruption-faut-il-plus-de-pouvoir accessed 12 June 2019.
197 CONAC Law, s 2(1).
198 CONAC Law, s 8(1).
199 CONAC Law, s 24(1).
200 CONAC Law, s 1(2).
201 CONAC Law, s 24(2)–(4).
202 Freedom House, 'Freedom in the World 2012 – Cameroon' (17 August 2012) https://www.refworld.org/docid/5033655537.html accessed 13 November 2019.
203 Transparency International, 'Overview of Corruption and Anti-Corruption' (n 176) 6, 7.
204 Thierry Amougou, *Biyaïsme: Le Cameroun au Piege de la Mediocrité Politique de la Libido Accumulative et de la Decivili* (L'Harmattan 2011).
205 Cited in Hond, 'De L'affirmation du Caractère Parlementaire' (n 39) 76.

References

Aba'a Oyono JC, 'L'insécurité Juridique en Matière Constitutionnelle: Questionnement Sélectif sur l'articulation et la Pratique Constitutionnelles au Cameroun' in Maurice Kamto, Stephane Doumbe-Bille and Brusil Metou (eds) *Regards Sur le Droit Public en Afrique* (L'Harmattan 2016).

Amnesty International, 'Impunity Underpins Persistent Abuse' (29 January 2009) www.amnesty.org/en/library/info/AFR17/001/2009 accessed 15 May 2012.

Amougou T, *Biyaïsme: Le Cameroun au Piege de la Mediocrité Politique de la Libido Accumulative et de la Decivili* (L'Harmattan 2011).

Ayah P, 'A Cameroonian Case Study: Executive Presidency versus Parliamentary Executive' (2004) *85*(4) *The Parliamentarian: Journal of the Parliaments of the Commonwealth* 318.

Bayart JF, *The State in Africa: the Politics of the Belly* (Longman 1993).

BBC News, 'Niger Leader Dissolves Parliament' (UK, 26 May 2009) http://news.bbc.co.uk/1/hi/world/africa/8067831.stm accessed 29 June 2011.

BBC News, 'Paul Biya: Cameroon's Absentee President' (5 October 2018) https://www.bbc.co.uk/news/world-africa-43469758 accessed 29 November 2019.

Bensimon C, 'Au Cameroun, Paul Biya, trente-cinq ans de pouvoir et d'absencess' (*Le Monde Afrique*, 6 October 2018) https://www.lemonde.fr/afrique/article/2018/10/06/au-cameroun-le-systeme-biya-promis-encore-a-de-beaux-jours_5365622_3212.html accessed 29 November 2019.

Bertelsmann Stiftung, 'Bertelsmann Transformation Index 2012 – Cameroon Country Report' (Gütersloh: Betlelsmann Stiftung, 2012) www.bti-project.de/fileadmin/lnhalte/reports/2012/pdf accessed 20 July 2012.

Bilong S, 'La Structure du Pouvoir de L'Etat au Cameroun: Une Analyse Socio-Juridique' (Morocco: African Training and Research Centre in Administration for Development, 2001) http://unpan1.un.org/introduc/groups/public/documents/cafrad...pdf accessed 16 July 2012.

Business Anti-Corruption Portal, 'Cameroon Corruption Report' (*Cameroon Intelligence Report*, December 2016) https://www.ganintegrity.com/portal/country-profiles/cameroon/ accessed 12 June 2019.

Cavatorta F and Elgie R, 'The Impact of Semi-Presidentialism on Governance in the Palestinian Authority' (2010) *63*(1) *Parliamentary Affairs* 22.

Commonwealth Secretariat, 'Report of the Commonwealth Expert Team: Cameroon Legislative and Municipal Elections, 30 September 2013' https://read.thecommonwealth-ilibrary.org/commonwealth/governance/cameroon-legislative-and-municipal-elections-30-september-2013_9781848599079-en#page3 accessed 29 April 2014.

Dicklitch S, 'Failed Democratic Transition in Cameroon: A Human Rights Explanation' (2002) *24*(1) *Human Rights Quarterly* 152.

Dougueli G, 'Paul Biya Remanie Son Gouvernement: Valse des Ministres à Yaoundé' (30 June 2009) www.JeuneAfrique.com/Article/ARTJAWEB20090630235233/-RDPC-Paul-Biya... accessed 12 November 2012.

Duverger M, 'A New Political System Model: Semi-Presidential Government' (1980) *8 European Journal of Political Research* 166.

Elgie R, 'A Fresh Look at Semi-Presidentialism: Variations on a Theme' (2005) *16*(3) *Journal of Democracy* 98.

Enonchong L, *'The Problem of Systemic Violation of Civil and Political Rights in Cameroon: Towards a Contextualised Conception of Constitutionalism'* (PhD Thesis, University of Warwick 2013).

Favoreu L, Ghevontian R, Scaffoni G and Pfersmann O, *Droits Constitutionnel* (Éditions Dalloz 2008).

Fombad C, 'Cameroon's Emergency Powers: Recipe for (Un)Constitutional Dictatorship' (2004) *48*(1) *Journal of African Law* 62.

Fombad C and Inegbedion N, 'Presidential Term Limits and Their Impact on Constitutionalism in Africa' in Charles Fombad and Christina Murray (eds) *Fostering Constitutionalism in Africa* (Pretoria University Law Press 2010).

Freedom House, 'Freedom in the World 2019: Cameroon Country Report' https://freedomhouse.org/report/freedom-world/2019/cameroon accessed 1 February 2020.

Freedom House, 'Freedom in the World 2012 – Cameroon' (17 August 2012) https://www.refworld.org/docid/5033655537.html accessed 13 November 2019.

Gabriel JM, 'Cameroon's Neopatrimonial Dilemma' (1999) *7 Journal of Contemporary African Studies*187.

Geschiere P, *The Perils of Belonging: Autochthony, Citizenship and Exclusion in Africa and Europe* (University of Chicago Press 2009).

Ginsburg T, Melton J and Elkins Z, 'On the Evasion of Executive Term Limits' (2011) *52 William and Mary Law Review* 1807.

Gross O, 'Constitutions and Emergency Regimes' in Tom Ginsburg and Rosalind Dickson (eds) *Comparative Constitutional Law* (Edward Elgar Publishing 2011).

Hansen K, 'The Politics of Personal Relations: Beyond Neopatrimonial Practices in Northern Cameroon' (2003) *73*(2) *Africa: Journal of the International African Institute* 202.

Hatchard J, 'Presidential Removal: Unzipping the Constitutional Provisions' (2000) *44*(1) *Journal of African Law* 1.

Head of State's New Year Message to the Nation, 31 December 2018 https://www.prc.cm/en/multimedia/documents/6986-message-de-se-paul-biya-a-la-nation-31-12-2018-en accessed 14 April 2019.

Hond JT, 'De L'affirmation du Caractère Parlementaire du Régime Politique Camerounaise au Regard de la Constitution du 18 Janvier 1996' in Maurice Kamto, Stephane Doumbe-Bille and Brusil Metou, *Regards Sur le Droit Public en Afrique* (L'Harmattan 2016).

Inter-Parliamentary Union, 'Cameroon National Assembly' https://data.ipu.org/node/31/elections?chamber_id=13357 accessed 5 November 2019.

Inter-Parliamentary Union, 'Cameroon (National Assembly)' (27 August 2007) www.ipu.org/parline-e/reports/Ctr/parlementaire/2053_F.htm accessed 2 February 2012.

Inter-Parliamentary Union, 'Cameroon-National Assembly: Information about the Parliamentary Chamber' (6 November 2013) www.ipu.org/parline-e/reports/2053.htm accessed 29 April 2014.

Journal du Cameroun, 'Anglophones Split over Atanga Nji's Ministerial Appointment' (6 March 2018) https://www.journalducameroun.com/en/anglophones-split-atanga-njis-ministerial-appointment/ accessed 29 April 2019.

Journal du Cameroun, 'Cameroon: Paul Biya Pledges FCFA 3 Billion for HIV, TB, Malaria Global Fund' (10 October 2019) https://www.journalducameroun.com/en/cameroon-government-contributes-3billion-to-fund-hiv-tb-malaria-prevention/ accessed 29 October 2019.

Jua N, 'Problematising a Transition: The Power Elite, the State and Transition Politics in Cameroon' in Julius Ihonvbere and John Mbaku, *Political Liberalisation and Democratisation in Africa: Lessons from Country Experiences* (Praeger Publishers 2003).

Kankeu J, *Droit Constitutionnel* (Tome 1, 1st edn, Presses Universitaires de Dschang 2003).

Kendemeh E, 'Cameroon: Parliament – Extending MP's Term of Office Examined' (28 March 2012) http://allafrica.com/stories/201203281240.html accessed 30 April 2014.

Kindzeka ME, 'Cameroon's Biya Declared Election Winner' (*Voice of America News*, 22 October 2018) https://www.voanews.com/africa/cameroons-biya-declared-election-winner accessed 14 January 2019.

Le Vine V, 'Leadership and Regime Changes in Perspective' in Michael Schatzberg and William Zartman (eds) *The Political Economy of Cameroon* (Praeger 1985).

Locka C, Bola F, Maurisse M et al, 'Paul Biya, Cameroon's Roaming President' (Organised Crime and Corruption Reporting Project, 18 February 2018) https://www.occrp.org/en/investigations/7653-paul-biya-cameroon-s-roaming-president accessed 29 November 2019.

Mbohou A, 'Lutte contre la corruption: faut-il Plus de pouvoir à la conac?' (Cameroon tribuneTribune, 14 January 2019) https://www.cameroon-tribune.cm/article.html/23561/fr.html/lutte-contre-la-corruption-faut-il-plus-de-pouvoir accessed 12 June 2019.

Mbuagbor O and Akoko R, 'Roll Back: Democratisation and Social Fragmentation in Cameroon' (2004) *13*(1) *Nordic Journal of African Studies* 1.

Monin M, *Textes et Documents Constitutionnels depuis 1958: Analyse et Commentaires* (Armand Colin 2001).

Morris C and Malone R, 'Regulations Review in the New Zealand Parliament' (2004) 2 *Macquarie Law Journal* www.austlii.edu.au/au/journals/MQLJ/2004/2.html accessed 12 June 2012.

Motala Z and Ramaphosa C, *Constitutional Law: Analysis and Cases* (Oxford University Press 2002).

Mulango V, 'Cameroon: MPs Speedily Adopt Bill Extending Mandate Again' (Yaoundé, 4 May 2013) http:// Cameroon-info.net/reactions/@,45736,7 accessed 30 April 2013.

National Democratic Institute, 'Interim Report: International Delegation to the Presidential Elections in Cameroon' (28 October 1992) 93 www.ndi.org/files/0822_cm_interim_102892.pdf accessed 5 January 2012.

Nji A, *Understanding the Politics of Jesus* (Friesen Press 2018) 343.

Nsom K, 'SDF Backs Biya's Presidential Immunity' (Buea, 11 April 2008) www.postnewsline.com/2008/04/sdf-backs-biyas.html#tp accessed 15 May 2012.

Pemunta NV, 'An Evaluation of European Union Development Aid to the Democratisation Project in Cameroon' (2020) *16(1) Democracy and Security* 1.

Posner R, *An Affair of State: The Investigation, Impeachment, and Trial of President Clinton* (Harvard University Press 1999).

Searcey D and Essomba F, 'Cameroon in Turmoil as Leader Holds onto Power After 36 years' *The Irish Times* (16 July 2018) https://www.irishtimes.com/news/world/africa/cameroon-in-turmoil-as-leader-holds-on-to-power-after-36-years-1.3566534 accessed 29 November 2019.

Shugart M, 'Semi-Presidential Systems: Dual Executive and Mixed Authority Patterns' (2005) *3 French Politics* 323.

Shugart M and Carey J, *Presidents and Assemblies: Constitutional Design and Electoral Dynamics* (Cambridge University Press 1992).

Skach, C, 'The "Newest" Separation of Powers: Semipresidentialism' (2007) *5*(1) *International Journal of Constitutional Law* 93.

Takougang J and Krieger M, *African State and Society in the 1990s: Cameroon's Political Crossroads* (Westview Press 1998).

Transparency International, 'Overview of Corruption and Anti-Corruption' https://knowledgehub.transparency.org/helpdesk/cameroon-overview-of-corruption-and-anti-corruption accessed 12 June 2019.

United Nations Human Rights Committee (HRC), 'Concluding Observations of the Human Rights Committee: Cameroon' (CCPR/C/CMR/CO/4, 4 August 2010) 5, para 18 www2.ohchr.org/english/bodies/hrc/docs/CCPR.C.CMR.CO.4.doc accessed 13 December 2010.

US Department of State, 'Cameroon Executive Summary' (31 March 2018) 6 https://www.state.gov/documents/organization/186385.pdf accessed 12 June 2018.

Yanou M, 'Democracy in Cameroon: A Socio-Legal Appraisal' (2013) *46*(3) *Law and Politics in Africa, Asia and Latin America* 303.

3 The electoral system and the legislature

Introduction

The 1996 Constitution introduced a bicameral parliament, consisting of the National Assembly and the Senate.[1] Despite that constitutional development, legislative power continued to be exercised solely by the National Assembly until 2013 when the first senators were appointed and elected. The period of the 1990s was also significant with respect to the momentous shift in the political landscape to embrace multiparty politics. Thus, the single-party parliament represented by the Cameroon People's Democratic Movement (CPDM) was soon open to other political parties such as the Social Democratic Front, which for a considerable period remained the most influential opposition party. Neither multipartism nor bicameralism have led to any meaningful democratic advancement. One of the greatest challenges that have repressed democratic development inheres in the continued existence of political structures, such as the electoral system, that were established in the framework of a one-party system. Intuitively, while the number of political parties has grown exponentially, the dynamics of representation within parliament has varied only marginally. A related obstacle is the predominance of the executive within the electoral system and parliament itself. With this entrenched structural inhibits, legislative power cannot be meaningfully exercised.

To compound the structural problems, there are social issues such as the political culture which is suffused with clientelism. The combined effect is a parliament which finds itself incapable of influencing executive policy, performing oversight of the executive or representing the popular will, despite its apparently wide ranging constitutional powers.

This chapter will attempt to develop the issues raised previously and provide a better appreciation of legislative power by examining the electoral system, the structure of the legislature, its powers and functions and the accountability of Members of Parliament (MP) and Senators.

Part I. The electoral system

The issue of devising a credible and efficient electoral system is one that preoccupies most jurisdictions in the world, not least Cameroon where historically the electoral system has consisted of a myriad of institutions with conflicting duties and a myriad of legislative texts often obscure and largely unknown to the electorate. An attempt to deal with some of these issues was made in 2000 when the National Elections Observatory (NEO) was created.[2] It soon proved to be ineffective in addressing the historical problems undermining the credibility of the electoral system due significantly to its lack of institutional independence.[3] It was subsequently replaced by Elections Cameroon (ELECAM) in 2008. In addition to the creation of ELECAM, an electoral code was adopted in 2012 which largely consolidated the disparate legislative texts regulating elections.[4] That approach implied that a completely new regime was not adopted to meet with the changing dynamics of the society or to reflect that commitment to democratic advancement. Instead, the old dispensation was perpetuated in the form of a new code. This section provides an overview of the electoral system and its institutions as regulated by the Electoral Code. That discussion is deemed relevant as it provides the contextual background to understand the election process, parliamentary dynamics and the political culture of legislators.

A. *Structure of the National Electoral Commission (ELECAM)*

Structurally, ELECAM is composed of the Electoral Board (EB) and the General Directorate of Elections (GDE).[5] The EB is the governing body of ELECAM and is composed of eighteen members[6] appointed by the President of the Republic.[7] The EB is headed by a chairperson and a vice chairperson who both assume the role of chair and vice chair of ELECAM.[8] ELECAM is represented locally by branches at the regional, divisional and council levels.[9]

The issue of the membership of ELECAM has often sparked controversy due in part to their method of appointment and the apparent lack of independence. Although the law indicates that there should be consultation with the National Assembly and civil society organisations, there is little evidence that such a process is actually carried out by the President prior to appointment or that any such consultation would result in robust scrutiny of the nominees. As a measure of safeguarding their independence, the law provides that their duties are incompatible with inter alia, duties as member of government or the central administrative services and membership of a political party.[10] Yet it has become customary that senior members of ELECAM tend to be either key figures in the government or central administrative services (appointed by the President) or members of the ruling CPDM party whose chairman is the President of the Republic. These features lend credence to accusations of lack of independence and presidential control or usurpation of the democratic process. This reputation was earned at its inception when its first twelve members were appointed in 2008,[11] ten of whom were members of the ruling CPDM party.[12] Although an attempt has been made to vary its membership, key figures of the central administration and the ruling CPDM party continue to make up its membership.[13]

I. Role and powers of ELECAM

ELECAM is prima facie responsible for the organisation, management and supervision of all election and referendum operations.[14] This is done principally through the EB and the DGE. These duties are summarised below.

A. THE DIRECTORATE GENERAL (AS PER SECTION 26(1))

Pre-election

- Organising or supervising the training of electoral personnel
- Drawing up, updating and publishing of the electoral register
- Issuing and distributing voter cards
- Distributing ballot samples to candidates and political parties
- Preparing and executing draft budgets of elections
- Receiving and forwarding to the EB candidacy papers for all elections

Election period

- Coordinating the work of approved observers
- Coordinating all bodies responsible for election operations

Post-election

- Documentation of materials emanating from the elections
- Coordinating the forwarding of election reports from polling stations to the EB

B. EB (AS PER SECTIONS 10 AND 11)

Pre-election

- Scrutinise candidacy papers and publish the final list of candidates for elections
- Publication and notification of the list of members of local polling commissions to the relevant persons or institutions
- Control the preparation of election materials and documents

Election period

- Hear and determine claims and petitions regarding pre-election and election operations (subject to the jurisdiction of the Constitutional Council and appropriate courts or authorities)

Post-election

- Forward election reports to the Constitutional Council or other relevant bodies.

It should be noted that ELECAM (through its DGE and EB) works in conjunction with other sub-commissions to ensure the organisation and management of the election process. As will become apparent later, the roles may sometimes be duplicated making the existence of multiple institutions in the electoral process questionable.

B. Sub-commissions

There are five sub-commissions in the electoral system – Electoral Register Revision Commission (ERRC), Voter Card Issuance and Distribution Commission (VCIDC), Local Polling Commissions (LPC), Divisional Supervisory Commissions (DSC)[15] and the National Commission for the Final Counting of Votes (NCFCV). Their membership and role in the electoral system is represented in Table 3.1.

Table 3.1 Jurisdiction, membership and role of sub-commissions

Institution	*Territorial jurisdiction*	*Membership*	*Responsibilities*
ERRC, ss 52, 52	Local council	Chair (representative of ELECAM), a representative of the administration, mayor or deputy mayor or municipal councillor, representative of each authorised political party in that local council	Revision of electoral registers (jointly with ELECAM)
VCIDC, s 53	Local council	Chair (representative of ELECAM), a representative of the administration, mayor or deputy mayor or municipal councillor, representative of each authorised political party in that local council	Supervising the issuance and distribution of voter cards (jointly with ELECAM)
LPC, ss 54, 61, 62	Nationwide	Chair appointed by ELECAM, representative of the administration, representative of each political party or election candidate	– Vote counting – Rule on any difficulties relating to the organisation and conduct of the poll and vote counting

Institution	*Territorial jurisdiction*	*Membership*	*Responsibilities*
			– Prepare a report on all polling operations which should be signed by the Chairperson and members present and forwarded to the divisional branch of ELECAM
DSC, ss 63, 64	Administrative Division	Chair (president of the High Court),[a] three representatives of the administration, three representatives of ELECAM and a representative of each political party or election candidate	– Supervise operations for drawing up, keeping and revising electoral registers and examine all claims relating thereto. – Supervise distribution of voter cards – Centralise and check returning operations carried out by LPCs and documents relating thereto and request regularisations by LPCs in case of minor irregularities
NCFCV, ss 68, 69	National	Chair (member of the Constitutional Council), two judicial officers, five representatives of the administration, five representatives of ELECAM, one representative of each political party or election candidate.	– Carry out the final counting of votes – Correct any clerical errors in the counting of votes – Draw up a report on all its operations – Forward report and appended documents to the Constitutional Council within five days

Note

[a] For senatorial elections, the chair is the president of the Court of Appeal.

I. Other electoral commissions

From the table, it can be seen that the pre-election role of ELECAM is largely duplicated by the sub-commissions. Moreover, ELECAM's role in the management and supervision of the election process is not quite clear and is obscured by its presence in all other sub-commissions involved in the election process. While its presence in the sub-commissions may be seen as a means by which it fulfils its mandate, it is not immediately clear that this approach actually enables it to do so.

Another observation that can be made is that there are quite many and apparently superfluous sub-commissions involved in the election process. The duties performed by these sub-commissions could be carried out by ELECAM. The creation of multiple sub-commissions does little to ameliorate historical problems relating to the electoral system. The current approach perpetuates the obscure system which facilitated the occurrence of irregularities undermining the credibility of elections. This assertion can be supported by a number of observations relating to the structure of various institutions and the processes involved.

Structurally, the composition of the sub-commissions leaves a lot to be desired. There is a heavy presence of the administration and presidential appointees in key commissions such as the DSC and the NCFCV. For instance, the chairperson of the DSC is a presidential appointee and so are the representatives of ELECAM.[16] The three representatives of the administration are appointed by the Senior Divisional Officer, who is a presidential appointee.[17] Similarly, the chairperson of the NCFCV, a member of the Constitutional Council, is a presidential appointee, including the two judicial officers and five representatives from ELECAM. Again, there are five representatives from the administration appointed by the Minister of Territorial Administration, a presidential appointee. It was noted earlier in the 'Introduction' section the ruling CPDM partisan composition of ELECAM. Besides the issue of the significant presence of presidential appointees, there is a disproportionate representation of the opposition in the sub-commissions, especially in the NCFCV which has thirteen apparent presidential appointees as opposed to one representative from each candidate in the elections.

In terms of the process, some sub-commissions have been ascribed roles which may provide the opportunity for electoral malpractices. The danger is potentially within the DSC and the NCFCV. Once the votes have been counted and results proclaimed at the LPC, the latter generates a report which is signed by all members present[18] and forwarded to the local branch of ELECAM.[19] ELECAM in turn forwards it to the DSC within 48 hours of the close of polling operations[20] and it forms the basis of the deliberations of the DSC.[21] Although members of the LPC are given a copy of the report which they would have signed,[22] the only authentic copy is the original which is retained by the local branch of ELECAM.[23] Thus, in case of a dispute, a candidate in the election may not be able to rely on their own copy to dispute any subsequent disparities. Interestingly, the DSC is authorised to 'correct', 'rectify' or 'adjust' corresponding reports in case of miscalculations and to explain that in its final report.[24] It is not clear why the DSC has to undertake further returning operations given that the results would have been proclaimed already at the stage of the LPC, particularly in the light of the fact that there is a further stage at which the votes would be tallied. The operations of the DSC at this stage appear superfluous and provide the opportunity for unwarranted or bogus 'correction' or 'adjustments'.

Once the DSC has completed its operations, it writes a report which is forwarded (together with documents from the LPC) to the NCFCV.[25] The NCFCV is a crucial institution in the election process as it has the responsibility to carry out the 'final counting of votes' on the basis of the reports and documents received from the DSC.[26] Like the latter, the NCFCV can 'correct any clerical errors in the counting of votes'.[27]

C. The Constitutional Council

The Constitutional Council (Council) may be considered to be at the apex of the electoral system. It has the mandate to proclaim the results of elections[28] and to hear and determine disputes arising therefrom.[29] Election petitions made to the Council must be submitted within 72 hours of the close of polls[30] and its rulings are final.[31] This poses a significant problem in respect of petitions relating to irregularities from final counting of votes. As mentioned previously, generally, it takes more than 72 hours for the final results of the election to be known. The reports from LPC are submitted to the NCFCV within 72 hours of the close of polls[32] and the latter in turn submits its own report to the Council, after tallying the votes within five days.[33] It is at this stage that some irregularities such as disparities with figures from the polling station and those from the various sub-commissions could become apparent. This is way beyond 72 hours implying that at this point, any candidate would be divested of the right to challenge the election results irrespective of the nature of the irregularity revealed. It is submitted that the provision on time limit is inherently detrimental to the democratic process as it precludes recourse to challenge unfair or irregular electoral practices. This is exacerbated by the fact that the decisions of the Council are not subject to appeal. A more democratic process would vest ordinary courts or special electoral tribunals with jurisdictions in electoral disputes allowing for a process where there is a final reviewing body such as the Council.

A further problem which can be seen as an obstacle to the transparency and independence of the Council's processes is the fact that the chair of the NCFCV is a member of the Council, which later sits to deliberate the report from the NCFCV.[34] Thus, not only is the chairperson scrutinising their own report, their presence in the Council may effectively deter an objective scrutiny by other members of the Council. There is no legal requirement that the chair of the NCFCV should recuse themselves from the deliberations of the Council. In addition, the composition of the Council is also rendered questionable by the heavy presence of presidential appointees who are loyal to the President and the ruling CPDM party.[35]

The entire electoral process and system appears to be one that is designed to consolidate incumbency advantages, inimical to a credible democratic process. It is therefore unsurprising that since the supposed democratic transition in the 1990s, the CPDM has dominated party politics, winning an overwhelming majority of seats in the National Assembly and since 2013, the Senate inclusive. The opacity of the electoral process and its domination by officials loyal to the government and the ruling CPDM makes it more likely than not that the CPDM will continue to dominate politics in Cameroon.[36] As will be demonstrated in the course of this chapter, the consequences of the inadequacies in the system are far reaching, particularly with respect to parliament's ability to act as a credible accountability and representative institution. It is against this background that the next section examines the election of members of parliament.

Part II. Election of members of parliament

Elections to both houses of parliament differs, warranting a separate discussion.

A. National Assembly

The National Assembly is composed of 180 MPs collectively representing the electoral constituencies in Cameroon.[37] Each administrative division in the country is a constituency,[38] although some electoral constituencies could be warded by decree of the President of the Republic on the ground of their 'peculiar circumstances'.[39] In terms of representation, it is ironical that additional constituencies could be created for such a nebulous reason by the President. The law provides no indication of what these 'peculiar circumstances' may be. Moreover, the number of MPs representing each constituency is determined unilaterally by presidential decree.[40] This is potentially a tool that can be applied to reduce representation in opposition strongholds.[41] It has been demonstrated that during the parliamentary elections in 1997, 16 special constituencies were created by presidential decree. The distribution of seats in the special constituencies was disproportionate in areas where the opposition would have otherwise enjoyed a majority.[42] In other areas, the creation of special constituencies was intended to make seats available to the ruling party in opposition strongholds. For instance, in the 1997 parliamentary elections, a special constituency was created in Balikumbat whose candidate (the *fon*) was member of the ruling CPDM. This constituency was carved in the North-West where the CPDM had no seats, but electoral manipulations ensured that the CPDM won that seat, providing its sole parliamentary representation in the North-West region.[43]

In terms of eligibility, candidacy is open to any Cameroonian citizen of at least twenty three years of age, irrespective of gender, who enjoys their civic rights, and literate in French and English and enrolled on the electoral register.[44]

In addition, foreign persons who have obtained Cameroonian nationality are eligible ten years after the acquisition of Cameroonian nationality.[45] Ineligible Cameroonians include serving members of the defence and security forces,[46] persons who have placed themselves in a position of dependency on a foreign organisation or sate, or a person acting as a security agent of the foreign state.[47]

MPs are elected for a term of five years by universal suffrage and direct and secret ballot, through a mixed system of majoritarian and proportional representation.[48] In constituencies that have only one seat, voting is for a single candidate and the first past the post system is applied where the candidate attracting the majority of votes wins the seat.[49] In case of a tie, the eldest candidate wins the seat.[50] It is a controversial provision due to the inherent unfairness and discriminatory approach because a younger candidate attracting an equal number of votes is prejudiced simply due to their age. In constituencies that apply the list system, the list obtaining an absolute majority of votes wins all the available seats.[51] Where no list obtains an absolute majority, the highest list is allocated half of the seats. A tie between two or more lists, results in the number of seats being allocated to the list with the highest average age.[52] The remaining seats are then allocated to the lists through the application of proportional representation to the list with the highest votes.[53] A list obtaining less than 5% of the votes is ineligible for allocation of a seat.[54] Once elected, their term of office commences on the second Tuesday following the proclamation of election results, when the National Assembly meets as of right in ordinary session.[55]

B. The Senate

The eligibility criteria for senatorial elections is similar to that of MPs except that the minimum age is forty years and the candidate must be habitually resident in the region concerned.[56] With respect to composition, it has one hundred senators representing electoral constituencies and each of the ten regions of Cameroon is an electoral constituency.[57] Each region is represented by ten senators, seven of which are elected whereas three are appointed by presidential decree, in both instances to serve for a term of five years.[58]

Unlike MPs, senators are elected indirectly by an electoral college comprising regional and municipal councillors.[59] Election is by a list system and a mixed single ballot comprising a majority and proportionate representation system.[60] Political parties taking part in the elections must present a list of seven candidates reflecting the gender and sociological components of the region.[61] A list obtaining an absolute majority of the votes is allocated all the seven seats.[62] However, where there is no absolute majority, the list obtaining a relative majority shall be awarded four of the seven seats and in case of a tie, the four seats are shared equally between the relevant lists.[63] Where necessary, the remaining seat is awarded to the list with the highest average age.[64] The three other seats are distributed proportionately among all the lists, including those that obtained a relative majority under the proportional representation system.[65] In case of a tie in the number of votes obtained where the last seat needs to be allocated, that seat is allocated to the eldest candidate. Here again, it can be noted that the age factor is being used to prejudice other lists or candidates who may be equally entitled to the seat.

With respect to the presidential appointees, it is worth noting that their appointment is made within ten days of the proclamation of senatorial election results.[66] At this stage, the President would have a clear indication of the level of representation of the ruling party and may well use this discretionary power to influence the representative capacity of the ruling party. It is rather ironical that besides the general eligibility criteria, the law provides no specific criteria which should guide the choice of appointees. More significantly, this power is exercised unilaterally without a requirement to confer or confirm with any other institution. As such, nothing deters the President from solely appointing representatives or supporters of the ruling party. In fact, the first cohort of thirty senators appointed in 2013 was predominantly members of the CPDM.[67] Although a very small number of representatives of opposition parties and traditional rulers were also appointed, they were notable supporters or allies of the ruling CPDM.[68] Most of the appointees had their mandate renewed in 2018 when their initial term ended.[69] One of the controversies surrounding such a discretionary power is the potential for abuse as it can be used by the President to subvert an elected opposition majority in the Senate or to consolidate the ruling majority to ensure a very firm control of the Senate. Understandably, in any political system, the ruling party would favour control of any of its houses of parliament.

One of the problems with the approach in Cameroon is that a system of appointment of representatives to sit with elected representatives does not augur well for a fragile democracy where the same representatives lack independence. In addition, the inadequacies of the electoral process as described earlier combine to ensure that the CPDM dominates both houses of parliament. Tables 3.2 and 3.3 depict the trend of electoral outcomes in Cameroon since the transition to multiparty democracy in the 1990s.

As shown in Tables 3.2 and 3.3, the CPDM has won the majority of seats in every election contested since the transition to multiparty democracy in 1990. This makes both the National Assembly and Senate overwhelmingly dominated by the CPDM. There was an opportunity in 1992 for the opposition to form a formidable alliance to outnumber the CPDM, considering that their cumulative number of seats put them at 51.1%. However, that was upset by the MDR entering into a suspect coalition with the CPDM, eliminating the potential for meaningful parliamentary reforms. In practice, there is a high level of party discipline within the CPDM and MPs or Senators are very loyal to the party. This is due in significant part to the need to preserve the benefits attached to their office.[70] The inevitable consequence is the inability of parliament to perform effective oversight of the government acquiring the reputation of a complacent institution that rubber-stamp government policies as defined by the President.[71]

Table 3.2 Results of legislative elections

Parties	*Number of seats*					
	Electoral period					
	1992	*1997*	*2002*	*2007*	*2013*	*2020*
CPDM	88	116	149	153	148	152
SDF	0	43	22	16	18	5
NUDP	68	13	1	6	5	7
UPC	18	1	3	–	3	–
CDU	–	5	5	4	4	4
MDR	6	1	1	1	1	2
Others	–	1	1	–	1	10
Total	180	180	180	180	180	180

Source: Inter-Parliamentary Union, http://archive.ipu.org/parline/reports/2053_E.htm; Inter-Parliamentary Union, 'Cameroon: National Assembly' https://data.ipu.org/node/31/elections?chamber_id=13357; Election Guide: Democracy Assistance and Election News: http://www.electionguide.org/elections/?inst=Assembly&cont=Cameroon&yr=2008.

Notes

Abbreviations: CDU, Cameroon Democratic Union; MDR, Movement for the Defence of the Republic; NUDP, National Union for Democracy and Progress; UPC, Union of the Peoples of Cameroon.

Table 3.3 Results of senatorial elections

Parties	*Number of seats*	
	Electoral period	
	2013	*2018*
CPDM	56	63
SDF	14	7
Total	70	70

Source: http://archive.ipu.org/parline-e/reports/arc/2054_13.htm; http://archive.ipu.org/parline-e/reports/2054_E.htm.

Part III. Structure of the legislature

A. The National Assembly

The National Assembly meets three times a year in ordinary sessions in March, June and November when convened by its Bureau and after consultation with the President of the Republic.[72] It can also be convened to hold extraordinary sessions with a fixed agenda at the request of the President of the Republic or one-third of its members.[73]

In terms of its organisational structure, it consists of a Bureau and a Chairmen's Conference which are the governing bodies of the institution. These are complemented by internal groups such as Party Groups, the General Committees, Ad Hoc Committees, Special Committees and Committees of Inquiry.

The Bureau is elected at the beginning of each legislative year. The Bureau is empowered to preside over the proceedings of the National Assembly and organise all its services.[74] It is additionally responsible for the drafting of minutes by the secretaries, drawing up of the list of speakers, evaluating, auditing and controlling the services of the National Assembly.[75] The Bureau is composed of a president, a senior vice president, five vice presidents, four questors, twelve secretaries and a secretary general, who is also a legal and parliamentary adviser of the National Assembly.[76]

The Chairmen's Conference is responsible for drawing up the agenda of the National Assembly,[77] ruling on the admissibility of bills, referring bills to the relevant parliamentary committees[78] and setting the dates for plenary sitting. It is composed of members of the Bureau, chairpersons of the nine General Committees and presidents of Parliamentary Groups. A member of government shall participate in their deliberations.[79]

The Standing Orders provide that MPs may organise themselves into Parliamentary Groups according to political parties and each group may not exceed fifteen members.[80] However, MPs who do not belong to any parliamentary groups may form an alliance with a group of their choice, although approval is required from the bureau of that group.[81] The groups form the basis for membership of the General Committees.[82]

There are nine General Committees and these are bodies through which the National Assembly carries out the substantive study of bills, the debates and the final drafting of bills.[83] The committees are as follows: the Committee on Constitutional laws, Human Rights and Freedoms, Justice, Legislation and Standing Orders and Administration; Finance and Budget; Foreign Affairs; National Defence and Security; Economic Affairs, Planning and Regional Development; Education, Vocational Training and Youths; Cultural, Social and Family Affairs; Production and Trade and the Committee on Resolutions and Petitions.[84] The General Committees are convened at the request of the Secretary General of the National Assembly to consider substantive aspects of bills referred by the Chairmen's Conference.[85] Only members of the Committee may vote on issues relating to that Committee, although its debates are open to members of other committees and to members of government (when the bill is relevant to their ministries).[86]

The Committees of Inquiry are set up with specific terms of reference,[87] for instance, to inquire into various issues, either internal issues of the National Assembly or external issues relating to public institutions, such as when exercising oversight of the government.[88] In the latter instance, the Committee is expected to report its findings to the National Assembly.[89] Members of the Committee are bound by secrecy and any defiance of the applicable rule will invoke sanctions pursuant to the applicable official secrecy legislation.[90]

B. The Senate

The two houses of parliament appear to have been conceived on an identical configuration. According to the Standing Orders of the Senate, that institution holds three ordinary sessions in March, June and November, respectively.[91] The opening date for the sessions shall be fixed by the Bureau of Senate after consultation with the President of the Republic. Extraordinary sessions can also be organised for a maximum period of 15 days at the request of the President of the Republic or one-third of Senators.[92]

In terms of its structure, Senate consists of a Bureau, a Chairmen's Conference, Parliamentary Groups and General Committees. Additionally, Special Committees and Joint Committees may be set up when the need arises.

The Bureau is made up of a president, a senior vice president, four vice presidents, three questors, eight secretaries and the secretary general who is ex officio member.[93] The Bureau is responsible for, inter alia, presiding over the proceedings of the Senate and to organise all its services and represent it in all public ceremonies.[94] Through the questors, the Bureau oversees the administrative and financial services of the Senate,[95] whereas the secretaries supervise the drafting of minutes, list of speakers and the internal voting process.[96]

The Chairmen's Conference is composed of presidents of Parliamentary Groups, chairpersons of General Committees and members of the Senate Bureau.[97] The duties of the Chairmen's Conference include drawing up the agenda of Senate,[98] ruling on the admissibility of bills referring them to the relevant parliamentary committees,[99] proposing the organisation of debates to the Senate[100] and setting the dates for plenary sittings.

As is the case with the National Assembly, Senators may organise into Parliamentary Groups according to their political parties, although in this case, the group size is a minimum of ten members.[101] Senators who do not belong to any group may form an alliance with a group of their choice with the consent of the Bureau of that group.[102] Group membership forms the basis for membership in the General Committees.[103]

There are nine General Committees in the Senate[104] corresponding with those of the National Assembly.[105] The committees may only sit during parliamentary sessions with the exception of the Finance and Budget Committee which may sit as and when necessary.[106] The reason for the exceptional dispensation is not stated in the law but one may assume that due to the particularly significant nature of its duties and the potentially evolving nature of a country's economy and finance, it would be necessary for the committee to meet should there be relevant changes in the financial and economic policy or situation of the country. This is the more so with respect to the finance laws which may be amended in the course of the financial year. The General Committees are convened at the request of the Secretary General of the Senate to consider substantive aspects of bills referred by the Chairmen's Conference.[107] Although a specific committee is allocated the duty to carry out the substantive study of a matter referred to it by the Chairmen's Conference, other committees may request to provide an opinion.[108] In which case, such an opinion would be subsequently submitted to the main committee carrying out the substantive study.[109] Only members of the Committee may vote on issues relating to that Committee, although its debates are open to members of other Committees and to members of government (when the bill relates to matters falling within the competence of their ministry).[110]

In relation to Special Committees, these are set up for 'specific purposes, particularly of major national interest'. What that entails is not stated in the law but it may be inferred from the wording of the law that these would be created as and when the need arises.[111] Membership of such committees would usually be determined by the resolution which precedes the setting up of the special committee.[112]

The Joint Committees are Committees from both houses of parliament which may meet on the premises of either house.[113] They may be convened by their eldest members or in relation to a specific matter and they determine their composition.[114] The rules of procedure are those generally applicable to committees, although in the event of a conflict in the rules of the two houses, the rule of the house hosting the committee shall take precedence.[115]

C. The relationship between the National Assembly and Senate

The Senate has sometimes been perceived with suspicion, as an institution introduced to dominate the National Assembly.[116] That perception might be influenced partly by the fact that 30% of senators are presidential appointees, indicative of the predominance of the executive in that institution. Although executive interference may arguably be discerned in practice, the supremacy of the Senate over the National Assembly is not overtly reflected in constitutional provisions or implicitly inferred from the roles attributed to both houses. In fact, in terms of their spheres of competence in relation to legislation, each house is not confined to legislating on specific thematic or territorial areas as would be found in countries such as Kenya, in which case, presumably, the Senate could be used to bypass the National Assembly.[117] Although in terms of representation they cover different geographical spheres,[118] the Constitution states that parliament (consisting of both houses) shall legislate and control government action and both houses shall meet on the same dates.[119] They can meet in congress at the request of the President of the Republic, to be addressed by him or to receive a message from him, to receive the oath of members of the Constitutional Council or to decide on a draft or proposed constitutional amendment.[120] In those instances, the Bureau of the National Assembly shall preside over the meeting. It can be seen that although there are opportunities to work together in congress, there is no explicit substantive hierarchy in favour of the Senate. In fact, one may argue to the contrary considering that the National Assembly's Bureau is given the task to preside over meetings in congress.

With respect to their role in the legislative process, the position is that, government bills and private members' bills are submitted to the Bureau of both houses at the same time to be studied by their relevant committees prior to debates in the plenary sessions.[121] When a bill has been passed by the National Assembly, it is forwarded to the Senate for consideration.[122] Within ten days of receiving the bill (or five days for a bill declared urgent by the government),[123] Senate may alternatively, adopt the bill, make amendments to it or fail to adopt the entire bill or parts of it. The procedure is simple where Senate adopts the bill as it is merely forwarded to the Speaker of the National Assembly who in turn forwards it, within 48 hours, to the President of the Republic for promulgation.[124] Where amendments are made by Senate, the bill is forwarded to the National Assembly for a second reading. It is worth noting that amendments to the text would only be admissible if approved by a simple majority of Senators.[125] In contrast, where Senate fails to adopt all or parts of the bill the procedure is more complex. First, such an objection requires an absolute majority of Senators for it to be valid.[126] Once that is determined, the Speaker of the Senate will return the bill to the National Assembly for a second reading. The National Assembly may in turn adopt the bill but only on the basis of an absolute majority of MPs voting in favour.[127] This demonstrates that a rejection from Senate is not definitive and does not completely prevent the adoption of a bill by the National Assembly. This aspect puts in doubt the supremacy argument. What is clear is that when Senate adopts, amends or fails to adopt a bill, it is exercising some review function and in that sense may be perceived as a house with the power to scrutinise legislation emanating from the National Assembly. Thus, one can accommodate the view that the Constitution creates an appellate hierarchy in the enactment of laws, which places the Senate at the top of that hierarchy as opposed to the National Assembly. Nevertheless, that view may be diluted by what ensues from the failure of the National Assembly to attain an absolute majority, following Senate's rejection of a bill.

Where the National Assembly fails to obtain an absolute majority, this calls for intervention by the President of the Republic. The latter may convene a joint commission composed of an equal number of members of both houses, to propose an alternative formulation of the specific provisions objected to by Senate.[128] The alternative draft is submitted by the President, to the two houses for approval where amendments may be made but may only be admissible on the endorsement of the President.[129] Here again, it can be seen that the approval of the alternative formulation is a collegiate matter rather than one that puts Senate at the helm of the approval process. Doubts as to the supremacy of Senate is further reinforced by the procedure in the event of a failure to reach a joint alternative or where both houses fail to adopt a joint alternative draft. In both cases, the President of the Republic may either request the National Assembly to reach a definitive conclusion or declare the bill null and void.[130]

A pertinent observation that can be made here is that it is the National Assembly that is required in the latter case to reach a definitive conclusion and not the Senate. This is commendable in terms of the majoritarian argument. Senate is composed of a mixture of elected and appointed representatives and therefore it cannot be said to be fully democratic. This is in contrast with the National Assembly where all MPs are elected and therefore that house may be considered more fully democratic as in theory, it represents the will of the electorate. From that perspective, it would be more rational for the National

Assembly to have a definitive say in the enactment of laws. What emanates from the aforementioned discussion is the fact that there is an appellate hierarchy in terms of the enactment of laws and a procedure which requires some level of collegiality.

An important question worth considering is the rationale for the intervention of the President of the Republic, in view of the role of the Constitutional Council in resolving disputes between institutions. Perhaps this can be explained by the typically presidential nature of the political system by virtue of which the President is largely in control of every aspect of the political life and the institutions. This can be contrasted with the position in Kenya where an impasse between the houses of parliament is mediated by a mediation committee consisting of an equal number of members of each house appointed by the speakers of each house.[131] Therefore, it is the houses of parliament, through their respective speakers, that attempt to deal with the impasse and not the president of the republic. Moreover, where a mediation committee fails to arrive at a joint formulation of a bill or a joint formulation is rejected by both houses, the bill automatically fails.[132] It does not depend on the president to make a declaration. In the case of Cameroon, it can be contended that it is unnecessary for the President of the Republic to intervene as this could be seen as an encroachment on the jurisdiction of the Constitutional Council.[133] The President of the Republic should be confined to promulgating laws passed by parliament, rather than interfering with parliamentary processes. It may, however, be argued that this does not constitute encroachment or unwarranted interference, as the Constitution vests on him, powers to 'ensure the proper functioning of public authorities' through his arbitration.[134] There appears to be a certain ambiguity here which works in favour of Presidential intervention. In any event, this goes further to demonstrate the pervasive influence of the institution of the President.

Part IV. Powers and functions of the legislature

A. The legislative domain and law making

One of the principal responsibilities of the legislative arm of government is law making and as stated earlier, the Constitution vests this power within the jurisdiction of both houses of parliament.[135] Peculiarly, parliament has been vested with powers to legislate in very specific areas and these include fundamental liberties, civil status, penal procedures, political, administrative and judicial organisation, financial and patrimonial matters, social and economic programme and the education system.[136] Beyond these areas, parliament has no competence to issue legislation. The reason for that restriction, as discussed in Chapter 2, emanates from the fact that the President is authorised to exercise statutory authority[137] and to issue rules and regulations in the areas which do not fall within parliament's competence.[138] The Prime Minister (PM) is also vested with statutory authority.[139] Thus, although parliament is the principal legislative institution, its legislative competence is severely restricted in favour of the executive.[140]

This approach to limiting the legislative domain of parliament is consistent with a highly presidential semi-presidential system which favours the vesting of exorbitant and largely uncontrolled powers on the president. Within the legislature, this is manifested in many ways including the admissibility criteria regulating the admission of bills in parliament. The admissibility criteria give pre-eminence to bills introduced by the President as they override all others in terms of the order of consideration.[141] However, private member bills (not supported by the government) are considered subsequently and this may only occur three subsequent sittings after a bill was originally admitted.[142] This is a formidable tool which can be used tactically to prevent the consideration of bills from the opposition by interminably postponing consideration.[143] A case in point is the opposition's proposals for the adoption of a harmonised electoral code which had been made repeatedly since 1991 on the basis that it was necessary for promoting the democratisation process.[144] Lacking support from the government and parliament, consideration of the reform bill was consistently postponed and was eventually rejected.[145] The debate was subsequently revived in 2005 and a code was finally adopted by parliament in April 2012.[146] It is worthy to note that the bill was introduced by the President.

Notwithstanding the aforementioned restrictions, parliament has the exclusive jurisdiction to examine bills admitted through the Chairmen's conference of each of its two houses. In the National Assembly, debates occur typically within the General Committees although in certain circumstances the Chairmen's Conference may decide to cause a bill to be considered by the entire house. When that applies, proceedings will be restricted to general discussions. In all circumstances, the substantive debates on a bill is undertaken within the General Committees which also have the mandate to produce a final draft of the bill. The Committees' debates are open to the movers of proposals and amendments and in case of government bills, the relevant government minister and their close aid(s) may attend and be heard at their request. Given that the composition of the General Committees allows for non-partisan representation such as Parliamentary Groups, there is scope for scrutiny of bills at the Committee stage. However, the potentials for meaningful debate may only be realised where there is a fairly equitable representation of different political parties within the Committees. This is relevant because a General Committee that is dominated by one party may tend to be sympathetic to the party's position, an aspect which might undermine objectivity in their scrutiny of bills. A fairly recent example is the Government's Bill to amend certain provisions of the Electoral Code to the effect that ninety councillors would be allocated to each of the geographic regions of Cameroon.[147] These councillors form an essential part of the governance structure of the regions and the Electoral College for the election of senators. When the Bill was debated in the Committee on Constitutional Laws, Legislation, etc, the opposition SDF objected to the proposed amendments on the basis of the inequitable distribution of representatives as it did not reflect the demographic disparities between the regions.[148] The MRC also objected additionally on the basis that it was a strategy adopted by the central government to infiltrate regional governance by filling it with pro-CPDM councillors. The Minister of Decentralisation defended the amendment on the basis that all regions, irrespective of their demographic size, should be given an equal number of representatives.[149] Lacking support for the opposition's objection, the SDF found it futile to continue with the Committee debates considering that, of the twenty members of that Committee, only three where from the opposition. Thus they abstained from further debates and from voting for the Bill.[150] Unsurprisingly, the Bill was passed by both houses[151] despite the arguments relating to the apparent inequality that it endorsed. That aspect of representation is perhaps one that would continue to undermine committee debates in parliament in view of the historically overwhelming domination of the ruling CPDM party in parliament.

Nevertheless, if the system operates effectively, a private member bill discussed at committee stage can be amended or substituted, if it is not adopted or rejected. A government bill is accorded special status as it cannot be substituted with an alternative drafted by the Committee that is considering it. A bill that has been adopted by a committee is presented at the plenary session where it is further debated. It may be referred back to the General Committee for reconsideration or it may be adopted. In the latter instance, the adopted bill is forwarded by the speaker of the National Assembly to the speaker of the Senate.

At the level of the Senate, a bill submitted by the President of the Republic or private member or government bills submitted by the speaker of the National Assembly is ultimately transmitted to the relevant General Committee through the Chairman's Conference after ruling on its admissibility.[152] The government or the Committee may request that the bill should be voted at the next plenary session without debating at the Committee level.[153] If the bill is included in the agenda of the next plenary session, either the government or a Senator (supported by twenty Senators) may request its withdrawal.[154] In which case, the bill will be withdrawn from the agenda and returned to the Committee which would be obliged to hear the objections raised.[155] This is an important intervention to maintain the quality of the democratic process. It is necessary that bills are properly scrutinised to ensure refinement and that issues which may affect their enforcement are dealt with at an early stage. A system that allows for bills to be adopted without debate undermines the oversight potentials of parliamentary debates. Nevertheless, once the Committee has considered the objections, it is expected to produce a report containing the substance of the objections raised. In the absence of an objection or where an objection is either defeated or declared inadmissible, a bill would be voted in the plenary session without debating at Committee level following the normal procedure in the Senate.[156]

At the Committee level, once a bill has been debated, a report is produced which forms the basis of the debate at the plenary session.[157] Prior to the plenary debate, a Senator may raise a preliminary objection with a view to deciding whether there should be a debate.[158] The objections may be made orally, to which only the relevant government minister or the president or rapporteur of the Committee may respond.[159] An objection may be adopted, in which case the bill will be rejected or where it fails, the bill will be debated.[160] Again, this may be seen as an important step in ensuring that if an objection at the level of the Committee failed, a bill should not be adopted at the plenary session without debate. Of course the benefits of such an intervention would be realised only where an objection succeeds in preventing the adopting of a bill without debate.

The procedure at the level of the Senate appears to take into account Senate's role in scrutinising bills adopted by the National Assembly as there is some intervention at various points and the process seems less straight forward than that of the National Assembly. A bill that has gone through preliminary objections (or where no objections were raised) is first debated generally during the plenary session.[161] Even at this stage, interlocutory motions may be tabled with the effect of adjourning the debate until certain conditions are met or referring the bill back to the General Committee that had considered its substantive issues or even referring to a different Committee for an advisory opinion.[162] This again is a commendable intervention which has the potential to reinforce the quality of scrutiny exercised by the Senate. A decision from the Committee in favour of rejecting the bill will invoke a vote immediately after the close of general debates.[163] That may also occur alternatively, where the Committee or its rapporteur fails to submit a conclusion or a report, respectively.[164] The Senate may vote whether or not to proceed to a substantive debate and a vote against debate will automatically defeat the bill.[165] Where a bill is not defeated, a general debate is followed by a more substantive debate during which each section of the bill is discussed by the Senators. At this stage any alternative bills (amendments to the original bill) that had been validly submitted and discussed at the Committee level would be considered.[166] Senate may either adopt the bill, reject or amend it and the procedure described earlier will apply.[167]

A law adopted by the National Assembly is promulgated by the President of the Republic within fifteen days of it being forwarded to him except where he requests a second reading or refers the law to the Constitutional Council.[168] Where the deadline elapses without promulgation by the President and upon establishing his failure to do so, the law may be promulgated by the speaker of the National Assembly.[169] In any case, a law that has been promulgated must be published in the Official Gazette of the Republic in English and French.[170]

B. Scrutiny of the executive

Another important role of parliament as per article 14(2) of the Constitution is to exercise oversight of the government. As discussed later, there are at least five principal mechanisms through which the legislature performs oversight of the executive. They include, oral and written questions, vote of no confidence and motion of censure, commissions of inquiry, fiscal oversight and impeachment.[171] These are typically powers exercised by the legislative arm of government in the pursuit of promoting accountable governance. However, in the case of

Cameroon, there are several challenges that impinge on the ability of the legislature to exercise meaningful oversight of the executive, despite the powers it has been vested with. These mechanisms and related issues are discussed later.

I. Oral and written questions

The Constitution provides that, 'Parliament shall control government action through oral and written questions'.[172] The government is under obligation to provide any explanation and information, however, subject to the important caveat of national defence, state security or the secrecy of criminal investigations.[173] In practice, this has been one of the fundamental ways by which executive officials have been subjected to some form of scrutiny to provide answers and justifications for government policies with respect to individual ministries. MPs or Senators intending to question executive officials are obliged to submit their questions to the speaker of the relevant house who ultimately transmits them to the relevant executive official.[174] Upon receipt of a question, the relevant executive official is given fifteen days to respond, although that period is reduced to three days when the National Assembly or Senate is in session.[175] An additional period of three days (or two days during sessions) may be allocated where further research is required to provide answers to the question(s).[176] The process of prior information provides scope for the executive officials in question to prepare answers prior to the parliamentary question and answer session.

A problem with the procedure for question and answer is that there appears to be no particular criteria in determining which questions are selected from among the multitude of questions submitted.[177] The decision is made by the Chairmen's Conference.[178] This is an important facet of the question and answer process because it is the stage at which potentially probing questions on controversial issues might be eliminated in order to shield the government. This weakness is further exacerbated by the requirement that precludes questions which raise allegations relating to named third parties.[179] Thus, a minister would not be questioned directly for actions by named third parties in their ministry. It is not surprising that although MPs have consistently questioned ministers on policies relating to their ministries, it is reported that such questions have been rarely critical.[180]

Another problem emanates from the fact that although ministers are under obligation to provide answers, there is no obvious mechanism to ensure compliance in practice.[181] A solution to addressing a refusal to answer questions is the tabling of a draft resolution on the refusal.[182] The law is not specific as to what follows a resolution[183] but one implication is that a vote on the resolution might lead to a rejection of the question at the Committee stage or at the plenary. The weakness of the parliamentary questioning system was demonstrated in June 2014 following the failure of the national football team in the World Cup football tournament in Brazil. There were other problems relating to financial arrangements for the national team which might have affected its performance. The Minister of Sports and Physical Education was questioned in the National

Assembly about these problems. MPs of the opposition SDF demanded a clear financial evaluation of the trip to Brazil. The Minister responded that it was not possible to provide a financial evaluation at the time because the national team had just returned home from Brazil. He went on to state that all other questions were likely to be answered by the results of an ongoing investigation led by the PM. Although the PM's investigation should not prevent Parliament from obtaining information from the Minister of Sports, the latter used that to evade scrutiny.

In addition to the aforementioned weaknesses, it is doubtful what effect parliamentary questions may have in streamlining executive action. The answers provided by ministers would usually relate to information on government policy and an explanation of how and why they have been adopted or executed. They do not necessarily provide any undertaking to alter or change policies that legislators deem to be harmful to the electorate. In June 2018 during the parliamentary session, the government was questioned on its handling of the Anglophone crisis which had left hundreds of civilians and scores of soldiers dead in the struggle for self-determination of the Anglophone regions of Cameroon. Responding to a question from an opposition MP from the CDU party in the National Assembly, relating to a call for dialogue on the Anglophone crisis, the PM replied that the default method of resolving sociopolitical disputes in Cameroon was dialogue. In that respect, the President of Cameroon had created a Commission on Bilingualism and Multiculturalism, an institution which undertakes to promote dialogue in times of peace and in times of crisis. He went further to state that everyone is obliged to respect the rule of law and that the government's resort to the use of proportionate force in the Anglophone regions was necessary to protect the rights of innocent civilians who were not participating in the violence that has characterised the conflict in those regions. In this instance, the oral questions provided an opportunity for the government to discuss this issue openly with parliamentarians. Yet, there was no undertaking to ensure that the government engaged in meaningful dialogue with a view to resolving the crisis. The failure of the the National Assembly to be proactive in discussing and seeking solutions to the Anglophone crisis has demonstrated its inability to act as a credible oversight institution.

Despite the limitations associated with the parliamentary question mechanism, in more recent times, the question and answer sessions have provided a platform for the opposition to expose incidents of maladministration and corruption in the government.[184]

II. Vote of no confidence and motion of censure

Motions of censure and confidence votes are important mechanisms through which a legislative body can perform oversight of the executive. According to Rodney Brazier, their real significance lies in the fact that they oblige every government to justify its actions and explain its policies to parliament and through parliament, to the entire country.[185] In Cameroon, only the National

Assembly (as opposed to the Senate) can adopt a motion of censure or vote of no confidence against the government. Although this should be a formidable mechanism by which the National Assembly could effect the accountability of the government, the relevant provisions have been so narrowly construed that they do not afford sufficient capacity for the mechanism to be effective.

The Constitution provides that, after the deliberations of the Council of Ministers, the PM may commit the responsibility of the government before the National Assembly on a programme or general policy statement.[186] In which case, voting shall take place at least forty eight hours after a vote of no confidence was requested and a successful vote shall be passed by an absolute majority.[187] Similarly, after the deliberations of the Council of Ministers, the PM may commit the responsibility of the government before the National Assembly on the adoption of a bill.[188] In which case, the bill may be considered adopted, except where a motion of censure tabled within twenty four hours is passed.[189]

There are doubts as to the effectiveness of this process as an oversight mechanism.[190] The procedure for vote counting appears to be an obstacle to obtaining the requisite majority as only the votes against the vote of no confidence are counted.[191] Thus, MPs who have abstained from voting for various reasons are counted as having voted against a vote of no confidence.[192]

Moreover, it would appear that rather than being a mechanism for oversight, a motion of no confidence initiated by the PM is a means by which the executive curbs legislative scrutiny. This is so because government bills initiated through this process can become law without a vote from parliament as long as a motion of censure has not been submitted.[193] This process can provide opportunity for the government to pass unpopular policies, while circumventing the legislative process. András Sajó has observed that, with reference to France (on which the Cameroonian system is modelled), the confidence vote is more a weapon of the sitting government than an exercise of government's responsibility to Parliament.[194]

In Cameroon, the National Assembly can also hold the government accountable through a motion of censure.[195] A motion of censure is only admissible if signed by at least a third of the MPs and shall be passed by a two-third majority.[196] Where the National Assembly passes a no confidence vote or adopts a motion of censure against the government, the PM is expected to tender the resignation of the government to the President of the Republic.[197] Nevertheless, the President may reappoint the PM and ask him to form a new government.[198] In the event of a rejection of a motion of censure, the signatories are prohibited from proposing another motion within one year, except where the PM commits the responsibility of the government on the adoption of a bill.[199] As an oversight mechanism, these arrangements are problematic for at least three reasons.

The first problem inheres in the fact that, although the PM and the cabinet implement national policy as defined by the President, the latter is not being censured as the authority from which the policy originates. Rather, it is the PM and the cabinet that are potentially being held accountable for implementing a policy initiated by the President. Admittedly, it is a commendable mechanism in terms of scrutinising the activities of the government. The limitation, however, is that it allows the President to deflect criticism and censure onto the Cabinet, while exculpating himself from parliamentary scrutiny.

The second problem stems from the possibility of the reappointment of the PM by the President. A PM who would have resigned from office following a censure from the National Assembly would be reappointed despite failing to command the support of that house.[200] An important implication is that parliamentary oversight is rather ineffective if it can be overridden by the reappointment of the PM.

The third problem can be gleaned from the fact that signatories to a motion of censure cannot propose another motion within one year in the event that their motion is rejected. This provision therefore has the potential to limit the frequency of parliament initiated censure.[201] Admittedly, it is unlikely that under the current dynamics in parliament with the ruling CPDM party controlling an overwhelming and largely disciplined majority in the National Assembly, with an increasingly fragmented opposition, a motion of censure or vote of no confidence has a fair chance of succeeding. The Inter-Parliamentary Union reports that, between 1990 and 2000, numerous motions of censure were tabled by the opposition but none were ever successful.[202] Paul Ayah contends that,[203] in practice, the constraints have made it impossible for parliament to hold the government to account.[204] He argues that MPs from the ruling party are usually disinclined to vote against party initiative as it may constitute grounds for disciplinary action.[205] That was the situation during the 2008 constitutional amendments which among other amendments, eliminated presidential term limits. Although proposals for the reforms met with stiff opposition from the electorate and the parliamentary opposition, it was widely voted for by the ruling majority. Paul Ayah was the only member of the ruling party who opposed the amendment and abstained from voting. Subsequently, in a press interview, he alleged threats to his life and that of his family and victimisation from security forces as a result of his criticism of the ruling party. He eventually resigned from the party to join the opposition.[206]

A further rationale for the reluctance of members of the ruling party to vote against party initiatives (even if they disagree with such initiatives) is the patronage advantage associated with membership of the party.[207] The CPDM party affords the best opportunity for patronage and according to the *Bertelsmann Stiftung*, candidate selection is based on 100% loyalty to presidential policy.[208] On account of those social circumstances, in addition to structural weaknesses, it is evident that the motion of censure and vote of no confidence are ineffective mechanisms for parliamentary oversight of the government.

III. Commissions of inquiry

Article 35(1) of the Constitution provides the basis for the creation of 'committees of inquiry' within parliament, with specific terms of reference.[209] In that respect, each of the houses of parliament may adopt a draft resolution to set up a commission of inquiry.[210] The draft resolution must outline the facts necessitating an inquiry or the government service(s) whose management is the subject of the inquiry.[211] Such commissions are not permanent and exist only for the purpose(s) for which they are created.[212] The members are appointed on the basis of a single round majority list ballot[213] and their duties terminate following the submission of their report to the relevant house.[214]

As commissions of inquiry within the context of the Constitution have specific terms of reference, their role is clearly outlined. This includes information gathering and the examination of administrative, financial or technical management of public services with a view to informing the relevant house.[215] Additionally, the commissions may inform the relevant house, on the status of some matters of national interest and assist the house to make appropriate proposals.[216]

Although commissions of inquiry may be empowered[217] to carry out their functions, they are subject to certain restrictions. Thus, where judicial proceedings have been instituted on the same matter the commission already investigating the matter is required to seize operations.[218] Similarly, a commission of inquiry cannot be established where judicial proceedings have already commenced.[219] Although the rationale is not specifically stated in the law, this approach can be argued, from a separation of powers perspective, to be an approach that allows the system of checks and balances to function appropriately without undue interference from another branch of the government.

A further restriction can be gleaned from the requirement to respect official state secrecy legislation, by virtue of which members of the commission are bound by secrecy.[220] This is perhaps to maintain the integrity of the investigation being undertaken on behalf of parliament. This also applies to the reports submitted to parliament following the conclusion of the investigation. No member of the commission or anyone else may publish in whole or in part, any reports from the commission or any information about its proceedings or acts.[221] Parliament alone has the mandate to publish any part of the report, following a special resolution by either house and proposed by the speaker of the relevant house or the commission concerned.[222]

Generally, parliamentary commissions of inquiry like those provided for by the Constitution should perform an important role in the checks and balances system of a government. Through their investigations, they act as a credible source of information which may be useful to the public and to the ultimate assessment of government policy.[223] In the latter role, they may trigger the process for government accountability to parliament.[224] However, the benefits of commissions of inquiry are yet to accrue to the checks and balances system in Cameroon. The reason reverts to the predominance of the ruling party in both houses of parliament. This poses an obstacle first in terms of the passing of a successful resolution to establish a commission of inquiry and second for the membership of the commission to be fairly representative and independent. This partly explains the absence of parliamentary scrutiny in the face of a significant number of incidents of maladministration or government high handedness towards the population. For instance in December 2018, the SDF Parliamentary Group petitioned the speaker of the National Assembly to open a parliamentary inquiry into the withdrawal of the football tournament, Africa Cup of Nations which was to be hosted by Cameroon in 2019. Cameroon lost its hosting rights in November 2018 following persistent delays in the completion of relevant infrastructural facilities, in breach of its commitment to the organising authorities (Confederation of African Football). The SDF Group was of the opinion that it was necessary for parliament to conduct an inquiry to understand what went wrong, to learn from the mistakes and hold those responsible to account. The incident was internationally embarrassing to Cameroon due to the international significance of the event and also in the light of the major financial commitments that the country had undertaken in that respect. Yet, the speaker of the National Assembly did not deem it necessary to open a parliamentary inquiry.[225] Similarly, the opposition have been unsuccessful is calling for a commission of inquiry to investigate the massive violations of human rights in the North-West and South-West regions. In the context of the current dynamics in parliament, successfully petitioning for the establishment of a parliamentary commission of inquiry remains a herculean task.[226]

C. Fiscal oversight

Budgetary scrutiny is the main mechanism through which parliament performs fiscal oversight of the government. An additional mechanism is through committees of inquiry appointed to investigate matters relating to public finance.[227] The rules governing such committees are identical to other committees of inquiry discussed earlier. The committee of inquiry for matters relating to public finance, however, may report cases to the budget disciplinary committee.[228]

The power to perform budgetary oversight is particularly vested in the National Assembly which adopts the state's budget as the finance law during one of its sessions.[229] The Committee on Finance and Budget of the National assembly is responsible for scrutinising the annual budget of the state which is presented as the finance bill. The performance of this role is underpinned by three main phases.[230] The first phase consists of a review process based on an examination of the execution of the previous budget which is presented as a settlement bill.[231] If adopted this becomes the settlement law.[232] The second phase is the approval of the budget based on an examination of allocations and projected income for the following financial year, presented as the initial finance bill.[233] The process is aimed at ensuring that revenue projection is realistic and budget allocations adequately reflect government policy priorities for the subsequent financial year. If adopted, this becomes the initial finance law.[234] The third phase involves quarterly auditing of government reports submitted to parliament on budget execution and the implementation of the initial finance law.[235] Amendments may be made to the initial finance law during this period but must be tabled before parliament following the procedure for the adoption of the initial finance law.[236] Any amendments made to the initial finance law at this stage are referred to as amendments to the finance law,[237] which together with the initial finance law and the settlement law, have the status of finance laws of the state.[238]

In terms of procedure, once the Chairmen's Conference deems a finance bill presented by the government admissible, it is transmitted to the Finance Committee for a substantive study.[239] The substantive study provides the opportunity for Committee members to scrutinise government action, for instance, scrutinising the projected revenue and expenditure stated in the initial finance bill. Additionally, each ministry represented by its minister or a designated representative would be required to make representations which include clarifications on issues raised by Finance Committee members and statements defending their budgets. The Minister of Finance takes centre stage in defending the overall budget of the state and in presenting a report on the execution of the previous budget. This is an important phase of the oversight process as it provides a means by which parliament, through the Finance Committee, probes the government for any perceived anomalies or discrepancies in projected revenues and to provide the rationale for expenditure on selected programmes. In the November 2018 session during which the finance bill for the year 2019 was discussed, the Finance Committee raised a number of concerns to the Minister of Finance. Some of these included the negative balance of trade due to the importation of food, despite the national production capacity and government subsidies to the local industry; the need to budget for actions aimed at restoring peace in the North-West and South-West regions and the reasons for the failure to involve domestic companies in the construction of stadia to host the 2019 AFCON.[240] In response, the Minister noted that reforms aimed at revamping production structures were currently being undertaken and stated that although it was difficult to quantify the action necessary in the North-West and South-West regions, to warrant separate budgeting, there were funds allocated under 'common expenditure' which could be used for that purpose should the need arise.[241] He also informed the Committee that, in relation to AFCON preparations, domestic companies were excluded due to possible delays and that in order to pre-empt this, the government had opted for companies that were capable of delivering 'prefabricated structures'.[242] It is not clear that the Committee was persuaded by these responses. Nevertheless, it provided some basis for evaluating the decision of the government.[243]

Although government ministers and their representative are required to defend their budget, the Committee is often unable to elicit sufficient cooperation or clarification from the government. A notable instance is during the scrutiny of the 2019 Initial Finance Bill, when the Finance Committee inquired as to the sufficiently of funds allocated to ELECAM to improve on the electoral process and the electoral system.[244] The relevant government representative opined that the Committee should concern itself with consideration of the budget for ELECAM and not with the budget for the organisation of elections.[245] It is difficult to see how these two heads should be considered in isolation in the process of scrutinising the projected expenditure relating to the institution that plays a key role in the election process, especially in the light of parliamentary and municipal elections which were expected in that financial year. Although it is clear that such lack of cooperation in practice undermines an effective oversight process, the Committee is not empowered to compel the government to co-operate. In those circumstances, it does appear that there is potential for the effectiveness of the process to be adversely affected.

As part of the process of scrutinising the budget, the Committee may make recommendations which could be accepted[246] or rejected by the government. Where recommendations are accepted, the relevant budget head would be amended before being adopted by the Committee. The Committee stage is followed by a presentation of the budget (as adopted by the Committee) to the plenary of the National Assembly. Very often at this stage, the house adopts the budget as the finance law for the subsequent financial year.[247] In view of the historic dominance of the CPDM and the entrenched party disicpline, the finance bill is usally adopted with ease. The 2018 finance bill was passed without much debate despite significant disturbances from the political opposition aimed at compelling the National Assembly to discuss the turbulent situation in the North-West and South-West regions. The Constitution, however, envisages a situation where the budget is not adopted before the end of the financial year. In which case, the President of the Republic is empowered to extend the current budget by one fifth until a new budget is passed.[248]

Another aspect that remains questionable in the oversight process is the scrutiny of the settlement bill. In that process, the National Assembly works in collaboration with the Audit Bench of the Supreme Court which is vested with powers to provide its opinion on the execution of the budget for the preceding financial year.[249] In addition, the Finance Committee may request the Audit Bench to conduct enquiries on the management of government services or entities.[250] One aspect which remains unclear is the extent to which parliament scrutinises the settlement bill, considering that the opinion of the Audit Bench should determine to a large extent whether the bill is passed or not. In the examination of the settlement bill for the 2017 financial year, the Audit Bench noted a number of significant inconsistencies in government income and expenditure resulting from problems relating to poor budget discipline.[251] Yet, its recommendation was for parliament to pass the bill as submitted by the government and it was indeed passed without parliament raising issues with the discrepancies.[252] While this is not necessarily suggestive of weaknesses in the parliamentary process, it may be indicative of the limited role of parliament as simply one of authenticating the opinion of the Audit Bench, rather than providing an additional tier of oversight.

The second aspects which may render doubtful, the effectiveness of the scrutiny of the settlement bill is the extent to which the government could be held accountable for the implementation of recommendations arising from the scrutiny. The Audit Bench noted with disapproval that during the process of auditing the settlement bill for the 2016 financial year, a number of specific recommendations were made to the government on improving efficiency and transparency in the execution of the budget.[253] However, these seemed not to have been implemented by the government as the same issues were noted in the settlement bill for 2017.[254] Neither the Audit Bench nor the National Assembly seemed to have been able to compel the government to respond favourably to the recommendations.

It appears from the aforementioned discussion that there is certainly a system which has potential to allow for effective scrutiny of the government. Yet, in practice, there are some difficulties orchestrated by the nature of the political system and party dynamics. While the Finance Committee may be empowered to carry out its functions, the issue of the overwhelming majority of the ruling party, coupled with party discipline might affect the ability or willingness of Committee members to be assertive in the oversight process. In the legislative period for 2013–2019, of the twenty-member Finance Committee, only five members were from the opposition.[255] The remaining fifteen members were from the CPDM. It is not difficult to see how or why finance bills would be passed with relative ease.

The lack of political capacity or the will to submit the executive to effective oversight is not uncommon in many countries in Africa and appears to be a product of the nature of the political culture in many African states. It has been noted that in sub-Saharan Africa, clientelism and neo-patrimonial politics compel MPs to retain the favour of the ruling party. Thus, party loyalties prevent them from articulating national interest and incentivises them to pass the budget quickly in order for funds to be allocated to their constituencies.[256] For parliamentary budget and finance committees such as that of Cameroon to be effective, in addition to legislative guarantees, there is need for a shift in political cultures to embrace a utilitarian approach by which MPs are motivated by the need to work for the greater good of their constituents, rather than self and party interests. Such an approach is not without merit. In Ghana, for instance, the parliamentary committees are said to be effective in performing their oversight functions, due significantly to the fact that at the committee level the collective interests of the MPs supersedes partisanship.[257] With respect to the Ghanaian Public Accounts Committee in particular, an additional factor that is said to enhance its clout is the fact that the chairperson is statutorily from a minority party represented in parliament.[258] This allows for the possibility of submitting the government's budget proposals to effective scrutiny as the chairman has no personal or partisan interest in unduly favouring the government.

Cameroon's parliament is not incognisant of its limitations and is taking steps to enhance its working relationship with the executive to inter alia improve on the oversight process and in particular, to enhance the transparency of the budgetary process. As part of that initiative, a Parliamentary Platform has been created which aims to provide MPs and Senators access to updated information on the Finance and Settlement Bills as well as information on the execution of different budgets. It is hoped that this would provide an additional and effective level of parliamentary fiscal oversight of the government.[259]

Part V. Parliamentary accountability

Having noted previously the powers and responsibilities of parliament and the constraints on the exercise of these powers, it is worth examining the extent of parliamentary accountability. Accountability is a basic requirement for public office in a democracy and owing to the nature of parliamentary functions, accountability is imperative. The position in Cameroon consists of vertical and horizontal accountability structures. Vertical accountability may be said to be embedded in the electoral process. In other words, MPs and Senators are held accountable by the electorates during elections. This should ordinarily be a useful and effective mechanism in a system that allows for free and fair elections, but as has been demonstrated earlier in this chapter, that is not often the case in Cameroon. The inevitable conclusion that may be drawn from this assertion is that the mechanism for vertical accountability is unreliable.

In contrast, parliament is horizontally accountable to the executive. This is not explicitly stated in the Constitution or any statutory instrument. Nevertheless, as discussed in more detail in the previous chapter, the National Assembly can be dissolved by the President of the Republic after consultation with the Government, the Bureau of the National Assembly and the Senate.[260] No further conditions are stipulated for the rationale to dissolve the National Assembly. As such, this may rely on the sole discretion of the President. Although it may be argued that this is not a method of accountability, it does seem, implicitly, that parliament is made answerable to the President as the decision to initiate a dissolution lies solely with him. The question to consider at this point is whether that provision leaves parliament vulnerable to the executive? An answer in the affirmative inherently suggests some form of accountability.

Parliament is nevertheless protected by immunity provisions, which consist of a blend of both the parliamentary non-accountability model and the parliamentary inviolability model.[261] Under the former model, parliamentary agency is protected by ensuring that MPs and Senators are immune from prosecution, investigation, arrests, detention or trial for speeches made or votes cast in the exercise of their duties.[262] The law on defamation further extends this protection by excluding from the offence of defamation, speeches made within any legislative assembly or reports and other documents printed on the orders of such an assembly.[263] It also excludes from the offence of defamation, 'Faithful accounts without malice' of the public sittings of such assemblies.[264] These provisions appear sufficiently wide to protect legislators. In a democracy, immunity is a necessary element aimed at safeguarding inter alia, the independence of legislators. On account of their role as largely elected representatives who collectively represent the public will, they must of necessity be granted scope for free and open debate. Despite this significant benefit, there remains the potential for human rights violations that may be facilitated by the non-accountability model.[265]

However, Cameroon's dual approach to an extent addresses that potential problem. Thus, the second model, the parliamentary inviolability model, allows for the lifting of parliamentary immunity with the authorisation of parliament. It follows that, parliament (when in session) or the Bureau of each house (when not in session) may authorise criminal prosecution against any legislator following the lifting of their immunity.[266] However, the authorisation of parliament is dispensed with in cases of offences committed in *flagrante delicto* or offences against the internal and external security of the state.[267] Nevertheless, parliament or the Bureau of the two houses can, through a motion, suspend the detention or prosecution of any legislator by a public prosecutor or the Minister of Defence where the matter falls within the jurisdiction of the military tribunals.[268]

The system which combines parliamentary non-accountability and inviolability is consistent with constitutional checks and balances to the extent that although parliamentary agency is protected, any excesses can be streamlined through the authorisation of parliament itself. The underlying idea is for legislators to be able to freely promote democratic ideals yet be constrained to act within the same democratic ideals which they purport to promote. In practice, the National Assembly has sometimes albeit reluctantly upheld these responsibilities by lifting the immunity of some MPs. A notable instance was in February 2005 when the Bureau of the National Assembly unexpectedly lifted the immunity of one of its influential members, Fon Doh Gwanyim, who was cumulatively the Mayor and MP for the Balikumbat Constituency under the banner of the ruling CPDM. The background to this relates to criminal investigations for the alleged murder of the district Chairman of the opposition SDF.[269] There have been other instances where MPs have been divested of their immunity, although some have been tainted by allegations of political motivations in support of aims pursued by the government and the ruling CPDM.[270]

Conclusion: democratisation and bicameralism in a one-party dominated state

For decades, the image of the National Assembly remained that of a feasible and compliant institution brimming with self-serving representatives who exercised public office at the pleasure of the President. This counter-intuitively produced a system of representation of the executive will, rather than the will of the people. According to the *Bertelsmann Stiftung* 2018 report, the legislature in Cameroon was described as weakened by overwhelming presidential influence.[271] The report further stated that the overwhelming majority held by the ruling party ensured that parliament was subject to the wishes of the executive and almost no initiative originated from parliament.[272] This is ironic as has been demonstrated previously in view of the functions and powers of parliament in holding the executive to account. A closer look at those powers and the dynamics within parliament explains to a large extent why the National Assembly remained a feeble institution. The change that was expected with the advent of multiparty politics and subsequently the establishment of a Senate has not been witnessed in any meaningful form. In fact, the composition of the Senate, in particular, militates against any meaningful political influence. In addition to the fact that it is infused with members of the CPDM and appointed ardent supporters of the regime, there is an age issue which makes the efficiency of that house questionable. The Senate has been described as being 'composed primarily of elderly former ministers and traditional chiefs'.[273] While age should not necessarily hinder the proper functioning of an institution, it can have an overall effect on the dynamism and innovativeness of that institution and its amenability to adapt to changing political circumstances. The doyen, Chief Victor Mukete, is over hundred years old and the Speaker of the house, Niat Njifenji, is eighty five years old (and constantly absent for health reasons). In fact, the minimum age eligibility limit for election or appointment of senators (forty years) already militates against a youthful senate. This is a pattern of the political system in Cameroon which is based on the 'recycling' of loyal political elite, to the exclusion of the younger generation that also has a perspective to offer in regards to the democratic advancement of the country and the development of national policy. Another pertinent observation with the age issue is that, most of the Senators especially the presidential appointees have been part of the regime for considerably lengthy periods and have operated in a system that is not receptive to change. In consideration of the benefits they obtain from the system through lavish allowances and other advantages, there is very little incentive for change.

Although bicameralism now exists in fact, in theory and practice, the challenges and ills that bedevilled monocameralism have transcended into the new dispensation. It remains the case of 'pouring new wine into old wineskins'. Both the National Assembly and Senate are institutions that are configured to consolidate presidential power and to ensure the survival of the regime. There is arguably no intention to represent the popular will as the electoral system itself eliminates that possibility. For parliament to emerge as a credible public institution, a number of factors would require transformation, notably the electoral system which inhibits meaningful democratic advancement and the reform of internal working systems through the committees to give the opposition substantial scope to influence parliamentary debates and decisions. Similarly, there needs to be a shift in the clientelist structure and political culture. This is a wider issue which affects other areas of public life and therefore an overhaul of the entire system, difficult as it may be, would be essential.

Notes

1 Constitution, art 14.

2 Law No. 2000/016 of 19 December 2000 to set up a National Elections Observatory.

3 Charles Fombad, 'Election Management Bodies in Africa: Cameroon's National Elections Observatory in Perspective' (2003) 3(1) *African Human Rights Law Journal* 25, 42–47; Michael Yanou, 'Democracy in Cameroon: A Socio-Legal Appraisal' (2013) 46(3) *Law and Politics in Africa, Asia and Latin America* 303–320.

4 Law No. 2012/001 of 19 April relating to the Electoral Code (Electoral Code).

5 Electoral Code, s 8.

6 Electoral Code, s 9(1).

7 Electoral Code, s 12(3).
8 Electoral Code, s 12(1)(4).
9 Electoral Code, s 30(1).
10 Electoral Code, s 17.
11 Decree No. 2008/463 of 30 December 2008 appointing Electoral Commission members.
12 Freedom House, 'Freedom in the World 2012 – Cameroon' (17 August 2012) https://www.refworld.org/docid/5033655537.html accessed 13 November 2019; US Department of State, 'Cameroon' in Background Notes: Central Africa 2011 (InfoStrategist.com 2011); Susan Dicklitch, 'The Southern Cameroons and Minority Rights in Cameroon' (2011) 29(1) *Journal of Contemporary African Studies* 49, 51. See also Tansa Musa, 'EU Condemns Elections Management Transfer in Cameroon' (15 November 2009) www.newstimeafrica.com/archives/6216 accessed 21 May 2012.
13 For instance, Dr Dorothy Njeuma is a well-known member of the CPDM and Delphine Tsanga has been associated with the CPDM as far back as 1969 when she was member of the then Cameroon National Union which became the CPDM. See also Cameroon Ministry of Justice, 'Report on Human Rights in Cameroon-2009' www.spm.gov.cm/uploads/media/Rapport_Minjustice_Ang_2009.pdf accessed on 12 March 2011, 14, s 3, para 73, in which the government rejected the UN Human Rights Committee's recommendation to amend the composition of ELECAM to conform to its laws.
14 Electoral Code, ss 3, 4(1), 7(1).
15 For senatorial elections, this becomes the Regional Supervisory Commission – Electoral Code, s 235(1).
16 Electoral Code, s 64(1).
17 Electoral Code, s 64(1). In the case of the Regional Supervisory Commission, the appointments are made by the Governor of the region who is a presidential appointee.
18 Electoral Code, s 115(1).
19 Electoral Code, s 62(2).
20 Electoral Code, s 62(2).
21 Electoral Code, s 67 (1).
22 Electoral Code, s 115(2).
23 Electoral Code, s 115(3). With the senatorial elections, only two copies of the report are made and retained by the local branch of ELECAM and the Regional Supervisory Commission, s 234(4).
24 Electoral Code, s 67(2).
25 Electoral Code, ss 62(2), 67(3).
26 Electoral Code, s 69(1).
27 Electoral Code, s 69(2).
28 Electoral Code, s 168(1).
29 Electoral Code, s 132.
30 Electoral Code, s 133(1).
31 Electoral Code, s 136.
32 Electoral Code, s 67(3).
33 Electoral Code, s 69(4).
34 Electoral Code, s 68(1).
35 This aspect is discussed in more detail in Chapter 5.
36 See below a table of political parties represented in Parliament from the 1992 to 2020.
37 Electoral Code, s 150(1).
38 Electoral Code, s 149(1).
39 Electoral Code, s 149(2).

40 Electoral Code, s 150(2).
41 Charles Fombad, *Constitutional Law in Cameroon* (Wolters Kluwer 2012) 109.
42 ibid.
43 David Mokam, 'The Search for a Cameroonian Model of Democracy or the Search for the Domination of the State Party: 1966–2006' (2012) 23 *Cadernos de Estudos Africanos* 85, 103.
44 Electoral Code, s 156.
45 Electoral Code, s 157.
46 Electoral Code, s 159(1).
47 Electoral Code, s 158(1).
48 Electoral Code, ss 148(1)(3), 152(1).
49 Electoral Code, s 152(2)(3)(a). It should be noted that, for every seat available, there is a substantive candidate and an alternate who are voted at the same time. The alternate can assume the position of the substantive in case of the latter's vacancy (ss 153–154).
50 Electoral Code, s 152(3)(a).
51 Electoral Code, s 152(3)(b).
52 Electoral Code, s 152(3)(b).
53 Electoral Code, s 152(3)(b).
54 Electoral Code, s 152(4).
55 Electoral Code, s 148(4)(5).
56 Electoral Code, ss 220 and 221, respectively.
57 Electoral Code, s 217(1).
58 Electoral Code, s 214(1)(5).
59 Electoral Code, s 222.
60 Electoral Code, ss 217(2), 218(1).
61 Electoral Code, s 218(2)(3). There must be a substantive and an alternative candidate for each seat (s 218(2)).
62 Electoral Code, s 218(4).
63 Electoral Code, s 218(5)(6).
64 Electoral Code, s 218(6).
65 Electoral Code, s 218(7).
66 Electoral Code, s 215(3).
67 Decree No. 2013/149 of 8 May 2013 Relating to the Appointment of Senators.
68 For instance, Mr Dakolle Daissala, leader of the MDR party, was a longstanding ally of the President, whereas Pierre Flambeau Ngayap is of the UNDP, which is in coalition with the government. Similarly, traditional leaders such as Chief Victor Mukete and Sultan Mbombo Njoya who were also appointed were fervent supporters of the ruling CPDM party.
69 Decree No. 2018/242 of 12 April 2018 relating to the Appointment of Senators. It is worth noting that no member of the main opposition SDF was appointed in 2018.
70 The CPDM offers the best opportunities for patronage. See 'Bertelsmann Transformation Index 2012 - Cameroon Country Report' (Gütersloh: Bertelsmann Stiftung, 2012) 9 www.bti-project.de/fileadmin/lnhalte/reports/2012/pdf accessed 4 April 2019.
71 ibid 7, 8.
72 Constitution, art 14(1)(a); Law No. 73/1 of 8 June 1973 on the Standing Orders of the National Assembly as amended (most current amendment is Law No. 2014/016 of 9 September 2014) Standing Orders (NA), ss 16(2), 3(3)(5).
73 Constitution, art 14(1)(b); Standing Orders (NA), s 3(7).
74 Standing Orders (NA), s 18.
75 Standing Orders (NA), s 19(3)(4).
76 Standing Orders (NA), s 16(1)(2).

77 Constitution, art 18(1); Standing Orders (NA), s 39(1).
78 Standing Orders (NA), s 24(1).
79 Constitution, art 18(2), Standing Orders (NA), s 39(2).
80 Standing Orders (NA), s 20(1).
81 Standing Orders (NA), s 20(2).
82 Standing Orders (NA), s 22.
83 Standing Orders (NA), s 21(1)(3).
84 Standing Orders (NA), s 21(1)(a)–(i).
85 Standing Orders (NA), s 25(1).
86 Standing Orders (NA), s 25 (2)(3)(4).
87 Constitution, art 35(1).
88 Standing Orders (NA), ss 38, 86(2)(5).
89 Standing Orders (NA), s 86(5)(a)–(c).
90 Standing Orders (NA), s 87(4).
91 Constitution, art 21(2); Law No. 2013/006 of 10 June 2013 on the Standing Orders of the Senate, s 4(1).
92 Constitution, art 21(3); Standing Orders of Senate, s 4(3) as amended by Law No. 2016/011 of 27 October 2016.
93 Standing Orders of Senate, s 16.
94 Standing Orders of Senate, s 12(2).
95 Standing Orders of Senate, s 14.
96 Standing Orders of Senate, s 15.
97 Constitution, art 23(2); Standing Orders of Senate, s 39(2).
98 Constitution, art 23(1); Standing Orders of Senate s 39(1).
99 Standing Orders of Senate, s 28(1).
100 Standing Orders of Senate, s 43.
101 Standing Orders of Senate, s 23(1).
102 Standing Orders of Senate, s 23(2).
103 Standing Orders of Senate, s 24.
104 Standing Orders of Senate, s 25.
105 See the names of committees mentioned previously under discussions of the National Assembly.
106 Standing Orders of Senate, s 25(3).
107 Standing Orders of Senate, s 28.
108 Standing Orders of Senate, s 28(2).
109 Standing Orders of Senate, s 28(4).
110 Standing Orders of Senate, s 29(2)(3)(4).
111 Standing Orders of Senate, s 36.
112 Standing Orders of Senate, s 36.
113 Standing Orders of Senate, s 37(1).
114 Standing Orders of Senate, s 37(1)(2).
115 Standing Orders of Senate, s 37(3).
116 Peter Fossungu, *Democracy and Human Rights in Africa: The Politics of Collective Participation and Governance in Cameroon* (Langaa Research and Publishing 2013) 119–203; Leslie Ngwa, 'What Cameroonians Should Know About a Senate' *The Post* (Buea, 11 March 2013) 4.
117 For instance, Constitution of Kenya, article 109(3) by virtue of which Senate cannot consider a bill which does not relate to county government, as it is only considered in the National Assembly.
118 MPs represent the entire nation, whereas senators represent the regions and local authorities.
119 Constitution, art 14(2)(3).
120 Constitution, art 14(4).

121 Constitution, art 29(1).
122 Constitution, art 30(1)(2); Standing Orders of Senate, s 67(1)(2).
123 Constitution, art 30(3); Standing Orders of Senate, s 67(3).
124 Constitution, art 30(3)(a); Standing Orders of Senate, s 67(3)(a).
125 Constitution, art 30(3)(b); Standing Orders of Senate, s 67(3)(b).
126 Constitution, art 30(3)(c); Standing Orders of Senate, s 67(3)(c).
127 Constitution, art 30(3)(c)(1); Standing Orders of Senate, s 67(3)(c).
128 Constitution, art 30(3)(c)(2); Standing Orders of Senate, s 67(4).
129 Constitution, art 30(3)(c)(2); Standing Orders of Senate, s 67(4).
130 Constitution, art 30(3)(c)(2); Standing Orders of Senate, s 67(5).
131 Constitution of Kenya, art 113.
132 Constitution of Kenya, art 113(4).
133 As per Constitution, arts 46, 47(1), para 3.
134 Constitution, art 18(2).
135 Constitution, art 14(1).
136 ibid art 26(2)(a)–(f).
137 ibid art 8(8).
138 ibid art 27.
139 ibid art 12(3).
140 Serges Vincent Ntonga Bomba, 'La Procédure Législative Devant L'Assemblée Nationale du Cameroun' (2002) 58 *African Administrative Studies* 43–61, 46–49.
141 Constitution, arts 18(4), 23(4), 29(2).
142 ibid art 18(4).
143 It has been reported that since 1991, all laws enacted have emanated from government bills and between 1992 and 2009, the President initiated all laws enacted. See Refworld, 'Freedom in the World 2011-Cameroon' (May 2011) https://www.refworld.org/docid/4dcbf51ec.html accessed 9 February 2012; Arch Puddington, Aili Piano and Katrina Neubauer, *Freedom in the World: Annual Survey of Political Rights and Civil Liberties* (Rowman & Littlefields 2009) 140; US Embassy in Cameroon, 'Human Rights Practices in Cameroon – 2006' (Yaoundé, March 2007) http://yaounde.usembassy.gov/cmr_human_rights.html accessed 12 March 2011, where it is argued that bills come rarely from the opposition and all the laws voted originate from the government. See also Joseph Kankeu, *Droit Constitutionnel* (Tome 1, 1st edn, Presses Universitaires de Dschang 2003) 171.
144 Didier Olinga, 'Politique et Droit Electoral au Cameroun: Analyse Juridique de la Politique Electorale' (1998) 6(2) *Polis: Revue Camerounaise de Science Politique* 40, 41–42.
145 ibid 41–42.
146 Law No. 2012/001 of 19 April 2012 relating to the Electoral Code.
147 The relevant provisions are sections 249, 250 and 257 of the Electoral Code debated in the March 2019 Parliamentary Session.
148 Franck Foute, 'Cameroun: L'Assemblée Nationale Approuve une Modification Partielle du Code Électoral' *Jeuneafrique* (Yaoundé, 31 March 2019) https://www.jeuneafrique.com/756521/politique/cameroun-lassemblee-nationale-approuve-une-modification-partielle-du-code-electoral/ accessed 4 April 2019.
149 ibid.
150 ibid.
151 Law No. 2019/005 of 25 April 2019 to amend some provisions of Law No. 2012/001 of 19 April relating to the Electoral Code.
152 Standing Orders of Senate, s 38(1)(a)(b), (5).
153 Standing Orders of Senate, s 40(1).
154 Standing Orders of Senate, s 41(1)(2)(3).
155 Standing Orders of Senate, s 41(3).
156 Standing Orders of Senate, s 42(3). That procedure is described at page 87.

157 Standing Orders of Senate, s 52.
158 Standing Orders of Senate, s 60(2).
159 Standing Orders of Senate, s 60(2).
160 Standing Orders of Senate, s 60(3).
161 Standing Orders of Senate, s 61(1).
162 Standing Orders of Senate, s 61(2).
163 Standing Orders of Senate, s 61(3).
164 Standing Orders of Senate, s 61(4).
165 Standing Orders of Senate, s 61(5).
166 Standing Orders of Senate, s 61(6)(7). It should be noted that as per section 63, the procedure for debates on the budget is slightly different.
167 See pp 82–83.
168 Constitution, art 31(1); Standing Orders of Senate, s 68(1)(3).
169 Constitution, art 31(2). It seems, however, that the speaker of the National Assembly has not yet promulgated a law despite numerous instances of the failure of the President of the Republic to do so. See Ntonga Bomba, 'La Procédure Législative' (n 140) 18.
170 Constitution, art 31(3); Standing Orders of Senate, s 68(1)(4).
171 Impeachment was discussed in Chapter 2.
172 Constitution, art 35(1).
173 Constitution, art 35(2); Standing Orders of Senate, s 83(4); Standing Orders (NA), s 79(1).
174 Standing Orders of Senate, s 81(1); Standing Orders (NA) s 76(1).
175 Standing Orders of Senate, s 81(4); Standing Orders (NA) s 77(1).
176 Standing Orders of Senate, s 81(4); Standing Orders (NA) s 77(1).
177 Lilian Atanga, *Gender, Discourse and Power in the Cameroonian Parliament* (Langaa RPCIG 2010) 17.
178 Standing Orders of Senate, s 83(1); Standing Orders (NA), s 78(2).
179 Standing Orders of Senate, s 81(3); Standing Orders (NA), s 76(2).
180 Bertelsmann Stiftung (n 70).
181 Fombad, *Cameroon Constitutional Law* (n 41) 100–101.
182 Standing Orders (NA) s 79 (2). See also Fombad, *Cameroon Constitutional Law* (n 41) 100–101.
183 Section 79(2) of the Standing Orders NA states that an examination of the draft resolution shall be according to ordinary procedures. The Senate's Standing Orders are silent on this.
184 Fombad, *Cameroon Constitutional Law* (n 41) 101.
185 Rodney Brazier, *Constitutional Practice* (2nd ed, Clarendon Press 1994) 213–213.
186 Constitution, art 34(2).
187 ibid.
188 ibid art 34(4).
189 ibid.
190 Fombad, *Cameroon Constitutional Law* (n 41) 98.
191 Constitution, art 34(2) para 4.
192 Fombad, *Cameroon Constitutional Law* (n 41) 98.
193 ibid 99–100.
194 András Sajó, *Limiting Government: An Exercise in Constitutionalism* (Central European University Press 1999) 186.
195 Constitution, art 34(3).
196 ibid.
197 ibid art 34(5).
198 ibid art 34(6).
199 ibid art 34(3).

200 Fombad, *Cameroon Constitutional Law* (n 41) 99.
201 ibid.
202 Inter-Parliamentary Union, 'Cameroon-National Assembly: Information about the Parliamentary Chamber' (6 November 2013) accessed 29 April 2014.
203 Paul Ayah was formerly a CPDM parliamentarian who defected to join the opposition. Prior to becoming a politician, he was a judge in the Court of Appeal.
204 Paul Ayah, 'A Cameroonian Case Study: Executive Presidency versus Parliamentary Executive' (2004) 85(4) *The Parliamentarian: Journal of the Parliaments of the Commonwealth* 318.
205 ibid.
206 Emmanuel Kendemeh, 'Hon. Ayah Paul Abine' *Cameroon Tribune* (Yaoundé, 10 January 2011) www.cameroon-tribune.cm/index.php?option=com_content&view=article&id=62972:hon-ayah-paul-abine-quits-cpdm&catid=1:politique&Itemid=3 accessed 29 August 2012; Reuters Africa, 'Cameroon Presidential Hopeful Quits Ruling Party' (11 January 2011) http://af.reuters.com/article/topNews/idAFJOE70A0HZ20110111 accessed 29 August 2012.
207 Jürg Martin Gabriel, 'Cameroon's Neopatrimonial Dilemma' (1999) 7 *Journal of Contemporary African Studies* 187; Susan Dicklitch, 'Failed Democratic Transition in Cameroon: A Human Rights Explanation' (2002) 24(1) *Human Rights Quarterly* 152.
208 Bertelsmann Stiftung (n 70) 6. See also a similar observation recorded by the US Department of State 'Human Right Practices in Cameroon - 2012', 22 http://www.state.gov/documents/organization/204309.pdf accessed 22 April 2014. See further, African Development Bank, '2004 Cameroon Country Governance Profile' (Country Operations Department: Central and West Region, September 2004) https://www.afdb.org/sites/default/files/documents/projects-and-operations/adb-bd-if-2004-211-en-cameroon-country-governance-profile.pdf accessed 19 October 2018.
209 The Standing Orders (NA) s 91 makes provision for a special public finance 'committee of inquiry' which will be discussed in the next section in the context of fiscal oversight.
210 Standing Orders of Senate, s 90(1); Standing Orders (NA) s 86(1).
211 Standing Orders of Senate, s 90(2); Standing Orders (NA) s 86(2).
212 Standing Orders of Senate, s 93(1); Standing Orders (NA) s 88(2).
213 Standing Orders of Senate, s 92; Standing Orders (NA) s 88(1).
214 Standing Orders of Senate, s 93(2); Standing Orders (NA) s 88(3).
215 Standing Orders of Senate, s 90(5)(a)(b); Standing Orders (NA) s 86(5)(a)(b).
216 Standing Orders of Senate, s 90(5)(c); Standing Orders (NA) s 86(5)(c).
217 Standing Orders of Senate, s 90(3); Standing Orders (NA) s 86(3).
218 Standing Orders of Senate, s 91; Standing Orders (NA) s 87.
219 ibid.
220 Standing Orders of Senate, s 93(3); Standing Orders (NA) s 88(4).
221 Standing Orders of Senate, s 95; Standing Orders (NA) s 89.
222 Standing Orders of Senate, art 94; Standing Orders (NA) s 90
223 Raanan Sulitzeanu-Kenan, 'Reflection in the Shadow of Blame: When Do Politicians Appoint Commissions of Inquiry? (2010) 40 *British Journal of Political Science* 613–634.
224 ibid.
225 As discussed in Part IIIC, Cameroon's hosting of the event and preparations there of preoccupied the Committee of Budget and Finance during the scrutiny of the 2019 budget.
226 Bertelsmann Stiftung notes that 'The opposition's demands for investigative commissions are routinely blocked by these parliamentary majorities'. See Bertelsmann Stiftung, 'Bertelsmann Transformation Index 2018 – Cameroon Country Report', 10 https://www.bti-project.org/fileadmin/files/BTI/Downloads/Reports/2018/pdf/BTI_2018_Cameroon.pdf accessed 20 November 2019.

227 Standing Order (NA) s 91.
228 Standing Orders (NA) s 92.
229 Constitution art 16(2)(b). In practice, this is usually in the November session.
230 As of 2018, a slightly modified system was introduced by laws intended to enhance transparency and accountability in the management of public finances. See Law No. 2018/011 of 11 July 2018 to Lay Down the Cameroon Code of Transparency and Good Governance in Public Finance Management, ss 13, 14(2), 40 and Law No. 2018/012 of 11 July 2018 Relating to the Fiscal Regime of the State and other Public Entities, ss 39(3), 57–61, 83(1), 85.
231 Fiscal Regime Law, ss 20, 22.
232 Fiscal Regime Law, s 20.
233 Fiscal Regime Law, s 13.
234 Fiscal Regime Law, ss 13.
235 Fiscal Regime Law, s 85(8).
236 Fiscal Regime Law, ss 17, 18.
237 For instance, Ordinance No. 2018/002 of 4 June 2018 to Amend and Complete Certain Provisions of Law No. 2017/021 of 20 December 2017 relating to the 2018 Finance Law of the Republic of Cameroon.
238 Fiscal Regime Law, s 12(3).
239 As per Standing Orders of the NA, ss 24, 28.
240 National Assembly, 'Report on Bill No. 1041/PJL/AN: Finance Bill of the Republic of Cameroon for the 2019 Financial Year Presented on Behalf of the Committee on Finance and Budget' Report No. 120/R/AN/9, November 2018, pp 3, 5.
241 National Assembly, 'Report on Bill No. 1041/PJL/AN', pp 7–8.
242 ibid 8.
243 As noted earlier, Cameroon's right to host the championship was revoked due significantly to delays.
244 National Assembly, 'Report on Bill No. 1041/PJL/AN', pp 14–16.
245 ibid 14–16.
246 In the 2019 session, two recommendations were suggested by the Committee and after discussions with the government, the relevant budget heads were amended with the consent of the government. National Assembly, 'Report on Bill No. 1041/PJL/AN', pp 83, 84.
247 The Guardian, 'Cameroon MP injured by Flying Debris in Parliament Amidst Anglophone Crisis' *The Guardian* (10 December 2017) https://www.theguardian.com/world/2017/dec/10/cameroon-mp-injured-parliament-anglophone-crisis accessed 15 March 2019.
248 Constitution art 16(2)(b).
249 Law No. 2006/016 of 29 December 2006 Relating to the Organisation and Functioning of the Supreme Court (Supreme Court Law), s 39(c).
250 Fiscal Regime Law, s 85(9).
251 Audit Bench of the Supreme Court, 'Avis No. 001/2018/CSC/CDC sur le Projet de Loi de Reglement – Exercise 2017' (26–29 October 2019) 59.
252 ibid 60.
253 ibid 42–43.
254 ibid.
255 The National Assembly, 'Committee on Finance and the Budget', http://www.assnat.cm/index.php/en/national-assembly/the-9-committees?showall=&start=1 accessed 2 April 2019.
256 See Lise Rakner, Luke Mukubvu, Naomi Ngwira, Kimberly Smiddy and Aaron Schneider , 'The Budget as Theatre: The Formal and Informal Institutional Makings of the Budget Process in Malawi' (Washington, DC: World Bank, 2004) 22.
257 Rick Stapenhurst and Riccardo Pelizzo, 'Improving Democracy and Accountability

in Ghana: The Importance of Parliamentary Oversight Tools' 25(2)(2012) *Governance: An International Journal of Policy, Administration and Institutions* 335, 339.
258 ibid 337.
259 Ministry of Finance and MINEPAT, 'The Parliamentary Platform: Connection Guide' (2019) pp 2–4. The URL for that platform is www.parliamentaryplatform.cm.
260 Constitution, art 8(12).
261 This system is a relic of French colonialism in Cameroon and can be contrasted with the British parliamentary system which adopts the non-accountability model.
262 Standing Orders of Senate, s 19(1)(2); Ordinance No. 72/12 of 26 August 1972 relating to the Immunity of Members of the National Assembly (National Assembly Immunity Ordinance), s 1.
263 Cameroon Penal Code, s 306(1).
264 Cameroon Penal Code, s 306(2).
265 For a good illustration of that danger, see the decision of the European Court of Human Rights in *A v United Kingdom* (35373/97) (2003) 36 EHRR 51; Nick Barber, 'Parliamentary Immunity and Human Rights' (2003) 119(4) *Law Quarterly Review* 557–560.
266 Standing Orders of Senate, s 19(3); National Assembly Immunity Ordinance, s 2.
267 ibid.
268 Standing Orders of Senate, s 19(3); National Assembly Immunity Ordinance, s 3 (a)(b).
269 Fombad, *Cameroon Constitutional Law* (n 41) 95; Jude Fokwang, *Mediating Legitimacy: Chieftaincy and Democratisation in Two African Chiefdoms* (Langaa Research & Publishing 2009) 77.
270 Fombad, *Cameroon Constitutional Law* (n 41) 95. See also, Inter-Parliamentary Union, 'Cameroon: Case No. CM/01 - Dieudonné Ambassa Zang' (IPU Governing Council 16.10.2014) http://archive.ipu.org/hr-e/197/CM01.pdf accessed 04 April 2019.
271 Bertelsmann Stiftung (n 226) 9.
272 ibid. See also Bertelsmann Stiftung 2012 Report (n 70) 7.
273 Bertelsmann Stiftung (n 226) 10.

References

African Development Bank, *'2004 Cameroon Country Governance Profile'* (Country Operations Department: Central and West Region, September 2004). accessed 19 October 2018.

Atanga L, *Gender, Discourse and Power in the Cameroonian Parliament* (Langaa RPCIG 2010).

Audit Bench of the Supreme Court, 'Avis No. 001/2018/CSC/CDC sur le Projet de Loi de Reglement – Exercise 2017' (26–29 October 2019).

Ayah P, 'A Cameroonian Case Study: Executive Presidency versus Parliamentary Executive' (2004) *85*(4) *The Parliamentarian: Journal of the Parliaments of the Commonwealth* 318.

Barber N, 'Parliamentary Immunity and Human Rights' (2003) *119*(4) *Law Quarterly Review* 557.

Bertelsmann Stiftung, 'Bertelsmann Transformation Index, 2018 - Cameroon Country Report' https://www.bti-project.org/fileadmin/files/BTI/Downloads/Reports/2018/pdf/BTI_2018_Cameroon.pdf accessed 20 November 2019.

'Bertelsmann Transformation Index, 2012 - Cameroon Country Report' (Gütersloh: Bertelsmann Stiftung, 2012) www.bti-project.de/fileadmin/lnhalte/reports/2012/pdf accessed 04 April 2019.

Brazier R, *Constitutional Practice* (2nd ed, Clarendon Press 1994).

Cameroon Ministry of Justice, 'Report on Human Rights in Cameroon - 2009' www.spm.gov.cm/uploads/media/Rapport_Minjustice_Ang_2009.pdf accessed 12 March 2011.

Dicklitch S, Failed Democratic Transition in Cameroon: A Human Rights Explanation (2002) *24*(1) *Human Rights Quarterly* 152.

Dicklitch S, 'The Southern Cameroons and Minority Rights in Cameroon' (2011) *29*(1) *Journal of Contemporary African Studies* 49.

Fokwang J, *Mediating Legitimacy: Chieftaincy and Democratisation in Two African Chiefdoms* (Langaa Research and Publishing 2009).

Fombad C, 'Election Management Bodies in Africa: Cameroon's National Elections Observatory in Perspective' (2003) *3*(1) *African Human Rights Law Journal* 25.

Fombad C, *Constitutional Law in Cameroon* (Wolters Kluwer).

Fossungu P, *Democracy and Human Rights in Africa: The Politics of Collective Participation and Governance in Cameroon* (Langaa Research and Publishing 2013).

Foute F, 'Cameroun: L'Assemblée Nationale Approuve une Modification Partielle du Code Électoral' *Jeuneafrique* (Yaoundé, 31 March 2019) https://www.jeuneafrique.com/756521/politique/cameroun-lassemblee-nationale-approuve-une-modification-partielle-du-code-electoral/ accessed 4 April 2019.

Freedom House, 'Freedom in the World 2012 – Cameroon' (17 August 2012) https://www.refworld.org/docid/5033655537.html accessed 13 November 2019.

Gabriel JM, 'Cameroon's Neopatrimonial Dilemma' (1999) *7 Journal of Contemporary African Studies* 187.

Inter-Parliamentary Union, 'Cameroon: Case No. CM/01 - Dieudonné Ambassa Zang' (IPU Governing Council, 16 October 2014) http://archive.ipu.org/hr-e/197/CM01.pdf accessed 04 April 2019.

Kankeu J, *Droit Constitutionnel* (Tome 1, 1st edn, Presses Universitaires de Dschang 2003).

Kendemeh, 'Hon. Ayah Paul Abine' *Cameroon Tribune* (Yaoundé, 10 January 2011) www.cameroon-tribune.cm/index.php?option=com_content&view=article&id=62972:hon-ayah-paul-abine-quits-cpdm&catid=1:politique&Itemid=3 accessed 29 August 2012.

Mokam D, 'The Search for a Cameroonian Model of Democracy or the Search for the Domination of the State Party: 1966–2006' (2012) *23 Cadernos de Estudos Africanos* 85.

Musa T, 'EU Condemns Elections Management Transfer in Cameroon' (15 November 2009) www.newstimeafrica.com/archives/6216 accessed 21 May 2012.

Ngwa L, *'What Cameroonians Should Know About a Senate' The Post* (Buea, 11 March 2013).

Ntonga Bomba SV, 'La Procédure Législative Devant L'Assemblée Nationale du Cameroun' (2002) *58 African Administrative Studies* 43.

Olinga D, 'Politique et Droit Electoral au Cameroun: Analyse Juridique de la Politique Electorale' (1998) *6*(2) *Polis: Revue Camerounaise de Science Politique* 40.

Puddington A, Piano A and Neubauer K (eds), *Freedom in the World: Annual Survey of Political Rights and Civil Liberties* (Rowman & Littlefields 2009).

Rakner L, Mukubvu L, Ngwira N, Smiddy K, Schneider A, 'The Budget as Theatre: The Formal and Informal Institutional Makings of the Budget Process in Malawi' (Washington, DC: World Bank, 2004).

Refworld, 'Freedom in the World 2011 – Cameroon' (May 2011) https://www.refworld.org/docid/4dcbf51ec.html accessed 09 February 2012.

Reuters Africa, 'Cameroon Presidential Hopeful Quits Ruling Party' (11 January 2011) http://af.reuters.com/article/topNews/idAFJOE70A0HZ20110111 accessed 29 August 2012.

Sajó A, *Limiting Government: An Exercise in Constitutionalism* (Central European University Press 1999).

Stapenhurst R and Pelizzo R, 'Improving Democracy and Accountability in Ghana: The Importance of Parliamentary Oversight Tools' *25*(2) (2012) *Governance: An International Journal of Policy, Administration and Institutions* 335.

Sulitzeanu-Kenan R, 'Reflection in the Shadow of Blame: When Do Politicians Appoint Commissions of Inquiry?' (2010) *40 British Journal of Political Science* 613.

The Guardian, 'Cameroon MP injured by Flying Debris in Parliament Amidst Anglophone Crisis' *The Guardian* (10 December 2017) https://www.theguardian.com/world/2017/dec/10/cameroon-mp-injured-parliament-anglophone-crisis accessed 15 March 2019.

The National Assembly, 'Committee on Finance and the Budget' http://www.assnat.cm/index.php/en/national-assembly/the-9-committees?showall=&start=1 accessed 02 April 2019.

US Department of State, 'Human Right Practices in Cameroon – 2012' http://www.state.gov/documents/organization/204309.pdf accessed 22 April 2014.

US Department of State, 'Cameroon' in *Background Notes: Central Africa 2011* (InfoStrategist.com 2011).

US Embassy in Cameroon, 'Human Rights Practices in Cameroon – 2006' (Yaoundé, March 2007) http://yaounde.usembassy.gov/cmr_human_rights.html accessed 12 March 2011.

Yanou M, 'Democracy in Cameroon: A Socio-Legal Appraisal' (2013) *46*(3) *Law and Politics in Africa, Asia and Latin America* 303.

4 The judiciary, judicial independence and power

Introduction

This chapter explores the judiciary as one of the 'powers' of the state, one of the major changes introduced in the 1996 Constitution. That innovation emerged from the 1990s' journey towards democratisation as a recognition of the relevance of a strong and independent judiciary to an effective democratic process. However, as with other aspects of governance discussed so far, the foundations of 'judicial power' have been laid on an executive-centric Constitution that limits the extent to which other arms of government can effectively exercise power. From the discussion that follows, it will be demonstrated that the way judicial power is structured, exercised and controlled belies any purported elevation of the status of the judiciary. Unlike some judiciaries in other countries that have promoted democratisation and respect for the rule of law, the judiciary in Cameroon has continued to be haunted by its past weaknesses and more contemporary challenges for which it is constitutionally ill-equipped to address.

This chapter will provide a basic description of the organisation of the judiciary and the jurisdiction of the respective courts. It will proceed to examine the status of the judiciary and the extent to which it can be considered independent. In the course of the discussion, the challenges that confront the judiciary will be identified.

Part I. Organisation of the judicial system and jurisdiction of the courts

According to the Judicial Organisation Law, judicial organisation shall comprise of the following[1]:

- The Supreme Court
- The Court of Appeal
- The Special Criminal Court
- Lower Courts of Administrative Litigation (Regional Administrative Courts)
- Lower Audit Courts (Regional Audit Courts)
- Military Tribunals

- High Courts
- Courts of First Instance
- Customary Law Courts

It can be seen from the above list that the Supreme Court is at the apex of the organisational structure of the courts. In the sections that follow, the relevance of that hierarchy will become apparent in discussing the jurisdiction of the courts and the appeals therefrom.

Pursuant to the constitutional and statutory provisions[2] regulating the judicial system, a dual classification of courts can be distinguished. The classification is often described in terms of courts of ordinary jurisdiction and courts with special jurisdiction as described briefly later.

A. *Courts of ordinary jurisdiction*

Courts of ordinary jurisdiction have general competence to settle all types of matters, be they criminal or civil. They include Customary Courts, Courts of First Instance, High Courts, Courts of Appeal and the Supreme Court.[3] Within this classification, there are courts with original jurisdiction and those with appellate jurisdiction.

I. Ordinary courts with original jurisdiction

These are courts with jurisdiction to hear matters at first instance. Thus, the Customary Courts, Courts of First Instance and High Courts have original jurisdiction in civil and criminal matters.[4] Regional Administrative Courts and Regional Audit Courts are also ordinary courts with original jurisdiction. The courts are discussed later in turn.

A. REGIONAL ADMINISTRATIVE COURTS

Regional Administrative Courts are an innovation introduced by a 2006 statute.[5] Although article 42 of the Constitution provided for lower Administrative Courts, these were not established until 2016. Prior to that period, the Supreme Court exercised both original and appellate jurisdiction in administrative matters.[6] The current position is that Regional Administrative Courts have exclusive ordinary jurisdiction in matters relating to administrative review, while appeals therefrom go to the Administrative Bench of the Supreme Court.[7] The courts are located in the regional headquarters, although a court may serve more than one region where service needs make it imperative.[8]

The courts are composed of a president, judges, a registrar in chief and registrars at the bench.[9] At the Legal Department (LD), the composition includes the *Procureur General* of the Court of Appeal for that region and one or more deputy *Procureur General*.[10] All matters are heard by a collegiate bench of three judges.[11] Unlike most ordinary courts which are composed exclusively of career judges, the law makes provision for the appointment of non-career judges such as senior civil servants and senior contract officers with a masters degree in law and fifteen years of work experience.[12] Law professors with a minimum of ten years' experience and lecturers with a minimum of fifteen years may also be appointed.[13] These appointments would be made under exceptional circumstances where service needs make it necessary and in all instances, the appointments are for a temporary period of five years.[14] The law does not state what these service needs may be, neither does it make provision for the training of the non-career judges. Perhaps this would be a matter to be dealt with internally by the individual courts concerned.

The courts have exclusive jurisdiction in matters relating to administrative authorities. In that respect, they are competent to hear and determine disputes emanating from municipal and regional elections and disputes between the state, decentralised public authorities and state institutions.[15] Administrative acts contemplated by the aforementioned provisions include petitions for the quashing of *ultra vires* acts, actions for damages resulting from administrative acts, disputes relating to public contracts and public utility concessions, disputes relating to state lands and the maintenance of law and order.[16] In the exercise of its jurisdiction, the court may, when faced with difficulties in interpreting or assessing the legality of a legislative act or a regulatory instrument, refer the matter to the Administrative Bench of the Supreme Court.[17]

B. REGIONAL AUDIT COURTS

Regional Audit Courts are also a creation of a 2006 statute.[18] They were first mentioned in article 41 of the 1996 Constitution but their establishment and functioning was dependent on a law which was enacted in 2006. The audit courts are in principle located in the regional headquarters, although due to service needs, their jurisdiction may cover several regions.[19]

In terms of their composition, at the Bench, they are composed of a president, section presidents, judges, registrars, registrars on special duty, judges on special duty, commissioners of audit and trainee commissioners of audit.[20] At the LD, there is the *Procureur General* of the Court of Appeal for that region, deputy *Procureur General* and deputies to the *Procureur General* on special duty.[21] Matters are heard in that court by a collegiate of three judges.[22] As with the lower Administrative Courts, provision is made for non-career judges fulfilling the same criteria as those described above, except that with the Audit Courts, the academic disciplines are broader and include, economics, public finance, management and accounting.[23] The Courts are organised in separate sections with each allocated respectively to regions and urban councils, rural councils, councils trade unions and councils or regional public establishments.[24]

The Courts are competent to control and adjudicate on public accounts and the accounts of regional and local authorities and public establishments within their area of territorial jurisdiction.[25] They shall also decide on matters of accounting expressly devolving upon them by law and those referred by the Supreme Court.[26]

It is worth noting that the Audit Courts are yet to be established. Their establishment shall be progressive, depending on service requirements and the state's available resources.[27] In the interim, the Audit Bench of the Supreme Court exercises original jurisdiction while appeals are heard by a joint session of all the sections within the Audit Bench of the Supreme Court.[28]

C. HIGH COURTS

High Courts are established in every administrative division[29] and are located in the headquarters of that division'.[30] However, for service purposes, its territorial jurisdiction may cover several divisions by decree of the President of the Republic.[31] The High Court is composed of a president, one or more judges, one or more registrars and a registrar in chief at the bench.[32] At the preliminary inquiry, there are one or more examining magistrates and one or more registrars.[33] At the LD, there is a state counsel and one or more deputy state counsels.[34] All cases brought before the High Court shall be heard by a single judicial officer, although some matters may be heard by a collegiate bench of three judges at the instance of the president of the Court or on the request of the LD or a party to the dispute.[35] The composition of the Court in labour matters is regulated by the Labour Code.[36] Following an amendment to the Judicial Organisation Law in 2011, the High Courts are organised into Benches and a General Assembly.[37] There are separate benches for civil, commercial, criminal and labour matters,[38] although the president of the Court of Appeal may by order merge two or more benches taking into account the service needs of the Court.[39] The General Assembly shall be composed of all the legal and judicial officers of the Court and the registrars in chief.[40] It shall have a judicial and an advisory jurisdiction and provide its opinion on issues relating to the functioning of the Court and in matters provided for by the law.[41]

In terms of its substantive jurisdiction, in criminal matters, the Court has competence to try felonies and related misdemeanours and to hear and determine bail applications, subject to the jurisdiction of the Court of First Instance.[42] It has competence to entertain civil matters relating to the status of persons, civil status, marriage, divorce, filiation, adoption and inheritance.[43] Other civil matters include claims where the damages exceed 10,000,000 CFA and recovery by way of the simplified recovery procedure, claims not exceeding 10,000,000 CFA.[44] Its competence in commercial matters includes collective proceedings for the cancellation of debts, unquestionable, liquidated and due commercial debts of any amount where the obligation arises from a cheque, a promissory note or a bill of exchange and disputes relating to commitments and transactions between businessmen and commercial establishments.[45] In addition, it can entertain disputes between shareholders of companies or economic interest groups relating to commercial companies and acts and bills of exchange between all persons as provided for by the Organisation for the Harmonisation of

Business Law in Africa (OHADA) Uniform Act on general commercial law, where the amount exceeds 10,000,000 CFA.[46] Its jurisdiction in labour matters includes claims which exceed 10,000,000 CFA.[47] Furthermore, the Court has jurisdiction in non-administrative matters, to issue the writs of mandamus, prohibition[48] and habeas corpus[49] and to hear petitions against administrative detention measures.[50] The Court can additionally, through its president or a judge designated by the president, hear disputes relating to the enforcement of the decisions of High Courts.[51]

D. COURTS OF FIRST INSTANCE

In principle, Courts of First Instance are found in every sub-division and located in the headquarters of that sub-division.[52] However, for service purposes, its territorial jurisdiction may cover several sub-divisions by decree of the President of the Republic.[53] The composition of the Court is as follows: at the bench, there is a president, one or more magistrates, one or more registrars and a registrar in chief.[54] At the preliminary inquiry, there are one or more examining magistrates and one or more registrars.[55] At the LD, there is a state counsel and one or more deputy state counsels.[56] All cases brought before the Court shall be heard by a single judicial officer,[57] although provision is made for a hearing by a collegiate bench of three magistrates when deemed necessary by the president or at the request of the LD or a party to the litigation.[58] In matters relating to minors, the composition of the Court is regulated by a special law[59] and in labour matters, it is regulated by the Labour Code.[60] The Courts of First Instance are also now organised into Benches and a General Assembly.[61] There are benches for civil, commercial and labour matters, benches for misdemeanours and simple offences and benches for matters relating to minors.[62] Where service needs make it necessary, the president of the Court of Appeal may by order merge two or more benches.[63] The General Assembly is comprised of all the legal and judicial officers of the Court and the registrars in chief.[64] It shall have a judicial and an advisory jurisdiction and provide its opinion on issues relating to the functioning of the court and in matters provided for by the law.[65]

The Court has substantive jurisdiction in criminal matters to try all offences classified as simple offences or misdemeanours and felonies committed by minors without adult co-offenders or accessories and to hear applications for bail.[66] In civil matters, it has jurisdiction to hear matters where the damages claimed does not exceed 10,000,000 CFA and to recover by way of the simplified recovery procedure, claims not exceeding 10,000,000 CFA.[67] In commercial matters, the court may hear disputes relating to commitments and transactions between businessmen and commercial establishments and disputes between shareholders of companies or economic interest groups relating to commercial companies and acts and bills of exchange between all persons as provided for by the OHADA Uniform Act on general commercial law, where the amount does not exceed 10,000,000 CFA.[68] The court also has jurisdiction in labour matters where the claim does not exceed 10,000,000 CFA.[69] Additionally, when hearing a criminal matter, the court has jurisdiction to entertain claims for damages resulting from the criminal act even where the amount claimed exceeds 10,000,000 CFA.[70]

E. CUSTOMARY COURTS

Customary Courts are the least influential in terms of the administrative and political governance of the country but they play an important role within the local communities in which they operate. They are found in administrative districts. Article 4(1) of the Judicial Organisation Law states that the organisation of courts including the Customary Courts shall be laid down by law. However, there are no new laws governing Customary Courts, so these continue to exist under the different regimes applicable in the Anglophone and Francophone Regions before 1972.[71] Nevertheless, customary courts have civil jurisdiction in customary marriages, divorce, custody, succession and inheritance, applying the local customs and traditions of the districts in which they operate. They can only entertain matters for which the claim does not exceed 69,200 CFA.

II. Ordinary courts with appellate jurisdiction

The courts with appellate jurisdiction are the Courts of Appeal and the Supreme Court.

A. COURTS OF APPEAL

The Courts of Appeal are located in the headquarters of each of the ten administrative regions in Cameroon.[72] As with the other courts, its territorial jurisdiction may cover other regions where the need arises.[73] The Court of Appeal is composed of a president, one or more vice presidents, one or more judges, one or more registrars and a registrar in chief at the bench.[74] The LD is composed of a *Procureur General*, one or more Advocates General, one or more deputies of the *Procureur General* and one or more Legal Assistants at the *Procureur General's* chambers.[75] The Court is organised into Benches and the General Assembly.[76] There are quite a number of benches, perhaps due to its appellate role to accommodate all matters of appeal from lower courts. There are separate benches for matters relating to motions and urgent applications, the enforcement of judgments, civil, commercial, criminal, labour and customary law matters and those relating to misdemeanours, simple offences and inquiry control.[77] Despite the number of benches, the president of the Court may by order merge two or more benches taking into account the service needs of the Court.[78]

Unlike the General Assembly for the High Courts and Courts of First Instance, that of the Court of Appeal is composed of all the judicial officers of the Court and the registrars in chief only.[79] It also has a judicial and an advisory jurisdiction and provides its opinion on issues relating to the functioning of the Court and in matters provided for by the law.[80] It is worthy to note that although section 20(2)(a) states that the Court is organised into Benches and a General

Assembly, subsequent provisions use the term 'General Meeting' instead. It is not clear why this discrepancy exists but both are interpreted to give effect to section 20(2)(a).

With respect to jurisdiction, a Court of Appeal is competent to hear appeals against decisions delivered by all courts (except those of other Appeal Courts and the Supreme Court), appeals against the rulings of Examining Magistrates and all other matters provided for by the law.[81] The 2011 amendments introduced some changes to the substantive jurisdiction of Appeal Courts. Previously, each Appeal Court was competent to hear disputes relating to the enforcement of its own decisions. The current position is that the president of the Appeal Court can hear and determine disputes relating to the enforcement of decisions of all Appeal Courts.[82]

All cases falling within the jurisdiction of the Court must be heard by three judges who are members of that Court.[83] However, when hearing appeals from the Military Court, one of the judges must be a military judge or a member of the armed forces where a military judge is unavailable.[84] In addition, when hearing appeals from military tribunals, a military magistrate shall be appointed to represent the LD.[85]

B. SUPREME COURT

There is one Supreme Court which has national jurisdiction and is located in Yaoundé, the capital city.[86] It is the highest court of record with final jurisdiction in judicial,[87] administrative and audit matters.[88] The Bench of the Supreme Court is composed of a First President (who is the president of the Supreme Court), presidents of the bench, justices, masters, puisne justices, the registrar-in-chief of the Supreme Court, registrars-in-chief of the bench and registrars.[89] The LD is composed of a *Procureur General*, a First Advocate General and advocates general.[90]

In terms of its organisational structure, the Supreme Court is made up of a Bureau, a General Secretariat and a Registry and five benches designated as follows[91]:

- *The Administrative Bench* (jurisdiction in administrative litigation)[92]
- *The Audit Bench* (jurisdiction in the auditing of public accounts)[93]
- *The Judicial Bench* (jurisdiction in civil, criminal, commercial and social matters and those relating to customary law)[94]
- *Panel of Joint Benches* (jurisdiction in matters relating to the regulation of judges, recusal and transfer of cases between courts)[95]
- *A Full Bench* (examines matters relating to the Court submitted to it by the First President, the *Procureur General* or by one third of the members of the Supreme Court)[96]

Each of the Benches is composed of divisions[97] which have a president, at least two justices of the Supreme Court and one or more Advocates General.[98]

A 2017 amendment to the Supreme Court Law introduced significant changes to the Judicial Bench and the composition of its relevant divisions.[99] The necessity for the changes stemmed from the protracted Anglophone crisis and the grievances of the common law lawyers regarding the insouciant treatment of the inherited English common law in Cameroon's bi-jural legal system. This move was intended to assuage some of the concerns of common law advocates by appearing to be according the common law an equal status with the civil law. Thus, in addition to its previous competence, the Judicial Bench is also now competent to hear and determine final decisions of tribunals on matters governed by the common law.[100] According to the new section 8, the Judicial Bench is composed of a civil division, a commercial division, a criminal division, a labour division, a customary law division and a common law division. The common law division is the innovation. It shall have jurisdiction, in matters relating to the common law, to hear appeals against final decisions of tribunals and judgments of Courts of Appeal.[101] To ensure professional competence, the law provides that judges appointed to the common law division must have 'an Anglo-Saxon legal background'. This is perhaps a response to one of the main grievances of the Anglophone lawyers in respect of the fact that the government has increasingly appointed civil law trained judges who have neither the language nor the professional competence to serve in courts in the Anglophone regions which apply the inherited English common law.

Despite the apparent attractiveness of the changes, one pertinent observation can be made here. The fact that all matters emanating from the Anglophone regions have to be heard by a single division in the Supreme Court, whereas appeals from lower courts from other regions applying the civil law are dispersed within the many divisions in the Supreme Court. The common law may seem to have been elevated because it now has a special division. This may not be an elevation in itself. In fact, it has been further relegated by giving it the same status as customary law. Note that, in the organisation of the Benches into divisions, the civil law is not mentioned as a division. A more appropriate approach would have been to increase the number of common law judges within the different divisions of the Court to ensure that every panel hearing an appeal has sufficient representation of judges from both legal traditions. By attempting to resolve a problem, the government might be creating another one in the sense that there is potential for the common law division to be overwhelmed by cases from the two Anglophone regions. This might lead to delays an aspect that is inimical to the efficient administration of justice.

As an appellate jurisdiction, the Supreme Court has specific provisions on the grounds for which its jurisdiction may be invoked. According to section 35, the grounds include:

- Want of jurisdiction
- Misinterpretation of facts
- Default, contradiction or insufficient grounds
- Irregularity

- Breach of the law
- Failure to respond to the submission of the parties or the LD
- Abuse of office
- Violation of a general principle of law
- Failure to comply with the jurisprudence of a panel of joint divisions or joint benches of the Supreme Court

With the establishment of the Constitutional Council, the Supreme Court has ceased to exercise jurisdiction in the review of legislation, the standing orders of parliament and international instruments, and the resolution of disputes emanating from parliamentary and presidential elections and the functioning of institutions.

B. Courts with special jurisdiction

These are courts with specialised jurisdiction in terms of the subject matter. They may also be limited in terms of the category of persons with standing to sue or those over whom the court has jurisdiction. These courts are Military Tribunals, the Court of Impeachment, the State Security Court and the Constitutional Council. Since 2011, the judicial landscape has extended to include the Special Criminal Court created by an act of parliament to try the offence of misappropriation of public funds. It should be noted that the law on judicial organisation does not mention the Court of Impeachment, the State Security Court and the Constitutional Council. Therefore, they may be considered as courts that operate outside of the ordinary judiciary. However, on account of the fact that they perform judicial functions, they will be discussed briefly here (except the Constitutional Council which is discussed separately in the next chapter).

I. Military tribunals

In relation to the military tribunals, the law specifically states that they are tribunals of special jurisdiction.[102] Like the other courts discussed previously, they are located in the regional headquarters.[103] Peculiarly, the tribunal in Yaoundé has a special status as it can exercise jurisdiction over the national territory during exceptional circumstances specified in article 9 of the Constitution[104] or during circumstances leading to a serious threat to public order and state security or acts of terrorism.[105] Additionally, it has competence to hear various type of offences committed by servicemen on official mission or during operations abroad.[106] The general competence of military tribunals is regulated by section 8 of the Military Justice Code. This provision gives the tribunals a very wide competence which includes crimes ranging from war crimes, crimes against humanity, genocide, terrorism-related offences, the purchase, importation, sale, use, keeping and wearing of military effects and insignia and offences committed with the use of fire arms, by both military and civilian persons.

Two of the main criticism against the military tribunals are the breadth of their competence especially in the area of terrorism which is very vaguely defined[107] and their jurisdiction over civilians, an aspect which contravenes international and regional instruments ratified by Cameroon.[108] In *Walter Numvi & others v The People*, the Court of Appeal in Bamenda confirmed that 'ordinary civilians' charged under the legislation on terrorism must be tried in a military tribunal.[109] In recent years, the military tribunal has received considerable attention due to its active role in the fight against terrorism orchestrated by *boko haram* in the northern parts of the country and its controversial role in the prosecution of terrorism-related offences committed by political dissidents and Anglophone separatist and federalist leaders.

II. Special Criminal Court

The Special Criminal Court was created by an act of parliament[110] as an accelerated means of combating corruption in Cameroon, principally the embedded criminal culture of misappropriation of public funds. The Court is located in Yaoundé, with jurisdiction over the entire country.[111] The Bench of the Court is composed of a president, one or more vice presidents, one or more advisers (judges) and one or more examining magistrate.[112] The LD is composed of a *Procureur General*, Advocates General and one or more deputy *Procureur General*.[113]

The Court is competent to hear and determine matters relating to the misappropriation of public funds and related offences provided for by the Penal Code and international conventions ratified by Cameroon, where the amount of the loss is a minimum of 50,000,000 CFA.[114] This in effect limits the competence of the High Court to try felonies such as misappropriation, to those that result in losses below 50,000,000 CFA. The jurisdiction of the Special Criminal Court is original and appeals from there are made directly to the Supreme Court.[115] A rationale for the direct approach (appealing directly to the Supreme Court) is partly to eliminate lengthy procedures and reduce trial times which remain an issue in the administration of justice in Cameroon. Whether the objective has been achieved remains a moot point.

III. Court of Impeachment

A Court of Impeachment is provided for under article 53 of the Constitution. This provision states very briefly the general competence of the Court.[116] According to article 53(4), the organisation, composition and conditions under which matters shall be referred to it, as well as the applicable procedure shall be laid down by law. This law is still to be enacted. Without further information, it is not clear whether this Court exists within or outside of the ordinary judiciary. One reason for the uncertainty is the role of parliament in indicting the President of the Republic. This question is likely to be answered by the enabling legislation. In any case, in light of the fact that it is not included in the Judicial Organisation

Law, it may be reasonable to presume that it exists outside of the ordinary judiciary.

IV. State Security Court

The State Security Court was provided for by a 1990 statute in the context of the democratic uprisings in the 1990s.[117] It has 'exclusive' competence to try felonies and misdemeanours against the internal and external security of the state.[118] The Court has both original and appellate (final) jurisdiction although appeals may be made exceptionally to the Supreme Court on matters of interpretation and application of the law.[119] Uncertainties now surround the role of the State Security Court considering the wide competence of the military tribunals in state security issues[120] and the exclusive competence in matters relating to terrorism.[121] It is not clear which of the courts will prevail in the relevant matters. However, the State Security Court has not been established, neither has the 1990 law been repealed. It has been argued that the Court is a tool to be used by the government to supress citizens.[122] This position can neither be supported nor refuted considering that the Court is yet to be established.

Part II. The status and independence of the judiciary

Prior to 1996, the status of the judiciary in relation to the executive and the legislature was doubtful. In particular, it could hardly be considered as equal to those two arms of the government. This affected in practice its relation with legislative and executive bodies and institutions. In addition, its independence was called into question in the light of its inferior status and the manner in which judges were appointed and made to progress within the judiciary. This section attempts to unravel the changes introduced principally under the 1996 Constitution and to determine the contemporary effects on the judiciary as a 'power'.

A. Structure and constitutional status of the judiciary

It is worth stating at the outset that discussions on the judiciary in this part exclude the customary courts, the Court of Impeachment, the State Security Court and the Constitutional Council. With the exception of the customary courts, these courts operate outside of the ordinary judiciary and they all differ (including the customary courts) in many respects from the ordinary courts. The discussion here may not necessarily be relevant to them.

I. Structure

Cameroon has a peculiar judicial structure which is based on the French civil law system and therefore different from other judicial systems, particularly those with an English common law orientation. It is deemed necessary to explain its peculiarities due to the fact that some of the terms have been used in the preceding sections of this chapter. The judiciary consists of two main category of judges, notably, judges 'of the bench'[123] and prosecutors.[124] The former are those engaged in the conventional function of adjudication. There is also a judge known as the examining magistrate (a judge of the bench) with responsibility to conduct preliminary investigations in criminal matters.[125] In contrast, prosecutors perform prosecutorial functions and form part of what is known as the LD. The LD is attached to all the courts.[126] In the appellate courts, the LD is headed by the *Procureur Général* (directly responsible to the Minister of Justice)[127] and a State Counsel[128] in the lower courts (directly responsible to the *Procureur Général* of the Court of Appeal within its territorial jurisdiction).[129] The role of the LD in criminal matters is to conduct investigations, issue warrants and carry out prosecution and generally to enforce laws, regulations and judgments.[130] The Ministry of Justice also has a LD through which it performs its supervisory duties on the judiciary.[131] Interestingly, judges may be appointed to serve on the bench or the LD during their career or even to the Ministry of Justice.[132] This has serious implications for judicial and prosecutorial independence as discussed subsequently.

II. Constitutional status

A major innovation of the 1996 Constitution with respect to the judiciary is the elevation of that institution from an 'authority' to a 'power' like the legislature and the executive. Both the 1961 and 1972 Constitutions referred to the judiciary as an authority. The elevation was described as a measure to establish 'the balance and separation of power'.[133] This was important in the context of the democratic revival in the 1990s to demonstrate concerted efforts at establishing a constitutional democracy. Article 37(2) of the Constitution further appears to enhance the position of the judiciary by providing that 'The judicial power shall be independent of the executive and legislative powers'. Despite the audacious statement, the actual transformation of that status is doubtful. This is partly evident in article 37(3) which provides controversially that judicial independence shall be guaranteed by the President of the Republic, who ironically is the executive. Admittedly, article 37(3) does not indicate a prima facie case of judicial subservience as it may be a positive duty imposed on the President to ensure that the necessary conditions exist for the judiciary to function independently. However, for that obligation to be meaningful, it should necessarily be backed by a mechanism to ensure that the President fulfils that obligation.[134]

As will become evident, predominantly in the discussion of the judicial tenure, the conditions for securing judicial independence are inimical to the exercise of actual judicial autonomy or power. It would seem that, while normatively, the status of the judiciary has been elevated to a power, substantively, it is still perceived as an authority.

B. The judicial tenure: appointment, career progression and discipline of judges

I. Appointment

Unlike common law systems where judges are appointed from senior lawyers in private practice, Cameroon follows a typical civil law approach where the judiciary is a career judiciary. Judges are appointed following the completion of two years of training in the National School of Administration and Magistracy (ENAM) in the Magistracy section.[135] Entrance into ENAM is dependent upon success in a competitive exam undertaken by candidates who have completed a master's degree in law or *maitrise en droit.*[136] Following their training, they are integrated into the civil service as members of the judicial corps and enjoy a fixed tenure until retirement.[137] In terms of their appointment, the Constitution provides that they shall be appointed by the President of the Republic, with the assistance of the Higher Judicial Council (HJC).[138] They may be appointed as judges on the bench, as prosecutors, investigating magistrates or to the Ministry of Justice.[139]

The appointment method is a co-operative one as it involves both the President and the HJC. Ideally, this method affords more opportunities for transparency and independence. Indeed, this method has been described by the government of Cameroon as part of the 'balancing mechanism'[140] to prevent exclusive executive control of the judiciary. In support of that assertion, the government asserts that the HJC is composed of distinguished personalities and characterised by broad representation and balance.[141] Yet, the co-operative method described earlier can be deemed ambiguous in terms of the statutory arrangements for the composition of the HJC. At the helm, there is the President of the Republic who is the chair, followed by the Minister of Justice as deputy chair. Other members are three parliamentarians, an independent personality appointed by the President, the President of the Supreme Court and three senior judges.[142] It can be seen that the President is member of the same institution that is supposed to assist him in the appointment of judges and with the exception of the parliamentarians, all the other members of the HJC are presidential appointees. Perhaps at the initial appointment stage into the judiciary, this poses no significant issues, considering that all graduates from ENAM must be appointed to commence service anyway. The situation may be different in terms of career progression and discipline.

II. Career progression

As career civil servants, judges progress through a certain hierarchy through various means, including promotions or transfers which may in effect be promotions. Consistent with the requirement for security of tenure, they have a fairly secured tenure as it is fixed until retirement.[143] However, a judge's term may be extended by presidential decree where necessitated by the nature or peculiarity of certain functions.[144] This is a rather vague provision which does not define the specific conditions under which an extension may occur. This is unfavourable to the basic tenets of judicial independence as it provides an opportunity to enhance the tenure of a conformist judge who may be more inclined to advance the political objectives of the executive.[145] The point is not that extensions are inherently objectionable, but that they should be based on clearly defined criteria with the aim of facilitating the administration of justice. Some executive authorities in other jurisdictions exercise this power, albeit under well-defined conditions. For instance, in Botswana, the tenure of a High Court judge can be extended by the President to permit the conclusion of proceedings that commenced before him prior to attainment of the retirement age.[146] This is clearly to allow for the efficient administration of justice and the power to extend that tenure is exercised in accordance with the advice of the Judicial Service Commission.[147]

In Cameroon, progression within the judicial hierarchy is further determined through promotions. Here again, the President of the Republic assumes a decisive role. He is responsible for promotions and is assisted by the HJC 'which shall give him its opinion on all nominations'.[148] Note here that the HJC is only required to give an 'opinion' as opposed to advice and the President is not bound by it. In terms of procedure, promotion is purportedly based on recommendations backed by the evaluation of individual judges. There is a separate system for judges in the appellate courts. Senior judges[149] within the Supreme Court, Courts of Appeal and the Ministry of Justice would be subject to evaluation by the Minister of Justice who subsequently recommends the judges for promotion on the advice of the Secretary General and directors at the Ministry of Justice.[150] Less senior judges are evaluated, respectively, by the presidents of the Supreme Court and Courts of Appeal.[151] Judges in the lower courts are evaluated by the president and *Procureur Général* of the Court of Appeal for that administrative region.[152] They must act on the advice of the presidents of the respective courts.[153] There is also provision for judges who have not been recommended by their superiors. In those circumstances, the individual judges may submit personal requests to the Minister, paradoxically through their hierarchical superior.[154] The reports from evaluations and subsequent recommendations are forwarded by the Minister to the HJC which must decide through a process of voting and the collation of a final list of nominees.[155] The list forms the basis of the recommendations to the President of the Republic who in principle promotes judges by presidential decree based on the nominations.[156]

The process is ostensibly rigorous and potentially objective. There are, however, a number of issues which emerge from further analysis. For instance, the fact that the Minister and other executive authorities in the Ministry are in charge of the evaluation process for senior judges. The extent of their knowledge of the performance of these judges is doubtful. Moreover, given the composition of the HJC, there is effectively no distinction between those who perform the evaluation and nominations, and the institution responsible for recommendations and final appointment. It is akin to making the same institution or personalities, judge and jury in the process. More poignantly, the evaluations do not seem to be based on an objective criteria, a situation which may engender arbitrariness. Cumulatively, the system appears to be one that is prone to abuse by the executive. In fact, within the judicial sphere, the system has been said to impede on the individual independence of judges.[157]

That is also the case with transfers which may sometimes be perceived as a double edge sword. Given the geographically decentralised nature of courts as described earlier, judges may be transferred to different geographical locations. In addition, they may be transferred functionally – between the bench, the LD and the Ministry of Justice. A major issue with transfers is the absence of specific criteria for selecting judges that should be transferred.[158] The HJC is also required to provide its opinion on transfers, but as with promotions, the opinion is not binding and the President of the Republic retains decisional authority.[159] This has prompted some senior judges to question the possibility of exercising judicial independence in the midst of such obscurity and executive control.[160] The uncertainties with transfers perhaps account for why they are sometimes seen as punitive measures towards errant judges. For instance, a transfer from the bench to the LD is often seen (particularly among common law judges) as a punitive measure on judges who exercise decisional independence against the executive.[161] The assumption is that, because the LD is directly answerable to the Minster of Justice, a judge so transferred would be 'cowed' or 'tamed' through direct subordination to the Minister. A transfer to a geographically remote area is similarly perceived as a punitive measure on an errant judge who decides against the executive. Courts in remote areas are presumably places where the judge would be removed from the most contentious cases where the executive has no particular interest to safeguard.[162] The judges are well aware of the potentially abusive nature of the systems of transfer. This was evident in the very controversial case of *The People v Nya Henry*[163] where a number of the Southern Cameroons National Council members were arrested during peaceful celebrations commemorating the end of British colonial rule in Southern Cameroons. Uncharacteristically, their application for bail was granted due to irregularities in the execution of the arrest by executive officials and to preserve the integrity of the judicial process. This decision was unfortunately reversed on appeal. The trial judge was conscious of the possible repercussions for his heroism and clearly noted in his judgements that, 'those who cherish the status of this country as a state of law should keenly follow-up … any developments in the career of this magistrate after this case'.[164] Unswervingly, he was transferred to another jurisdiction to serve in the LD.[165] A similar outcome was registered in *Wakai v The People*[166] where a panel of judges ruled against the executive in favour of granting bail to members of the opposition Social Democratic Front (SDF) party. They had been arrested under very irregular circumstances during nationwide protest at allegedly rigged presidential election results in favour of the incumbent President Biya. The judges' decisional independence was sanctioned by the transfer of the president of that court (who was a member of the panel) to the LD and the transfer of the other two judges to remote areas.[167] In both cases, the transfer of the judges was an overt reaction to their decisional independence.

A further controversy with transfers is that it can sometimes be used by the executive as a tool to manipulate the judicial process especially in political cases. This was the situation with the recent protracted trial of some Anglophone separatist leaders in the Yaoundé Military Tribunal for secession, terrorism and other related offences. The case suffered a number of adjournments, with a disquieting adjournment on 10 January to reconstitute the panel of judges due to the transfer of a panellist to another region.[168] This caused further delays in the trial with the result that the accused remained in prolonged pre-trial detention. A pertinent question in relation to the transfer is whether it was absolutely necessary to transfer the judge at that point. Another case in point is the trial of Titus Edzoa in the Mfoundi High Court for embezzlement of public funds, a trial widely believed to be politically motivated as Edzoa was seen as a potential contender for the presidency.[169] On 18 July 2012 when the Court was expected to arrive at a decision, the matter was adjourned.[170] It transpired that one of the judges in the panel was summoned the previous night to be ordered to take up an appointment elsewhere. Ironically, the judge had been appointed in April 2012 by presidential decree and it was not until this crucial moment that their effective transfer was deemed necessary. The intention of the executive here was very dubious as it had the effect of delaying the trial given that the case had to be heard all over by a new panel which had to be constituted.

III. Discipline

Although judges enjoy a fixed term until retirement, they are subject to disciplinary sanctions. This is necessary to maintain their accountability, a quality that is essential to the proper administration of justice. There are a number of breaches of professional conduct that can attract disciplinary sanctions. These include lack of professionalism, lack of integrity, impropriety, failure to adhere to the law, breach of duty to the state[171] and breach of the judicial oath.[172] While most of these conducts may seem easy to identify, others such as 'breach of duty to the state' may be controversial. For instance, what amounts to a judge's duty to the state is unclear. Such a nebulous conduct cannot objectively form the basis of a disciplinary sanction.

As with the progression system, the President of the Republic and the HJC play yet an important role.[173] The disciplinary procedure is essentially adversarial in nature. A potential disciplinary complaint received by the Minister is referred to the HJC for further investigation by an ad hoc committee of HJC's members, appointed by the President.[174] This would be followed by a hearing at which the judge in question may represent themselves or be represented by counsel or even a colleague.[175] This process is thus dominated by the HJC which acts both as judge and prosecutor thereby undermining the objectivity of the process. Subsequent to the hearing and further deliberations by the HJC, the latter makes a recommendation which is transmitted to the President by the

Minister.[176] This provision is controversial on the basis of the composition of the HJC. If the President and Minister are chair and vice chair, respectively, they would be expected to be part of the same deliberations and recommendations which are meant to be subsequently transmitted to the same President. The President may act on the recommendations or bypass them to sanction the judge in question by presidential decree.[177]

There are a number of possible sanctions ranging from less severe to more severe sanctions, including elimination from the promotion list, a freeze on promotion for a maximum of two years, declassification, early retirement, temporary suspension for a maximum of two years, a reprimand or caution[178] and dismissal[179] with or without pension.[180] Despite the wide variety of possible sanctions, it is unclear what misconduct attracts specific disciplinary sanctions. There is no way of foreseeing the corresponding sanctions for a misconduct particularly because the presidential decrees do not often indicate the provision of the relevant law that has been breached. For instance, the decree sanctioning Pascal Magnaguemabe, a once reputed 'Paul Biya super magistrate'[181] contained the reasons for his dismissal – 'extortion of powers of attorney' and misappropriation of the funds for the estate.[182] The decree did not mention under what provision of the law he was being sanctioned or whether the sanction corresponded with the impugned actioned. Given the unfavourable reputation of the judge in the public sphere and his controversial role in the fight against corruption by the Biya regime, it would have been prudent for the decree to be more specific in order to dispel conspiracy theories.[183] The obscurity of the system for sanctioning is a weakness that can create room for arbitrariness in the way judges are sanctioned by the executive. A recent example of executive arbitrariness in applying disciplinary sanctions was the summary retirement of Paul Ayah SCJ, a fierce critic of the government and former leader of the opposition Peoples Action Party. He was arrested during the Anglophone crisis on charges of terrorism after fiercely condemning the government for grossly mishandling the crisis in the Anglophone regions.[184] He was quickly sent on retirement after a session of the HJC. The government argued that he was due for retirement anyway. However, this move was widely seen as a sanction for his criticism of the executive partly because as noted earlier, the retirement age can be extended by the executive. In view of the political context surrounding his retirement, allegations of executive arbitrariness in his abrupt retirement did not seem unfounded.

Judicial independence under the current arrangements in Cameroon has been severely compromised by the specific arrangements to guarantee a secure judicial tenure. With the executive firmly in control of appointments, progression and discipline, there is little scope for judges to exercise decisional independence. These aspects have not gone unnoticed by the judges as a Court of Appeal judge affirmed that the judicial career is the 'sole prerogative of the executive' who exercises this role 'without the restraints of transparent and objective selection procedures'.[185] More recently, in ironically, a protracted habeas corpus hearing,[186] an advocate commented on the influence of the executive on the decisional independence of judges. The case concerned, a journalist arrested in connection with the Anglophone crisis and accused of supporting armed separatists. The advocate remarked that the inability of the judge to exercise decisional independence in that case was indicative of their lack of independence.[187]

C. *Judicial independence versus accountability: a tenuous relationship*

Stephen Burbank asserts that judicial independence and accountability can be more appropriately described as 'different sides of the same coin'[188] due to their complementary relationship. Judicial independence is instrumental in providing the medium through which judges can render justice impartially, promote the rule of law and secure human rights. In contrast, accountability is necessary in order to avoid undermining the same goals that independence aims to achieve. An unaccountable judiciary stands the risk of exercising power in an abusive way which does not afford impartiality or promote any of the goals described earlier. The importance of that relationship has been reflected in the Constitution which vests the President of the Republic with the duty to guarantee judicial independence.[189] In addition, judges are required to render justice in accordance with the law and their conscience.[190] Moreover, judicial decisions are required to be in writing, well-reasoned and supported in law and in fact.[191] This is to pre-empt judicial arbitrariness and provide scope for accountability through a process of appeal or through public scrutiny.[192]

Despite the complementarity of the two concepts, accountability and independence are inherently conflicting, primarily because it is not always possible to determine the appropriate balance between the two concepts. Excessive independence can lead to an unaccountable judiciary whereas an overly accountable judiciary is likely to be deprived of the requisite level of independence. The latter scenario is feasible where the mechanisms to secure independence have been conceived or structured in ways that render the judiciary almost exclusively accountable to one institution, for instance, the executive. Moreover, where the tenure and career progression are exclusively controlled by one institution, the judiciary is unlikely to have the capacity to act independently, at least towards that institution.[193] Independence can be further compromised in a system that is devoid of an objective or transparent mechanism for judicial accountability.

The judiciary in Cameroon exhibits that tension between accountability and independence.[194] As demonstrated earlier, the judiciary is excessively reliant on the executive for appointment, tenure and discipline. Moreover, the disciplinary system is obscure and lacks objectivity. This is a situation that does not augur well for judicial independence. Epuli SCJ, Fonachu JA and Evande J, have condemned the accountability system which lacks objectivity and its punitive focus for which disciplinary files are left interminably open.[195] The judges assert that the system engenders a sense of constant apprehension, a fact which affects a judge's ability to be independent.[196] During a ceremony to mark the beginning of the judicial year in 2011, Martin Rissouk à Milong, then *Procureur Général* at the Supreme Court, questioned whether judges could be independent and act impartially towards the executive when the judiciary is structurally attached to the executive, the career of judges is dependent on the executive and judges have to measure all the consequences of the decisions they make.[197] It may be argued that the inclusion of the HJC in the determination of the judicial tenure is a cooperative mechanism aimed at balancing the oversight of the judiciary. Yet, as already discussed, this is doubtful given the composition of the HJC and its nominal role of making recommendations rather than binding decisions. This fact was condemned in *Kevin Mgwanga Gunme et al v Cameroon*,[198] a complaint to the African Commission on Human and Peoples' Rights against the government of Cameroon. The complainants, the SCNC and Southern Cameroons Peoples' Organisation (SCAPO),[199] complained inter alia about the lack of judicial independence in Cameroon, in breach of article 26 of the African Charter on Human and Peoples' Rights. On that point, the African Commission held that the presence of the President of the Republic and the Minister of Justice and their respective roles in the HJC are 'manifest proof that the judiciary is not independent'.[200] It stated further that '[t]he composition of the HJC by other members is not likely to provide the necessary "checks and balances" against the chairperson, who happens to be the President of the Republic'.[201] The Commission recommended the restructuring of that institution to remove the President and the Minister. That recommendation resonates with the approach taken by the French government in restructuring its equivalent institution to eliminate the role of the President and the Minister[202] as a means of reinforcing the independence of the judiciary.[203] A more objective judicial service institution relies little on the executive. Such arrangements are more prevalent in common law oriented systems where judicial service commissions are predominantly independent of the executive and are more influential in overseeing the judiciary.[204]

A further means by which the accountability of the judiciary undermines its independence is through its financial dependence on the executive. The funding of the judiciary is an important aspect by which the proper administration of the courts can be obtained and also a means to enhance the administration of justice. A system of funding based on transparent and objective criteria makes the judiciary as an institution less susceptible to undue influence and promotes the integrity and competence of individual judges. One way of enhancing financial independence is by charging the judiciary's budget to a consolidated fund which is not controlled exclusively by one institution.[205] A judiciary that is dependent on one institution for its funding and lacks the qualities of objectivity and transparency is likely to be susceptible to undue influence from that institution.[206]

That is regrettably the position in Cameroon where the judiciary's budget is not a fixed percentage of the national budget. As a department in the Ministry of Justice, its budget is inextricably linked to that of the Ministry. That invariably impacts on the mechanisms for providing the remuneration and allowances of judges which are determined by the executive through decrees that are susceptible to erratic changes.[207] The lack of objectivity and transparency provides an additional dimension through which the independence of the judiciary is undermined[208] and judges have described the situation as objectionable and a threat to their independence.[209] This has been noted in relation to the discriminatory augmentation of the salaries and allowances of judges involved in presidential and parliamentary elections.[210] Prior to the establishment of the Constitutional Council, the *Bertelsmann Stiftung* reported that Supreme Court judges who were involved in overseeing electoral processes received regular salary increases.[211] In response to the challenges facing the judiciary, Maurice Kamto has advocated for the creation of an independent institution with competence in matters relating to the funding of the judiciary.[212] He contends that such an approach has potential to secure judicial independence.

D. The prosecutor in the judicial landscape

Prosecution and adjudication are inherently separate functions, although in Cameroon that distinction is increasingly blurred. As noted earlier, judges assume the role of adjudicators or prosecutors at different points in their career. There is, however, a normative distinction particularly in terms of the hierarchical relationship between the Ministry of Justice and the LD. The judiciary is considered a department in the Ministry and is hierarchically linked to it through the LD which is made up of prosecutors. The *Procureur Général* who is head of the LD is central to that relationship as he provides the hierarchical link with the Ministry.[213] The relationship is underpinned by the principle of subordination to hierarchy which proceeds on the assumption that prosecutors are answerable to the Minister (through the hierarchy of the *Procureur Général*).[214] That relationship is sometimes perceived as a good accountability mechanism.[215] Emmanuel Ndjere, for instance, asserts that the hierarchical relationship between the judiciary and the Ministry is an instrumental one.[216] It is the means by which the Minister, as the representative of the executive in the Judiciary, can coordinate and harmonise judicial politics in his department to conform to public policy objectives such as maintaining peace and public order, which are necessary for economic development.[217] Similarly, Kamto is of the view that it is a system of accountability that ensures the consistent and impartial application of the law.[218] While acknowledging the excessive dependence of the judiciary on the executive, he argues further that the relationship would be necessary to maintain law and order and to prevent the development of an errant judiciary.[219] This may well be the case if the prosecutorial service were distinctively separated from the judicial services. Thus, while those arguments may sound compelling, there is need to take into account further implications for the judiciary.

A principal implication of that relationship of subordination is that prosecutors are required to act in accordance with the instructions of the Minister,[220] failure of which may attract a disciplinary sanction. That position was confirmed by the government in its Fourth Periodic Report to the UN Human Rights Committee when it reiterated that prosecutors were 'bound to respect the principle of subordination to hierarchy' since they represent the executive in the judiciary.[221] This may be contrasted with judges of the bench who are required to act according to the law and their conscience. A problem with the hierarchical subordination of the LD is that prosecutors act only at the instance of the Minister who must give them specific instructions on matters relating to prosecution of criminal offences, particularly those involving senior public officials.[222] The effect is to limit the independence and initiative of prosecutors.[223] It also creates room for the political interference of the executive in cases where it has a specific interest to prosecute.

A further controversy of the system inheres in the fact that prosecutors can become judges of the bench who should hear and determine cases applying the law and their conscience impartially. The problem is that a prosecutor who has been subordinated to the executive due to the requirement to be subordinate may not necessarily be disposed to independent initiative when they sit on the bench. Moreover, as demonstrated earlier, it is the same executive that determines important aspects of their career. Those two factors combine to provide an environment that is unconducive to independence. Irrespective of whether the former prosecutor is now a judge of the bench and no longer required to submit to the will of the Minister, it is still a fact that judges of the bench belong to a judiciary that is dependent on the executive. Their tenure is still determined by the executive through arbitrary processes. Fonachu JA notes that due to the dependence of the judiciary on the Ministry of Justice, 'a judge feels compelled to respond positively to the dictates' of those that determine their career.[224] Moreover, it is not very convincing that psychologically, a former prosecutor would feel completely detached from the LD or the Minister. According to Anyangwe, judges who have served as prosecutors cannot 'suddenly become independent and fearless' and are more likely to act as prosecutor than impartial judges.[225] This resonates with the argument relating to the transfer of judges to the LD as a disciplinary measure aimed at 'cowing' judges into submission.

The International Bar Association has condemned this system noting that the inter-changeability of judicial functions creates insecurity in the judicial tenure and severely compromises the independence of judges.[226] In France where a similar system applies, empirical research has demonstrated that some judges have found it difficult to determine their actual status and assert that the problem results from the fact that they 'have multiple functions'.[227] As such, they sometimes question whether they are judges or prosecutors.[228] A recent decision of the Court of Justice of the European Union regarding the relationship between the prosecutor and the judiciary in Germany and Lithuania unveils the international perspective on the issue. In Germany, in particular, the Court held that the prosecutor's office in not an independent judicial authority on the basis that the prosecutor is part of an administrative hierarchy headed by the Minster of Justice and therefore exposed to the risk of political interference.[229] This decision makes it even more problematic to argue, as Kamto has done, in favour of the relationship between the LD and the Ministry of Justice and the alternating functions of judges in Cameroon. As discussed, this relationship is inimical to judicial independence conceptually and as a matter of its practical application to Cameroon.

E. Judicial scrutiny of the executive

The main mechanism by which the judiciary performs oversight of the executive is through judicial review of administrative acts. The system of review is closely modelled on that of France which has a specialised jurisdiction for administrative authorities. This is partly an upshot of the French approach to the principle of separation of power which has the effect of subordinating the judiciary to the executive. A necessary implication is that executive or administrative authorities must be tried by a specialised court rather than the ordinary judiciary. In Cameroon, jurisdiction in administrative review is vested in lower Administrative Courts with appeals going exclusively to the Administrative Bench of the Supreme Court.[230] This section will discuss some of the most salient issues relating to judicial review such as the scope of review, matters exempt from review and the problem of lack of judicial power.[231]

I. Scope of review

Administrative courts have jurisdiction to hear petitions emanating from the acts of administrative authorities carried out in their capacity as administrative officials. Thus, they have competence to entertain petitions for the annulment of ultra vires or unlawful acts, claims for damages resulting from an administrative act, disputes emanating from contracts or public service concessions, disputes relating to state land and disputes emanating from the application of procedures on the maintenance of law and order.[232] Ultra vires acts include acts that are bad in form, acts made without jurisdiction, acts that infringe a legal provision or constitute an abuse of authority.[233] Additionally, a decision which is materially inaccurate or based on an inaccurate interpretation of the law constitutes a breach of authority.[234]

The administrative Bench of the Supreme Court, sitting at first instance in *Cameroon Music Corporation (CMC) v Ministry of Culture*[235] has applied its powers to annul an administrative decision. This action was initiated by the Cameroon Music Corporation (CMC), an organisation responsible for regulating copyright and related rights of musical artists in Cameroon. It challenged an earlier decision[236] of the Minister of Culture, Ama Muna, dissolving the CMC on the basis of inefficient management. The Minister had arbitrarily taken over the management of the CMC and subsequently, unilaterally created a separate organisation to replace the defunct CMC. The Court held that the Minister's decision was not taken in the interest of public order or public security and instead had the potential to cause permanent damage to the CMC. As a result, the decision was annulled.[237]

An essential criteria which must be fulfilled is that the impugned act must be performed by a respondent in their capacity as an executive or administrative official.[238] Where the impugned acts are not performed in an official capacity, they will still be subject to judicial scrutiny. However, the competent courts would be the ordinary courts such as the high courts.[239] Impugned acts performed under that category are known as *voies de fait,* a doctrine of French administrative law. It was introduced in Cameroon in *Nve Ndongo v Ngaba Victor*[240] and incorporated into the legal order under the 1972 Supreme Court Ordinance.[241] The doctrine proceeds on the understanding that the action of an administrative authority can be challenged in the ordinary courts on the basis that it is so irregular or arbitrary that it loses its administrative character. In that context, it is considered as the personal act of that individual because it has lost its administrative character. It is a formidable means by which executive arbitrariness can be curbed particularly in an effort to protect human right.[242]

A classic example was demonstrated in the *Wakai case* mentioned earlier. In that case, as a result of the upheavals following the proclamation of the presidential election results, a state of emergency was proclaimed. Executive officials proceeded to effect mass arrests of supporters of the main opposition party SDF, among whom where the plaintiffs. They made an application to the Mezam High Court to be released on bail. Their arrest and detention was tainted by irregularities which included arrests without warrants and night arrests contrary to the law and the issuing of backdated warrants to legalise unlawful detentions. Irregularities also included detentions beyond the limit imposed by the emergency legislation. Moreover, some individuals were arrested in different jurisdictions but were transferred to the restive zones to be made subject to the emergency legislation. In the view of the court, the irregularities were so severe that they lost their administrative character; therefore, the bail application could be heard in the Mezam High Court, an ordinary court.

The doctrine of *voies de fait* has also been applied in *Senior Divisional Officer (SDO) Oku v Shey Ndifon & Oku Rural Radio Association (ORRA),*[243] where the Senior Divisional Officer for Oku repeatedly and unlawfully interfered with the operation of the Oku Rural Radio. He unlawfully formed a commission to audit the accounts of the ORRA, appointing himself as chair of the commission with remuneration of 180,000 CFA from the accounts of that Association. He subsequently suspended the Board of ORRA and when a new Board was appointed by ORRA's coordinating committee, the SDO issued an administrative order dissolving that and indefinitely suspending the Station Manager. Due to the repeated interference, ORRA was pre-empted from its broadcasting service. The Court held that the acts of the SDO were manifestly arbitrary and that he had no authority to interfere with the management of a private entity such as the ORRA. He was held personally liable for the damages to the Association and ordered to desist from further interference.

It can be seen from the aforementioned information that the actions of executive officials can be subject to judicial scrutiny whether they act in their official capacity or where they act arbitrarily.

II. Exemptions from judicial scrutiny: actes de gouvernement

In spite of the jurisdiction of the courts in scrutinising executive officials, not all executive acts can be subject to scrutiny. There is a specific category of acts known as *actes de gouvernement* which are exempt from judicial scrutiny. According to section 4 of the Administrative Courts Law, no court shall have jurisdiction over acts of the government. The doctrine of *actes de gouvernement* is an ancient French doctrine which pre-empts judicial review of regulatory measures taken by executive officials such as the President, the Prime Minister and Minister of External Relations.[244] The acts or measures are those taken in the context of the constitutional relationship between the executive and the legislature and the government's foreign or diplomatic relations.[245] Their essential characteristic is that they are politically motivated.[246] According to the Supreme Court in *Kouang Guillaume*, the rational for jurisdictional immunity is the preservation of the state and the maintenance of public order.[247] The Court went further to state that, by granting such wide powers to the executive, the legislator intended to allow political authorities to act without interference from the judiciary and without the apprehension of acrimonious conflicts with political powers. The effect is that the administrative judge is given powers over ordinary administrative acts, while allowing political powers some degree of jurisdictional immunity which is indispensable for them to act without constraints. It follows that if measures are taken to preserve the state or public order, submitting them to review can have severe consequences.[248]

Although the law does not identify or outline any specific acts or measures in that category, the Supreme Court (embracing the approach in France) has provided some indication of what they may be.[249] They include regulatory measures relating to parliamentary elections, convening of the electoral college prior to legislative elections, convening of the first session of a new parliament, the government's right to initiate bills in parliament, requesting a second reading and withdrawal of a bill or failure to introduce a bill, negotiating or ratifying international treaties or agreements, treaty enforcement measures and instructions to diplomatic officials.[250] The Court in a later decision considered that category incomplete and not specifically reflective of the political context of Cameroon or the discretionary powers of the President.[251] The Court held that it did not take into account some powers which have no distinctive legal or political character such as discretional powers to award damages to victims of terrorism.[252] Other measures which have been identified in the jurisprudence of the Court include the appointment of officials to government and other public institutions[253] and measures taken in the context of the suppression of terrorism.[254]

In view of the nature of the acts exempt from scrutiny, it can be argued that it is a weakness in the governance and checks and balances system in Cameroon. Those are acts that can have significant consequences on individual rights and effective public administration. Yet, the acts cannot be scrutinised irrespective of the potential severity of their consequences. Consider, for instance, the fact that as discussed in Chapter 3, the President of the Republic is almost unaccountable legally or politically despite his overwhelming powers. The President is vested with extensive regulatory powers which have been exercised to circumscribe some fundamental rights and the independence of institutions such as ELECAM charged with the responsibility of overseeing the exercise of some democratic rights. Moreover, unlike the clearly defined scope of the legislative competence of parliament, the legislative scope of the President is indeterminate such that he can assume competence over every aspect which is not under parliament's responsibility. Considering the breadth of those powers it is important that some oversight mechanism is available to regulate their effective exercise to ensure that regulatory powers are not used arbitrarily, particularly to undermine fundamental constitutional rights and principles. In *Social Democratic Front v État du Cameroun*,[255] the main opposition party (SDF) petitioned the Supreme Court to declare null and void the 2008 presidential decree appointing ELECAM members.[256] The petitioner argued that the appointment of members of the ruling CPDM party to that institution contradicted the incompatibility, neutrality and impartiality safeguards provided in sections 11 and 13 of the ELECAM Law. The petition was dismissed on the basis that the impugned decree was issued by the President in the exercise of his regulatory powers. That constituted an act of the government for which no court was vested with powers of review.[257] That decision is disappointing bearing in mind the potentially negative effect an impartial composition of ELECAM may have on free and fair elections, thereby undermining democratic rights. Similarly, in *Mvogo Jean-Marie v État du Cameroun*,[258] a presidential decree appointing a consular officer was held to be an act of the government, which could not be subjected to judicial review.

The position in Cameroon is at odds with contemporary international standards which require executive decrees to be subject to review as a means of preventing executive arbitrariness. This requirement was affirmed in *Civil Liberties Organisation v Nigeria*,[259] where the African Commission on Human and Peoples' Rights condemned the ousting of the jurisdiction of the courts from reviewing executive decrees as an 'invidious attack on human rights'. In France, the courts have attempted to limit the effect of the exemption when fundamental rights are threatened. Thus, regulatory acts emanating from the executive can be challenged in the *Conseil d'État* and the *Cour de Cassation* where they adversely affect the exercise of fundamental rights.[260] Perhaps, a similar approach can be adopted by the courts in Cameroon to ensure at least that fundamental rights and other fundamental constitutional principles are not jeopardised. The rigorous application of such a controversial doctrine in Cameroon only serves to entrench excessive executive hegemony.

F. *Judicial power and the enforceability of judgments*

In addition to the problem of lack of individual and institutional independence, judicial power to effectively exercise oversight of the executive is limited by the inability to enforce judgments rendered against executive officials.[261] The latter aspect has been partially demonstrated in some cases discussed earlier.[262]

The inability to enforce judgments against the executive results from the deep-seated culture of executive contempt of the courts[263] which explains why judges are sometimes harassed by security forces.[264] In January 2011, for instance, a State Counsel for Tignere, Faro and Deo Division in the Adamawa region was severely beaten by soldiers of the Rapid Intervention Battalion (BIR) when he attempted to stop them from harassing a civilian.[265] One area where executive contempt is prominent is in matters relating to arbitrary detention. This was demonstrated in *D S Oyebowale v Company Commander Fako*[266] where a Nigerian sailor was arbitrarily arrested by the Company Commander of the Gendarmerie Company for Fako Division, on the high seas, on his way to Cameroon. There were no apparent reasons for his arrest, neither were any charges read to him at the time of the arrest. He was later detained in Cameroon, still without being informed of the reasons for his arrest or detention. He made an application for bail to the State Counsel but the process was thwarted by the failure of the respondent to report in Court when summoned. The applicant then made an application for habeas corpus (immediate release) on the basis of his unlawful detention. The respondent was summoned to appear in Court for the hearing and again he failed to do so. The Court considered the circumstances of the applicant's arrest and determined that the arrest was lawful. It consequently ordered the immediate release of the applicant. Yet, this order was flouted by the respondent. Regrettably, his repeated contemptuous conduct was neither condemned by the LD nor the Governor of the South-West region, his administrative superior. Such unbounded contempt for the judiciary was also demonstrated in *Albert Chidi v The People*,[267] where a Nigerian resident in Cameroon was arrested and detained by security officers and was allegedly tortured while in detention. His resident permit and passports were confiscated by the officers, although they alleged that he was an illegal immigrant. He successfully applied to the Court for bail and the return of his documents. However, the security officers failed to release him.

The culture of executive disregard for court orders is symptomatic of the subordinate relationship of the judiciary in relation to the executive and the fact that the enforceability of court decisions is dependent on the executive. As with a classic separation of powers system, the execution of judgment is the responsibility of the executive. The system in Cameroon is that, the Ministry of Justice supervises and controls the execution of judgments pronounced by criminal courts[268] and this is done through the LD which has the responsibility to supervise the enforcement of judgments.[269] To exercise that role, the LD acts in conjunction with security forces such as the police.

A major problem with the dependence of the judiciary on the executive is that due to the subordinate position of the LD to the Ministry, there is a limit on the extent to which it can enhance enforceability. Bearing in mind that the career of judges depends on the executive, their actions have to accord with the instructions of the executive in order to avoid jeopardising their career. In that context, enforcing a decision against the executive is problematic particularly where this has been implicitly or expressly forbidden. In *Nya Henry*, for instance, although the trial judge acted heroically in deciding against the government in such a politically contentious case, the judgment was not enforced. The reason as it later emerged was that the *Procureur Général*, head of the LD, instructed the LD not to enforce the decision.[270] This, sadly, was confirmed by the clerk of the Court and the prosecution, which is part of the LD.[271]

In addition to the unwillingness or the apathy of the LD to facilitate enforcement of court orders, security forces who are mandated to assist the LD[272] also exhibit a similar reluctance or unwillingness. The attitude of the security forces may be explained by their subordination to the President of the Republic who is their Commander in Chief.[273] As discussed in Chapter 2, he is responsible for their appointments and career development and controls them through the Minister of Defence.[274] As with the judiciary, the processes are neither transparent nor objective. Given their dependence on the executive, security officers would naturally be inclined to protect the executive in order to secure their career. In addition, as executive officials themselves, there is a tendency to reinforce the historical subordination of the judiciary to the executive. Thus, police and armed forces as executive officials have the tendency to showcase their political ascendancy by portraying themselves as being accountable to the executive hierarchy rather than the judiciary. In fact in the *Oyebowale case*, the respondent made it clear that he was answerable to the regional Governor (an executive authority) rather than the courts.[275]

The attitude of the executive is symptomatic of a general culture of the absence of the rule of law in Cameroon. Without the political will of the executive, the execution of decisions from the courts remains a herculean task. That explains why Evande J (a High Court judge) was of the view that, where a judgment affects the interest of the government, enforcement is only possible with the executive's cooperation.[276] Regrettably, despite the pervasiveness of the problem, there appears to be limited attempts to eradicate it. Epuli SCJ, once lamented why, '[s]tate officials who maliciously resist the enforcement of court decisions, are not brought to book?'.[277]

Conclusion

The judiciary as demonstrated previously lacks independence as an institution. Its excessive dependence on the executive limits the extent to which it can act as a credible institution and discharge its constitutional mandate effectively. The individual independence of judges is also constrained by their methods of appointment, promotion and discipline. Their dependence on the executive, through mechanisms that are neither objective nor transparent contributes significantly to their inability to be assertive towards the executive. As noted by Fonachu JA, that position of dependence creates 'an unbalanced state of affairs where the executive imposes its will and has significant control over the judiciary'.[278] In effect, although the status of the judiciary was elevated to a 'power' equal to the executive and the legislature, its status continues to be framed by a culture of subordination and dependence on the executive. In its

2017 Report on Human Rights in Cameroon, the Ministry of Justice implicitly affirmed the subordinate role of the judiciary and confirmed that Cameroon's international partners:

> were concerned about the interference of the Executive Power in the management of the Judicial Power through the appointment of Judges, disciplinary procedures and the possibility of the Executive Power to stop proceedings pending before the courts. They recommended that the composition and functioning of the Higher Judicial Council be amended and ensure that the Executive Power does not in any way interfere in the activities of the Judicial Power.[279]

Until such recommendations are heeded, the judiciary remains an institution severely influenced by the executive. Although it has sometimes exercised its independence, such circumstances have been limited and the general environment obviates against that. As a result, the judiciary is not in a position to influence meaningful change in accountable governance and the protection of human rights and fundamental liberties.

Notes

1 Law No. 2006/015 of 29 December 2006 on the Organisation of the Judiciary (Judicial Organisation Law [JOL]) as amended by Law No. 2011/027 of 14 December 2011, s 3.
2 Constitution, art 37–42; Law No. 2006/015 of 29 December 2006 on the Organisation of the Judiciary (JOL); Law No. 2006/016 of 29 December 2006 on the Organisation and Functioning of the Supreme Court (Supreme Court Law).
3 JOL, s 3.
4 JOL, ss 15(1), 18(1).
5 Law No. 2006/022 of 29 December 2006 on the Organisation and Functioning of the Administrative Courts (Administrative Courts Law).
6 Constitution of Cameroon, art 40; Supreme Court Law, s 9.
7 Administrative Courts Law, s 2(1).
8 Administrative Courts Law, s 5(1)(2).
9 Administrative Courts Law, s 6(a).
10 Administrative Courts Law, s 6(b).
11 Administrative Courts Law, s 13 (1).
12 Administrative Courts Law, s 8(2)(c).
13 Administrative Courts Law, s 8(2)(b)(c).
14 Administrative Courts Law, s 8(2).
15 Administrative Courts Law, s 2(2).
16 Administrative Courts Law, s 2(a)(a–e).
17 Administrative Courts Law, s 14(2).
18 Law No. 2006/017 of 29 December 2006, to Lay Down the Organisation, Duties and Functioning of Regional Audit Courts (Regional Audit Courts Law), ss 1, 2(1).
19 Regional Audit Courts Law, s 2(2)(3).
20 Regional Audit Courts Law, s 3(a).
21 Regional Audit Courts Law, s 3(b).
22 Regional Audit Courts Law, s 8(1).

23 Regional Audit Courts Law, s 4(2)(a)(c).
24 Regional Audit Courts Law, s 12.
25 Regional Audit Courts Law, s 9(1).
26 Regional Audit Courts Law, s 9(2)(3).
27 Regional Audit Courts Law, s 67(1).
28 See Constitution, art 41; Regional Audit Courts Law, s 67(2)(b).
29 JOL, s 16(1).
30 JOL, s 16(2).
31 JOL, s 16(1).
32 JOL, s 17(1)(a).
33 JOL, s 17(1)(b).
34 JOL, s 17(1)(c).
35 JOL, s 17(7).
36 JOL, s 17(8).
37 JOL, s 17(9)(a).
38 JOL, s 17(9)(b).
39 JOL, s 17(9)(c).
40 JOL, s 17(9)(f).
41 JOL, s 17 (9)(g).
42 JOL, s 18(1)(a).
43 JOL, s 18(1)(b).
44 JOL, s 18(1)(b).
45 JOL, s 18(1)(b).
46 JOL, s 18(1)(b).
47 JOL, s 18(1)(b).
48 JOL, s 18(1)(c).
49 JOL, s 18(2)(b).
50 JOL, s 18(2)(b).
51 JOL, s 18(2)(a).
52 JOL, s 13(1)(2).
53 JOL, s 13 (1).
54 JOL, s 14(1)(a).
55 JOL, s 14(1)(b).
56 JOL, s 14(1)(c).
57 JOL, s 14(2)(a).
58 JOL, s 14(2)(b).
59 JOL, s 15(4).
60 JOL, s 14(3).
61 JOL, s 14(4)(a).
62 JOL, s 14(4)(b).
63 JOL, s 14(4)(c).
64 JOL, s 14(4)(f).
65 JOL, s 14(4)(g).
66 JOL, s 15(1)(a).
67 JOL, s 15(1)(b).
68 JOL, s 15(1)(b).
69 JOL, s 15(1)(b).
70 JOL, s 15(3)(a)(b).
71 Charles Fombad, *Cameroon Constitutional Law* (Wolters Kluwer 2012) 132.
72 JOL, ss 19(1) (2).
73 JOL, ss 19(1).
74 JOL, s 20(1)(a).
75 JOL, s 20(1)(b).

76 JOL, s 20(2)(a).
77 JOL, s 20(2)(b).
78 JOL, s 20(2)(c).
79 JOL, s 20(2)(f).
80 JOL, s 20(2)(g).
81 JOL, s 22(a)(b)(c), respectively.
82 JOL, s 22(3).
83 JOL, s 21(1).
84 JOL, s 21(2).
85 JOL, s 20(3).
86 Supreme Court Law, s 3.
87 These include, civil, criminal, commercial and social matters and those relating to customary law.
88 Constitution, arts 38(1), 39; Supreme Court Law, s 2.
89 Supreme Court Law, s 4(a).
90 Supreme Court Law, s 4(b).
91 Constitution of Cameroon, art 38(2); Supreme Court Law, s 7(1).
92 Constitution of Cameroon, art 40; Supreme Court Law, s 9.
93 Constitution of Cameroon, art 41; Supreme Court Law, s 10.
94 Constitution of Cameroon, art 39; Supreme Court Law, s 8.
95 Supreme Court Law, s 41(1).
96 Supreme Court Law, s 20.
97 Supreme Court Law, s 7(2).
98 Supreme Court Law, ss 11(1), 12(1).
99 Law No. 2017/14 of 12 July 2017 to amend and supplement some provisions of Law No. 2006/16 of 29 December 2006 to lay down the Organisation and Functioning of the Supreme Court.
100 Supreme Court Law, s 37(a) as amended.
101 Supreme Court Law, s 37-1.
102 Law No. 2017/012 of 12 July 2017 to lay down the Code of Military Justice (Military Justice Code), s 2(1). This law repeals Law No. 2008/015 of 12 December 2008 to Organise Military Justice and to lay down Rules of Procedure before the Military Tribunals.
103 Military Justice Code, s 3(1). However, according to section 3(2), the President of the Republic may set up more than one tribunal in a region or extend the territorial jurisdiction of a tribunal to cover other regions as per service needs.
104 These circumstances are states of emergency and states of siege which may threaten the nation's territorial integrity or its existence, its independence or institutions.
105 Military Justice Code, s 4(1).
106 Military Justice Code, s 4(2).
107 This area of its competence is complemented by Law No. 2014/028 of 14 December 2014 on the Repression of Acts of Terrorism (Terrorism Law).
108 For instance, African Charter on Human and Peoples' Rights, art 7(1)(d); International Covenant on Civil and Political Rights, art 14(1).
109 *Walter Numvi, Che Nji & Kongnso Lawrence v The People*, Suit No. CANWR/MA/3C/2015, SLR 6[2017] 10, 16–17.
110 Law No 2011/28 of 14 December 2011 relating to the creation of the Special Criminal Court as amended by Law No 2012/011 of 16 July 2012, s 1.
111 Special Criminal Court Law, s 3.
112 Special Criminal Court Law, s 4.
113 Special Criminal Court Law, s 4.
114 Special Criminal Court Law, s 2.
115 Special Criminal Court Law, s 11(1).

116 This has been discussed in Chapter 3 in the context of executive accountability.
117 Law No. 90/60 of 19 December 1990 to set up and organise the State Security Court (State Security Court Law).
118 State Security Court Law, s 4(1).
119 State Security Court Law, s 8.
120 See, for instance, Terrorism Law, ss 1–8; Military Justice Code, s 8. For a discussion of that point, see Marc Stéphane Mgba Ndjie, 'De l'application du principe du double degré de juridiction en procédure pénale Camerounaise' (2017) 13 *MISIÓN JURÍDICA: Revista de Derecho y Ciencias Sociales* 93, 102–103.
121 Terrorism Law, s 1(3).
122 Norman Taku, 'Cameroon' in Christof Heyns (ed) *Human Rights Law in Africa* (Kluwer Law International 1997) 140.
123 The French language version of the Constitution refers to *magistrat du siège* to distinguish from prosecutors (art 37(2)). This is the categorisation applied in the judiciary in France and the explanation of that distinction according to the French Ministry of Justice is that while judges 'of the bench' preside over cases, prosecutors otherwise known as '*magistrats debout*' (standing judges), who share the same status as judges 'stand' during judicial proceedings. See Ministère de la Justice (République Française), 'Les Magistrats' www.ado.justice.gouv.fr/php/page.php?ref=3a accessed 10 February 2019.
124 There are also personnel such as clerks, registrars, notaries, bailiffs and judicial police officers, known as auxiliaries of justice who assist in the entire administrative system.
125 Criminal Procedure Code 2006 (hereafter, CPC), art 142(3); JOL, ss 14(1)(b), 17(1)(b).
126 JOL, ss 14(1)(c), 17(1)(c), 20(1)(b); Supreme Court Law 2006, s 4(b); CPC, s 127; Military Justice Code, s 5(1)(c).
127 JOL, s 30(1).
128 State Prosecutor in the Military Tribunals – Military Justice Code, s 5(1)–(c).
129 JOL, s 30(2). In the military tribunals, they are responsible to the Minister of Defence – Military Justice Code, s 6.
130 JOL, s 29(1)(2).
131 Decree No. 2005/122 of 15 April 2005 Organising the Ministry of Justice (hereafter, OMJ), ss 8, 32(1) para 1.
132 Carlson Anyangwe, *The Magistracy and the Bar in Cameroon* (CEPER 1989) 41–42.
133 Augustin K Kouomegni, 'Minister of Communication's Introductory Note to the 1996 Constitutional Amendment' *Fundamental Legal Texts* (vol 1, National Printing Press 1996).
134 Constitution, arts 37(3), 42.
135 Decree No. 95/048 of 8 March 1995 on the Status of the Magistracy (SOM), s 11(1)(b).
136 SOM, ss 11(1), (2).
137 Judges retire at various ages: fifty eight years for first- and second-grade judges, sixty for third-grade judges and sixty five for fourth grade, and judges 'hors hiérarchie'. See SOM, art 71(2) as amended.
138 Constitution of Cameroon, s 37(3).
139 SOM, s 11(1)(a)(b) as amended. See also SOM, s 6(1).
140 United Nations Human Rights Committee (HRC), 'Consideration of Reports Submitted by States Parties under Article 40 of the Covenant on Civil and Political Rights: Fourth Periodic Report of Cameroon' (19–20 July 2010) CCPR/C/CMR/Q/4/Add.1, p 62, para 176–177.
141 ibid 62, para 177.
142 HJC Law (as amended), s 1(1)(2)(3).

143 Judges retire at various ages: fifty eight years for first- and second-grade judges, sixty for third-grade judges and sixty five for fourth grade, and judges 'hors hiérarchie'. See SOM, s 71(2) as amended.

144 SOM, s 71(4).

145 For instance, a previous first president of the Supreme Court (Dipanda Mouelle) had his tenure extended for considerable periods without sufficient justification. His political inclination was apparent in 1992 when he declared the incumbent President Biya winner of the presidential election, in spite of the numerous irregularities that he noted but declared that the Court could do nothing about them. See Charles Fombad, 'The New Cameroonian Constitutional Council in a Comparative Perspective: Progress or Retrogression?' (1998) 42(2) *Journal of African Law* 172, 186.

146 Constitution of Botswana, s 96(4).

147 Constitution of Botswana, s 96(4). The Ghanaian Constitution, ss 144, 145(5), goes even further by laying a more prescriptive time limit for a permissible extension (a maximum of six months for both judges of lower and superior courts).

148 Constitution of Cameroon, art 37(3).

149 Includes the Procureur Général of the Supreme Court and the Courts of Appeal and judges in the Ministry who have attained the level of director or secretary general.

150 SOM, s 31(1) (a)-(f), (2)–(4).

151 SOM, s 32(2), 34(1).

152 SOM, s 34(1).

153 SOM, s 34(2).

154 SOM, ss 36, 39.

155 SOM, s 40; SOM, s 42(3)(4).

156 SOM, s 6(1). See also SOM, s 29(3).

157 Mathias Epuli SCJ, 'Opening Address' (Seminar on 'The Independence of Justice and the Fight Against Corruption in the Judicial System', Yaoundé, March 2006) www.coursupreme.cm/index.php?csc=allocution10 accessed 16 March 2011; Helen Fonachu JA, 'The Criminal Justice System in Cameroon: Problems Faced with regard to Corruption' (Tenth International Training Course on Criminal Justice Response to Corruption, Tokyo, December 2008) 150 www.unafei.or.jp/english/pdf/PDF_rms_all/no76.pdf accessed 16 March 2011; Muambo Evande J, 'Empowering the Judiciary: Making Judicial Power Possible' (2001) 1 *The Imperial Judge: SOWEMAC Judicial Journal* 42, 47–48.

158 Epuli SCJ, 'Opening Address' (n 157); Fonachu JA 'The Criminal Justice System' (n 157) 150; Evande J, 'Empowering the Judiciary' (n 157) 47–48.

159 Constitution, art 37(3) and SOM, art 6(2).

160 Epuli SCJ (n 157); Fonachu JA (n 157) 150; Evande J (n 157) 47–48.

161 Anyangwe (n 132) 42–43; Nelson Enonchong, 'Human Rights Violations by the Executive: Complicity of the Judiciary in Cameroon' (2003) 47 *Journal of African Law* 265, 270; Charles Fombad, 'Cameroon's Emergency Powers: A Recipe for (Un)Constitutional Dictatorship?' (2004) 48 *Journal of African Law* 62, 79.

162 Anyangwe (n 132) 43; Enonchong 'Human Rights Violations' (161) 270; Fombad, 'Cameroon's Emergency Powers' (n 161) 79.

163 *The People v Nya Henry & 4 Others* (2005) 1CCLR, 61.

164 ibid.

165 Enonchong, 'Human Rights Violations' (n 161) 270; Fombad, 'Cameroon's Emergency Powers' (n 161) 79.

166 *Wakai & 172 Others v The People*, 1997 (1CCLR) 127.

167 Fombad, 'Cameroon's Emergency Powers' (n 161) 80; Evande J (n 157) 47.

168 Abdur Shaban, 'Trial of Cameroon Separatist Leaders Ajourned to February 07' *Africa News* (14 January 2019) https://www.africanews.com/2019/01/14/trial-of-cameroon-separatist-leaders-adjourned-to-feb-7// accessed 24 July 2019.

169 Lucien Embom, 'Droits de l'Homme: Amnesty International Épingle le Cameroun' (Yaoundé, 16 December 2012) www.cameroon-info.net/stories/0,39576,@,droits-de-l-homme-amnesty-international-epingle-le-cameroun.html accessed 16 December 2012; Michel Tong, 'Amnesty International Appelle à la Libération de M. T. Atangana et Titus Edzoa' *Journal l'Actu* (17 December 2012) www.camerounactu.net/en/social/social-pool/3078-amnesty-international-appelle-a-la-liberation-de-m-t-atangana-et-titus-edzoa accessed 10 February 2019.

170 Georges Dougueli, 'Cameroun: Atangana et Edzoa, Procès à durée Indéterminée' *Jeune Afrique* (Paris, 27 July 2012) www.jeuneafrique.com/Article/JA2689P018.xmlo/cameroun-justice-process-paul-biyacameroun accessed 13 August 2012; Rodrigue Tongue, 'Rouleau Compresseur: Laurent Esso bloque le verdict de l'affaire Edzoa et Atangana' *Le Messager* (Yaoundé, 19 July 2012) http://cameroon.info.net/stories/0,36115,@,rouleau-compresseur-laurent-esso-bloque-... accessed on 19 July 2012; Nadine Bella, 'Affaire Thierry Atangana: L'Etat fait reprendre le procès' *La Météo* (Yaoundé, 19 July 2012) http://cameroon-info.net/stories/0,36114,@,affaire-thierry-atangana-l-etat-fait-reprendre... accessed 19 July 2012.

171 SOM, art 46.

172 The judicial oath is taken by judges upon their first appointment as members of the judiciary. They swear before God and man to render justice impartially, equally and with regard to the laws and customs of the Cameroonian people, without fear or favour and to conduct themselves with dignity and loyalty. See SOM, art 23.

173 Constitution, art 37(3); HJC Law, s 13(1)(2).

174 SOM, ss 61(2), 50(1)(a); HJC Law, s 26(2).

175 HJC Law, ss 30, 31, 32.

176 SOM, ss 59(3), 60(1); HJC Law, s 34.

177 HJC Law, s 13(2). This is because the recommendations are not binding. Examples of presidential disregard for recommendations of the HJC where demonstrated in 2005 when two judges were sanctioned by presidential decree, despite the HJC's recommendations to sanction 13. See Decrees No. 2006/001 and Decree No. 2006/002 of 3 January 2006 to dismiss a Magistrate. *Cameroon Tribune*, Issue No. 8509/470 (Yaoundé, 4 January 2006).

178 SOM, s 49(1).

179 For instance, Decree No. 2012/208 of 23 April 2012 dismissing a judge of the Audit Bench of the Supreme Court for influence peddling and Fraud.

180 SOM, s 47(1)(c)–(j). For instance, Decree No. 2018/763 of 10 December 2018 dismissing Mrs Marthe Souksouna with forfeiture of pension rights.

181 The judge gained that reputation for sending high-profile executive officials to jail for embezzlement of public funds in the context of the controversial government fight against corruption. He was later alleged to have fallen out of favour with the President for exercising decisional independence. Journal du Cameroon, 'Paul Biya Fires Top Brass Judge, Pascal Magnaguemabe' (7 July 2017) https://www.journalducameroun.com/en/biya-fires-top-brass-judge-pascal-magnaguemabe/ accessed 21 June 2018.

182 Decree No. 2017/359 of 6 July 2017 to Inflict a Disciplinary Sanction on a Legal Officer.

183 Tedlapidus, 'Cameroun-Corruption endémique dans la magistrature: Un premier auteur tout trouvé, Pascal Magnaguembe' (7 July 2017) https://www.cl2p.org/cameroun-corruption-endemique-dans-la-magistrature-un-premier-auteur-tout-trouve-pascal-magnaguembe/ accessed 21 June 2018.

184 Wilson Musa, 'Cameroon: Ayah Paul Abine Sent on Retirement, Son Arrested' *Cameroon-info.net* (Yaoundé, 8 June 2017) http://www.cameroon-info.net/article/cameroon-ayah-paul-abine-sent-on-retirement-son-arrested-290787.html accessed 15 July 2019.

185 Fonachu JA (n 157) 150.

186 Suit No. HCF/HB/002/19.

187 Atia Azohnwi, 'Cameroon: Former Special Criminal Court Judge, Emmanuel Nkea Casts Fresh Doubts over Independence of Cameroon's Judiciary, Says Accountability Remains Farfetched' (6 November 2019) http://www.cameroon-info.net/article/cameroon-former-special-criminal-court-judge-emmanuel-nkea-casts-fresh-doubts-over-independence-of-cameroons-355191.html accessed 20 November 2019.

188 Stephen Burbank, 'The Achitecture of Judicial Independence' (1999) 72 *Southern California Law Review* 315–351; Stephen Burbank, 'The Past and Present of Judicial Independence' (1996) 80(3) *Judicature* 117, 117–118.

189 Constitution, art 37(3).

190 Constitution, art 37 (2). See also SOM, s 5(1) (as amended). Affirmed by the Supreme Court in *Woundjou Samuel v Ministère Public & Kamdem Emillienne*, Arrêt No. 102 of 20 November 2014.

191 JOL, ss 6(4), 7.

192 Laura-Stella Enonchong, 'Judicial Independence and Accountability in Cameroon: Balancing a Tenuous Relationship' (2012) 5(3) *African Journal of Legal Studies* 319.

193 Nuno Garoupa and Tom Ginsburg, 'Guarding the Guardians: Judicial Councils and Judicial Independence' (2009) 57(1) *American Journal of Comparative Law* 103–134

194 For a more exhaustive discussion, see Enonchong, 'Judicial Independence and Accountability' (n 192). See also Jean Calvin Aba'a Oyono, 'L'insécurité Juridique en Matière Constitutionnelle: Questionnement Sélectif sur l'articulation et la Pratique Constitutionnelles au Cameroun' in Maurice Kamto, Stephane Doumbe-Bille and Brusil Metou (eds) *Regards Sur le Droit Public en Afrique* (L'Harmattan 2016) 49–53.

195 Epuli SCJ (n 157); Fonachu JA (n 157) 150; Evande J (n 157) 47–48.

196 ibid.

197 Aba'a Oyono, 'L'insécurité Juridique en Matière Constitutionnelle' (n 194) 52.

198 Kevin Mgwanga *Gunme et al v Cameroon*, Communication No. 266/2003 ACHPR (05/2009), Ex.CL/529(XV) Annex 4.

199 Political organisations advocating secession of the Anglophone minority from the francophone regions.

200 *Gunme et al v Cameroon* (n 198) 39, para 211.

201 ibid 40, para 212.

202 French Constitution, art 65 (as amended). See also la Loi Organique no. 2010-830 du 22 Juillet 2010 which gives effect to French constitutional reforms introduced in 2008. The Minister of Justice retains observatory status in all sessions except disciplinary hearings. Similar amendments have been made to the system in Congo. See DRC Constitution 2006, art 152(2).

203 Vincent Lamanda, 'Discours de M. Vincent Lamanda, Premier Président de la Cour de cassasion' (Audience Solennelle de la Cour de Cassation, Paris, 7 January 2011) www.conseil-superieurdelamagistrature.fr accessed 11 March 2011.

204 For instance, the judicial service commissions of South Africa (Constitution, s 178) and Ghana (Constitution, s 153).

205 This is the approach adopted in some countries like Botswana (Constitution of Botswana, s 117) and Uganda (Constitution of Uganda, s 128(5).

206 For instance, in Malawi and Zimbabwe, the executive has been able to exert undue pressure on the judiciary due to its control of budgetary allocations to the judiciary. See Charles Fombad, 'A Preliminary Assessment of the Prospects for Judicial Independence in Post-1990 African Constitutions' (2007) 2 *Public Law* 233, 247.

207 SOM, s 10(3). See also Evande J (n 157) 48.

208 Maurice Kamto, 'Les Mutations de la Justice Camerounaise à la Lumière des Développements Constitutionnels de 1996' (2000) 1(1) *Reveu Africaine des Sciences Juridiques* 9, 15–16; Anyangwe (n 132) 44.

209 Evande J (n 157) 48.
210 Fombad, 'A Preliminary Assessment' (n 206) 255
211 Bertelsmann Stiftung, 'Bertelsmann Transformation Index 2012- Cameroon Country Report' (Gütersloh: Betlelsmann Stiftung, 2012) 6 www.bti-project.de/fileadmin/Inhalte/reports/2012/pdf accessed 20 July 2012.
212 Kamto, 'Les Mutations de la Justice Camerounaise' (n 208) 15–16.
213 Criminal Procedure Code, ss 60, 128 and 133(2). See also OMJ, ss 8, 32(1), para 1.
214 SOM, s 3(1)
215 Kamto, 'Les Mutations de la Justice Camerounaise' (n 208) 17–18. In relation to the position in France, see Jacqueline Hodgson, *French Criminal Justice: A Comparative Account of the Investigation and Prosecution of Crime in France* (Hart Publishing 2005) 80.
216 Emmanuel Ndjere, *Le Ministère Public ou Parquet* (Volume I, Presses de l'UCAC 2012) 45.
217 ibid.
218 Kamto, 'Les Mutations de la Justice Camerounaise' (n 208) 17–18.
219 ibid.
220 SOM, s. 3(2).
221 United Nations Human Rights Committee (HRC), 'Consideration of Reports Submitted by States Parties under Article 40 of the International Covenant on Civil and Political Rights: 4th Periodic Reports of States Parties: Cameroon' (CCPR/C/CMR/4, 11 May 2009) www.unhcr.org/refworld/docid/4a891ec10.html accessed 10 February 2019, art 104, para 386.
222 Ndjere, *Le Ministère Public* (n 216) 49. See also Fonachu JA (n 157) 150
223 ibid.
224 Fonachu JA (n 157) 150.
225 Anyangwe (n 132) 43.
226 International Bar Association (IBA), 'Review of the Draft Criminal Procedure Code of Cameroon' (IBA Human Rights Institute 2003) 5 www.ibanet.org/Human_Rights_Institute/Work_by_regions/Africa/Cameroon.aspx accessed 9 March 2019.
227 Jacqueline Hodgson, *French Criminal Justice* (n 215) 70.
228 ibid.
229 Joined Cases C-508/18 OG (Public Prosecutor's office of Lübeck) and C-82/19 PPU PI (Public Prosecutor's office of Zwickau) and in Case C-509/18 PF (Prosecutor General of Lithuania).
230 Administrative Courts Law, s 2; Supreme Court Law, s 38.
231 Neville Brown and John Bell, *French Administrative Law* (5th ed, Oxford University Press 1998) 127–128; John Allison, *A Continental Distinction in the Common Law: A Historical and Comparative Perspective on English Public Law* (Oxford University Press 1996) 142.
232 Administrative Courts Law, s 2 (3) (a)-(e).
233 Administrative Courts Law, s 3(a). See for instance *Eglise Presbytérienne du Cameroun*, Ordonnace No. 02/CS/CA of 26 October 1994, where a provincial governor's order prohibiting a religious meeting was annulled for abuse of authority.
234 *Mbarga Symphorien v Etat du Cameroun*, Judgment No. 29/ CS/CA of 03 May 1990.
235 *Cameroon Music Corporation (CMC) v Ministry of Culture*, Judgment No. 192/2011/CS/CA of 07 September 2011.
236 Minister of Culture, Decision No. 0088/MINCULT/CAB of 12 May 2008.
237 Ordonnance No. 0341 Ose/CS/CA/2008 of 19 February 2009.
238 *Jesco Manga Williams v Chantier Naval* (2005) 2 CCLR 99.
239 Administrative Courts Law, s 3(2).
240 *Nve Ndongo v Ngaba Victor*, Decision of the Full Bench of the Federal Supreme Court No. 10 of 17 October 1968.
241 Supreme Court Ordinance 1972, s 9(4).
242 *James* v *Tchoussongou*, (2001) 1 CCLR 730.

243 *Senior Divisional Officer (SDO) Oku v Shey Ndifon & Oku Rural Radio Association*, Suit No. HCB/05M/2003–2004, affd (2005) BCA/17/2005 (unreported).
244 *Kouang Guillaum v État du Cameroun*, Judgment No 66 ADD/CS/CA of 31 May 1979 (unreported). See also John Bell, Sophie Boyron and Simon Whittaker, *Principles of French Law* (2nd ed, Oxford University Press 2009) 179–180; Réné Chapus, 'L'acte de Gouvernement: Monstre ou Victime?' (1958) *Recueil Dalloz*, Chronique II, 5.
245 ibid.
246 ibid.
247 *Kouang Guillaume v État du Cameroun*, Jugement No 53/CS/CA of 26 June 1980 (unreported). See also Jean de Noel Atemengue, 'Les *Actes de Gouvernement* Sont-ils une Catigorie Juridique? Discussion Autour de leur Origine Francaise et de leur Reception Camerounaise' (2000) 12 *African Journal of International and Comparative Law*144, 149–150.
248 Atemengue, 'Les *Actes de Gouvernement*' 149–150.
249 *Kouang Guillaum* (1979) (n 244).
250 ibid.
251 *Kouang Guillaume* (1980) (n 247).
252 ibid.
253 *Social Democratic Front (SDF) v État du Cameroun*, Ordonance No. 01/OSE/CCA/CS/2009 (unreported); *Mvogo Jean-Marie v État du Cameroun*, Judgment No. 1203/CS/CA/1999–2000 (unreported).
254 *Société Forestière de la Sanaga v État du Cameroun*, Arrêt No. 5/CFJ/AP of 15 March 1967 (unreported).
255 *Social Democratic Front (SDF) v État du Cameroun*, Ordonance No. 01/OSE/CCA/CS/2009 (unreported).
256 Decree No. 2008/463 of 30 December 2008. Discussed in Chapter 3.
257 *Social Democratic Front* (n 255) 4–6.
258 *Mvogo Jean-Marie v État du Cameroun*, Judgment No. 1203/CS/CA/1999–2000 (unreported).
259 *Civil Liberties Organization v Nigeria* ACHPR Communication No. 129/94 (1995).
260 Brown and Bell, *French Administrative Law* (n 231) 219–220; Martin Rogolf, 'A Comparison of Constitutionalism in France and the United States' (1997) 49 *Maine Law Review* 21, 75–78.
261 This problem has been discussed extensively in Laura-Stella Enonchong, 'Habeas Corpus under the New Criminal Procedure Code of Cameroon: Progress or Status Quo?' (2014) 14(1) *Oxford University Commonwealth Law Journal* 47.
262 For instance, *Nya Henry*, *Wakai* and *SDO v Shey* discussed previously.
263 See also *Namondo Makake v Bernard O Bilai* Suit No: HCF/164/IR/04–05 (where a senior divisional officer failed to comply with a habeas corpus summons); *Etengeneng J T v The Governor of South West Province*, (1998) 1CCLR, 9 (where a governor failed to comply with a habeas corpus summons). See further *Nji Ignatius v The People*, HCF/22M/03–04 (where security officers refused to release confiscated property contrary to a court order); *Bonu Innocent v Bakongo Simon* (1997) 1 CCLR 142 (where the orders of a State Counsel were disobeyed by a police officer), *Benjamin Itoe v Joseph Ncho*, Suite No. BCA/1/81 of 13 July 1981 (unreported) where an executive officer failed to comply with an injunction.
264 Commonwealth Lawyers Association, 'Statement on the Arrest and Detention of Lawyers and Judges in the Cameroon' (7 February 2017) https://www.ganintegrity.com/portal/country-profiles/cameroon/ accessed 16 November 2019.
265 United States Department of State, 'Country Reports on Human Rights Practices for 2011: Cameroon'. https://cm.usembassy.gov/wp-content/uploads/sites/240/18081420l1Cameroon-HR-report.pdf. accessed 18 December 2018.

266 *D S Oyebowale v Company Commander of Gendarmerie for Fako*. Suit No. HCF/0040/HB/09 (unreported).
267 *Albert Chidi v The People*, Suit No. LM/98/M/2002 (unreported).
268 OMJ, art 32(1), para 3.
269 CPC, s 11.
270 *Nya Henry* (n 163) 64.
271 ibid.
272 CPC, s 11.
273 Constitution, art 8(2).
274 Constitution, art 8(10).
275 Laura-Stella Enonchong, 'Habeas Corpus' (n 261) 57 esp n 68.
276 Evande J (n 157).
277 Epuli SCJ (n 157).
278 Fonachu JA (n 157) 150.
279 Ministry of Justice, 'Report of the Ministry of Justice on Human Rights in Cameroon in 2017' (Yaoundé, October 2018) 220 http://www.minjustice.gov.cm/components/com_flexicontent/uploads/rapport_minjustice_2017_en.pdf accessed 2 June 2019.

References

Aba'a Oyono JC, 'L'insécurité Juridique en Matière Constitutionnelle: Questionnement Sélectif sur l'articulation et la Pratique Constitutionnelles au Cameroun' in Maurice Kamto, Stephane Doumbe-Bille and Brusil Metou (eds) *Regards Sur le Droit Public en Afrique* (L'Harmattan 2016).

Allison J, *A Continental Distinction in the Common Law: A Historical and Comparative Perspective on English Public Law* (Oxford University Press 1996).

Anyangwe C, *The Magistracy and the Bar in Cameroon* (CEPER 1989).

Atemengue JN, 'Les *Actes de Gouvernement* Sont-ils une Catégorie Juridique? Discussion Autour de leur Origine Francaise et de leur Reception Camerounaise' (2000) *12 African Journal of International and Comparative Law* 144.

Azohnwi A, 'Cameroon: Former Special Criminal Court Judge, Emmanuel Nkea Casts Fresh Doubts over Independence of Cameroon's Judiciary, Says Accountability Remains Farfetched' (6 November 2019) http://www.cameroon-info.net/article/cameroon-former-special-criminal-court-judge-emmanuel-nkea-casts-fresh-doubts-over-independence-of-cameroons-355191.html accessed 20 November 2019.

Bell J, Boyron S and Whittaker S, *Principles of French Law* (2nd ed, Oxford University Press 2009).

Bella N, 'Affaire Thierry Atangana: L'Etat fait reprendre le procès' (*La Météo*, Yaoundé, 19 July 2012) http://cameroon-info.net/stories/0,36114,@,affaire-thierry-atangana-l-etat-fait-reprendre... accessed 19 July 2012.

Bertelsmann Stiftung, 'Bertelsmann Transformation Index 2012 – Cameroon Country Report' (Gütersloh: Bertlelsmann Stiftung, 2012) www.bti-project.de/fileadmin/lnhalte/reports/2012/pdf accessed 20 July 2012.

Brown N and Bell J, *French Administrative Law* (5th ed, Oxford University Press 1998).

Burbank S, 'The Past and Present of Judicial Independence' (1996) *80*(3) *Judicature* 117.

Burbank S, 'The Achitecture of Judicial Independence' (1999) *72 Southern California Law Review* 315.

Chapus R, *'L'acte de Gouvernement: Monstre ou Victime?' Recueil Dalloz* (Chronique II 1958) 5.

Commonwealth Lawyers Association, 'Statement on the Arrest and Detention of Lawyers and Judges in the Cameroon' (7 February 2017) https://www.ganintegrity.com/portal/country-profiles/cameroon/ accessed 16 November 2019.

Dougueli G, 'Cameroun: Atangana et Edzoa, Procès à durée Indéterminée' *Jeune Afrique* (Paris, 27 July 2012) www.jeuneafrique.com/Article/JA2689P018.xmlo/cameroun-justice-process-paul-biyacameroun accessed 13 August 2012.

Embom L, 'Droits de l'Homme: Amnesty International Épingle le Cameroun' (Yaoundé 16 December 2012) www.cameroon-info.net/stories/0,39576,@,droits-de-l-homme-amnesty-international-epingle-le-cameroun.html accessed 16 December 2012.

Enonchong L, 'Habeas Corpus under the New Criminal Procedure Code of Cameroon: Progress or Status Quo?' (2014) *14*(1) *Oxford University Commonwealth Law Journal* 47.

Enonchong L 'Judicial Independence and Accountability in Cameroon: Balancing a Tenuous Relationship' (2012) *5*(3) *African Journal of Legal Studies* 319.

Enonchong N, 'Human Rights Violations by the Executive: Complicity of the Judiciary in Cameroon?' (2003) *47 Journal of African Law* 265.

Epuli M, 'Opening Address' (Seminar on 'The Independence of Justice and the Fight Against Corruption in the Judicial System', Yaoundé, March 2006) www.coursupreme.cm/index.php?csc=allocution10 accessed 16 March2011.

Evande M, 'Empowering the Judiciary: Making Judicial Power Possible' (2001) *1 The Imperial Judge: SOWEMAC Judicial Journal* 42.

Fombad C 'The New Cameroonian Constitutional Council in a Comparative Perspective: Progress or Retrogression?' (1998) *42*(2) *Journal of African Law* 172.

Fombad C 'Cameroon's Emergency Powers: A Recipe for (un)constitutional Dictatorship?' (2004) *48 Journal of African Law* 62.

Fombad C 'A Preliminary Assessment of the Prospects for Judicial Independence in Post-1990 African Constitutions' (2007) *2 Public Law* 233.

Fombad C, *Constitutional Law in Cameroon* (Wolters Kluwer 2012).

Fonachu H, 'The Criminal Justice System in Cameroon: Problems Faced with regard to Corruption' (Tenth International Training Course on Criminal Justice Response to Corruption, Tokyo, December 2008) www.unafei.or.jp/english/pdf/PDF_rms_all/no76.pdf accessed 16 March 2011.

Garoupa N and Ginsburg T, 'Guarding the Guardians: Judicial Councils and Judicial Independence' (2009) *57*(1) *American Journal of Comparative Law* 103.

Hodgson J, *French Criminal Justice: A Comparative Account of the Investigation and Prosecution of Crime in France* (Hart Publishing 2005).

International Bar Association (IBA), *'Review of the Draft Criminal Procedure Code of Cameroon'* (IBA Human Rights Institute 2003) 5 www.ibanet.org/Human_Rights_Institute/Work_by_regions/Africa/Cameroon.aspx accessed 9 March 2019.

Journal du Cameroon, 'Paul Biya Fires Top Brass Judge, Pascal Magnaguemabe' (7 July 2017) https://www.journalducameroun.com/en/biya-fires-top-brass-judge-pascal-magnaguemabe/ accessed 21 June 2018.

Kamto M, 'Les Mutations de la Justice Camerounaise à la Lumière des Développements Constitutionnels de 1996' (2000) *1*(1) *Reveu Africaine des Sciences Juridiques* 9.

Kouomegni AK, *'Minister of Communication's Introductory Note to the 1996 Constitutional Amendment' Fundamental Legal Texts* (vol 1, National Printing Press 1996).

Lamanda V, 'Discours de M. Vincent Lamanda, Premier Président de la Cour de Cassassion' (Audience Solennelle de la Cour de Cassation, Paris, 7 January 2011) www.conseil-superieurdelamagistrature.fr accessed 11 March 2011.

Ministère de la Justice (République Française), 'Les Magistrats' www.ado.justice.gouv.fr/php/page.php?ref=3a accessed 10 February 2019.

Ministry of Justice, 'Report of the Ministry of Justice on Human Rights in Cameroon in 2017' (Yaoundé, October 2018) 220 http://www.minjustice.gov.cm/components/com_flexicontent/uploads/rapport_minjustice_2017_en.pdf accessed 02 June 2019.

Musa W, 'Cameroon: Ayah Paul Abine Sent on Retirement, Son Arrested' *Cameroon-info.net* (Yaoundé, 08 June 2017) http://www.cameroon-info.net/article/cameroon-ayah-paul-abine-sent-on-retirement-son-arrested-290787.html accessed 15 July 2019.

Ndjere E, *Le Ministère Public ou Parquet* (vol I, Presses de l'UCAC 2012).

Ndjie MSM, 'De l'application du principe du double degré de juridiction en procédure pénale Camerounaise' (2017) *13 MISIÓN JURÍDICA: Revista de Derecho y Ciencias Sociales* 93.

Rogolf M, 'A Comparison of Constitutionalism in France and the United States' (1997) *49 Maine Law Review* 21.

Shaban A, 'Trial of Cameroon Separatist Leaders Ajourned to February 07' *Africa News* (14 January 2019) https://www.africanews.com/2019/01/14/trial-of-cameroon-separatist-leaders-adjourned-to-feb-7// accessed 24 July 2019.

Taku N, 'Cameroon' in Christof Heyns (ed) *Human Rights Law in Africa* (Kluwer Law International 1997).

Tedlapidus, 'Cameroun-Corruption endémique dans la magistrature: Un premier auteur tout trouvé, Pascal Magnaguembe' (07 July 2017) https://www.cl2p.org/cameroun-corruption-endemique-dans-la-magistrature-un-premier-auteur-tout-trouve-pascal-magnaguembe/ accessed 21 June 2018.

Tong M, 'Amnesty International Appelle à la Libération de M. T. Atangana et Titus Edzoa' *Journal l'Actu* (17 December 2012) www.camerounactu.net/en/social/social-pool/3078-amnesty-international-appelle-a-la-liberation-de-m-t-atangana-et-titus-edzoa accessed 10 February 2019.

Tongue R, 'Rouleau Compresseur: Laurent Esso bloque le verdict de l'affaire Edzoa et Atangana' *Le Messager* (Yaoundé, 19 July 2012) http://cameroon.info.net/stories/0,36115,@,rouleau-compresseur-laurent-esso-bloque-... accessed on 19 July 2012.

United Nations Human Rights Committee (HRC), *'Consideration of Reports Submitted by States Parties under Article 40 of the Covenant on Civil and Political Rights: Fourth Periodic Report of Cameroon'* (19–20 July 2010) CCPR/C/CMR/Q/4/Add.1.

United States Department of State, 'Country Reports on Human Rights Practices for 2011: Cameroon' https://cm.usembassy.gov/wp-content/uploads/sites/240/1808142011Cameroon-HR-report.pdf. accessed 18 December 2018.

5 The Constitutional Council and democratic advancement

Introduction

The Constitutional Council (the Council) is one of the institutions created by the 1996 Constitution in the context of the 1990s transition to multi-party democracy. As would be demonstrated in the subsequent section, it appeared to have been given a significant role in promoting the rule of law and in harnessing the democratisation process. Although the Constitution made provision for the establishment of a Constitutional Council, its first organic law was only enacted in 2004,[1] while the Supreme Court continued to exercise its jurisdiction temporarily.[2] It was not until February 2018 that the first members of the Council were appointed and it eventually went into operation. Part I of this chapter will discuss the structure of the Constitutional Council, examining its composition and jurisdiction as well as the rules on standing and the procedures in the Council. It will additionally examine the role of the Council in protecting constitutional rights and in promoting the democratic advancement of the country. Part II delves into an exploration of a possible alternative approach to constitutional review, in view of the limited mechanism applied by the Council.

Part I. Structure and competence of the Constitutional Council

A. Composition

The Council is composed of eleven members[3] appointed by the President of the Republic for a renewable term of six years.[4] The appointments are based on nominations by the executive, the legislature and the judiciary as follows:

- Three members including the president of the Council, by the President of the Republic
- Three members by the Speaker of the National Assembly (with the Bureau's approval)
- Three members by the speaker of the Senate (with the Bureau's approval)
- Two members by the Higher Judicial Council

In addition to the eleven regular members, former presidents are ex officio members for life.[5] This category would presumably be more relevant when there has been a change of political leadership in Cameroon. The willingness of former presidents to contribute to the debates in the Council and the extent or effect of their contributions, however, remain uncertain. In France, from which the Cameroonian model was adopted, a number of former French presidents have either never sat on the French *Conseil Constitutionnel* or have sat infrequently and others have made minimal contributions.[6] So, in Cameroon, the presence of former presidents may add little to the dynamism of the composition. In addition to the preceding reservations, it is not clear what the role of this category is. For instance, do they have voting rights or merely observer status? What is clear though, in terms of membership, is that it is inconsistent with any other public office whether elected or appointed.[7]

Although members have a six-year term with a possibility for renewal, it may be terminated at the request of the nominating authority or the Council itself for incompatibility of functions or abuse of office, or loss of civil or political rights and for violation of the regime.[8] Nevertheless, the termination must be approved by a two-third majority of the Council. A member is also permitted to terminate their term by resignation.[9]

Members are accorded a number of immunities, including immunity from civil or criminal prosecution.[10] There are, however, circumstances under which arrest or detention may be permitted, but this must occur with the approval of the Council.[11] The circumstances contemplated include where a crime has been committed in flagrante delicto and in the event of a final decision from the courts.[12] In all other circumstances, the Minister of Justice must refer the matter to the president of the Council as soon as possible.[13]

Another important aspect relating to composition is the qualification of members. The Cameroonian approach unsurprisingly clearly mirrors that of France, which favours a wider representation with no specific requirements for legal qualifications. The law only requires nominees to be persons of integrity, with an established professional reputation and renowned competence.[14] In fact, the first members appointed in February 2018 could be said to be persons who are renowned as they have occupied significant administrative positions for decades. In addition, there are notable legal professionals such as the president, Clement Atangana, who has served as president of the Administrative Bench of the Supreme Court[15]; Florence Arrey, a senior judge, who has served both in the Supreme Court of Cameroon and at the International Criminal Tribunal for Rwanda as its vice president[16]; Joseph-Marie Bipoun-Woum, a public law professor, former Dean of the Faculty of Law and Political Science of the University of Yaoundé II and former Minister of Culture and Bah Oumarou Sanda, a trained judge, who has served in the National Assembly and the diplomatic services.[17] Thus, although not specifically required, there is a significant presence of members with a legal background.

There is still a question of whether constitutional jurisdictions in general should, as a matter of principle, be made exclusively of legal professionals. There is some merit in this suggestion. Due to their legal training and experience in the profession, legal professionals and career judges can be deemed to have acquired the relevant competence in the practical interpretation and application of the law. In the particular case of professional judges, they have specific training and competence in judicial reasoning. These are indispensable qualities and skills in carrying out a constitutional court's functions in constitutional review, adjudication and dispute resolution. These skills and qualities have potential to enrich the quality of debates.[18] It has been argued that because legislators are not involved in the practical application of the law, they are not necessarily aware of some of the constraints that may arise from formal application but professional judges have this exposure in the course of their career through adjudicating concrete cases.[19] Thus, the argument that the judges in constitutional jurisdictions should have a professional legal qualification or judicial experience seems justified and widely accepted. This is reflected in the composition of constitutional institutions in other jurisdictions. For instance, the Italian Constitutional Court has fifteen judges selected from retired judges, law professors and lawyers with at least twenty years of experience in practice.[20] Similarly, the South African Constitutional Court is made up of the Chief Justice and Deputy Chief Justice and nine other judges, at least four of whom must have been serving judges at the time of their appointment.[21] Other jurisdictions, however, include diverse professions but give predominant place to legal professionals. This can be seen in the Constitutional Court of Benin, which has seven judges, three of whom are magistrates and two others are law professors or prominent jurists or legal practitioners, with a minimum professional experience of fifteen years.[22] Another example is the German Constitutional Court, which has two panels,[23] each composed obligatorily of six Supreme Court judges and two other judges either law professors and former politicians who, in practice, have usually been regional or federal ministers of justice.[24]

In Cameroon, although the law does not prescribe a specific background and training, the professional background of the first members demonstrates that an important place is accorded to the legal profession. Additionally, professional diversity is recognised through the appointment of members outside of the legal profession. For instance, Paul Nchoji Nkwi, a renowned professor of anthropology. Is that approach necessarily problematic? There is no definitive answer to that question. Perhaps it is best to focus on what diversity may bring to the deliberations of the Council. A diverse composition may enrich deliberations in other ways that are unfamiliar to the legal profession and potentially resulting in a more holistic approach to interpretation and in ensuring compliance with constitutional principles. However, the benefits of diversity may accrue to a system if among other conditions, the members are permitted to express their opinion whether affirming or dissenting with the majority. The value of diversity would be lost where members are constrained by circumstances that prevent them from freely expressing their views. In a typical Kelsenian style constitutional court, dissenting or separate opinions are impermissible.[25] This approach is consistent with the civil law tradition and exemplified by the constitutional courts of Austria, France and Italy where decisions are formally 'unanimous'.[26] This approach has been justified on the basis that the authority of law is perceived to be better protected by a unified voice.[27] Another view, however, is that the practice inherently conceals contentious issues.[28] In Cameroon, there is no express provision on dissenting judgments but the procedure within the Council makes dissenting unfavourable. For every matter that is referred to the Council, a rapporteur is appointed whose role is partly to produce a report on the matter and a draft decision.[29] The members have to demonstrate collegiality, which means presenting a united front. This is partly reflected in the provision that prevents members from abstaining from voting.[30] Once a rapporteur's report has been produced, the members must vote, not necessarily in favour of the Council's position, but a dissenting opinion is not generally expressed or published. This is partly a reason to emphasise the value of legal training as a rapporteur without any form of legal training and experience in reviewing legislation, in adjudication or dispute resolution may potentially render a report, which does not sufficiently or satisfactorily deal with the issues raised in a petition to the Council. The argument is not that a member with a legal background can identify and exhaustively deal with all the potential issues. Nevertheless, their training and experience lend more support to the contention that judicial reasoning and interpretation would form a significant basis for their decisions.

B. Jurisdiction

As a specialised jurisdiction, the Council has a complex amalgamation of duties, both adjudicatory and advisory. However, the three main areas of its jurisdiction include reviewing the constitutionality of laws, the standing orders of parliament and international treaties and conventions[31]; regulating the functioning of state institutions and the regions[32]; and ensuring the regularity of presidential and parliamentary elections and referendum operations (ruling on electoral disputes).[33] These roles are discussed in the subsequent sections in turn.

I. Constitutional review

The framework for constitutional review under the 1996 Constitution replicates many aspects of the 1972 Constitution, although that jurisdiction is now exercised by the Council rather than the Supreme Court. Article 47(1) of the Constitution envisages a preventative control of the constitutionality of laws. At least three main categories of control are contemplated under the current system.

The first category relates to parliament's internal regulations. According to article 47(1), the Council shall give a final ruling on the constitutionality of the Standing Orders of the National Assembly and the Senate, 'prior to their implementation'. Here, there is an obligation for the speaker of the relevant house to refer its Standing Orders to the Council, whether these are newly adopted Orders or amendments to existing Orders.[34] A referral to the Council automatically suspends the enactment of the Standing Orders.[35]

The second category relates to international treaties and agreements. The President of the Republic is vested with authority to negotiate and ratify international treaties and agreements where these fall within the executive's regulatory domain defined by article 27 of the Constitution.[36] Treaties or agreements that fall within parliament's competence as defined by article 26 shall be referred to parliament for authorisation to ratify.[37] The role of the Council is to make a final ruling on the constitutionality of the treaties or agreements prior to their ratification.[38] Unlike the Standing Orders, referral to the Council in this instance is not obligatory. Considering the increasing normative importance of international treaties within the legal system, it is submitted that this is one area where a mandatory referral should have been constitutionally prescribed. The presence of an international treaty with unconstitutional provisions in the domestic legal order may pose significant problems in its implementation and further uncertainties in the application of related domestic provisions. This was the situation with the (old) article 42 of the OHADA Treaty,[39] which originally prescribed French as its working language.[40] This Treaty was ratified by Cameroon despite the inherent unconstitutionality of article 42. This is so because Cameroon is a bilingual country, with both English and French as official languages having an equal constitutional status.[41] A treaty that recognises only one of the official languages of Cameroon is inconsistent with the linguistic equality enshrined in the Constitution. The old article 42 of the OHADA inevitably excluded English-speaking Cameroonians, rendering the practical application of the Treaty problematic. Advocates trained in the common law system, whose working language is English, were vehemently opposed to its application and viewed it with suspicion, contending that it was a 'neo-colonial' imposition from the predominantly French-speaking government of Cameroon.[42] In addition, while judges trained in the French civil law system were inclined to applying it, some trained in the common law system had objections to its application.[43] For instance, in *Akiangan Fombin Sebastian v Foto Joseph & Others*,[44] Paul Ayah, J (as he then was), refused to apply the OHADA Treaty noting emphatically that due to its French-language prescription, the Treaty suffered from self-exclusion in the English-speaking regions of Cameroon. Prior to the revision of article 42 in 2008, this created uncertainty and chaos due to the different approach of the judiciary and indeed the Bar in Cameroon. Although it may be argued that a compulsory review may not have precluded the ratification of the OHADA Treaty, it would have provided the Council, at least, the opportunity to engage with the constitutional issues raised by the Treaty. Moreover, a compulsory review is still a valuable process from a constitutional perspective for the purpose of preserving the supremacy of the Constitution.

The third category of constitutional review relates to the review of legislation. As with the first two categories, the Council shall give a final ruling on the constitutionality of laws prior to their promulgation. It is worthy to note that, 'law', in this instance, is confined to statutory instruments and not regulatory instruments such as executive decrees. This position has been confirmed by the

Council in a matter relating to a regulatory instrument on social security.[45] Although the application was declared inadmissible for want of standing, in its decision, the Council stated that assuming however that the applicant had standing, the subject matter was beyond the jurisdiction of the Council because its competence did not extend to regulatory instruments.

The system of review envisaged by the Constitution is the a prior (pre-legislative) system. An implication is that a challenge is made in the absence of a concrete case. More importantly, a challenge relates to laws that have been adopted by parliament prior to their promulgation,[46] indicating that the scope of constitutional review precludes the review of legislation already in force.[47] There are a number of advantages attributed to this system, although in the specific case of Cameroon, these advantages are outweighed by disadvantages equally attributed to the system. In terms of the advantages, one is that it promotes the idea of constitutionality especially with respect to human rights legislation, on the basis that the issue of its constitutionality would have been determined prior to the enactment of the relevant law.[48] Another advantage inheres in the fact that it adds another dimension to the checks and balances in the constitutional system, since parliament is made to 'police' itself by referring its legislation for review.[49] Additionally, as argued by Louis Favoreu (with respect to the system in France), it can accord a reasonable degree of cohesion within the legal order and its pre-emptive nature has the potential to reduce a floodgate of litigation that can occur with post-legislative review in concrete cases.[50]

Despite the advantages outlined earlier, a closer examination of the system in Cameroon demonstrates that those advantages are notional rather than real, particularly given the fact that (as discussed later) the opportunities for referral to the Council are almost non-existent. Therefore, most often, laws would enter the legal order without scrutiny from the Council. Thus, the disadvantages of the a prior review system tend to be more real for Cameroon. From a human rights perspective, one significant disadvantage is that an unconstitutional provision breaching human rights may continue to apply without any possibility of subjecting it to scrutiny, until such a time as the legislature or the executive may deem its amendment or repeal necessary. Charles Fombad also asserts that the a prior system deprives Cameroon of the potential for review to contribute to the adaptability of legislation to reflect evolving conceptions of rights.[51] A notable example relates to the contemporary understanding of freedom from discrimination that has evolved under international law to include discrimination on the grounds of sexual orientation.[52] Although the Constitution prohibits discrimination,[53] the first harmonised post-independence Penal Code, which entered into force in 1967,[54] prohibited homosexuality and imposed a maximum custodial sentence of five years and a fine of up to 200,000 CFA.[55] This was inherently in breach of the constitutional right to equality and freedom from discrimination. A number of independent reports have indicated a high level of arrests and detention of persons perceived to be homosexuals in Cameroon.[56] Despite the unconstitutionality of that provision of the Penal Code and objurgating from the domestic and international human rights community, it was re-enacted in the new Penal Code promulgated in 2016.[57] It is argued that a mechanism for post-legislative review could provide the opportunity to challenge such impugning provisions, thereby, potentially contributing to the development of the constitutional right to equality and freedom from discrimination. It is recognised that homosexuality is a criminal offence in some Commonwealth African countries, which have mechanisms for post-legislative review. Nevertheless, the recent Botswana case of *Letsweletse v Attorney General*, in which the High Court in Gaborone declared similar provisions of the Botswana Penal Code unconstitutional, lends support to the role of post-legislative review in contributing to the development of constitutional rights. In that case the High Court in Gaborone stated that it was incumbent upon the courts 'that exercise posterior control' to give effect to constituional rights by taking into account the 'expanding scope, content and horisons of human rights'.[58]

The a prior system of review is a heritage of French colonialism in Cameroon and can be seen in other French civil law jurisdictions in Africa. Yet, it must be emphasised that the pitfalls of that system have been noted by France and other African countries. Thus, France in 2008, as part of a broader initiative to modernise the institutions of the fifth French Republic, introduced post-legislative review vesting the *Conseil Contitutionnel* with the authority to review the constitutionality of legislation[59] through a system referred to as *La Question Prioritaire de Constitutionnalité* (QPC).[60] This is similar to the system adopted by other civil law jurisdictions in Africa such as Benin,[61] Congo and Senegal, known as *l'exception d'inconstitutionnalité* (EI). In these systems, an individual involved in proceedings in court may raise the issue of the constitutionality of a statute on the basis that it infringes on their fundamental rights guaranteed by the constitution. The determination of the substantive matter is suspended and the constitutional question is referred by the court to the constitutional jurisdiction for a ruling on constitutionality. The post-legislative nature of the procedure provides the basis for individuals to assert their fundamental rights by challenging legislation that has been enacted and is being enforced.

Cameroon's Constitution provides no such opportunities for post-legislative review. Moreover, the ordinary courts have been clear in affirming their lack of jurisdiction in engaging in QPC or EI.[62] Perhaps the closest mechanism could be through the provision of an advisory opinion. The problem with that mechanism is that it would depend on a referral by political actors who are often unconcerned with the application or interpretation of the law and would most likely have initiated the laws in the first instance. The Council may, however, raise such issues on its own initiative.[63] There is some normative basis for that proposition as the Council has powers to automatically raise issues of public policy and to inform the relevant authority.[64] Therefore, if a matter of public policy is underpinned by a legislative provision that is unconstitutional and the Council finds this to be so, it may raise the issue and inform the relevant authority. It is not clear though, how the authority is required to react to the issue raised by the Council. It may nevertheless provide the basis for a change of public policy to bring it in line with the Constitution.

II. Regulating the functioning of state institutions and the regions

Section 30 of the Constitutional Council Law reiterates the constitutional role of the Council in giving final rulings on disputes between state institutions, between the state and the regions and between the regions. Not much information is provided to elaborate on this role. It is nevertheless an important attribute in the light of the decentralised system provided for under the Constitution. It is feasible to envisage conflicts between existing state institutions and regions in terms of how powers have been devolved and how responsibility is defined within the devolved system. This is not limited to decentralisation. The semi-presidential system of Cameroon and in particular the ambiguous distribution of powers between the executive and the legislature could equally be cause for concern. An interesting question to explore is what happens when the conflict is between the Council itself and another institution such as ELECAM in determining the scope of their powers in regulating elections? Such a controversy has not yet been an issue for determination but it is possible to assume that the Council would still act as an arbiter given that it already performs such an ambiguous role (through its president) in the Commission on the Final Counting of Votes.[65]

III. Ensuring the regularity of elections

By virtue of article 48(1) of the Constitution, the Council shall ensure the regularity of presidential elections, parliamentary elections and referendum operations and proclaim the results thereof.[66] Section 40 of the Constitutional Council Law provides additionally and, perhaps, controversially that the Council shall ensure that voting is free and fair. This, as has been noted, may come into conflict with ELECAM as it has similar responsibilities in that respect.[67] Both provisions, vesting the Council with responsibilities to ensure the 'regularity' and the free and fair nature of the process, appear, upon further examination, to be stating the same objective. Regularity may relate to the expectation that the elections are carried out following the relevant procedures. If so, that ensures freedom and fairness, at least to the extent provided by the law. To discharge that mandate, the Council has been vested with pre- and post-electoral duties that arguably may not provide sufficient scope to do so.

The Council's pre-electoral responsibility in presidential and parliamentary elections is to confirm the eligibility of candidates for presidential and parliamentary elections.[68] In that respect, any aspiring candidate whose candidacy has been rejected can petition the Council for a determinative ruling.[69] Here, it can be seen that the Council's ruling on eligibility can make a difference between a fair process and an unfair one by ensuring at the outset that candidates are not unfairly excluded from contesting the elections.

The Council's role in the post-electoral process evokes considerable controversy. First, the president of the Council is the chair of the National Commission for the Final Counting of Votes (NCFCV), which has the pivotal responsibility of carrying out the final collation and counting of votes from all other electoral sub-commissions.[70] The NCFCV forwards the reports containing, among other things, the result of the elections to be proclaimed by the Council. It is objectionable that the Council is then vested with the monumental responsibility of hearing and giving final rulings on petitions contesting the regularity of the same elections. How can it possibly do so impartially if, as chair of the NCFCV, it has already affirmed the results and subsequently proclaimed them? It is submitted that both subjectively and objectively, justice cannot be seen to be done if the status quo is maintained. Perhaps a more acceptable approach would be to completely exclude the president of the Council from the NCFCV.

C. Access

Access to the Council is one of the features that lend credence to a perception that it is an institution that serves the political organs of the state. To what extent is that view accurate? That question can be answered through a closer examination of the standing requirements. There is a limited category of officials who have standing in the Council, depending on which substantive jurisdiction is being invoked. Thus, in matters relating to the constitutionality of laws, these are the President of the Republic, the speaker of the National Assembly, the speaker of the Senate, one-third of MPs or Senators[71] and heads of regional executives (where the interest of their regions is likely to be affected by legislation).[72] In electoral matters, political parties and candidates who took part in elections have standing, including any persons or officials who acted as representatives of the government during elections.[73] It is obvious from the discussion that the ordinary citizen is excluded from this institution, which may potentially be of great benefits in securing their constitutionally guaranteed rights and ensuring their meaningful participation in the democratic process.

A closer analysis of the system of restriction on standing further demonstrates the factual alienation of the ordinary citizen as a major deficiency of the institutional architecture of the Council. Despite being accessible to certain political actors, their inclination to invoke the jurisdiction of the Council is doubtful. This is particularly so with constitutional adjudication. The President of the Republic is unlikely to challenge any laws as they would have been initiated by the executive (of which he is the head) and or the government. In the light of the fact that the parliament is composed of a largely disciplined and overwhelming majority of the ruling CPDM party, it is also improbable that they would attempt to challenge laws which they would have voted for, in the first place. Regional executives may also challenge laws that affect their regions. This would be a very limited category of laws with very limited scope of application. Additionally, considering that they are appointed by the President of the Republic and they lack institutional independence, they are hardly potential contenders for challenging any laws. Access is further limited as the parliamentary opposition can only succeed in initiating a challenge by obtaining a one-third majority in the National Assembly or Senate. This is not an easy majority to obtain in any democracy and in the specific case of Cameroon, it may be considered a herculean task on account of the current overwhelming CPDM majority in parliament, as discussed in Chapter 3.[74] This is further compounded by the fact that some opposition parties are in coalition with the government. Numerically, the opposition cannot initiate a challenge and their difficulty has been a source of frustration. This was noted in the period leading to the enactment of the Electoral Code. The draft bill contained several provisions implicitly undermining civil and political rights and granting electoral advantages to the incumbent.[75] Despite fierce objections from the opposition, they were unable to use constitutional adjudication to challenge the constitutionality of the specific provisions in the Council.[76] More recently, in relation to the 2019 law[77] on decentralisation, which, among other things, grants a special autonomy status to the North-West and South-West regions, the opposition was unable to mount any meaningful challenge. In spite of their objection to the bill for reasons including the constitutionality of some provisions, no constitutional challenge was initiated. It may be that lacking the requisite numbers to initiate a challenge, the parliamentary opposition considered it worthless to even contemplate that option.

Thus, in terms of constitutional adjudication, the ordinary citizen who is more likely to be affected by legislation, especially those limiting fundamental human rights, has no recourse to challenge unconstitutional provisions. This limitation was evident in a matter[78] challenging the constitutionality of section 322-1 of the Penal Code brought by an ordinary citizen. The impugned provision provides a custodial sentence for a tenant who defaults in their contractual obligation to pay rents on a property for two months. That provision is contrary to the right to personal liberty guaranteed by the Constitution[79] and other international instruments to which Cameroon is a party.[80] Article 11 of the ICCPR in particular prohibits the imprisonment of a person 'merely' on the ground of inability to fulfil a contractual obligation (including payment of a debt). Rent arrears are considered to be debts and while a landlord can take steps to recover such a debt, the steps should be proportionate. The law in Cameroon allows for action that is arguably disproportionate, especially as freedom from imprisonment under article 11 of the ICCPR is absolute. Despite the apparent inconsistency of section 322-1 of the Cameroonian Penal Code with the Constitution and international law, the Council dismissed the application on the basis that the applicant had no standing. This demonstrates clearly the vulnerability of the ordinary citizens and their subjection to possibly oppressive legislation that may continue to apply to them despite their unconstitutionality. The restriction on standing compels dependence on the same politicians who are unlikely and unwilling to challenge the laws that they have initiated or enacted. This can be demonstrated by reference to the 2019 Law on the National Human Rights Commission.[81] The government bill introducing the law stated among other things that the law was intended to strengthen the Commission, to enhance its independence and to comply with the Paris Principles.[82] However, the bill had a number of flaws that undermined several Paris Principles and the independence of the Commission with the effect of undermining its ability to effectively protect human rights guaranteed by the Constitution.[83] These observations were raised by a consortium of civil society human rights organisations, which called on parliament to have the bill reviewed and to have an open consultation process before the law was passed.[84] These calls, of course, were ignored by parliament and the law was passed with neither an open consultation nor submission for constitutional review. If access to the constitutional jurisdiction were open to individuals or groups, the civil society consortium would have had the opportunity to refer the bill to the Council.

With respect to restriction on individual access, Jean Aba'a Oyono has stated that the restriction can be understood on the basis that individuals are not privy to the bills and the debates in parliament prior to promulgation of a law.[85] While this may be the case, it is submitted here that from the perspective of the right to information, a government bill is a public document, which individuals in society should have the freedom to access and to comment on. Human rights law particularly affects individuals and they should be well informed about any government proposals that may potentially affect their rights. From the perspective of democracy, the government should be open and transparent in a way that people can understand the basis of government decisions and policies. In addition, good and effective governance requires that the government should gauge the effect that proposed policies and legislation would have on the public. One way of doing so is to make government bills accessible to the public prior to debates in parliament. Oyono, however, acknowledges that the restriction of standing to a specific class of politicians or authorities potentially renders constitutional justice less dynamic because of the overwhelming influence of the regime and the political system, which is structured in a way that prevents opposition to presidential policy implemented through laws.[86] This argument can be supported by the fact that, as described earlier, even the selected politicians or authorities that have access to the Council in practice would face considerable obstacles in referring matters to the constitutional jurisdiction. In effect, it would appear that only the President can realistically access that jurisdiction. This perhaps explains why Oyono, citing François Mbome, asserts that the notion of constitutional supremacy only exists to the extent that the President recognises it.[87] As such, in his view, the supreme legal order of the state is no longer the Constitution but the President who is the sole guardian of the constitutional hierarchy and therefore the supremacy of the Constitution.[88]

Although this approach of restricting standing to the political branches was adopted from the French model and transplanted to other civil law jurisdictions, the weaknesses of the approach have been acknowledged and countries like France have made significant constitutional reforms allowing individual access to their constitutional jurisdictions. Ordinary citizens can now challenge the constitutionality of laws and a challenge can be raised in the course of litigation in the ordinary courts.[89] In some civil law-oriented jurisdictions in Africa such as Benin[90] and the Democratic Republic of Congo[91], individuals have direct access to the constitutional courts. In view of the fact that the Cameroonian Constitutional Council was created to enhance the democratic process and to strengthen the rule of law in Cameroon, it is disappointing that the 'drafters' of the 1996 Constitution opted for such a restrictive system. In fact, during the constitutional reform process, a proposal for open access to the Council was made to the Technical Committee on Constitutional Matters headed by Joseph Owona.[92] It was rejected by the Committee on the basis that it will lead to a floodgate of petitions that will encumber the Council.[93] That position seems unsupported as similar institutions in other jurisdictions that have open access tend not to be encumbered with a floodgate of cases. In Benin, in particular, individual access has been described as the 'key' aspect that permits the court to discharge its mandate as a protector of human rights.[94] In Cameroon, there is insufficient evidence to support a contention that the Council will be flooded with constitutional petitions.

The position in Cameroon undermines the effective enforcement of fundamental human rights and other constitutional obligations. This is not limited to constitutional adjudication as problems of access can be identified in electoral matters. For instance, section 132(2) of the Electoral Code allows an electoral petition to be lodged by an official who acted as a representative of the government during elections, but does not allow access to representatives of other political parties. This provision undoubtedly grants incumbency advantages and there appears to be no basis to justify the discriminatory treatment of party representatives in electoral procedures. The limitation of this system was exposed when a representative of the SDF opposition party brought a petition against ELECAM, the CPDM and two other opposition parties challenging the results of the 2018 senatorial elections for Lebialem, Kupe-Manengouba and the entire South-West region on the basis of gross irregularities.[95] The petitioner had acted as the SDF representative for the Regional Supervisory Commission. Some of the irregularities complained against included the closing of the polling station before the statutory time thereby disenfranchising voters, the CPDM representative being the sole signatory of the report from the polling station, excluding the other members of the polling commission, none of whom received a copy of that report,[96] in violation of the Electoral Code,[97] the tally sheet accompanying the report being riddled with cancellations that were not endorsed or signed by any of the members of the polling commission.[98] The Council held that, as the petitioner was a representative of an opposition party, he had no standing by virtue of section 132(2) of the Electoral Code. Despite the irregularities that may have marred the legality and credibility of the elections, a representative of an opposition party who witnessed these irregularities was unable to successfully request the intervention of the Council to discharge its mandate in ensuring the regularity of the election process.

D. Procedures before the Constitutional Council

In relation to the procedure in the Council, generally, to deliberate, the minimum composition is nine of its eleven members,[99] while a simple majority can arrive at a binding decision, with every judge voting.[100] Where there is a tie, the president of the Council has the casting vote.[101] The Council is seized by means of a simple application that should generally contain details of the applicant and respondent and well-supported legal and factual grounds for the petition, submitted within specified deadlines.[102] A petition that is manifestly inadmissible would be rejected by a reasoned decision of the Council without further investigations or adversarial procedures.[103] Where a petition is deemed admissible, the president appoints a rapporteur among the members whose role is to examine the petition, to hear the parties (where necessary), to make a report and issue a draft decision.[104] The rapporteur's report is based on an analysis of the facts and legal grounds submitted by the petitioner(s), on documentary evidence provided and investigations carried out.[105] The report and draft decision are submitted to the president who forwards them to the secretary general.[106] The latter, in turn, distributes them to the members as these form the basis of deliberations in the Council, a date for which is fixed by the president.[107] During the hearing, the rapporteur is required to read out the report after which deliberations will follow.[108] The Council may adopt the decision of the rapporteur or amend and adopt it as the decision of the Council.[109]

In addition to the general procedure, there are specific procedural issues relating to the different areas of competence of the Council. In that regard, there are at least two specific areas of interest – constitutional review and electoral petitions.[110] These are examined in the following sections.

I. Constitutional review

In constitutional adjudication, the Council may be seized through a simple petition signed and dated by the petitioner.[111] The petitioner must state their complaint and the legal and factual grounds in support thereof.[112] The President of the Republic and the two houses of parliament must be informed of the petition and a copy thereof sent to them.[113]

A law referred to the Council for review has the effect of suspending its promulgation until the Council has arrived at a decision,[114] which must be rendered within fifteen days or reduced to eight days at the request of the President of the Republic.[115] Following the rapporteur's report, and voting, the Council arrives at a decision declaring the law to be either in conformity with the Constitution or not. In the former case, the suspension on enactment is uplifted and the statutory enactment deadline becomes applicable.[116] In the latter case, there are two possibilities. First, a provision of a law may be declared unconstitutional but it does not affect other provisions of the law. The result is that the parliament would be authorised to pass the law without the expunged provision.[117] Alternatively, the law may be referred to parliament for a new reading.[118] Second, a provision may affect the constitutionality of the entire legislation to the effect that, it would be declared unconstitutional.[119] In that case, the Council makes a declaration prohibiting the enactment or enforcement of the law.[120] The outcome of the declaration of unconstitutionality of an international treaty or agreement is different in that authorisation to sign the agreement or treaty would be deferred until the Constitution is amended.[121]

II. Electoral petitions

Electoral petitions must be addressed to the Council within seventy-two hours of the close of polling.[122] Petitions should be dated and should include the name, address and status of the petitioner and the respondent(s).[123] They must contain the factual and legal grounds on which they are based and the relevant supporting documents.[124] Once received by the secretariat of the Council, they must be posted within twenty-four hours of their filing and notified to the relevant parties who are expected to file their written submissions within forty-eight hours of receipt of the notification.[125] Where necessary (as determined by the Council), the parties may be heard or the Council may order the production of evidence and written submissions or investigations.[126] It should be noted that the hearings of the Council in electoral matters are public.[127] Following the report of the rapporteur and the public hearing, the Council renders its decision.

The requirement for public hearings is an important aspect of transparency, which is vital for democracy. In the electoral petitions relating to the November 2018 presidential election, the public hearings proved to be a significant factor in providing the public the opportunity to witness and appreciate the procedures of the Council. The public hearings demonstrated, among other things, how the Council strenuously avoided engagement with substantive issues relating to the complaints of the petitioners. This was followed live by members of the public who received the information directly without the risk of dilution by second- or third-party reporting. In that respect, the public hearings helped to formulate and, in some cases, reinforce the perception of the Council as an institution that lacked credibility and existed primarily to lend legitimacy to an undemocratic regime.

III. Effect of the Council's decisions

The decisions of the Council are final[128] and binding on all public, administrative, judicial and military authorities, as well as natural and corporate entities.[129] Additionally, they must be enforced without delay.[130] Despite the fact that the decisions are not subject to appeal, they can be amended in the event of a 'material error'.[131] There is no definition of what 'material error' entails but, presumably, this will be determined as the jurisprudence of the Council develops. It is not clear how this may affect the finality of the Council's decision. In terms of dissemination, the law provides that the decisions should be read in public, notified to the interested parties and published in the Official Gazette.[132]

E. Protecting constitutional rights and promoting democratic advancement

As noted earlier, the Council was created in the context of a democratic uprising as part of the strategy to harness the democratic process. The earlier discussion has highlighted several weaknesses in the institutional framework that make it difficult for the Council to achieve that objective. Nevertheless, it also identified areas where the Council can apply its constitutional and statutory powers to adjudicate more positively in favour of democratic advancement. The problem seems to be a convergence of political and institutional factors and the absence of 'judicial activism'.

In addition to the institutional weaknesses discussed earlier, the appointment process militates against the independence of members, a factor which has a potential for enhancing the promotion of party interest rather than the Council acting in the national interest. Although the appointment system discussed earlier appears diverse in the sense that it involves all three arms of the government, a cursory examination reveals significant anomalies, akin to those relating to the appointment of judges in the ordinary judiciary. The President of the Republic has a preponderance in the nomination of members. Of the eleven members, he appoints three, in his capacity as the President of the Republic, including the president of the Council who has the casting vote. As Chair of the Higher Judicial Council (HJC), it can be said that he is also responsible for the two members nominated by the HJC, as a nomination cannot be made without his approval. In addition, as the leader of the CPDM ruling party, he exerts some influence in the nominations made by parliament particularly in the context of the overwhelming influence of the ruling party in the Bureaus of each house, which makes the nomination. This is even the more so with the Senate where 30% of Senators are appointed by the President directly and the speaker of Senate is among the appointees. While this is not per se an indictment on the members' independence, the particular context of Cameroon demonstrates the overwhelming influence of the President on almost all major aspects of political life such that members, who depend on the institution of the presidency for their tenure, tend to be more disposed to act favourably to policies advanced by the ultimate authority in power.[133] Moreover, as the members do not have life tenure, they may be interested in preserving good relations with the nominating authorities in the hope of securing feature appointments.[134] We saw in Chapter 2, the extent of the presidential appointment powers that give the latter significant control over many public and para-public institutions. In addition to that, the Council's members are endowed with a number of benefits and allowances that are determined solely by presidential decree,[135] a situation unfavourable to their independence.

The inadequate institutional system for securing their independence may explain why, in many of the cases decided so far, the Council has adopted an avoidance technique, by shying away from the substantive aspects of complaints and instead favoured a very textual approach to the interpretation of the law. This tendency was apparent in a number of electoral petitions challenging the March 2018 senatorial elections[136] and the November 2018 presidential election[137] where the Council ruled against the petitioners partly on the basis that the irregularities would have no effect on the results as per the relevant statute. The Council failed to delve deeply into what these irregularities were or to attempt to deliver well-reasoned decisions capable of developing the law in the specific areas complained about. An important role of the Council is to ensure the regularity of elections, an element which is important for both present and future elections, as part of the process of enhancing democracy in Cameroon. As such, even where the Council determines that the irregularities would have no effect on the results, it is still important to probe into the problem to ensure that the irregularity does not develop into an institutional practice capable of having more severe consequences in the future. In some of the petitions, the complaints included stuffing of ballot boxes in the presence and in plain sight of electorates,[138] registration of some voters on several electoral registers with the provision of several voter cards.[139] These were serious complaints violating provisions of electoral laws and therefore required further investigations. Yet the Council concerned itself more with the statutory provisions that enabled it to dismiss the petitions rather than taking alternative steps to probe into the irregularities. A failure to at least condemn such unorthodox practices enhanced the Council's perfidiousness. It is submitted that, in such cases, the Council should mandatorily refer the matter to ELECAM for further investigations, and where the allegations relate to possible criminal offences, these should be referred to the prosecutor. The aversive approach of the Council can be contrasted with the approach of the Supreme Courts in Kenya[140] and Malawi,[141] which recently took a firm stance against electoral malpractices by cancelling presidential election results that were fraught with irregularities. In adopting such an approach, both courts demonstrated their willingness to support the rule of law and to promote progressive democratic practices in their countries. The Council in Cameroon is far removed from such activism.

In fact, the Council also adopted the avoidance technique when ELECAM was accused of collusion in the 2018 presidential election,[142] and the petitioner demonstrated that in violation of the Electoral Code,[143] some local polling stations under the supervision of ELECAM permitted high-ranking executive officials such as the Prime Minister, who are supporters of the CPDM, to vote outside of their constituencies. In addition, other authorities who are supporters of the CPDM (for instance, the speaker of the Senate) were allowed to change their constituencies after the time permitted by law and under circumstances that were not contemplated by the law. The petitioner argued that the irregularities cumulatively indicated collusion by ELECAM to favour the CPDM party. Even on that point indicting the impartiality of the national electoral institution, the Council made `no substantive comments, except a referral to the provision of the law that allows it to reject a petition on the ground that it has no effect on the election results. Its role is not only to police the results, but also importantly, the regularity of the *process* that has a bearing on the credibility of the results. The Council appeared disappointingly disingenuous when petitioners complained about the security situation in the North-West and South-West regions, which contributed to a significantly low voter turnout in those regions.[144] The SDF presidential candidate, in particular, argued inter alia that the failure of the government to provide adequate security measures resulted in disenfranchising these populations and, therefore, the results emanating therefrom could neither be representative nor credible given the irregular circumstances in which the election took place.[145] Many voters were also internally displaced due to insecurity and could not access their polling stations. The Council upheld the counterargument of ELECAM that the government had provided adequate security, whereas the petitioner had provided substantial evidence to demonstrate the insecurity in these regions, including the fact that the Prime Minister, Head of Government and other state officials could not vote in their constituencies in the North-West region and had publicly cited insecurity as the reason for their demand to ELECAM to change their polling stations. In addition, the Council was undaunted in affirming that the low voter turnout was only indicative of the popular exercise of the freedom to vote or to abstain from voting and could not be attributed to the insecurity in these regions.[146] It stated further that, in any case, there was no legally prescribed minimum threshold for participation.[147] The Council was, in effect, resisting to acknowledge a matter of fact relating to the insecurity in the North-West and South-West regions, which even the Prime Minister acknowledged. It was clear that the Council was determined to err on the side of caution in order to protect the incumbent regime.

In avoiding to deal with substantive issues, the Council fails to develop statutory and constitutional principles and, instead, entrenches a system that endows considerable advantages to the incumbent government and the ruling CPDM. In another matter initiated by the MRC presidential candidate challenging the impartiality of the Council's members,[148] the Council was disappointingly technical in its approach and overtly keen to maintain the status quo. The petitioner alleged that the members lacked the capacity to be independent and impartial to oversee the regularity and transparency of the presidential election. The grounds raised in support of the allegations included the fact that some of the identified members, including the president of the Council have some affinity with the ruling CPDM party. Others exercised additional functions that were incompatible with their role as Council members. The petitioner requested the Council to forward the petition to the relevant nominating authority, for the 'replacement' of the members to be recused in application of their nominating power under article 51(3) of the Constitution. In the meantime, the Council should apply its powers under section 18 of the Constitutional Council Law, which empowers it, on its own initiative and in regards to 2/3 of its members, to terminate the functions of a member for incompatibilities. The Council did not object to any of the allegations and in particular, in relation to the issue of incompatibilities, the Council failed to examine the specific allegations relating to the incompatibilities of its memebers. Instead, it was keen to highlight that there was no statutory provision dealing with recusal of members of the Council. It determined that recusal must be done through a special procedure. Surprisingly, the Council neither outlined the procedure nor provided the normative basis for it. Nevertheless, it stated that the petitioner lacked standing to initiate that procedure even though it did not outline what the procedure was and the basis for determining that the petitioner had no standing. As a result, the petition was dismissed. Given the significance of the complaint, and the factual grounds raised by the applicant, it is disappointing that the Council did not probe further into the substance of the petition. Although there may not be a statutory provision relating to the recusal of Council members, the implications of the issues raised warranted some judicial activism – a more profound exploration of the issue, and it gave the Council the opportunity to engage in a positive analysis and development of the law on the subject. The Council did not, even in good faith, undertake to explore the matter in the future to obtain clarity. Moreover, it failed to refer to its powers under section 18 of the Constitutional Council Law to determine its applicability in this case.

The Council appears to favour textualism in the interpretation of laws and one of the weaknesses of that approach is that it has the potential to allow members to advance personal preferences especially where constitutional texts are vaguely or broadly worded or where the text is silent on important constitutional provisions.[149] This approach only lends further credence to the perception of the Council as an institution that exists to lend legitimacy to the incumbent regime. The Council can adopt more objectivity in its reasoning, taking into account other considerations such as those based on moral reasoning, practical consequences and structural relationships.[150] This approach promotes the rule of law and arguably will help to dispel perceptions of arbitrariness because its decisions will be well reasoned and objective. The Council should be at the forefront of democratic reform in Cameroon by shaping electoral rules and other relevant rules, by vigorously enforcing constitutional and fundamental human rights and democratic principles. It should demonstrate sincerity in its efforts to resolve electoral disputes. This cannot be done through an avoidance technique or through a focus solely on textualism.

Part II. International treaties and the alternative to constitutional review

A. International law and the domestic legal order

International law plays an important role in the domestic legal order, not least because it extends the range of rights in the country. As noted earlier, the President of the Republic is vested with powers to ratify international treaties and agreements that fall within the reserved legislative domain.[151] For those that fall within the legislative competence of parliament, the latter may authorise the President to ratify the treaty or agreement.[152] Where the Constitutional Council finds a treaty provision incompatible with international law, ratification is deferred until the Constitution is amended.[153] For a treaty to become applicable once duly ratified, it must be published in the official gazette.[154] Application is also subject to reciprocity. However, that requirement may be dispensed with in the application of human rights instruments.[155]

Cameroon operates a monist system, which implies that once the appropriate procedures for ratification and publication have been complied with, an international treaty becomes directly applicable. In addition, international law takes

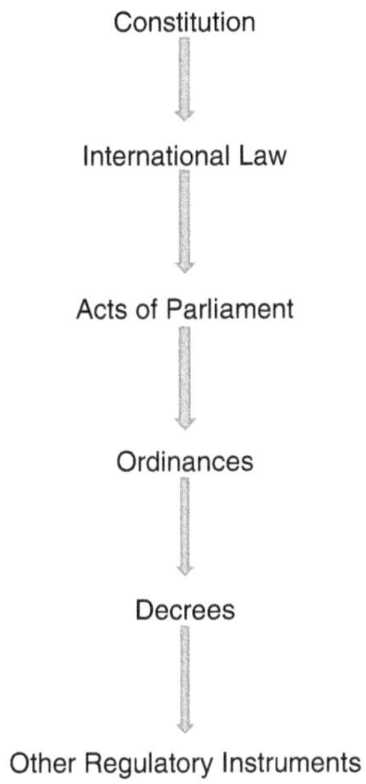

Figure 5.1 Hierarchy of norms in the domestic legal order.

precedence over domestic law (legislative acts ordinances and regulatory instruments). The basis for supremacy is article 45 of the Constitution, which states that, 'Duly approved or ratified treaties and international agreements shall, following their publication, override national laws'. In terms of hierarchy, the position is represented in Figure 5.1.

B. Le contrôle de conventionnalité des lois

The hierarchy depicted earlier, has important implications for issues relating to consistency within the domestic legal order. The Constitution is at the apex of that hierarchy and all other norms obtain their validity from it and, therefore, must be consistent with the Constitution. It can be seen that international law is second in that hierarchy. As international law takes precedence over domestic law, there is a necessary implication that domestic law should comply with international law in order to maintain consistency within the legal order. This may affect the ways in which domestic courts deal with provisions of domestic law that appear to be inconsistent with international law. Although there is no statute expressly empowering the courts to exclude domestic provisions that are incompatible with international law, the courts can adopt such a practice by an implicit reading of article 45 of the Constitution, as requiring compatibility of domestic law with duly ratified international instruments.[156] This practice, known as *Le contrôle de conventionnalité des lois* (*conventionnalité*), has been developed by the ordinary courts in France (the *Cour de Cassation* and the *Conseil d'Etat*) through a reading of article 55 of the French Constitution, which accords precedence to international law.[157] The ordinary courts in France have determined that an implication of article 55 is the requirement of compatibility of domestic law with international law.[158] As a result, through *conventionnalité*, the courts can exclude provisions of domestic law that are incompatible with international law. This has been a very important mechanism for the protection of human rights in France, primarily prior to the constitutional amendments in 2010 that paved the way for the introduction of post-legislative constitutional review.

Conventionnalité is particularly important in Cameroon for at least two specific reasons. First, due to the limited mechanism for constitutional review (pre-legislative) performed by the Council and second, due to the limitation on standing. In Cameroon, because article 45 of the Constitution grants international law precedence over domestic law, there is a constitutional basis for arguing that implicitly, the Constitution requires the compatibility of domestic law with international law.[159] Like their French counterparts, the courts in Cameroon can adopt the practice of *conventionnalité* to review domestic law for compatibility with international law. This will play a significant role in the protection of human rights, particularly in the present context where a number of provisions which infringe on human rights, are being enforced without the possibility of challenging their constitutionality.

The courts are not completely adverse to the application of international law. However, it has not been routinely applied as the basis to exclude the application of domestic provisions that infringe international law.[160] Nevertheless, a recent decision of the Supreme Court demonstrates judicial awareness of the practice of *conventionnalité*. In *Zouhair Fadoul v Omaïs Kassim*,[161] the Supreme Court affirmed the constitutional basis for *conventionnalité*.[162]

The appellant in that case appealed against the decision of the Littoral Court of Appeal rejecting the enforcement in Cameroon of a deed notarised by a notary public in the Republic of Benin. The Appeal Court submitted the notarised deed to an authentication procedure and declared it unenforceable. The Court had based its decision on section 10 of the Law on the Enforcement of Foreign Judgments in Cameroon.[163] That provision requires foreign judgements and other judicial orders and instruments such as notarised deeds to be subjected to additional authentication procedures before they became enforceable in Cameroon. On appeal to the Supreme Court, the appellants argued that section 10 of that domestic law was incompatible with the provisions of article 29 of the General Convention on Judicial Cooperation ratified by Cameroon and Benin. Article 29 provides a list of documents including notarised deeds that are directly enforceable within members states provided they have been issued and certified by the relevant authorities in the member states. This was sufficient to establish authenticity. As the notary public in Benin was the relevant authority, article 29 had been satisfied.

To address the issue, the Supreme Court referred to article 45 of the Constitution that gives international law precedence over domestic law. The Court stated that article 45 implied a system of hierarchy by which subordinate legislation was required to be consistent with superior legislation. Thus, in the present case, section 10 of the Law on Foreign Judgment had to be consistent with article 29 of the General Convention on Judicial Cooperation. In the light of the inconsistency, article 45 of the Constitution empowered the Court to exercise *le contrôle de la conventionnalité* to make the provision of the Convention to prevail over domestic law.[164] The effect of *conventionnalité* was to exclude section 10 of the domestic law from application to the present case. It followed that the notarised deed from Benin should have been enforceable without additional authentication procedures. The Supreme Court, thus, annulled the decision of the Court of Appeal.

Fadoul is important for at least two reasons. Foremost is the fact that is has given effect to the supremacy clause of the Constitution, thus affirming the constitutional basis for *conventionnalité*. Second, it has set a precedent for other ordinary courts in determining the compatibility of domestic law with international law.[165] This implies that domestic provisions, especially those that impinge on the exercise of human rights, can be challenged where they are incompatible with international human rights law.

One significant advantage of *conventionnalité* is that it is exercised by ordinary courts such as the High Courts, the Courts of Appeal and the Supreme Court, which are accessible to ordinary citizens. This is an advantage because the limited system of constitutional review of legislation performed by the Council is only accessible to a defined class of politicians. A further advantage is that it is post legislative. It can be used to exclude the application of legislation that is already in force. Therefore, *conventionnalité*, if well developed, may provide a suitable alternative mechanism to post-legislative constitutional review in Cameroon.

Conclusion

Constitutional jurisdictions are known to play an important part in upholding the rule of law and in protecting constitutional rights and democratic values. This perhaps explains why the 'drafters' of the 1996 Constitution thought that by introducing a Constitutional Council, such values would be promoted or at least it would appear so to the restive populations. After long decades of waiting expectantly for the actual establishment and functioning of the Council, it has become clear that the institution, like many others created under the 1996 Constitution, is a smoke-screen. This chapter has demonstrated that the Council is significantly politicised in terms of its appointment mechanism, which accords very limited de facto independence to the members. In addition, its mandate, especially in the area of constitutional review, is very limited. In electoral matters, the system appears to be a finely tuned web attached to ELECAM to preserve incumbency advantages. It is clear from the Council's institutional structure and its mandate that it serves better the political branches and in particular, like the ordinary judiciary, is very much under the influence of the President of the

Republic. While the Council is still witnessing its embryonic years and thus an argument can be made in support of the fact that it is still on the learning curve, early signals reveal that this institution has limited capacity to develop into a positively influential institution in the political landscape. From its early decisions in the electoral petitions, it has been clear that the Council has neither the independent capacity nor the will to be objective or to embark on a strategy to develop meaningful constitutional jurisprudence.

Notes

1 Law No. 2004/004 of 21 April 2004 on the Organisation and Functioning of the Constitutional Council (Constitutional Council Law).

2 Constitution, art 67(4).

3 The Constitution and organic laws use the term 'members' following the French model. It may be that the term 'judges' is not used because the composition is not limited to professional judges and the institution is not a court, although it adjudicates and interprets the law like an ordinary court.

4 Constitution, art 51; Constitutional Council Law, s 7(1).

5 Constitution, art 51(2); Constitutional Council Law, s 7(3).

6 For instance, Charles De Gaulle never sat on the Council, whereas Sakorzy sat between 2012 and 2013 but resigned after the Council's decision against funding for his presidential campaign bid in 2012 (Decision 2013-156 PDR of 4 July 2013).

7 Law No. 2004/005 of 21 April 2004 relating to the Status of Constitutional Council Membership (Constitutional Council Membership Status Law), art 8.

8 Constitutional Council Membership Status Law, ss 9, 10(1), 19.

9 Constitutional Council Membership Status Law, s 19.

10 Constitutional Council Membership Status Law, ss 11, 12.

11 Constituional Council Membership Status Law, s 10 (1).

12 ibid.

13 Constitutional Council Membership Status Law, s 10 (2).

14 Constitution, art 51(1); Constitutional Council Membership Status Law, art 2.

15 Conference of the Constitutional Jurisdictions of Africa, 'The Constitutional Council of Cameroon Enters into Operation' (7 February 2018) http://www.cjca-conf.org/blog/the-constitutional-council-of-cameroon-enters-into-operation/ accessed 17 June 2019.

16 United Nations International Residual Mechanism for Criminal Tribunals www.irmct.org/en/about/judges/judge-florence-rita-arrey accessed 17 June 2019.

17 Cameroun Tribune, 'Bah Oumarou Sanda: Retour a la Mission' *Cameroun Tribune* (8 February 2018) https://www.cameroon-tribune.cm/article.html/16331/en.html/article-CT accessed 17 June 2019.

18 John Arthur, 'Judicial Review, Democracy and the Special Competency of Judges' in Richard Bellamy (ed) *Constitutionalism, Democracy and Sovereignty: American and European Perspectives* (Aldershot 1996) 68–70; Tom Ginsburg, *Judicial Review in New Democracies: Constitutional Courts in Asian Cases* (Cambridge University Press 2003) 42–43.

19 Alec Stone Sweet, *Governing with Judges: Constitutional Politics in Europe* (Oxford University Press 2000) 196.

20 Constitution of Italy, art 135.

21 Constitution of South Africa, s 174(5).

22 Constitution of Benin, art 115. Members of the Beninese Constitutional Court lauded the fact that its composition also includes non-judicial members adding that

they bring new perspectives to the decision-making process. See Anna Rotman, 'Benin's Constitutional Court: An Institutional Model for Guaranteeing Human Rights' (2004) 17 *Harvard Human Rights Journal* 281, 296.
23 German Constitutional Court Law, art 2(1).
24 German Constitutional Court Law, arts 2(2), (3), 3(2).
25 Tom Ginsburg and Nuno Garoupa, 'Building Reputation in Constitutional Courts: Political and Judicial Audiences' (2011) 28(3) *Arizona Journal of International and Comparative Law* 539, 548.
26 ibid.
27 András Jakab, 'Judicial Reasoning in Constitutional Courts: A European Perspective' (2013) 14(8) *German Law Journal* 1215, 1267.
28 ibid.
29 Constitutional Council Law, s 60.
30 Constitutional Council Law, s 13(4).
31 Constitution, art 47(1); Constitutional Council Law, ss 2 and 3(1).
32 Constitution, art 47(1); Constitution of Cameroon, art 47(1); Constitutional Council Law, ss 3, 30.
33 Constitution, art 48; Constitutional Council Law, s 3(2); Electoral Code, s 132(2).
34 Constitutional Council Law, s 21.
35 Constitutional Council Law, s 22.
36 Constitution, art 43.
37 Constitution, art 43.
38 Constitution, art 47(1); Constitutional Council Law, s 20.
39 This provision was amended in 2008 in Quebec and adopts French, English, Spanish and Portuguese as its working languages, although the French version of the Treaty remains authentic.
40 See, in that respect, Nelson Enonchong, 'Harmonisation of Business Law in Africa: Is Article 42 of the OHADA Treaty a Problem?' (2007) 51(1) *Journal of African Law* 95; Martha Tumnde, 'Harmonization of Business Law in Cameroon: Issues, Challenges and Prospects' (2010) 25 *Tulane European and Civil Law Forum* 119.
41 Constitution of Cameroon, art 1(3).
42 Tumnde notes, for instance, the significant number of conferences organised by common law lawyers to discuss some of the constitutional, procedural and practical issues raised by OHADA. See Tumnde, 'Harmonisation of Business Law in Cameroon' (n 40) 127.
43 Tumnde, 'Harmonisation of Business Law in Cameroon' (n 40) 124–125.
44 *Akiangan Fombin Sebastian v Foto Joseph & Others*, Suit No. HCK/3/96 of 6 January 2000 (unreported).
45 Decision No. 02/SCCL/G/SG/CC of 12 February 2019. The application concerned Decree No. 2016/072 of 15 February 2016 relating to certain aspects of the social security system managed by the National Social Insurance Fund.
46 Charles Fombad, 'The New Cameroonian Constitutional Council in a Comparative Perspective: Progress or Retrogression?' (1998) 42(2) *Journal of African Law* 180, 171.
47 For an opposing view, see Enonchong, 'Harmonisation of Business Law in Africa' (n 40) 108.
48 For a general view, see Cynthia Vroom, 'Constitutional Protection of Individual Liberties in France: The *Conseil Constitutionnel* Since 1971' (1988–1989) 63 *Tulane Law Review* 266, 272; Cyril Adjei, 'The Comparative Perspective and the Protection of Human Rights à la Française' (1997) 17(2) *Oxford Journal of Legal Studies* 281, 294–295.
49 Adjei, 'The Comparative Perspective' (n 48) 295.
50 Louis Favoreu, 'Actualité et Légitimité du Contrôle Juridictionnel des Lois en Europe Occidentale' (1984) *Revue du Droit Public et de la Science Politique* 1147, 1187.

51 Charles Fombad, 'Protecting Constitutional Values in Africa: A Comparison of Botswana and Cameroon' (2003) 36(1) *The International and Comparative Law Journal of Southern Africa* 83, 100.
52 For instance, the International Covenant on Civil and Political Rights (ICCPR), arts 2(1), 26. The prohibition of discrimination under articles 2(1) and 26 have been held to include prohibition of discrimination on the grounds of sexual orientation. See the UN Human Rights Committee in *Toonen v Australia*, Communication No. 488/192 UN Doc. (CPR/C/50/D) 488/1992 (1994); *Young v Australia* Communication No. 94/2000 UN Doc. (CCPR/C/78/D/941/2000).
53 Constitution, Preamble paras 5(1)(13), (25).
54 Law No. 67/LF/1of 12 June 1967 Introducing the Cameroonian Penal Code (Penal Code).
55 Penal Code, s 347-1; 200,000 CFA is approximately £270.
56 Human Rights Watch, 'Cameroon: Court Upholds Unjust 'Homosexuality' Conviction' (18 December 2012) www.hrw.org/news/2012/12/18/cameroon-court-upholds-unjust-homosexuality-conviction accessed 18 December 2012; Amnesty International, 'Cameroon Urged to Overhaul Laws Criminalising Gay Relationships' (5 March 2012) www.amnesty.org/en/for-media/press-releases/cameroon-urged-overhaul-laws-criminalizing-gay-relationships-2012-03-05 accessed 29 August 2012; Alternatives Cameroun et al, 'The Status of Lesbian, Gay, Bisexual and Transgender Rights in Cameroon: A Shadow Report' (June 2010) www2.ohchr.org/english/bodies/hrc/docs/ngos/LGBTI_Cameroon_HRC99.pdf accessed 29 August 2012.
57 Law No. 2016/007 of 12 July 2016 relating to the Penal Code, s 347-1.
58 *Letsweletse Motshidiemang v Attorney General* [2019] MAHGB000591-16 (High Court of Botswana at Gaborone).
59 French Constitution 1958, art 61-1 as amended in 2008.
60 QPC translated as Preliminary Rulings on Constitutionality.
61 Constitution of Benin, art 122; Benin Law No. 91/009 of 4 March 1991 relating to the Constitutional Court (as amended by Loi No. 91/009 of 31 May 2001), s 24.
62 Jean Calvin Aba'a Oyono, 'L'insécurité Juridique en Matière Constitutionnelle: Questionnement Sélectif sur l'articulation et la Pratique Constitutionnelles au Cameroun' in Maurice Kamto, Stephane Doumbe-Bille and Brusil Metou (eds) *Regards Sur le Droit Public en Afrique* (L'Harmattan 2016) 60.
63 The Constitutional Council of Benin, interestingly, can, on its own initiative, raise issues of irregularities pertaining to elections. Constitution of Benin, art 117, para 6.
64 Constitutional Council Law, s 19(6).
65 This was discussed in Chapter 3 at pp 6–7.
66 See also Constitutional Council Law, ss 3(2), 40; Electoral Code, s 209.
67 See sections 10 and 11 of the Electoral Code.
68 Constitutional Council Law, ss 43 and 47, respectively.
69 Constitutional Council Law, ss 43, 47.
70 See Chapter 3 at pp 6–7. See also Electoral Code, ss 68, 69.
71 Constitution, art 47(2)(3); Constitutional Council Law, s 19(1).
72 Constitution, arts 57–60.
73 Electoral Code, s 132(2).
74 See Tables 3.1 and 3.2 in Chapter 3.
75 For instance, the restrictive time limit for submitting electoral petitions discussed in Chapter 3 at p 75.
76 Donat Suffo, 'Forum sur le Code Électoral: Le G7 Opte pour une Dynamique Inclusive' *Le Messager* (Douala, 27 August 2012) www.cameroon-info.net/stories/0,37086,@,cameroun-l-opposition-se-taille-un-code-electoral-un-forum-a-regroupe-la-societe.html accessed 27 August 2012.

77 Law No. 2019/024 of 24 December 2019 to Institute the General Code of Regional and Local Authorities.
78 Décision No. 01/SCCL/G/SG/CC of 10 January 2019.
79 Constitution, Preamble, para 10.
80 For instance, ICCPR art 9 and, in particular, art 11.
81 Law No. 2019/014 of 19 July 2019 relating to the Establishment, Organisation and Functioning of the Cameroon Human Rights Commission.
82 Principles relating to the status of National Human Rights Institutions (Paris Principles) (adopted 20 December 1993) UNGA Res 48/134.
83 Centre for Human Rights and Democracy in Africa, 'Concerns over the Bill to Establish a New Cameroon National Human Rights Commission' (Yaoundé, 3 July 2019) https://www.chrda.org/wp-content/uploads/2019/07/CHRDA-Press-Release-Relating-to-National-HR-Commission-Bill.pdf accessed 11 October 2019.
84 ibid.
85 Aba'a Oyono, 'L'insécurité Juridique en Matière Constitutionnelle' (n 62) 58.
86 ibid.
87 ibid.
88 ibid.
89 Loi Organique No. 2009-1523 of 10 December 2009 on the application of article 61-1 of the French Constitution, arts 23(1), (2). The new procedure has been acknowledged as one that empowers ordinary citizens to assert their rights. Edouard Balladur and Hugues Hourdin, 'Comité de Réflexion et de Proposition sur la Modernisation et Le Rééquilibrage des Institutions de La Ve Republique, Une Ve République plus Démocratique' (Documentation Française October 2007) www.ladocumentationfrancaise.fr/rapports-publics/074000697/index.shtml accessed 12 March 2011.
90 Constitution of the Republic of Benin 1990, art 122; Law No. 91/009 of 4 March 1991 (as amended, art 22).
91 Constitution of the Democratic Republic of Congo 2005, art 162.
92 Marcelin Nguélé Abada, 'L'independance des Juridictions Constitutionnelles dans le Constitutionnalisme des Etats Francophone Post Guerre Froide: l'exemple du Conseil Constitutionnel Camerounais' (2010) 4 *Palabres Actuelles: Revue de la Fondation Raponda-Walker pour la Science et la Culture* 47, 61.
93 ibid.
94 Rotman, 'Benin's Constitutional Court' (n 22) 294; Armand Tanoh and Horace Adjolohoun, 'International Law and Human Rights Litigation in Côte d'Ivoire and Benin' in Magnus Killander (ed) *International Law and Domestic Human Rights Litigation in Africa* (PULP 2010) 116–117.
95 Decision No. 008/CE/CC/2018 of 3 April 2018.
96 Decision No. 008/CE/CC/2018 of 3 April 2018, pp 4–6.
97 Electoral Code, ss 115(1), (2).
98 Decision No. 008/CE/CC/2018 of 3 April 2018, p 5, para 2.
99 Constitutional Council Law, s 13(1). However, in the absence of a quorum, a report of that must be made and signed by the president and secretary general of the Council; s 13(2).
100 It should be noted that abstention from voting is impermissible. Constitutional Council Law, s 13(4).
101 Constitutional Council Law, s 13(4).
102 Constitutional Council Law, s 55(1).
103 Constitutional Council Law, s 59(1). Affirmed in Decision No. 001/G/SCT/CC/2018 of 30 July 2018.
104 Constitutional Council Law, s 60.
105 Constitutional Council Law, s 61(1).
106 Constitutional Council Law, s 61(2).

107 Constitutional Council Law, ss 61(2), 62.
108 Constitutional Council Law, s 63.
109 Constitutional Council Law, s 63.
110 Others include referendum operations, opinions and dispute resolutions between institutions and the regions. These are not dealt with here partly because the Council has not been particularly active in these areas. There has been a single referendum operation since independence and the regional authorities are still being set up.
111 Constitutional Council Law, s 19(1).
112 Constitutional Council Law, s 19(2).
113 Constitutional Council Law, s 19(3).
114 Constitution of Cameroon, art 47(3); Constitutional Council Law, art 22.
115 Constitutional Council Law, s 19(4).
116 Constitutional Council Law, art 23. The statutory enactment deadline is fifteen days from the time a law passed by parliament is forwarded to the President of the Republic. Constitution, art 31.
117 Constitutional Council Law, s 26.
118 Constitutional Council Law, s 26.
119 Constitutional Council Law, s 25.
120 Constitution, art 50(2); Constitutional Council Law, s 24.
121 Constitution, art 44.
122 Constitutional Council Law, s 42(1).
123 Constitutional Council Law, s 49.
124 Constitutional Council Law, ss 42(3), 49.
125 Constitutional Council Law, s 42(3).
126 Constitutional Council Law, s 42(2).
127 Constitutional Council Law, s 64.
128 Constitution, art 47(1).
129 Constitution, art 50(1); Constitutional Council Law, s 15(3).
130 Constitutional Council Law, s 15(4).
131 Constitutional Council Law, s 16(1).
132 Constitutional Council Law, s 15(1)(2).
133 A similar view has been expressed by Ginsburg and Garoupa in relation to the appointment of constitutional court judges. See Ginsburg and Garoupa, 'Building Reputation in Constitutional Courts' (n 25) 541.
134 ibid.
135 Constitutional Council Membership Status Law, s 13.
136 See, for instance, Decision No. 09/CE/CC/2018 of 3 April 2018.
137 See, for instance, Decision No. 28/CE/CC/2018 of 16 October 2018; Decision No. 028/G/SRCER/CC/2018 of 17 October 2018; Decision No. 30/CE/CC/2018 of 18 October 2018.
138 Decision No. 28/CE/CC/2018 of 16 October 2018.
139 Decision No. 30/CE/CC/2018 of 18 October 2018.
140 John Mukum Mbaku, 'Kenya: Presidential Elections and the Rule of Law' *The Brookings Institute* (6 September 2019) https://www.brookings.edu/blog/africa-in-focus/2017/09/06/kenya-presidential-elections-and-the-rule-of-law/ accessed 13 December 2019.
141 Golden Matonga and Joseph Cotterill, 'Malawi Court Overturns 2019 Presidential Election Result' *Financial Times* (3 February 2020) https://www.ft.com/content/fbd09b8e-46c2–11ea-aeb3–955839e06441 accessed 3 February 2020.
142 Decision No. 30/CE/CC/2018 of 18 October 2018.
143 ss 74, 82, 83.
144 Decision No. 028/G/SRCER/CC/2018 of 17 October 2018; Decision No. 30/CE/CC/2018 of 18 October 2018.

145 Decision No. 30/CE/CC/2018 of 18 October 2018, p 7–14.
146 Decision No. 30/CE/CC/2018 of 18 October 2018, p 51–52.
147 Decision No. 30/CE/CC/2018 of 18 October 2018, p 52.
148 Decision No.024/CE/CC/2018 of 16 October 2018.
149 Lee Epstein and Thomas Walker, *Constitutional Law for a Changing America: Rights, Liberties, and Justice* (8th edn, CQ Press 2013) 26; Philip Bobbitt, *Constitutional Fate: Theory of the Constitution* (OUP 1982) 26, 37–38.
150 On the role of judicial reasoning and interpretation, see Jakab, 'Judicial Reasoning and Constitutional Courts' (n 27) 1218, 1221.
151 Constitution, art 43.
152 Constitution, art 43.
153 Constitution, art 44.
154 Constitution, art 45.
155 Confirmed in Ministry of Justice of Cameroon, 'Report of the Ministry of Justice on Human Rights in Cameroon 2005' (October 2006) 22 www.minjustice,gov.com accessed 27 April 2010. See also Alioune Sall, 'Le Droit International dans les Nouvelles Constitutions Africains' (1997) 3 *Revue Juridique et Politique, Indépendance et Coopération* 339, 350.
156 For a more in-depth discussion of the application of *conventionnalité* in Cameroon, see Laura-Stella Enonchong, 'International Constitutional Law and Judicial Review of Domestic Human Rights Legislation' (2019) 13(2) *The Vienna Journal on International Constitutional Law* 87.
157 For a brief account of the development of conventionnalité in France, see Enonchong, 'International Constitutional Law' (n 156) 95–97.
158 *Syndicat Général des Ingénieurs-conseils* & *Administration des Douanes v Société des Cafés Jacques Vabre*, Judgment of 24 May 1975, CC (chamber mixte), 1975, DS Jur (Fr) 497; CE, Ass. 20 October 1989, *Nicolo*, Rec. Lebon, 190.
159 Enonchong, 'International Constitutional Law' (n 156) 103–104.
160 ibid 105–108.
161 *Michel Zouhair Fadoul v Omaïs Kassim et Société Omaïs Selecta Sarl*, Arrêt No. 21/Civ/CS/CJ of 15 July 2010 (Ohadata J-12-242) http://www.ohada.com/jurisprudence/ohadata/J-12–242.html accessed 16 March 2017.
162 For a discussion of the case, see Enonchong, 'International Constitutional Law' (n 156) 104–105.
163 Law No. 2007/001 of 19 April 2007 to institute a Judge in Charge of Litigation Related to the Execution of Judgments and Lay Down Conditions for the Enforcement in Cameroon of Foreign Court Decisions, Public Acts and Arbitral Awards.
164 *Fadoul* (n 161) 4.
165 Enonchong, 'International Constitutional Law' (n 156) 109.

References

Aba'a Oyono JC, *'L'insécurité Juridique en Matière Constitutionnelle: Questionnement Sélectif sur l'articulation et la Pratique Constitutionnelles au Cameroun' in Maurice Kamto, Stephane Doumbe-Bille and Brusil Metou* (eds) *Regards Sur le Droit Public en Afrique* (L'Harmattan 2016).

Abada MN, 'L'independance des Juridictions Constitutionnelles dans le Constitutionnalisme des Etats Francophone Post Guerre Froide: l'Exemple du Conseil Constitutionnel Camerounais' (2010) *4 Palabres Actuelles: Revue de la Fondation Raponda-Walker pour la Science et la Culture* 47

Adjei C, 'The Comparative Perspective and the Protection of Human Rights à la Française' (1997) *17*(2) *Oxford Journal of Legal Studies* 281.

Alternatives Cameroun et al, 'The Status of Lesbian, Gay, Bisexual and Transgender

Rights in Cameroon: A Shadow Report' (June 2010) www2.ohchr.org/english/bodies/hrc/docs/ngos/LGBTI_Cameroon_HRC99.pdf accessed 29 August 2012.

Amnesty International, 'Cameroon Urged to Overhaul Laws Criminalising Gay Relationships' (5 March 2012) www.amnesty.org/en/for-media/press-releases/cameroon-urged-overhaul-laws-criminalizing-gay-relationships-2012-03-05 accessed 29 August 2012.

Arthur J, *'Judicial Review, Democracy and the Special Competency of Judges'* in Richard Bellamy (ed), *Constitutionalism, Democracy and Sovereignty: American and European Perspectives* (Aldershot 1996).

Balladur E and Hourdin H, 'Comité de Réflexion et de Proposition sur la Modernisation et Le Rééquilibrage des Institutions de La Ve Republique, Une Ve République plus Démocratique' (Documentation Française, October 2007) www.ladocumentationfrancaise.fr/rapports-publics/074000697/index.shtml accessed 12 March 2011.

Bobbitt P, *Constitutional Fate: Theory of the Constitution* (OUP 1982).

Cameroun Tribune, 'Bah Oumarou Sanda: Retour a la Mission' Cameroun Tribune' (8 February 2018) https://www.cameroon-tribune.cm/article.html/16331/en.html/article-CT accessed 17 June 2019.

Centre for Human Rights and Democracy in Africa, 'Concerns over the Bill to Establish a New Cameroon National Human Rights Commission' (Yaoundé, 3 July 2019) https://www.chrda.org/wp-content/uploads/2019/07/CHRDA-Press-Release-Relating-to-National-HR-Commission-Bill.pdf accessed 11 October 2019.

Conference of the Constitutional Jurisdictions of Africa, 'The Constitutional Council of Cameroon Enters into Operation' (7 February 2018) http://www.cjca-conf.org/blog/the-constitutional-council-of-cameroon-enters-into-operation/ accessed 17 June 2019.

Enonchong L, 'International Constitutional Law and Judicial Review of Domestic Human Rights Legislation' (2019) *13*(2) *The Vienna Journal on International Constitutional Law* 87.

Enonchong N, 'Harmonisation of Business Law in Africa: Is Article 42 of the OHADA Treaty a Problem?' (2007) *51*(1) *Journal of African Law* 95.

Epstein L and Walker T, *Constitutional Law for a Changing America: Rights, Liberties, and Justice* (8th edn, CQ Press 2013).

Favoreu L, *'Actualité et Légitimité du Contrôle Juridictionnel des Lois en Europe Occidentale'* (1984) *Revue du Droit Public et de la Science Politique* 1147.

Fombad C 'The New Cameroonian Constitutional Council in a Comparative Perspective: Progress or Retrogression?' (1998) *42*(2) *Journal of African Law* 180.

Fombad C, 'Protecting Constitutional Values in Africa: A Comparison of Botswana and Cameroon' (2003) *36*(1) *The International and Comparative Law Journal of Southern Africa* 83.

Ginsburg T, *Judicial Review in New Democracies: Constitutional Courts in Asian Cases* (Cambridge University Press 2003).

Ginsburg T and Garoupa N, 'Building Reputation in Constitutional Courts: Political and Judicial Audiences' (2011) *28*(3) *Arizona Journal of International and Comparative Law* 539.

Human Rights Watch, 'Cameroon: Court Upholds Unjust 'Homosexuality' Conviction' (18 December 2012) www.hrw.org/news/2012/12/18/cameroon-court-upholds-unjust-homosexuality-conviction accessed 18 December 2012.

Jakab A, 'Judicial Reasoning in Constitutional Courts: A European Perspective' (2013) *14*(8) *German Law Journal* 1215.

Matonga G and Cotterill J, 'Malawi Court Overturns 2019 Presidential Election Result'

Financial Times (3 February 2020) https://www.ft.com/content/fbd09b8e-46c2–11ea-aeb3–955839e06441 accessed 3 February 2020.

Mbaku JM, 'Kenya: Presidential Elections and the Rule of Law' *The Brookings Institute* (6 September 2019) https://www.brookings.edu/blog/africa-in-focus/2017/09/06/kenya-presidential-elections-and-the-rule-of-law/ accessed 13 December 2019.

Ministry of Justice of Cameroon, 'Report of the Ministry of Justice on Human Rights in Cameroon 2005' (October 2006) 22 www.minjustice,gov.com accessed 27 April 2010.

Rotman A, 'Benin's Constitutional Court: An Institutional Model for Guaranteeing Human Rights' (2004) *17 Harvard Human Rights Journal* 281.

Sall A, 'Le Droit International dans les Nouvelles Constitutions Africains' (1997) *3 Revue Juridique et Politique, Indépendance et Coopération* 339.

Suffo D, 'Forum sur le Code Électoral: Le G7 Opte pour une Dynamique Inclusive' *Le Messager* (Douala, 27 August 2012) www.cameroon-info.net/stories/0,37086,@,cameroun-l-opposition-se-taille-un-code-electoral-un-forum-a-regroupe-la-societe.html accessed 27 August 2012.

Sweet AS, *Governing with Judges: Constitutional Politics in Europe* (Oxford University Press 2000).

Tanoh A and Adjolohoun H, 'International Law and Human Rights Litigation in Côte d'Ivoire and Benin' in Magnus Killander (ed) *International Law and Domestic Human Rights Litigation in Africa* (PULP 2010).

Tumnde M, 'Harmonization of Business Law in Cameroon: Issues, Challenges and Prospects' (2010) *25 Tulane European and Civil Law Forum* 119.

United Nations International Residual Mechanism for Criminal Tribunals www.irmct.org/en/about/judges/judge-florence-rita-arrey accessed 17 June 2019.

Vroom C, 'Constitutional Protection of Individual Liberties in France: The *Conseil Constitutionnel* Since 1971' (1988–1989) *63 Tulane Law Review* 266.

6 Managing diversity

The Anglophone struggle for self-determination

Introduction

Since 2016, Cameroon has been embroiled in a crisis that has led to the resurgence of the Anglophone problem. As we saw in Chapter 1, the problem can be traced to historical grievances against the marginalisation of the Anglophones by the predominantly Francophone government. Despite persistent calls from the Anglophone minority for better recognition by the government, these calls have been largely unheeded. Historically, the government embarked on a strategy of denial of the existence of that problem and promoted a divide and rule policy pitting the South-West region against the North-West region. For many Anglophones, the federal structure that was adopted in 1961, upon reunification, was the ideal form of the state to guarantee the protection of their minority status and to ensure the preservation of their distinctive identity, specifically in the linguistic, education and judicial spheres. For others, a genuine preservation of that identity can only be secured through secession. The government has maintained that the decentralised structure of the state introduced in the 1996 Constitution constitutes the only acceptable approach which underscores the government's policy to unify the country against a single Cameroonian identity and to guarantee respect for difference through circumscribed regional autonomy. This policy has been largely unsuccessful and matters came to a head in 2016 when sectoral demands by teachers and lawyers in the Anglophone regions degenerated into armed struggles between the government and radical secessionist groups. As part of a wider governance initiative to enhance the autonomy of the administrative regions and in particular to resolve the Anglophone crises, a special autonomy status was granted to the North-West and South-West regions within the context of decentralisation.

This chapter examines the opposing approaches to governance proposed relentlessly as solutions to resolving the Anglophone problem. The first section provides a synopsis of the immediate triggers of the armed struggle that has engulfed the North-West and South-West regions. This will be followed by an examination of the government's approach to decentralisation and an analysis of the legislative provisions granting a special autonomy status to the North-West and South-West regions. The two other dominant ideological strands, federalism and secession, are also discussed. The chapter concludes with an outlook for holistic strategies to manage minority grievances in the midst of armed conflicts.

Part I. The immediate triggers of the Anglophone crisis in brief

The current explosion of tension in the Anglophone regions originated on 11 October 2016 when lawyers from the North-West and South-West regions went on strike in protest at the repeated failure of the Ministry of Justice to respond to their grievances, arising from the imposition of civil law trained judges and other judicial personnel on the essentially common law oriented courts and judicial procedures in those regions.[1] Their grievances related to the fact that the judicial personnel in question understood neither the common law system nor the English language to serve effectively within these regions. On 21 November, the lawyers were joined by teachers in the same regions with similar complaints relating to the lack of recognition of the 'Anglo-saxon' nature of education in the Anglophone regions and the deployment of teachers without proficiency in the English language or knowledge of the education system in those regions and could therefore not effectively educate students without the ability to communicate. While these protests were peaceful, security forces and gendarmes dispersed the protesters by violently beating and injuring some, while others were arrested and a few shot dead.[2] The repressive stance adopted by the government precipitated violent exchanges between the security forces and unarmed protesters, compelling the government to attempt to seek solutions. An ad hoc committee was appointed, composed of four Francophone ministers under the supervision of the Prime Minister (PM), to seek solutions to the problem.[3] It immediately suffered from a legitimacy crisis given that it was composed predominantly of Francophone ministers. The situation was exacerbated by the fact that prominent Anglophones such as the Minister of Territorial Administration and the former PM Peter Mafany Musonge maintained that there was no 'Anglophone problem'.

The lawyers and teachers subsequently formed the Cameroon Anglophone Civil Society Consortium (CACSC) led by Felix Nkongho Agbor Balla. Between December 2016 and January 2017, CACSC and the government committee entered into negotiations to which only the teachers were initially invited. The committee acceded to some demands in the education sector such as measures to recruit over 1000 bilingual teachers and the redeployment of some Francophone teachers from the Anglophone regions.[4] Other concessions subsequently made included the creation of a common law division within the Judicial Bench of the Supreme Court,[5] the creation of a department in the National School of Administration and Magistracy (ENAM) for judicial training in the common law system, complemented by an increase in Anglophone instructors in ENAM, and the recruitment of more Anglophone judges. A fifteen member National Commission for Bilingualism and Multiculturalism (the Bilingualism Commission) was also created in January 2017.[6] These measures were, however, seen as cosmetic and insufficient to address the root causes of the Anglophone problem. The government's intentions were also seen as dubious due to its objection to adopting systematic changes with potential to address more substantive grievances. For instance, it objected to demands for the unconditional release of protesters arrested during peaceful demonstrations and resisted demands for the adoption of a five-year development plan and the reintroduction of federalism.[7] Although the protests began initially with sectoral demands, at this stage, CACSC leaders where under pressure from the public to make wider demands relating to general issues affecting the Anglophone population. That explains the reasons for the last three demands that were shunned by the government. The government felt betrayed into negotiations for the alteration of the form of the state for which the committee had no mandate.[8] Mistrust between the negotiating parties and further repressive practices by security forces in January led to the breakdown of negotiations on 14 January 2017. CACSC declared a two-day civil disobedience campaign known as 'Operation Ghost Town' in the Anglophone regions. The government banned the Southern Cameroons National Council (SCNC) and CACSC and proceeded to arrest their leaders while other members of CACSC went into exile in Nigeria, South Africa and the USA.[9] The government embarked on a spate of arrest of journalists, members of civil society organisations and Anglophone activists, including the prominent Supreme Court Judge and politician, Ayah Paul.[10] Due to the influence of information technology in publicising the Anglophone crisis and the atrocities of the security forces, the government shut down internet access in the Anglophone regions between January 2017 and March 2018 for 240 days, branding social media as a new form of terrorism. That was interpreted as a further demarcation of and discrimination against the Anglophone regions.[11] The Anglophone regions remained heavily militarised with the deployment of the Rapid Intervention Battalion (BIR) noted for the use of brute force and for perpetrating atrocities such as torching of villages, enforced disappearances, torture, arbitrary arrests and extra judicial executions.[12]

Following the arrest of CACSC leaders in January 2017, provisional leadership was handed over to activists in the diaspora. Fuelled by increased government atrocities and pressure from the population, some of the leaders insisted on a complete secession of the Anglophone regions. Other CACSC leaders in exile severed links with the moderates to form the Southern Cameroons Ambazonia Consortium United Front (SCACUF), a group that advocates secession.[13] An unrecognised Interim Government of Ambazonia was formed with Julius Ayuk as the president. On 1 October 2017, SCACUF prematurely declared the independence of the South-West and North-West regions, with the aspiration to form a Federal Republic of Ambazonia. Despite the abortive declaration, the move inevitably prompted more repression from the government. There was a further twist in events when Julius Ayuk and forty-six members of the Interim Government were arrested in Nigeria in January 2018 and unlawfully[14] taken to Cameroon where they remained incommunicado for close to six months.[15] They were eventually tried by the military tribunal in Yaoundé and sentenced to life imprisonment in August 2019, a move that further strengthened demands for secession.

The humanitarian fallouts have been phenomenal with an estimated casualty of over 2000 people.[16] According to the United Nations, since 2016, about 530,000 people have been forced to flee their homes due to the insecurity in the Anglophone regions.[17] More than 35,000 of the displaced persons have fled to neighbouring Nigeria and the UNHCR estimated that by the end of 2019, that number would increase by more than 20,000.[18] In the education sector, 80% of the schools in the region have been closed affecting an estimated 600,000 children.[19] Many schools have been burned down, while others have not functioned effectively for three academic cycles.[20]

What began as simple sectoral demands, morphed into a political crisis that led to the resurgence of the Anglophone problem, which could no longer be ignored by the government. It required some decisive action to deal with the historical grievances that have continued to mar the relationship with the government.

Part II. Responses to the Anglophone problem

The Anglophone problem is one without an obvious solution and has arguably been made more problematic with the emergence of the armed struggle. While proponents of federalism and secession have persisted in their demands, the government has added another angle to its decentralisation scheme by granting a special status to the North-West and South-West regions. This section analyses the major ideological strands and attempts to identify their potential to serve as lasting solutions to the Anglophone problem.

A. Decentralisation

Decentralisation (through devolution) is the governance option adopted by the government of Cameroon, introduced partly as a concession to the Anglophones' demand for federalism in the early 1990s.[21] The 1996 Constitution describes Cameroon as a 'decentralised unitary state',[22] composed of a central government with autonomous subnational units represented by the ten administrative regions, and 360 councils.[23] Although this governance structure was introduced in 1996, the first implementing legislation only emerged in 2004 and further legislative instruments were enacted between 2008 and 2009.[24] It was not until 2010 that some aspects of decentralisation began to be implemented slowly. On 2 March 2018, the Ministry of decentralisation and local development was created by presidential decree as part of the initiative to expedite the process of decentralisation.[25] Further strides were made on 19 December 2019 when parliament passed a law on decentralised regional and local authorities, amidst the raging crisis in the Anglophone regions.[26] As per the government's explanatory statement accompanying the bill that was tabled before parliament, that law combines all the previous legislative instruments regulating decentralisation.[27] At the time of writing this monograph, that law had not come into force. In the subsequent discussions, the new provisions will be highlighted.

I. Justifying decentralisation

The government of Cameroon has advanced both a legal and a functional basis for decentralisation.

From a legal perspective, the argument is that the form of the state is inviolable. Reference is often made to article 64 of the Constitution, which provides that:

> No procedure for the amendment of the Constitution affecting the republican form, unity and territorial integrity of the State and the democratic principles which govern the Republic shall be accepted.

According to the government and proponents of decentralisation, the form of the state is provided for in article 1(2) of the Constitution, which makes Cameroon a decentralised unitary state. Read together with article 64, the form of the state is inviolable and any procedure that has the effect of altering that form, and indeed the territorial integrity of the state, is unlawful. Two pertinent observations warrant consideration. First, article 64 does not preclude a discussion of other forms of the state that do not alter its unitary nature or its territorial integrity. For instance, federalism does not imply a disintegration of the state. While it entails some devolution of powers, just like decentralisation, it preserves the unity of the state and its territorial integrity. The United States, for instance, is a unitary state with a federal structure. Federalism has not undermined the 'unitary' nature of the United States.

Second, an argument that article 64 prohibits any proposal for altering the form of the state stands at risk of questioning the lawfulness of decentralisation itself. Article 64 is a re-enactment of article 37 of the 1972 Constitution.[28] Moreover, article 1 of the 1972 Constitution described Cameroon as a 'Unitary State'. The 'decentralised unitary' form of the state was introduced through the 1996 amendment of the Constitution. If a discussion of the form of the state is not acceptable now on the basis of article 64, the same argument could be made that article 37 of the 1972 Constitution prohibited the kind of amendment or alteration of the form of the state introduced under article 1(2) of the 1996 Constitution, vis decentralisation. It is submitted here that article 64 does not prohibit discussions of or proposals on the amendment of the form of the state (for instance, federalism), which do not impair the unity of the state or its territorial integrity. Therefore, from a constitutional perspective, decentralisation should not be the only acceptable form of the state.

From a functional perspective, the government has often argued that decentralisation within a unitary state is a more suitable form of government, due to

Cameroon's multi-ethnic context. Decentralisation is perceived as the basic driving force for the promotion of development, democracy and good governance at the local level.[29] There is some merit in the argument in support of decentralisation as a functional tool for a multi-ethnic country like Cameroon. Decentralisation is credited with promoting a number of virtues, including democracy and sustainable development[30] and the reduction of ethnic conflict and secessionism by bringing the government closer to the people.[31] The potential outcome is that it increases the opportunities for local populations especially threatened or embattled minority groups to participate in government, giving them control over their social, economic and political affairs. Ultimately, there will be fewer incentives for local communities or regional minorities to seek their own independent status.[32] Thus, as a multi-ethnic community with pressing needs for the Anglophone identity to be respected and protected within the decentralised unitary state, it can be argued cautiously that decentralisation can accomplish some favourable outcomes.[33]

These benefits, however, do not accrue automatically. They are dependent on the existence of a number of factors including clearly defined constitutional and legal frameworks, the extent and nature of the devolved powers, institutional capacity, implementing processes and monitoring mechanisms.[34] More fundamentally in relation to conflicts and minorities, the extent of their protection within the decentralised framework and the governing principles of the implementing process are of primary importance. The absence of some of the vital factors or their ill-conceptualisation may have the reverse effect. This partly explains why decentralisation is sometimes viewed with much scepticism. Thus, other scholars have argued that decentralisation on the contrary amplifies the risk of ethnic division, conflict and demands for secession.[35] Decentralisation has often been advanced as the cause of the failure of integrationist projects in countries such as Kosovo and Yugoslavia.[36] The literature, thus, demonstrates that the evidence on the merits of decentralisation is inconclusive[37] and in regards to the resolution of conflicts, the potential for decentralisation to amplify conflict depends on the nature of the conflict and the role of ethnic tensions as a source of the conflict.[38] As Benjamin Edwards and Serdar Yilmaz note, '[w]hile decentralisation can serve to mitigate or reduce conflict, the processes involved can also exacerbate conflict. It all depends on country context and, especially, on the nature of the conflict itself'.[39] These competing perspectives indicate that the government of Cameroon must approach decentralisation with caution, focusing on the factors and conditions likely to promote economic and political development and, in particular, in resolving the Anglophone problem.

One can note, for instance, the restrictive nature of the principles of subsidiarity and complementarity[40] governing devolution and power sharing, which have inevitably contributed to a flawed decentralisation architecture and process. The subsidiarity principle demarcates the powers exercised by the central government and the devolved units and is based on the idea of 'transfer and exercise of authority at the territorial level which is most suitable or closest to the people concerned'.[41] Thus, the state shall devolve to local authorities, the powers necessary for their economic, social, health, educational, cultural and sports development.[42] In that respect, regional and local authorities shall have administrative and financial autonomy in the management of their interest and have separate assets, staff, property and services from the state.[43] Moreover, they shall have their own budget and resources prepared and voted by them and receive all or part of the proceeds from exploitation of natural resources within their territorial jurisdiction (under conditions laid down by law).[44] They shall also receive resources from the state and generate the resources necessary for the promotion of economic, social, health, educational, cultural and sports development in their jurisdictions.[45]

Despite the purported autonomy in the management and administration of their affairs and resources, their powers are restricted to those that are 'necessary' to achieve the previously mentioned objective and are to be exercised concurrently with the state under certain conditions.[46] For instance, the state may exercise devolved powers on an ad hoc basis to ensure the balanced development of the territory or to address an emergency, or where there has been a 'failure' duly established by the minister in charge of local authorities or a two-third majority of the deliberative organ of the region.[47] The law does not define a 'failure', as such, the implications are unclear. Again, although the devolved units are purportedly autonomous in the preparation and management of their budget and resources, some decisions, like those relating to budgets, accounts, special expenditure authorisation, loans, execution of public contracts, staff recruitment and international cooperation, are subject to the prior approval of the representative of the state, a presidential appointee.[48]

The other underpinning principle, the complementarity principle, as described by a Minister Delegate at the former Ministry of Territorial Administration and Decentralisation, relates to the idea that, 'authority transferred by the state does not exclude the fact that the latter continues to *exercise same*'.[49] Both principles are indicative of the extent to which the state may be reluctant to relinquish power to the devolved units and keen to interfere unduly in their affairs.[50] This is reflected in a number of provisions of the relevant normative instruments. For instance, presidential appointees, such as regional governors and senior divisional officers, are empowered to exercise supervisory duties over elected regional and council officials.[51] The RLA Code creates the position of the Secretary General, a presidential appointee responsible for coordinating regional administrative services, handling the business of the regions and implementing the decisions of the regional council president.[52] He is authorised to attend Bureau and regional council meetings for which he shall provide secretarial services.[53] The autonomy and stability of regions are further undermined by the fact that the President of the Republic can interfere with local governance by creating, renaming and re-defining geographical boundaries of local authorities *unilaterally*.[54] Further, under certain circumstances, the regional councils may be suspended by the President of the Republic or dissolved by the same in 'consultation' with the Constitutional Council.[55] In the context of such restrictions, there can hardly be any meaningful exercise of autonomy, therefore restricting the extent to which local populations can influence their governance and development. This is a factor that can further antagonise local communities and inflame their demands for greater autonomy and secession. However, the new law purports to grant local communities opportunities to participate in local governance through neighbourhood and village communities[56] and through consultative processes in the preparation of local budgets.[57]

Section 9(2) of the 2004 Law on Decentralisation also included the progressiveness or gradualism principle, which has partly determined the slow pace of decentralisation. According to that principle, 'transfer of authority is spread over time and is done in packages or levels'.[58] One of the problems affecting the pace of decentralisation, as explained by the Minister Delegate, is the 'lack of a local governance and participatory democracy culture'.[59] That has not been mitigated by legislative provisions, which, in effect, stymie participatory democracy. This factor, as well as others already outlined, makes for a decentralisation process that does not accord the devolved units meaningful autonomy to address the issues that are of concern to them. With respect to the Anglophone problem, the pre-December 2019 laws on decentralisation attempted to deal with issues such as education and culture. However, there were no specific provisions that went to the heart of the preservation of the elements that comprise the distinctive Anglophone identity. At the constitutional level, decentralisation did not address these issues in a clear and distinctive way. The closest it came was in article 62(2), which provides vaguely that, 'the law may take into consideration the specificities of certain Regions with regard to their organisation and functioning'. That was, however, not reflected in any of the implementing legislative texts before December 2019. Hence, as a means of achieving the objectives intended by the government, the decentralisation process and the normative framework seemed fundamentally flawed. There was, therefore, a need for reconsidering an alternative or, at least, reassessing the process of decentralisation with a view to amending the constitutional and legislative provisions to ensure that decentralisation could achieve favourable outcomes, including resolving the Anglophone problem. That was not a matter overtly contemplated by the government. However, it became even more necessary following the resurgence of the Anglophone problem.

B. Special autonomy status

On 10 September 2019, in a rare address to the nation, President Biya announced plans to convene a broad-based national dialogue to seek solutions to the crisis rocking the Anglophone regions.[60] The dialogue was preceded by a pre-consultation phase during which the PM, as the designated chair, received various delegations to obtain views that would inform the discussions during the dialogue itself. This was in line with the process stipulated in the presidential speech. The delegations included representatives of national groups and institutions and government representatives and institutions.[61] Government appointed delegations were dispatched abroad to consult diaspora groups and community representatives.

The main dialogue took place between 30 September and 4 October 2019. It is worth noting that this was organised, chaired and supervised by the government. No independent organisation was given any of the aforementioned duties to steer the process. To facilitate the discussion, a Dialogue Bureau was set up with a president/chair (the PM), four vice presidents – two of which were Anglophones – four rapporteurs – three of which were Anglophones – and eight themed commissions, as stated in the following list.

- Bilingualism, Cultural Diversity, and Social Cohesion
- Educational System
- Judicial System
- Assistance to Returning Refugees and Displaced Persons
- Reconstruction and Development of Regions Affected by Crisis
- Disarmament, Demobilisation and Reinsertion of Ex-Combatants
- Role of the Diaspora in the Crisis and Contribution to the Country's Development
- Decentralisation and Local Development

These commissions were the intended fora for 'inclusive' discussions with a view to developing proposals and recommendations to resolve the issues identified in the presidential speech. As a conflict-mediation strategy, the dialogue process seemed flawed at its very inception. For instance, the agenda seemed pre-determined. Major actors, such as the separatist leaders, were still incarcerated while the discussions were ongoing and diaspora separatist groups and leaders were excluded from discussions. Although they were purportedly invited, no special guarantees were provided to ensure their safety or their personal liberty and security. In addition, Anglophone representatives who attended the discussions perceived the process as inadequate in many respects but particularly because the dialogue was stage-managed without the opportunity for them to express their genuine concerns and proposals. For instance, when Agbor Balla (the first leader of the proscribed CACSC) and the National Chairman of the Social Democratic Front (SDF) Fru Ndi mentioned federalism in their speech, they were heavily criticised and heckled. The perceived inadequacies caused prominent figures like Barrister Akere Muna to withdraw from the dialogue.

Nevertheless, a number of recommendations were made at the end of the process aimed at resolving the Anglophone crisis. According to the Rapporteur General of the Dialogue, some of the recommendations need to be particularly highlighted and these include recommendations to:

> Grant a special status to the North-West and South-West Regions, in conformity with Section 62 Sub 2 of the Constitution; Take specific measures to ensure equality of English and French in all aspects of national life; Reinforce the autonomy of Decentralised Local Entities; Improve upon the infrastructure of judicial services throughout the country …[62]

While these recommendations, if implemented, may go some way to address the root causes of the Anglophone problem, critics still perceive the dialogue and the recommendations as a smokescreen.[63] It is worth noting that parliament passed a law on bilingualism, which emphasises the government's policy on the equal status of the two national languages.[64] It also promotes their compulsory use in public institutions and enshrines the rights of citizens to communicate with public institutions in their (official) language of choice. The bilingualism law is purportedly a complementary instrument to the special status arrangements.

I. An overview of the special status for the North-West and South-West Regions

The proposal for a special autonomy status for the North-West and South-West regions, unsurprisingly, was not without controversy. Some critics initially objected to the suggestion on the basis that it is an inferior arrangement for these regions and symbolises subjugation. One reason that may account for the objection is perhaps the fact that the proposal originated from pro-government supporters who were members of the Decentralisation Commission at the Dialogue, notably, Constitutional Council member Akame Mfoumou. The objection relates to the contention that the proposal was used to forestall any discussions of federalism. This was reinforced by the fact that the proposed special status would be granted within the context of article 62(2) of the Constitution, which makes provision for laws on decentralisation to take into account the specificities of certain regions.

The SDF opposition party initially backed the proposal emphasising that the implication was that,

> the regions will have to enjoy autonomy characterised by constitutionally entrenched Executive, Legislative and Judicial Powers with an administrative set up that reflects the aspirations of the people of these regions.[65]

The SDF made reference to the special status granted to the minority French-speaking province of Quebec in Canada as a model for the establishment of a special status for the Anglophone regions of Cameroon. In their view, the arrangements in Quebec would be suitable to Anglophone Cameroon as there is some resonance with the cultural heritage of the two entities. Although the similarities between Quebec and the Anglophone regions of Cameroon might be overstated, the SDF's optimism was not totally unfounded. That optimism was, however, short lived. In December 2019, parliament passed the Code on Regional and Local Authorities (RLA Code), which made provisions for a special status for the North-West and the South-West regions.[66] Some of the substantive provisions are analysed in the subsequent section. Attention is also accorded to the normative framework and the procedural mechanisms through which special status has been granted.

II. Substantive provisions

According to the government's Explanatory Statement preceding the bill to institute the RLA Code,[67] one significant advantage is that it compiles all the related laws on decentralisation in one document. The RLA Code regulates the general framework of decentralisation, the status of the local elected representatives, rules applicable to councils and regions and the financial regime applicable to regional and local authorities.[68] It states that the local authorities shall be regions and councils and shall carryout their activities with due respect for national unity, solidarity, territorial integrity and the primacy of the state.[69]

The specificities of the Anglophone regions are recognised at the outset. Thus, section 3(1) provides that, '[t]he North-West and South-West Regions shall have a special status based on their language specificity and historical heritage'. That provision is reiterated in section 327(1), which states additionally that the North-West and South-West shall have a special status in accordance with the provisions of article 62 of the Constitution. The Law states further that the special status shall be reflected in the context of decentralisation, 'in specificities in the organisation and functioning of these two regions'[70] and 'shall also entail respect for the peculiarity of the Anglophone education system and consideration of the specificities of the Anglo-Saxon legal system based on common law'.[71] Those provisions indicate clearly that there is acknowledgment of the distinct nature of some key features that constitute the core of the Anglophone identity.[72] In terms of devolution of powers, how does the RLA Code reflect those specificities?

A. DEVOLVED POWERS

The powers devolved on all the ten regions of the state are covered in sections 267 to 273. They include defined competencies in the areas of economic development, health and social development and education, sports and cultural development. All are not discussed here. This subsection focuses exclusively on some of the powers related to the central theme of this chapter. Specifically in the area of education, regions have, among other competencies, powers to participate in drawing up and implementing the *regional* portion of the national school map.[73] In the area of culture and promotion of national languages, regions are empowered, inter alia, to collect and translate works of oral tradition with a view to facilitating their publication, to encourage functional command of national languages and to produce the regional linguistic map.[74] In addition, they have powers to participate in the promotion of publishing and broadcasting in the national languages.[75]

According to section 328(1), in addition to the powers exercised by all regions, the North-West and South-West shall exercise the following powers:

- Participating in the formulation of *national* public policies relating to the Anglophone education subsystem
- Setting up and managing regional development authorities
- Participating in defining the status of traditional chiefdoms

This is commendable in that the law explicitly attempts to reflect the specificities of the Anglophone regions in certain areas such as its distinct education system. In the education sphere, all other regions have a limited scope in determining education policies as their role is restricted to participating 'in drawing up and implementing the *regional* portion of the national school map'.[76] Whereas, the local authorities in the Anglophone regions can participate in formulating '*national*' education policies that relate to the Anglophone system. The implication is that there is potential for local authorities to ensure the continued respect and the preservation of the Anglophone education system through national policies and to influence developments in that area.

Anglophone regional authorities can also set up and manage local development initiatives that promote local economic development in their regions. For instance, the creation of a local produce marketing board as in the federal era when the West Cameroon Marketing Board existed to facilitate the marketing of local cash crops such as cocoa, coffee, tea and palm oil.[77] On the strength of section 328(1), such initiatives would be created at the behest of the local authorities and managed by them, taking into account issues that are specifically relevant to their local populations.[78]

The Law also recognises the distinct legal tradition based on the common law system. Thus, section 328(2) provides that the Anglophone regions may be consulted in the formulation of judicial policies in the common law sub-system. That recognition is novel as no other existing statute specifically vests consultative powers on any Anglophone representatives in the formulation of judicial policies relating to the common law. As such, there is some scope for the reinforcement of the equality of the common law system and its preservation, an aspect that has gained renewed significance since the onset of the crises in 2016. As discussed in previous chapters,[79] as part of that recognition, a common law division was established in the Judicial Bench of the Supreme Court. In ENAM, a special section for the training of judicial officers with a common law background was established.

In spite of the apparent special powers granted to the Anglophone regional authorities, in terms of devolution, they do not appear to go far enough to allow sufficient scope for the authorities to significantly influence the management and development of those features that are specific to their regions. For instance, although they can participate in the formulation of national policy relating to the Anglophone education system, to what extent can they influence the development, amendment or adoption of these policies? If the regional authorities, reflecting current public opinion, proposed to the relevant minister that teachers without training in the Anglophone education system should not be routinely transferred to schools in the Anglophone regions, what weight would that proposal carry? The law only states that they shall participate but does not state in what capacity nor does it require the relevant national authority to be bound by the proposals emanating from the authorities of the Anglophone regions.

Similarly, with respect to the formulation of judicial policy relating to the common law, the North-West and South-West regional authorities 'may' only be 'consulted'. This formulation raises two important questions. First, why 'may' the authorities be 'consulted' as opposed to a requirement that they should 'participate' in the formulation of national policy? The latter formulation is applied in the case of the formulation of education policy and provides more scope to influence policy in that area. Second, the use of the term 'may' indicates that consultation is not mandatory. Rather, it provides opportunities for national authorities to apply their discretion to exclude regional authorities from the formulation of policies in that area. That approach can be contrasted with section 277(5), which provides, in relation to all regional councils, that they '*shall mandatorily* be consulted' in the implementation of development projects in their region. It is curious that a similar approach was not adopted in the crucial area of formulating judicial policies in the Anglophone regions in the context of their 'special status'. An argument that the adoption of that less-meaningful approach was deliberate, may be compelling. In terms of devolution of powers, this does not go very far in attempting to vest Anglophone regional authorities with sufficient powers to control the development and preservation of the common law tradition, especially in the training of legal and judicial personnel and the administration of the court system. These aspects would continue to be regulated at the national level without a mandatory contribution from the Anglophone regional authorities. In fact, in reacting to these supposedly special powers, a number of Anglophone MPs and Senators, both from the opposition and the ruling CPDM party, expressed doubts as to the significance of the 'participatory' and 'consultation' powers. In their view, it gave the North-West and South-West no influence in the development of education and judicial policies at the national level.[80] They were of the opinion that a special status should empower the regions to 'determine' policies in education and judicial administration and those relating to the legislative and the executive system, both at the national and the local level.[81]

III. *Institutional structures*

A. DELIBERATIVE AND EXECUTIVE ORGANS

With regard to the organisational structure of the regions, the relevant organs are the Regional Council and the President of the Regional Council, both charged with the administration of the region.[82] The Regional Council is the deliberative organ and is composed of 90 councillors elected for a term of five years.[83] The Regional Council consists of the divisional representatives elected by indirect universal suffrage and representatives of traditional rulers elected by their peers.[84] It comprises four committees, namely, Committee on Administrative and Legal Affairs, and Standing Orders; Committee on Education, Health, Population, Social and Cultural Affairs, Youth and Sports; Committee on Finance, Infrastructure, Planning and Economic Development; and Committee on Environment, Regional Development, State Property, Town Planning and Housing.[85] The President of the Regional Council is the executive organ of the region[86] elected from among members of the Regional Council.[87] The president is assisted by a bureau comprising a senior vice-president, a vice-president, two questors and a secretary.[88]

Unlike the other eight regions, the North-West and South-West Regions, pursuant to their special status, have a 'specific organisational and operational regime' as per section 327(2). In that respect, the organs of the region are the Regional Assembly (RA) and the Regional Executive Council (REC).[89] The RA is the deliberative organ,[90] composed of 90 members elected for a five-year term.[91] It comprises two houses, the House of Divisional Representatives (seventy members) and the House of Chiefs (twenty members).[92] The former are elected by the municipal councillors of the region through a one-round mixed list vote, comprising a majority system and a proportional representation system,[93] while the latter are elected 'in accordance with the laws in force'.[94] The House of Divisional Representatives rules on all matters falling within the competence of the Regional Assembly.[95] It comprises of five committees, namely,[96] the Committee on Administrative and Legal Affairs and Standing Order; Committee on Education; Committee on Health, Population, Social and Cultural Affairs, Youth and Sports; Committee on Finance, Infrastructure, Planning and Economic Development; and the Committee on Environment, Regional Development, State Property, Town Planning and Housing. The House of Divisional Representatives shall be chaired by the president of the REC.[97]

The House of Chiefs also rules on all matters falling within the competence of the Regional Assembly.[98] Additionally, it provides opinions on the status of traditional chiefdom, the management and conservation of historical sites, monuments and vestiges, the organisation of cultural and traditional events in the region and the collection and translation of elements of oral tradition.[99] It is composed of two committees, namely, the Committee on Administrative and Legal Affairs and Standing Orders, Education, Health, Population, Social and Cultural Affairs, Youth and Sports; and the Committee on Finance, Infrastructure, Planning, Economic Development, Environment, Regional Development, State Property, Town Planning and Housing.[100] The House of Chief is chaired by the vice-president of the REC.[101]

On the other hand, the REC is the executive organ of the region and comprises a president, a vice-president, a commissioner – each for economic development; for health and social development and for educational, sports and cultural development , two secretaries and a questor.[102] Members of the REC are elected from members of the Regional Council for the term of the Council.[103] Curiously, both the president and the vice-president of the REC are elected from members of the RA[104] (divisional representatives and traditional rulers, respectively).[105] The president of the REC is the executive organ of the region.[106]

A cursory glance at the provisions of the law demonstrates that, structurally, there is a marked distinction between the organs of the special regions and those of other regions. Notably, the deliberative organ of the North-West and South West regions is the RA as opposed to a Regional Council in other regions. Moreover, the executive organ of the North-West and South-West is the REC whereas the other regions have the institution of a President of the Regional Council. Remarkably, the RA of the North-West and South-West have the much desired House of Chiefs, an iconic institution representative of both the cultural and institutional identity of the Anglophones. As discussed in Chapter 1, the Southern Cameroons House of Chiefs from the colonial era morphed into the West Cameroon House of Chiefs as one of the houses of the bicameral legislature of West Cameroon. It played an important role in the governance of the Anglophone regions under both the colonial and immediate post-independence periods. There have been repeated calls for its re-institution as far back as the time of the AAC I and AAC II and, more recently, during the Major National Dialogue. Therefore, its reintroduction as a distinct feature of the special status can be perceived as a positive response to that call.

However, a more profound analysis of some specific provisions indicates that the differences may be more in terms of structural design. Substantively, the institutions, though different in appellation, are endowed with analogous personalities and competencies. For instance, the RAs in the special regions is composed of ninety members and partitioned into two houses – House of Divisional Representatives and House of Chiefs, with the latter elected from among regional councillors. The Regional Councils in the other regions are also composed of ninety members and divided into two sub-organs, Divisional Representatives and Traditional Rulers elected from among regional councillors. Although different in terminological designation, the composition is the same. In effect, the executive organs in all the regions are composed of councillors, some of whom are traditional rulers with the obvious difference that in the special regions, the traditional rulers are in a House of Chiefs. The fact of applying the terminology of 'House' in the case of the sub-organs of the RAs in the special regions is not sufficient to distinguish them substantively from the sub-organs in the other regions. Similarly, from the provisions of the law, there is no apparent substantive difference between the appellation, 'Regional Assembly' and 'Regional Council', particularly in view of the fact that the rules relating to regional administration[107] and operating procedures[108] are the same for Regional Assemblies and Regional Councils and there are corresponding committees through which their duties are exercised.[109] Moreover, in terms of competencies, the deliberative organs in all regions are vested with analogous competencies and functions, as per section 278 of the RLA Code. Although the law specifically provides that the House of Chiefs shall give its opinion in certain areas relating to culture and traditions (as defined in section 337(2)), this is not exclusive to them. The Regional Councils in other regions also have competencies in those areas.[110] It implies that traditional rulers, as part of the Regional Council, are likely to provide their opinion in the relevant areas, similar to their peers in the House of Chiefs.

Parallel arguments can be made in terms of the structure and competence of the executive organs. For instance, the president of the REC of the special regions performs similar functions to those of the president of the Regional Councils in other regions,[111] with the exception that the former chairs the sessions of the RA or the House of Divisional Representatives when it seats separately from the House of Chiefs.[112] Similarly, according to section 361, the rules relating to the president of the Regional Council in other regions shall apply to the president of the REC in the special regions.

B. THE PUBLIC INDEPENDENT CONCILIATOR

Perhaps the most distinctive and innovative institution is that of the Public Independent Conciliator (PIC).[113] The law provides that – the PIC shall be a highly experienced personality with reputed integrity and proven objectivity.[114] He shall be appointed for a non-renewable term of six years, by presidential decree pursuant to a 'concerted proposal' of the representative of the state in the region and the president of the REC.[115] As a public official, the PIC's role is incompatible with other public duties or employment or the exercise of any paid professional activity.[116] To safeguard his independence, the PIC shall neither seek nor receive instructions in the exercise of his duties.[117] The law also provides that, 'professional secrecy shall not be enforceable against him'.[118]

The duties of the PIC include the amicable resolution of disputes between 'users' and regional and council administration; defending and protecting the rights and freedoms of citizens from encroachment by regional and council authorities; ensuring that regional and local authorities comply with ethical obligations and designing; and implementing measures to prevent and combat discriminatory practices that may affect service users.[119] It has further oversight powers to conduct investigations on the functioning of regional and council public services and to prepare reports thereto. The PIC may receive complaints from natural or legal persons alleging infringement of their rights or from persons alleging to be victims of discriminatory practices forbidden by domestic and international instruments ratified or approved by Cameroon.[120] This is commendable because it allows complainants to use both domestic law and the expansive range of rights under international law, to hold local government to account where individual rights have been breached. In addition to dispute resolution and oversight powers, the PIC may propose legislative and regulatory amendments to the President of the Republic.[121] The law is silent on the corresponding action to be taken by the President.[122]

In terms of admissibility, the relevant complaints must be between a natural or legal person or public employee and a regional or council public authority.[123] The complainant must also have initially submitted an appeal to the authority concerned and the matter must not have been adjudicated by the courts.[124] Following investigation of the complaint, the PIC shall make recommendations to the relevant authority with a view to ensuring respect for the complainant's rights and freedoms, settling the dispute and preventing reoccurrence.[125] Where the authority fails to comply with the recommendations, the PIC may issue an order mandating compliance within a specified period.[126] Further non-compliance will result in the preparation of a report by the PIC, which will be forwarded to the authority concerned and the representative of the state.[127] The report may be published together with any response from the authority.[128]

From the preceding discussion, it would seem that the PIC intervenes where the public authority has initially failed to resolve the complaint. It provides that additional level of support to complainants before any legal action is instituted. In that respect, the PIC may be seen as an institution with the potential to protect the rights of ordinary citizens against encroachment by public institutions. Additionally, through its oversight mechanisms, it can ensure the proper functioning of public institutions for the benefit of the local populations. This would prove particularly useful in services such as education and the judiciary, if service users were not being guaranteed certain rights such as their linguistic rights. However, a major weakness of that institution is that the PIC has no powers of compulsion. It can only make recommendations, which are not binding. In circumstances where the public authority fails to implement the recommendations, the PIC can only forward a report to the representative of the state. The law is silent on what the latter may do with the report or what sanctions may be imposed on the recalcitrant authority. Moreover, the law does not prescribe any specific time limits for the investigation of complaints or the implementation of recommendations. This implies that a complainant may potentially wait interminably for a complaint to be resolved.

One further observation is that, given the role of the PIC, it seemed more judicious to vest such responsibilities on an institution such as a commission or a board rather than an individual. In the government's Explanatory Statement accompanying the bill, it is anticipated that the PIC would ensure the observance of regional specificity in the area of use of the English language, the practice of the common law and the implementation of the English education sub-system. For reasons relating to objectivity, wider expertise and time constraints, such duties are arguably more effectively discharged by a team. For instance, the Bilingualism Commission, which was established in the wake of the Anglophone crisis, is composed of a team of personalities rather than an individual. Due to the weaknesses described earlier, the ability of the PIC to influence the relationship between public authorities and the populations remains questionable.

IV. Procedural considerations

The RLA Code, which makes provision for the special status of the North-West and South-West regions, as already noted, was a response to recommendations from the Major National Dialogue. Besides that consultative phase, there is no indication that the law itself was a product of consultation and negotiation between the government and the populations of the Anglophone regions and their elected representatives. As such, their hopes and aspirations for the governance of their regions were not directly sought and, arguably, not fully represented in the ensuing law. The democratic deficit in the procedure for instituting special autonomy status has resulted in uncertainty and, in some cases, outright rejection. When the bill was tabled in parliament, Anglophone MPs were indignant at the lack of consultation by the government.[129] According to Jean Michel Nitcheu, an SDF MP, the law would not resolve the conflict and it was not a product of a dialogue.[130] Uncharacteristically, some MPs of the ruling party objected to the fact that they could neither make recommendations nor amendments to the bill.[131] It is unsurprising, therefore, that many Anglophones, even the most moderate, regard the special status provision as a 'derogatory status'[132] and insist on federation, while the separatist refuse to acknowledge the existence of the special status provisions and object to the application of the relevant law in the Anglophone regions.[133]

This undesirable outcome warrants a brief exploration of some of the factors that should guide a successful process for a peaceful resolution of self-determination conflicts, which results in the carving out of a special status for a conflict ridden region.

A. NEGOTIATING A SPECIAL STATUS AGREEMENT

The process of conflict resolution and determination of minority issues is as important as the outcome. This observation warrants a reconsideration of the traditional approach to political decision making in Cameroon, which is often a unilateral process, involving exclusively the government and its close allies. In this regard, the process must be underpinned by broad-based participation, negotiation and balancing (mutual compromise). The determination of the key issues to underpin the special status arrangements must include a process of negotiation between the government and the people of the two regions concerned (elected representatives of these regions). In addition, considering the rather complex circumstances (armed conflict) in which special status was contemplated, the armed separatist leaders should have constituted an essential part of any negotiation process. Experience elsewhere has demonstrated that failure to negotiate with broader sections of the society including armed separatist leaders is likely to lead to a rejection of concessions that are made by the government.[134] This was the case with the granting of special status for Aceh and Papua by the Indonesian government. The government hastily granted concessions to these two provinces without engaging in a systematic process of bargaining and negotiating with broad-based elements of the civil society. Although the substantive content of the arrangements amounted to significant concessions, the process of developing, adopting and enacting these arrangements into law excluded larger elements of the civil society and pro-independence leaders in both provinces.[135] Instead, provincial elites and the national parliament unilaterally adopted these concessions, which lacked a link to the main political forces that were advocating for independence in the two provinces.[136] A key consequence was that autonomy received little public support in both provinces and the autonomy laws offered few incentives to actually persuade pro-independence leaders to abandon their separatist claims.[137] Important parallels were also observed in Sri Lanka where the government's efforts to grant autonomy in the 1980s were not complemented by negotiation with the Tamil rebels.[138] Despite concessions granted by the government, the conflict continued unabated due, in significant part, to the government's failure to negotiate a broad-based agreement.[139] The outcome in Cameroon reflects this pattern, indicating that a different approach should have been adopted.

There is a need for broad-based participation in order to allow the local populations and pro-independence leaders to claim ownership of both the process and the outcome. It provides the space and opportunity to articulate their aspirations and how they desire these aspirations to be protected by the autonomy arrangements. Additionally, a broad-based process has the advantage of allowing room for compromise and balancing in order to pre-empt the domination of the process by one segment of the negotiating parties. Balancing ensures that the position of the relevant parties is well represented and, therefore, there is potential for greater ownership of the process and outcome. Marc Weller notes that balancing self-determination claims 'overcomes the mutually exclusive positions of both sides in a self-determination conflict'.[140] It allows both sides to claim prevalence and preservation of their views. He concludes that the secret behind the success of the Good Friday Agreement in Northern Ireland is balancing of the self-determination claims.[141]

The Cameroon government's initial 'negotiation' with the CACSC in December 2016 and the Major National Dialogue had already demonstrated that the relevant parties could not be excluded from negotiating the eventual framework agreement for the special status. It is unsurprising that the special status provisions have struggled to gain legitimacy and indeed to persuade separatist leaders to discontinue their demands for independence. Neither has it lessened demands for federalism. A genuine and credible broad-based participation process should not translate into the inclusion of old Anglophone barons of the regime who are not deemed to represent the Anglophones as they have lost legitimacy among the population. Moreover, the government should desist from usurping the process and allow Anglophone representatives to articulate the specific ways in which the minority rights of the Anglophones should be protected within a special status framework. As part of the negotiated process and to reinforce its legitimacy, these regions should be demilitarised or, at minimum, there should be a reduction of troops. A free and equitable process of negotiation cannot be achieved with one side having the barrel of the gun over the head of the other.

B. NORMATIVE FOUNDATIONS OF THE SPECIAL STATUS AGREEMENT

A further weakness embodying the special status of the Anglophone regions is that there is no independent document dealing with the special status arrangements. Instead, the relevant provisions appear as part of the general law on decentralised regional and local authorities.

It should be stated at the outset that the foundation document embodying any special status arrangement should preferably be incorporated into the Constitution or be established by an autonomy statute (act of Parliament).[142] This is the approach adopted by several special status regions such as Aceh and Papua, the Åland Islands, Hong Kong, South Tyrol, Quebec and Zanzibar where the arrangements are either embodied in the constitution or a separate autonomy statute or both. More importantly, the sanctity of the arrangements must be preserved. This has traditionally been done through entrenchment – providing special and more stringent mechanisms for their amendment or repeal. One important reason for entrenching fundamental principles or foundation documents is for their preservation, hence affording them stability and security. One can also add that entrenchment is indicative of the relative importance of specific constitutional or statutory arrangement and principles. Entrenchment is particularly desirable for a fragile democracy characterised by legal instability and disregard for the rule of law.[143] In such circumstances, entrenchment potentially acts as a barrier to unilateral action by a party seeking to alter foundational agreements to suit their whims and caprices. In the particular case of Cameroon, amendment provisions must also ensure that the consent of the autonomous regions is imperative. Considering the circumstances preceding the adoption of a special status agreement, their entrenchment is a means of pre-empting a recession into the violence, insecurity and economic stagnation that has been characteristic of the last three years. The country's constitutional development is undermined by an unresponsive government that often acts unilaterally, introducing important changes through regulatory instruments and its constitutional history is characterised by legal instability (in terms of the simplicity of the constitutional amendment procedure). Provisions that can be amended with ease may render otherwise progressive arrangements illusory. This was exemplified by the amendment to the presidential term limit provision in 2008. Article 6(2) of the Constitution, which limited the presidential term to two mandates, was adopted at a time when the demand for democratic change in Cameroon had led to considerable insecurity and paralysis of governance and the economy. It was an important provision to diffuse tensions at the time and to indicate the government's commitment to introducing democratic change. The ease with which it was reversed in 2008 lends support to the contention that any arrangements arrived at in a bid to secure the special autonomy status of the North-West and South-West need special protection in other to provide insulation from regressive government action.

In Hong Kong, for instance, the arrangements that grant significant autonomy to the Special Administrative Region are not entrenched.[144] Despite the high level of autonomy arrangements made for the Special Administrative Region, the provisions are enshrined in the Basic Law that was passed by the National Peoples' Congress (NPC) and can be amended unilaterally by the NPC, implying that the arrangements are not secure.[145] Recent events in Hong Kong demonstrate how that weakness has provided the opportunity for the government in Beijing to intefer with the administration of Hong Kong, thereby undermining its autonomy. By contrast, the autonomy of the Åland Islands is embodied in article 120 of the Finnish Constitution 'in accordance with what is specifically stipulated in the Act on the Autonomy of the Åland Islands'.[146] In addition, there is a separate procedure for amendment of the Constitution and the Act, which provides considerable security for the Åland autonomy arrangements. Thus, the

Act can only be amended through a bilateral process resulting from a joint decision of the Finnish Parliament and the Parliament of the Åland Islands. Any such decision requires a super majority of the votes cast in the Finnish Parliament, (or a 2/3rd majority in the second reading) and 2/3rd majority of votes cast in the Åland Parliament.[147] The provisions on Åland autonomy can, therefore, be said to be entrenched since the procedure for their amendment is stringent. It provides security in the sense that the Finnish government or Parliament cannot unilaterally abrogate the rights of the Åland populations or alter centre and state relationship without the latter's consent. This was demonstrated prior to Finland's accession to the European Union (EU). In arriving at the decision to join the EU, the Helsinki government was obliged to consult with the Åland Islands, since their interests would be affected and this involved extensive discussions and negotiations with Åland authorities. The agreement was sealed in a referendum during which the Åland Islands voted overwhelmingly in favour of joining the EU, under a separate protocol from that which governed the EU/Finnish relations.[148]

In Cameroon, the fact that the special status is embodied in a general law on regional and local authorities is unsatisfactory. Moreover, it is not specifically entrenched and can be amended at any time without the consent of the people of those regions or their representatives.

By and large, the architecture of decentralisation offered by the government and its accompanying special status arrangements appear unsuited to the distinct nature of the Anglophone problem. As discussed previously, there are elements in the current system that can be enhanced in order to more effectively address the problem. The Anglophone populations remain unconvinced by the government's approach as it does not appear to provide meaningful autonomy to these regions. That perhaps accounts for the persistence in demands for federalism and secession discussed in the subsequent sections.

C. Federalism

In Chapter 1, it was demonstrated that the option of federalism dominated the Anglophone struggle for identity even in the late 1990s when some radical political groups began to emerge. Renewed calls for federalism often alluded to Cameroon's brief experience with federalism from 1961 to 1972 and its potentials in the protection of the Anglophone minority and its cultural, social, political and legal heritage. This section will briefly explore some of the legal arguments that have been advanced in favour of a return to federalism, something that has remained unchanged despite the granting of a special status to the North-West and South-West regions.

I. Justifying a return to federalism

Despite the misgivings about Cameroon's experience of federalism, discussed in Chapter 1, proponents of federalism still see it as the best alternative to resolving the Anglophone crisis in the long and short term.[149] At least three major arguments are often advanced in support of federalism. The first argument hinges on the basis of the establishment of a union in 1961, while the second argument is underpinned by the questionable legality of the dissolution of the union in 1972.[150] The third argument, a more pragmatic one, focuses on the values of federalism in providing a reasonable degree of self-determination for the Anglophone regions. Notable figures, like emeritus archbishop Cardinal Christian Tumi, affirm that federalism is the best option to maintain unity and stability in Cameroon.[151]

On the first issue, the argument is that the very foundation of the union in 1961 was on the basis of a federation.[152] Although Southern Cameroons was not eventually accorded the loose federation that it advocated for, their understanding on entering the union was that it would be on the basis of a federation. Foncha's campaign during the prelude to reunification was framed around the idea of a federation through which the interest of Southern Cameroons as a minority would be protected.[153] During Ahidjo's visit to Buea in 1960, Foncha declared that the union with the Republic of Cameroon (The Republic) will not be similar to Southern Cameroons' experience with Nigeria, which was characterised by domination. Instead, he was certain that the union would be on the basis of equality (as of two brothers) in a federation.[154] That, as we now know, was overly optimistic and illusive. Yet, it was a key aspect in determining the basis of a union between Southern Cameroons and The Republic.

The second argument is founded on a literal interpretation of article 47 of the Federal Constitution.[155] Article 47(1) provides that,

> Any proposal for the revision of the present constitution which impairs the unity and integrity of the federation shall be inadmissible.

This provision has been interpreted to mean that a proposal which entailed an alteration or dissolution of the federation was inadmissible.[156] In that respect, the word federation referred to the form of state – its federal structure.[157] In which case, article 47(1), in effect, prohibited any change to that form. On that basis, it was unlawful for the federal parliament to have admitted Ahidjo's proposal to dissolve the union given that its effect would 'impair' the federal structure of the state. Carlson Anyangwe states emphatically that article 47(1) 'declared sacrosanct the federal form of the state', 'and was meant to prevent the transformation of the structure of the State from federal to unitary', the former of which provided protection from majority domination.[158] According to him, that provision was a 'special' (inviolable) provision, which had the purpose of preventing a change of the very basis upon which a union was negotiated. Relatedly, it has been argued that, even if the Constitution had to be amended, a referendum was not the valid process for the amendment.[159] Article 47(3) provided for a special procedure by virtue of which proposals for amendment were to be adopted by a majority vote of the members of the Federal National Assembly, provided that the said majority included the majority of the representatives of each of the federated states. The referendum bypassed that procedure, therefore, making it unlawful. Anyangwe contends that Ahidjo's resort to a referendum was treacherous in itself because the process that brought about the union (the plebiscite) involved only the people of the former Southern Cameroons. They voted to join the union on the basis of a federation. In that respect, a genuine decision to abrogate the federation should have involved only that part of the country.[160] He concludes that Ahidjo's decision to also involve East Cameroonians was a calculated move to ensure that even if the Anglophones rejected the change, they would be outnumbered by the Francophone majority.[161] The strength of the latter assertion is, however, doubtful considering that the results of the referendum seemed predetermined in the context of the authoritarian nature of Ahidjo's regime.[162] In that respect, the Anglophone regions were unlikely to have determined the outcome of the referendum.

In brief, those are some of the legal arguments challenging the validity of the abrogation of the federation in 1972. Of course, they have not gone unchallenged.[163] Assuming, however, that the federalist views were incontrovertible, the question is, what next? How are these arguments to be translated into binding recommendations or decisions for the government to return to federal arrangements? Referendum complaints fall within the jurisdiction of the Constitutional Council and in such matters, only the President of the Republic, the speakers of the two houses of parliament and one-third majority of Senators and MPs can make a complaint to the Constitutional Council.[164] This leaves out the majority of those ordinary persons such as proponents of federalism. In addition, we have seen that the Constitutional Council lacks independence and is unlikely to declare the 1972 referendum null and void. More importantly, there is the issue of whether the Constitutional Council will have jurisdiction taking into account the timing of the referendum (*ratione temporis*). The referendum occurred in 1972, whereas, the Constitutional Council was created in 1996 with its first organic law in 2004. Both the Constitution and the organic laws are silent on the issue of timing. This is unchartered territory and the possibilities are likely to be problematic and unfavourable to proponents of federalism. Moreover, considering that the organisation of a referendum is often a domestic affair, international jurisdictions would be disinclined to entertain any complaints, even those framed in the context of self-determination.[165]

Arguably, such matters can realistically be resolved through a political process provided that the relevant actors are open to such ideas and perceive federalism as a credible solution to addressing the issue of diversity management. The third argument advanced by some proponents of federalism is based on the latter point. Federal systems are credited for their potential to resolve a number of issues including achieving vertical and horizontal political accountability, enhancing democratic processes and managing diversity.[166] The values of federalism are noted to be focused on celebrating diversity, mutual respect, reciprocity and a general determination for cooperation and cohabitation.[167] In light of that focus, federalism has the potential to offer solutions in countries where territorially concentrated minorities demand greater recognition, autonomy and representation in central institutions.[168] Federalism has emerged as a useful tool for balancing the competing demands for autonomy and unity and diversity management in countries like Nigeria, India, Belgium and Malaysia.[169] Thus, proponents of federalism in Cameroon, embrace its potentials to resolve the current impasse and to provide meaningful autonomy to the North-West and South West regions. For instance, reference is made to the fact that federalism will entail independent regional executive and legislative organs with specific powers to regulate issues affecting these regions and a judiciary that is more reflective of the inherited common law tradition in theory and in practice. Such a system does not necessarily eliminate the powers of the central government if based on self-rule and shared rule, where the powers are clearly defined, providing sufficient scope for territorial autonomy and joint decision making at the centre. The African Commission on Human and Peoples' Rights has indicated that federalism can be an option for self-determination of the Anglophone regions.[170] It remains a colossal mission to convince the government of Cameroon to consider that possibility. Moreover, there are also doubts as to the kind of federal system that is suited to the Cameroonian context.

D. Secession

The secessionist agenda propagated by Gorji Dinka for which he was arrested and tried for treason in 1985 remained unobtrusive for some time, although not completely unsupported.[171] The AAC I did not advocate an overt secessionist agenda. That came after the AAC II following the Bamenda Proclamation and the resort to a secessionist agenda was prompted by the government's failure to respond to the Anglophones' demands for meaningful political dialogue. The secessionist agenda has gradually gained traction and, since 2016, has become widespread. The violence that has engulfed the Anglophone regions since 2016 is largely due to the secessionist taking up arms to advance that struggle for Anglophone autonomy, due to the high handedness of the government and its failure to resort to meaningful dialogue to address the Anglophone grievances. This has also been aggravated by the apparently closed international avenues to resolve the dispute.

As far back as 1995, proponents of secession endeavoured to seek peaceful means such as diplomatic offensive to garner support for the autonomy of the Anglophone regions. In May 1995, the SCNC deployed a nine-man delegation (including JN Foncha and ST Muna, the architects of federalism) to the UN to make the case for a residual responsibility of the UN to assist with the struggle for autonomy.[172] Needless to say that did not lead to a UN resolution or recommendation for the independence of the Anglophone regions.

I. Justifying secession

Proponents of secessionist discourse identify unitarism with the theme of subordination – a continuity of the colonial sate in the guise of autonomy and unity.

There have been attempts at achieving autonomy by secession through judicial processes advancing arguments often framed in the context of self-determination. Two major cases discussed in this section summarise the legal arguments underpinning the secessionist agenda. Notably, in 2002, twelve Anglophone nationalists, acting on behalf of themselves and the Southern Cameroonian people, brought a claim against the Federal government of Nigeria in the Federal High Court of Abudja.[173] Briefly,[174] their claim related to the issue of the marginalisation of the Anglophone regions, which they referred to as Southern Cameroons and the failure of the government of Cameroon to respect their right to self-determination under the African Charter on Human and Peoples' Rights. The applicants sort an order for the Federal Government of Nigeria (as party to the African Charter) to assist the people of Southern Cameroons in their quest for self-determination and independence, by presenting their case before the International Court of Justice (ICJ) and the United Nations General Assembly. The Attorney General for the Federal Government of Nigeria objected to the jurisdiction of the Court to hear the complaint. However, that argument was rejected by the Court. In view of that outcome, the parties eventually reached a settlement and the proceedings were discontinued. Pursuant to the settlement, Nigeria agreed to institute proceedings before the ICJ on terms that were clearly outlined in an order issued by the Federal High Court, requiring Nigeria to request the ICJ to determine five key issues.[175] These were whether the 1961 plebiscite was conducted in accordance with the relevant UN Resolutions; whether the termination of the trusteeship by the United Kingdom without ensuring constitutional arrangements between Southern Cameroons and The Republic had been effected in regards to their impending union, was in breach of Articles 3 and 6 of the Trusteeship Agreement for the Southern Cameroons; whether the assumption of sovereign powers over Southern Cameroons by The Republic on 1 October 1961 and its continued exercise are legal and valid; whether the people of Southern Cameroons are not entitled to self-determination separate from *The Republic*; and finally whether it is the Southern Cameroons and not *La Republique* that shares a maritime boundary with the Federal Republic of Nigeria. It must be noted that the last point was prompted by the fact that the complaint was made at the time when the case between Nigeria and Cameroon over the Bakassi Peninsula was before the ICJ. It has been argued that overall that might have influenced the outcome of this case as Nigeria had an interest in the determination of the question of sovereignty over Bakassi.[176] What must be questioned, however, is that although the case was based on Nigeria's obligations under the Africa Charter, the complainants sought an order to compel Nigeria to approach the ICJ. The Court itself did not question that but proceeded to make the order. The decision was a victory for the complainants although it may be argued that their euphoria was short lived. Needless to say, the government of Nigeria has not carried out that order, and has also not been pursued by the complainants.

Nevertheless, the quest for secession did not stop in the Federal High Court of Nigeria. In 2003, Anglophone nationalists represented by SCNC and SCAPO made an application to the African Commission on Human and Peoples' Rights in *Kevin Mgwanga Gunme and 13 ors v Cameroon.*[177] In their application, they rehashed the catalogue of human rights abuses perpetrated on the people of Southern Cameroons by the government of Cameroon and the issue of self-determination. Of interest here are the arguments advanced in support of their bid for autonomy and the response of the Commission. It is worthy to note, however, that the Commission found the government of Cameroon in breach of a good number of fundamental rights protected by the African Charter on Human and Peoples' Rights, including the rights to equality, life, personal liberty, fair trial, education, assembly and freedom from torture.[178]

The basis of their claim for self-determination centred on the potent history of the reunification of Southern Cameroons with The Republic in 1961. On that issue, the complainants argued that the 'unlawful and forced annexation and colonial occupation' of Southern Cameroons by the government of Cameroon constituted a violation of their right to self-determination protected under article 20 of the African Charter. In support of that claim, they alluded to the fact that prior to the reunification of Cameroon, an overwhelming majority of Southern Cameroonians preferred independence but the UN failed to give them that option insisting instead on Southern Cameroons achieving independence by joining Nigeria or the Republic of Cameroon. By failing to give them the option they desired for their independence, the UN denied them the right to self-determination. They argued that, although Southern Cameroons voted in the 1961 plebiscite to join The Republic, this was 'premised on certain conditions, including the convening of a conference of equal representative delegations from The Republic and Southern Cameroons to work out the conditions for the transfer of sovereign powers to the future federation'.[179] Moreover, the arrangement should have been agreed by representatives of the parliaments of both entities before the transfer of sovereignty to a single entity representing both sides. They challenged the validity of the 1961 Federal Constitution on the basis that it was never endorsed by the Southern Cameroons House of Assembly, which implies that there was never an act of union between the two entities. Interestingly, the complainants went further to challenge the 1972 referendum, which brought an end to the federation arguing that it was a breach of the arrangements under the 1961 Federal Constitution (a constitution that they challenged anyway). As a result of the transition to a unitary state, the protections for the Southern Cameroonian minority enshrined in the 1961 Constitution were no longer available. Consequently, they have been marginalised in all spheres and the specificity of the peoples of Southern Cameroons in terms of social life, political administration, culture, language, education and legal traditions were either being undermined or gradually eroded.

Despite the 'unlawful annexation' and marginalisation, the complainants averred that they have attempted to negotiate with the government of Cameroon for better arrangements for the protection of the peoples' of Southern Cameroons, particularly through the 1993 Buea Declaration ensuing from the AAC I and the 1994 Bamenda Proclamation from the AAC II. However, the government proceeded to adopt a new Constitution in 1996, ignoring the Southern Cameroons proposals and their calls for negotiation. According to the complainants, the failure of the government to engage in negotiations and the adoption of the 1996 Constitution without public debate, 'meant that the door was being finally closed on any future constitutional links between Southern Cameroons and *La Republique du Cameroun'*.[180] They noted further that the approach of the government prompted the complainants to conduct a signature referendum from 1 to 30 September 1995 in which 99% of Southern Cameroonians revealed a preference for 'full independence by peaceful separation'.[181] They requested the Commission to determine if the 1961 plebiscite was conducted in accordance with the pre-plebiscite UN resolutions[182] and to determine the right of the Southern Cameroons to self-determination through secession as a result of the massive violations of human rights, marginalisation and domination by the Cameroonian government in breach of article 20 of the African Charter.

After upholding its jurisdiction to hear the complaint and affirming the status of Southern Cameroons as 'a people' (two objections raised by the government of Cameroon), the Commission proceeded to analyse the claim for self-determination. It adopted an avoidance tactic at the outset by declining to address the pertinent question on the compliance of the 1961 plebiscite. It stated that, in determining the question of self-determination of Southern Cameroons,

> it shall contextualise the question by dealing, not with the 1961 UN Plebiscite, or the 1972 Unification, but rather the events of 1993 and 1994 on the constitutional demands vis-à-vis the claim for the right to self-determination of the Southern Cameroonian people.[183]

It is not clear why the Commission evaded the thorny issues of 1961 and 1972. One view is that there was a danger of 'emboldening' the government of Cameroon by declaring that the 1961 arrangements did not amount to an international agreement, a decision which would further antagonise the disillusioned Southern Cameroonians.[184] Alternatively, it may be that 'the Commission holds that determining whether or not the "union" was effected in accordance with UN resolutions, international treaty obligations and indeed international law is irrelevant … and that even if the change amounted to a breach of international law, it did not cause a prejudice worth redressing'.[185] It is submitted that the Commission missed an opportunity to possibly lay to rest a fundamental question in the determination of the Anglophone problem. Presumably, the Commission was careful not to engage in a debate that could possibly be interpreted as interfering with the internal political arrangements of Cameroon or, worst still, engaging in a debate with the danger of implicitly declaring parts of the 1961 or 1972 arrangements challengeable, therefore strengthening the claim for self-determination by secession. This would, in fact, pose a threat to Cameroon's territorial integrity. The Commission's approach to the issue of secession in the end bears testimony to these assertions.

The Commission confirmed the fact that, as a people, Southern Cameroons had the right to self-determination under article 20 of the African Charter and secession was not the sole means of exercising that right. Their autonomy could be exercised within a sovereign state, in the form of self-government, confederacy or federation, while preserving the *integrity* of the state. To demonstrate its commitment to maintaining the territorial integrity of its member states, the Commission held that the African Charter could not be invoked to 'threaten the sovereignty and territorial integrity of a State party'.[186] It stated further that,

> The Commission is obliged to uphold the territorial integrity of the Respondent State. As a consequence, the Commission cannot envisage, condone or encourage secession, as a form of self-determination for the Southern Cameroons. That will jeopardise the territorial integrity of the Republic of Cameroon.[187]

The Commission seems emphatically averse to upheaving the territorial integrity of its member states and in fact has a mandate to the contrary.[188] Individuals such as the complainants have a duty under the African Charter to maintain the territorial integrity of their states.[189] It is surprising that this duty was not alluded to by the Commission. Understandably, this is a difficult duty to exercise and in the context of the present complaint, it would have been immensely provocative to the complainants. The Commission also conflated the issue by stating that the matter of self-determination is not only an issue for Southern Cameroons. In its view, 'the various forms of governance or self-determination such as federalism, local government, unitarism, confederacy and self-government can be exercised only subject to conformity with state sovereignty and territorial integrity of a State party' taking 'into account the popular will of the entire population'.[190] It fails to acknowledge that the complaint specifically related to the self-determination of the people of Southern Cameroons. By making self-determination a national agenda, the Commission gave credence to an infamous government refrain relating to a common 'Cameroonian identity' justifying its decentralisation agenda. Decentralisation, as discussed earlier, has failed to resolve the key grievances of the Anglophone minority.

The Commission did not, however, close the door to secession. It alluded to standards set in *Katangese Peoples' Congress v Zaire*,[191] which requires a complainant to demonstrate two conditions under article 20(2) – oppression and domination. Thus, a right to secession is predicated on a complainant demonstrating that they are being dominated and oppressed through the commission of massive violation of human rights. Despite the importance of these standards, they were not defined by the Commission. Domination nevertheless relates to foreign domination rather than domination within a state. The Commission held that the allegations of violations of the rights of the people of Southern Cameroons did not meet that threshold of 'massive violations'. Failing to fulfil the article 20(2) criteria implied that the complainants could not engage in secession as secession was not a variant of self-determination recognised under the African Charter.[192]

II. What next for the secessionist agenda?

Understandably, the Commission's decision dealt a blow to the secessionist, who have since sought to advance their cause by peaceful and legal means. The approach of the Commission to the right to self-determination finds support in international law and resonates with avoidance tactics sometimes adopted by international jurisdictions. For instance, in the East Timor case involving Portugal and Australia, the ICJ passed an opportunity to create jurisprudence on secession by refusing to answer a question on sovereignty over East Timor. A response to that issue would have determined whether East Timor had a right to self-determination and whether it belonged to Portugal or Indonesia.[193] A similar approach was adopted by the ICJ in its advisory opinions on Kosovo and Western Sahara. In the former, although the ICJ was of the opinion that Kosovo's declaration of independence on 17 February 2008 did not breach international law because such a declaration was not prohibited under international law, it avoided making a declaration on secession on the basis that it was not required to address that issue in the Kosovo advisory opinion.[194] More significantly, in the latter case, the ICJ declined to rule on the legality of the claims by Mauritania and Morocco of sovereignty over Western Sahara but it affirmed their right to self-determination and the importance of territorial integrity. It stated that the principle of territorial integrity could prevail over self-determination, in instances where there is solid evidence of the existence of a territorial claim over a particular region, *irrespective* of the wishes of the people of that region not to be governed by the entity asserting such a territorial claim.[195]

It is clear from the aforementioned discussion that debates on self-determination and secession will always be infused with the primacy of territorial integrity. Even Principle V of the Friendly Relations Declaration makes clear that the principle of self-determination must be balanced with a state's territorial integrity.[196] All of these do not herald glad tidings for the secessionist agenda of the SCNC, SCAPO and the more recent secessionist groups in the Anglophone regions of Cameroon that see this as the only option. The ICJ, which, according to the order of the Federal High Court of Nigeria, could have heard their complaint, had Nigeria honoured the agreement, seems unlikely to have answered the questions in the affirmative, assuming that it answered the questions at all. As with the aforementioned cases (Kosovo and Western Sahara), it is unlikely that the ICJ will unequivocally affirm any right of the Southern Cameroons to secede. Perhaps the jurisprudence of the ICJ has dissuaded the Southern Cameroonians from pursuing the government of Nigeria to honour the agreement to present their case before the ICJ.

Despite the prominence of the principle of territorial integrity, like the African Charter, the right to secede has been recognised elsewhere and similarly under very limited circumstances. The Supreme Court of Canada in the matter on the secession of Quebec identified three circumstances.[197] These are – where a people are governed as part of a colonial empire, or subject to alien subjugation, domination or exploitation or where a people are denied the meaningful exercise of their right to self-determination within the state. In the Åland Island Question, it was stated that the circumstances that could justify secession included 'where a state lacks either the will or the power to enact and apply just and effective guarantee'.[198] In both instances, as with the African Charter, there is an emphasis on alien/colonial domination rather than domination within a state. With respect to the failure to guarantee the meaningful exercise of rights, the threshold would be very high as the interpretation of 'meaningful' can be very subjective. The threshold would be akin to that of 'sustained massive violations of human rights' under the African Charter. But even in all of these circumstances, including under the African Charter, secession is only exercised as an *ultima ratio*. Reverting to the decision of the African Commission in the *Gunme case*, could it be worth pursuing another line of arguments relating to new evidence of violations of human rights in the Anglophone regions? In other words, in the light of the egregious violations of human rights committed by security forces since 2016, could the secessionist successfully argue before the Commission that the violations are so severe that they call into question the integrity of the Cameroonian government and therefore have attained the threshold stipulated in the *Katangese case*? The answer is probably in the negative, particularly in the light of the special status granted to the restive regions. In view of the decision of the African Commission, which, in effect, denies that the Anglophone regions are not guaranteed any *meaningful* exercise of their right to internal self-determination, it would be a herculean task for the Anglophone secessionist to satisfactorily demonstrate in any international jurisdiction that those exceptional circumstances apply to the peoples of the Anglophone regions.

The difficulties for the Southern Cameroonian secessionist organisations in establishing the stringent criteria for secession may partly account for the current armed struggle between the separatists and the government's military and security forces. The justification may be that some successful stories of secession occurred after armed struggle. Two things must be noted here. First, not all armed liberation struggles have been successful. An example close to home is that of neighbouring Biafra, which failed in its bid to secede from the rest of Nigeria. Their liberation struggle received very limited support and was instead a subject of international condemnation.[199] Second, the few successful stories stemmed from decades of protracted armed conflict with overwhelming casualties and substantial economic costs. South Sudan, for instance, started its armed liberation struggle as far back as 1955 and it was only in July 2011 that it gained its independence.[200] This came after the Comprehensive Peace Agreement in 2005 in which transitional arrangements for self-rule were agreed and followed by a referendum in January 2011 in which almost 99% of Southern Sudanese voted for independence from Sudan.[201] In the case of Eritrea, independence was attained following a protracted armed struggle by the Eritrean Liberation Movement that spanned three decades and after an ultimate acknowledgement of Eritrea's right to external self-determination by Ethiopia.[202] Notwithstanding, the final process had to be sealed by a UN sponsored plebiscite in April 1993 in which Eritreans voted 99.8% in favour of independence from Ethiopia. These two instances of successful secession demonstrate not only that armed struggle is likely to be protracted and costly, but also that the people will ultimately have to decide through a lawful process whether they wish to secede. Bearing in mind the current divisions among Anglophone Cameroonians between those who favour independence or federalism and those who favour decentralisation (special autonomy status), it cannot be said with absolute certainty that secession is the preferred option of the majority.

Conclusion

This chapter has analysed the main contending views on the governance structure best suited to mediating the Anglophone quest for self-determination. The government's decentralisation option has thus far been unsuccessful and the practical effects of the new special status arrangements would no doubt be discernible in due course. Though imbued with prospects for effectively accommodating diversity, federalism has not appealed to the government. Despite its violent resurgence, secession has proved extremely uncertain and costly. Based on the analysis in this chapter, the following broad conclusions can be made.

First, it is clear that, historically, there is a democratic deficit in the mechanisms applied by the government to mediate the Anglophone problem. There is need for a paradigm shift that will allow genuine participatory processes capable of providing platforms for all the relevant parties to articulate the specific ways in which the Anglophone problem can be resolved and to mutually agree on common solutions. A comprehensive dialogue process should equally be open to various governance options, including those not yet explored and opposing parties must be disposed to concessions. A genuine and open participatory process will go a long way to create ownership and establish legitimacy of both the process and the outcome.

Second, the normative framework for mediating and institutionalising change is currently inadequate. Establishing genuine and effective solutions would require a new normative framework that is reflective of the new dispensation. The constitution currently limits the scope for expansive and innovative autonomy arrangements for the Anglophone regions. For instance, legislative and executive powers have already been allocated in the Constitution such that any autonomy arrangements intended to enhance regional governance cannot entail the granting of much desired legislative and executive powers at the regional level. This partly accounts for the very circumscribed special autonomy status that has to exist within the confines of a flawed decentralised system. Arguably, a new constitution is imperative for change, not only with respect to the Anglophone problem, but also for governance in general.

Lastly, there is need for systemic solutions that address the core issues in the Anglophone struggle for self-determination. Cosmetic solutions have proven to be ineffective. Solutions must necessarily envisage establishing the legal, political and institutional framework that guarantees effective governance at the regional level to enhance social, cultural and economic development and guarantee the protection of minority rights.

Notes

1 National Commission on Human Rights and Freedoms (NCHRF), 'Report on the State of Human Rights in Cameroon in 2016' (Ets Messie Printers and Publishers 2017) 154; International Crisis Group, 'Cameroon Anglophone Crisis at the Crossroads' (2 August 2017, Africa Report No. 250) 9 https://d2071andvip0wj.cloudfront.net/250-cameroons-anglophone-crisis-at-the-crossroads_0.pdf accessed 24 June 2018.
2 NCHRF, 'Report on the State of Human Rights' (n 1) 154–156; International Crisis Group, 'Cameroon Anglophone Crisis' (n 1) 9–10.
3 Order No. 124/CAB/PM of 29 November 2016.
4 International Crisis Group, 'Cameroon Anglophone Crisis' (n 1) 12.
5 Discussed in Chapter 4 at p 117.
6 Decree No. 2017/013 of 23 January 2017 on the creation of the National Commission for Bilingualism and Multiculturalism.
7 International Crisis Group (n 1) 12.
8 International Crisis Group (n 1) 11.
9 International Crisis Group (n 1) 11–12; Jon Lunn and Louisa Brooke-Holland, 'The Anglophone Cameroon Crisis: April 2019 Update' (17 April 2019, UK House of Commons Briefing Paper Number 8331) 8–9 https://researchbriefings.parliament.uk/ResearchBriefing/Summary/CBP-8331#fullreport accessed 19 July 2019.
10 Some CACSC leaders like Agbor Balla and other activists like Paul Ayah were subsequently released after several months in detention.
11 Freedom House, 'Freedom in the World 2019: Cameroon Country Report' https://freedomhouse.org/report/freedom-world/2019/cameroon accessed 10 September 2019.
12 US Department of State, '2018 Country Reports on Human Rights Practices: Cameroon' (13 March 2019) 5, 15 https://www.state.gov/wp-content/uploads/2019/03/Cameroon-2018.pdf accessed 10 September 2019.
13 International Crisis Group (n 1) 15.
14 The Federal High Court of Abuja (Nigeria) declared their arrest and detention unlawful, and their expulsion to Cameroon unlawful and unconstitutional in *Sisiku Ayuk Tabe & 11 Ors v The National Security Adviser & Anor* (Suit No./FHC/ABJ/CS/85/2018) and *Wilfred Tassang & 50 Ors v The National Security Adviser & Anor* (Suit No./FHC/ABJ/CS/147/2018).
15 US Department of State, '2018 Country Reports' (n 12) 9.
16 Francesca Grandi, 'Why Cameroon's Conflict Matters for Regional Security' (International Research Institute, 6 November 2018) https://www.iiss.org/blogs/analysis/2018/11/cameroon accessed 20 December 2019.
17 United Nations Department for the Coordination of Humanitarian Affairs, 'Cameroon: North-West and South-West Crisis, Situation Report N°8 as of 30 June 2019' https://www.humanitarianresponse.info/en/operations/cameroon/document/cameroon-north-west-and-south-west-crisis-situation-report-n%C2%B08–30-june accessed 9 September 2019.
18 UNHCR, 'Cameroon Situation: Responding to the Needs of IDPs and Cameroonian Refugees in Nigeria' (1 March 2019) http://reporting.unhcr.org/sites/default/files/UNHCR%20Cameroon%202019%20Supplementary%20Appeal%20%28March%202019%29.pdf accessed 11 September 2019; OHCHR, 'Opening Statement and Global Update of Human Rights Concerns by UN High Commissioner for Human Rights Zeid Ra'ad Al Hussein at 38th Session of the Human Rights Council' (18 June 2018) https://www.ohchr.org/EN/HRBodies/HRC/Pages/NewsDetail.aspx?NewsID=23206&LangID=E accessed 10 September 2019. See also, Nna-Emeka Okereke, 'Analysing Cameroon's Anglophone Crisis' (2018) 10(3) *Counter Terrorist Trends and Analyses* 8, 12.
19 UNESCO, 'Cameroon: Joint Statement of UNICEF and UNESCO on Abduction of Education Personnel and Attacks Against Schools in The South-West Region

of Cameroon' (1 June 2018) http://cm.one.un.org/content/unct/cameroon/en/home/presscenter/communiques-de-presse/cameroon–joint-statement-of-unicef-and-unesco-on-abduction- accessed 10 September 2019.

20 Victor Afoni, 'Anglophone Crisis: Ghost Towns and Social Unrest Hamper Education' N0.042, April 2018 *Born Free* (Magazine of the NCHRF) 15.

21 It was also influenced by the Bretton Woods Institutions. See Ndiva Kofele-Kale, 'Local Governance under Cameroon's Decentralisation Regime: Is It All Sound and Fury Signifying Nothing?' (2011) 37(3) *Commonwealth Law Bulletin* 513, 515; Janet Kathyola and Oluwatoyin Job (eds), *Decentralisation in Commonwealth Africa: Experiences from Botswana, Cameroon, Ghana, Mozambique and Tanzania* (Commonwealth Secretariat 2011) 64; Oben Mbuagbo, 'Cameroon: Flawed Decentralisation and the Politics of Identity in the Urban Space' (2012) 12(11) *Global Journal of Human Social Science, Sociology, Economics & Political Science* 14, 15–22.

22 Constitution, art 1(2).

23 Constitution, art 55(1).

24 Law No. 2004/017 of 22 July 2004 on the Orientation of Decentralisation (Law on Decentralisation); Law No. 2004/018 of 22 July 2004 to lay down Rules Applicable to Councils; Law No. 2004/019 of 22 July 2004 to lay down Rules Applicable to Regions; Law No. 2009/011 of 10 July 2009 on the Financial Regime of Regional and Local Authorities.

25 S. 4(1) of Decree No. 2018/190 of 2 March 2018, amending Decree No. 2011/408 of 9 December 2011 to organise the Government.

26 Law No. 2019/024 of 24 December 2019 to institute the General Code of Regional and Local Authorities (RLA Code).

27 RLA Code, s 500 repeals previous provisions.

28 This provision can, in fact, be traced to article 47 of the Federal Constitution, which had similar prescriptions and did not preclude the transformation of the form of the state from federal to unitary. See pp 199–200.

29 Law on Decentralisation, 2004, s 2(2), now reproduced in s 5(2) of the RLA Code.

30 Harry Blair, 'Participation and Accountability at the Periphery: Democratic Local Governance in Six Countries' (2002) 28(1) *World Development* 21.

31 Dawn Brancati, 'Decentralisation: Fueling the Fire or Dampening the Flames of Interstate Conflict?' (2006) 60(3) *International Organisation* 651, 655–656; Benjamin Edwards and Serdar Yilmaz, 'Decentralisation as a Post-Conflict Stabilisation Tool: The Case of Sierra Leone' (2016) 36 *Public Administration and Development* 347.

32 Ian Lustick, Dan Miodownik and Roy Eidelson, 'Secessionism in Multicultural States: Does Sharing Power Prevent or Encourage It?' (2004) 98(2) *American Political Science Review* 209.

33 Jude Ndzifon Kimengsi and Solange Akhere Gwan, 'Reflections on Decentralisation, Community Empowerment and Sustainable Development in Cameroon' (2017) 1(2) *International Journal of Emerging Trends in the Social Sciences* 53, 55.

34 Dawn Brancanti, *Peace By Design: Managing Intrastate Conflict through Decentralisation* (Oxford University Press 2008).

35 Thomas Chapman and Philip Roeder 'Partition as a Solution to Wars of Nationalism: The Importance of Institutions' (2007) 101(4) *American Political Science Review* 677; Svante Cornell, 'Autonomy as a Source of Conflict: Caucasian Conflicts in Theoretical Perspective' (2002) 54(2) *World Politics* 245; Jack Snyder, *From Voting to Violence: Democratisation and Nationalist Conflict* (Norton: New York 2000); Brancati, 'Decentralisation: Fuelling the Fire' (n 31) 656.

36 Francis Loh, 'Ethnic Diversity and the Nation State: From Centralisation in the Age of Nationalism to Decentralisation Amidst Globalisation' (2017) 18(3) *Inter-Asia Cultural Studies* 414, 416.

37 See generally, Charles Tiebout, 'A Pure Theory of Local Expenditures' (1957) 64 *Journal of Political Economy* 416.
38 Edwards and Yilmaz, 'Decentralisation as a Post-Conflict Stabilisation Tool' (n 31) 348.
39 Edwards and Yilmaz, 'Decentralisation as a Post-Conflict Stabilisation Tool' (n 31) 349.
40 Law on Decentralisation, 2004, s 9(2) now RLA Code, s 20(1).
41 Emmanuel Edou, 'Implementation of Decentralisation in Cameroon: Problems, Challenges and Strategies' (Working Paper Presented by Minister Delegate at the Ministry of Territorial Administration and Decentralisation, in charge of Local Councils) 5 unpan1.un.org › intradoc › groups › public › documents › unpan030738 accessed 28 July 2018.
42 Law on Decentralisation, 2004, s 2(2), now RLA Code, s 17.
43 RLA Code, ss 8 and 9.
44 RLA Code, s 11(1).
45 ibid.
46 Law on Decentralisation, 2004, s 4, restated in RLA Code, ss 17 and 18.
47 See, for instance, RLA Code, s 18(2).
48 For instance, RLA Code, s 76(1). The representative of the state in the regions is the Governor and the Senior Divisional Officer in the councils (RLA Code, ss73(1) and 73(5), respectively). Under the 2004 Law on Decentralisation, it was the Government Delegate and the Senior Divisional Officer.
49 Edou, 'Implementation of Decentralisation in Cameroon' (n 41) 5.
50 Kofele-Kale, 'Local Governance' (n 21) 521–527; Mbuagbo, 'Cameroon: Flawed Decentralisation' (n 21) 17–21.
51 Constitution, art 58. See also RLA Code, s 73. This was the situation under ss 67 and 115(1) of the 2004 Law on Decentralisation.
52 RLA Code, s 323(1)(2).
53 RLA, s 323(3).
54 Constitution, art 61(2).
55 Constitution, art 59(1)(2). See also, RLA Code, ss 296 and 297, respectively.
56 RLA Law, s 182(1).
57 RLA Law, s 416(2).
58 Edou, 'Implementation of Decentralisation in Cameroon' (n 41) 5.
59 ibid
60 The speech is available at https://www.prc.cm/en/news/speeches-of-the-president/3777-the-head-of-state-s-message-to-the-nation-10-sept-2019.
61 A comprehensive list can be obtained from 'Office of the Prime Minister: Official Program of Consultations of the Prime Minister, Head of Government, in View of the National Dialogue' https://www.spm.gov.cm/site/sites/default/files/version_anglaise_planning_des_consultations_du_pmcg.pdf accessed 23 October 2019.
62 An excerpt of the report of the Rapporteur General of the Major National Dialogue reproduced in 'Major National Dialogue: Recommendations to Restore Peace, Stability and Development' (*Cameroon Tribune* 7 October 2019) cameroon-tribune.cm/article.html/28306/en.html/major-national-dialogue-recommendations-restore-peace-stability accessed 24 October 2019.
63 See, for instance, Fred Muvunyi, 'Cameroon's Stillborn Dialogue for Peace' (*Deutsche Welle* 30 September 2019) dw.com/en/opinion-cameroons-stillborn-dialogue-for-peace/a-50638224 accessed 12 December 2019.
64 Law No. 2019/019 of 24 December 2019 on the Promotion of Official Languages in Cameroon.
65 John Fru Ndi, Press Release. Secretariat of the National Executive Committee of the Social Democratic Front, Ref. 060/S2/SDF.NF/033 of 6 October 2019.

66 Law No. 2019/024 of 24 December 2019 to Institute the General Code of Regional and Local Authorities.
67 Bill No. 1065/PJL/AN to institute the General Code of Regional and Local Authorities.
68 RLA Code, s 1.
69 RLA Code, s 2(1)(2).
70 RLA Code, s 3(2).
71 RLA Code, s 3(3).
72 See, for instance, RLA Code, s. 327(2), which mentions 'historical, social and cultural values'.
73 RLA Code, s 271(a).
74 RLA Code, s 273(a)(b).
75 RLA Code, s 273(b).
76 RLA Code, s 271(a).
77 See generally, Kingsly Awang, 'The National Produce Marketing Board in Cameroon, 1978–1991: An Analysis of its Origin, Performance and Collapse' (2014–2015) 22, 23 *AfrikaZamani* 101.
78 It may be possible to infer that such powers may also be exercised by other regions pursuant to section 38 of the RLA Code, broadly interpreted.
79 See Chapter 4 at 117.
80 Silja Fröhlich, 'Cameroon: Anglophone's Special Status – too little, too late?' (*Deutsche Welle*, 23 December 2019) dw.com/en/Cameroon-anglophones-special-status-too-little-too-late/a-51747683 accessed 7 January 2020.
81 ibid.
82 RLA Code, s 274(1).
83 RLA Code, s 275(1)(2).
84 RLA Code, s 275(3).
85 RLA Code, s 282(1).
86 RLA Code, s 306.
87 RLA Code, s 307(1)(2).
88 RLA Code, s 307(1).
89 RLA Code, s 330.
90 RLA Code, s 331(1).
91 RLA Code, s 332(1).
92 RLA Code, s 332(2).
93 RLA Code, s 333(1).
94 RLA Code, s 336.
95 RLA Code, s 334(1).
96 RLA Code, s 334(2).
97 RLA Code, s 335(1).
98 RLA Code, s 337(1).
99 RLA Code, s 337(2).
100 RLA Code, s 338.
101 RLA Code, s 339(1).
102 RLA Code, s 352(1)(2).
103 RLA Code, s 353(1).
104 RLA Code, s 353(2)(3).
105 RLA Code, ss 359(2) and 360(1), respectively.
106 RLA Code, 359(1).
107 RLA Code, ss 366, 323 and 324.
108 RLA Code, s 351.
109 RLA Code, ss 282(1) and 334(2).
110 See, for instance, RLA Code, s 273(a).

111 RLA Code, ss 359(1) and 312(1).
112 RLA Code, s 359(1) lines 3 and 4.
113 RLA Code, s 367(1).
114 RLA Code, s 367(2).
115 RLA Code, s 368(1).
116 RLA Code, s 368(2).
117 RLA Code, s 368(3).
118 RLA Code, s 368(4).
119 RLA Code, s 367(3).
120 RLA Code, s 369(1)(2).
121 RLA Code, s 369(1)(2).
122 RLA Code, s 370(4).
123 RLA Code, s 369(3).
124 RLA Code, s 369(3).
125 RLA Code, s 370(1).
126 RLA Code, s 370(2).
127 RLA Code, s 370(3).
128 RLA Code, s 370(3).
129 Fröhlich, 'Cameroon: Anglophone's Special Status?' (n 80); Josiane Kouagheu, 'Cameroon Grants Special Status to the Anglophone Regions' (*Reuters*, 20 December 2019) https://www.reuters.com/article/us-cameroon-separatists-lawmaking/cameroon-grants-special-status-to-anglophone-regions-idUSKBN1YO24S accessed 5 January 2020; Moki Edwin Kindzeke, 'Cameroon MPs Approve Law Giving Special Status to English-Speaking Regions' (*Voice of Africa News*, 21 December 2019) https://www.voanews.com/africa/cameroon-mps-approve-law-giving-special-status-english-speaking-regions accessed 10 January 2020.
130 Kouagheu, 'Cameroon Grants Special Status to the Anglophone Regions' (n 129).
131 Fröhlich, 'Cameroon: Anglophone's Special Status?' (n 80).
132 Sylvain Andzongo, 'Draft Law Submitted for the Special Status of Anglophone Regions' (Business in Cameroon, 13 December 2019) businessincameroon.com/public-management/1312–9769-exclusive-draft-law-submitted-for-special-status-of-anglophone-regions accessed 10 January 2020.
133 Kindzeke, 'Cameroon MPs Approve Law Giving Special Status' (n 129); Kouagheu, 'Cameroon Grants Special Status to the Anglophone Regions' (n 129).
134 Michelle Ann Miller, 'The Problem of Armed Separatism: Is Autonomy the Answer?' in Michelle Miller (ed) *Autonomy and Armed Separatism in South and Southeast Asia* (ISEAS Publishing 2012) 2–9.
135 Rodd McGibbon, 'Secessionist Challenges in Aceh and Papua: Is Special Autonomy the Solution?' (2004) 10 *Policy Studies* vii, 5–6, 25–27.
136 ibid 5–6, 25–27.
137 ibid 6, 68.
138 Ted Gurr, *Peoples versus States: Minorities at Risk in the New Century* (USIP 2000) 210.
139 ibid.
140 Marc Weller, 'Settling Self-determination Conflicts: Recent Developments' (2009) 20(1) *European Journal of International Law* 111, 140.
141 Weller, 'Settling Self-determination Conflicts' (n 140) 140.
142 See in that regard, Weller, 'Settling Self-determination Conflicts' (n 140) 115.
143 It has sometimes been argued that entrenchment may undermine democracy. However, this may arguably be so only in a democratic society where free and equal participation is guaranteed. See, for instance, Richard Albert, 'Constitutional Handcuff' (2017) 1 *Intergenerational Justice Review* 18. See also Eric Posner and Adrian Vermuele, 'Legislative Entrenchment: A Reappraisal' (2002) 111(7) *Yale Law Journal* 1665.

144 Albert Chen, 'Constitutional Adjudication in Post-1997 Hong Kong' (2006) 15(3) *Pacific Rim Law and Policy Journal* 627, 631–632.
145 ibid. See art 159 of the Basic Law of the Hong Kong Special Administrative Region.
146 Constitution of Finland, art 120.
147 Act on the Autonomy of Åland 1992, s 69.
148 Elisabeth Nauclér, 'Autonomy and Multi-Level Governance: Experience in Nordic and Central European Cooperation' in Marc Weller and Stefan Wolff, *Autonomy, Self-Governance and Conflict Resolution: Innovative Approaches to Institutional Design in Divided Societies* (Routledge 2005) 94.
149 Atia Azohnwi, 'Cameroon Anglophone Crisis – Agbor Balla, "I am a chief apostle of a two state federation … I am not a fan of separation"' 15 May 2019 *Cameroon-info.net.* http://www.cameroon-info.net/article/cameroon-anglophone-crisis-agbor-balla-i-am-a-chief-apostle-of-a-two-state-342672.html accessed 12 September 2019.
150 See 'The Buea Declaration: All Anglophone Conference, 2nd & 3rd April, 1993' (Nooremac Press 1993) 29.
151 The Crux, 'Cardinal Backs Federal Union to End Cameroon's Anglophone Crisis' (*The Crux*, 3 August 2019) https://cruxnow.com/church-in-africa/2019/08/03/cardinal-backs-federal-union-to-end-cameroons-anglophone-crisis/ accessed 12 September 2019.
152 This is emphatically stated in the Buea Declaration.
153 Frank Stark, 'Federalism in Cameroon: The Shadow and the Reality' (1976) (10)3 *Canadian Journal of African Studies* 423, 425–427.
154 Stark, 'Federalism in Cameroon' (n 153) 427.
155 Piet Konings, 'The Anglophone Struggle for Federalism in Cameroon' in Lidija Basta and Jibrin Ibrahim (eds) *Federalism and Decentralisation in Africa: The Multicultural Challenge* (Fribourg: Institute of Federalism 1999) 303; Carlson Anyangwe, *Betrayal of Too Trusting a People: The UN, the UK and the Trust Territory of the Southern Cameroons* (Langaa 2009) 120–126; Ngwa Nfobin, 'The Francophone/Anglophone Split over Article 47 of the Constitution of the Federal Republic of Cameroon: An Abiding Malaise with an Explosive Charge' (2017) 25(4) *African Journal of International and Comparative Law* 538. See also Yuhniwo Ngenge, 'Cameroon's Political Crisis: Why a Onetime Peace Haven Might Be Headed for the Unknown' (CONSTITUTIONNET, 24 November 2017) http://constitutionnet.org/news/cameroons-political-crisis-why-onetime-peace-haven-might-be-headed-unknown accessed 12 February 2018.
156 As discussed at p 182, a similar argument is made by the government in support of decentralisation, pursuant to article 64 of the 1996 Constitution.
157 A contrasting view has been expressed by Alain Didier Olinga, 'La Question Anglophone dans le Cameroun d'aujourd'hui' (1994) 48(3) *Revue Juridique et Politique, Indépendance et Coopération* 292.
158 Anyangwe, 'Betrayal of Too Trusting a People' (n 155) 124.
159 Anyangwe, 'Betrayal of Too Trusting a People' (n 155) 122; Konings, 'The Anglophone Struggle' (n 155) 303.
160 Anyangwe, 'Betrayal of Too Trusting a People' (n 155) 119.
161 ibid.
162 Stark, 'Federalism in Cameroon' (n 153) 40–41; Konings, 'The Anglophone Struggle' (155) 303–304.
163 See, for instance, Olinga, 'La Question Anglophone dans le Cameroun d'aujourd'hui' (n 157) 292–303.
164 Electoral Code, ss 209 and 210.
165 This will be explored further in the next section.
166 Rosalind Dixon, Ron Levy and Mark Tushnet, 'Theories and Practices of Federalism in Deeply Divided Societies' (2018) 46(4) *Federal Law Review* 481.

167 See generally, Michael Burgess, *Comparative Federalism: Theory and Practice* (Routledge 2006).
168 Soeren Keil, 'Federalism as a Tool of Conflict-Resolution: The Case of Bosnia and Herzegovina' (2012) 1(363) *Centre International de Formation Européenne* 205, 206.
169 Keil, 'Federalism as a Tool of Conflict-Resolution' (n 168) 205; Michael O'Neill, 'Re-Imagining Belgium: New Federalism and the Political Management of Cultural Diversity' 1998 51(2) *Parliamentary Affairs* 241.
170 *Kevin Mgwanga Gunme and 13 ors v Cameroon,* Communication No. 266/2003 ACHPR (05/2009), Ex.CL/529(XV) Annex 4, paras 188 and 191.
171 See Chapter 1 at p 20.
172 Francis Nyamjoh and Piet Konings, *Negotiating an Anglophone Identity: A Study of the Politics of Recognition and Representation in Cameroon* (Brill 2003) 92–95.
173 *Gunme & Ors v Attorney General of the Federal Republic of Nigeria.* Suit No. FHC/ABJ/CS/30/2002.
174 This case has been discussed extensively in Nelson Enonchong, 'Foreign State Assistance in Enforcing the Right to Self-determination under the African Charter' (2002) 46(2) *Journal of African Law* 246.
175 The terms of the order have been reproduced in Enonchong, 'Foreign State Assistance' (n 174) 250–251.
176 Enonchong, 'Foreign State Assistance' (n 174) 255–257.
177 *Gunme v Cameroon* (n 170).
178 *Gunme v Cameroon,* para 214.
179 *Gunme v Cameroon,* para 164.
180 *Gunme v Cameroon,* para 16.
181 *Gunme v Cameroon,* para 17.
182 See Chapter 1 at p 9–11 for a discussion of the resolutions.
183 *Gunme v Cameroon,* para 182.
184 Ngwa Nfobin and Nchotu Veraline Minang, 'The Cameroon Anglophone Question in International Law' (2014) 22(2) *African Journal of International and Comparative Law* 234, 252.
185 Nfobin and Minang, 'The Cameroon Anglophone Question' (n 184) 253.
187 *Gunme v Cameroon,* para 190.
186 *Gunme v Cameroon,* para 191.
188 AU Constitutive Act, arts 3(b) and 4(b), respectively, enshrine the principles of territorial integrity and *uti possidetis* and the African Commission as an institution of the AU must respect and promote this.
189 African Charter, art 29(5).
190 *Gunme v Cameroon,* para 199.
191 *Katangese Peoples' Congress v Zaire,* Comunication No. 75/92, 1 HRL 174 (ACHPR 1995).
192 *Gunme v Cameroon,* para 200.
193 East Timor (*Port. v Austl.*), 1995 ICJ 90 (30 June). http://www.worldcourts.com/icj/eng/decisions/1995.06.30_east_timor.htm accessed 15 February 2019.
194 International Court of Justice, 'Accordance with International Law of the Unilateral Declaration of Independence in Respect of Kosovo: Advisory Opinion of 22 July 2010' 403 https://www.icj-cij.org/files/case-related/141/141-20100722-ADV-01-00-EN.pdf accessed 13 February 2019.
195 Western Sahara, Advisory Opinion of 12 October 1975 (International Court of Justice) http://www.worldcourts.com/icj/eng/decisions/1975.10.16_western_sahara.htm accessed 15 February 2019.
196 Declaration on Principles of International Law Concerning Friendly Relations and Cooperation Among States in Accordance with the Charter of the United Nations, UNGA Res 2625 [XXV] 24 October 1970.

197 Reference re Secession of Quebec (SCR) 2(1998), 217, para 133.
198 The Åland Islands Question, Report submitted to the Council of the League of Nations by the Commission of Rapporteurs. Document du Conseil B7, 21/68/106, of 16 April 1921, 28.
199 See, for instance, OAU Resolution on Situation in Nigeria, AHG/Res 51 (IV) (1967) condemning Biafran Secession.
200 See generally, Anthony J Christopher, 'Secession and South Sudan: An African Precedent for the Future?' (2011) 93(2) *South African Geographical Journal* 125–132.
201 This has ironically not led to internal self-determination of the people of South Sudan. See, Ltje de Vries and Mareike Schomerus, 'Fettered Self-determination: South Sudan's Narrowed Path to Secession' (2017) 19(1) *Civil Wars* 26, 26–45.
202 Bereket H Selassie, 'Comment: Self-Determination in Principle and Practice: The Ethiopian-Eritrean Experience' (1997) 29 *Columbia Human Rights Law Review* 91.

References

Afoni V, 'Anglophone Crisis: Ghost Towns and Social Unrest Hamper Education' N0.042, April 2018 *Born Free* (Magazine of the NCHRF).

Albert R, 'Constitutional Handcuff' (2017) *1 Intergenerational Justice Review* 18.

Andzongo S, *'Draft Law Submitted for the Special Status of Anglophone Regions'* (Business in Cameroon, 13 December 2019) businessincameroon.com/public-management/1312-9769-exclusive-draft-law-submitted-for-special-status-of-anglophone-regions accessed 10 January 2020.

Anyangwe C, *Betrayal of Too Trusting a People: The UN, the UK and the Trust Territory of the Southern Cameroons* (Langaa 2009).

Awang K, 'The National Produce Marketing Board in Cameroon, 1978-1991: An Analysis of its Origin, Performance and Collapse' (2014–2015) *22 and 23 AfrikaZamani* 101.

Blair H, 'Participation and Accountability at the Periphery: Democratic Local Governance in Six Countries' (2002) *28*(1) *World Development* 21.

Brancati D 'Decentralisation: Fueling the Fire or Dampening the Flames of Interstate Conflict?' (2006) 60(3) *International Organisation* 651.

Brancati D, *Peace By Design: Managing Intrastate Conflict through Decentralisation* (Oxford University Press 2008).

Burgess M, *Comparative Federalism: Theory and Practice* (Routledge 2006).

Chapman T and Roeder P 'Partition as a Solution to Wars of Nationalism: The Importance of Institutions' (2007) *101*(4) *American Political Science Review* 677.

Chen A, 'Constitutional Adjudication in Post-1997 Hong Kong' (2006) *15*(3) *Pacific Rim Law and Policy Journal* 627.

Cornell S, 'Autonomy as a Source of Conflict: Caucasian Conflicts in Theoretical Perspective' (2002) *54*(2) *World Politics* 245.

de Vries L and Schomerus M, 'Fettered Self-Determination: South Sudan's Narrowed Path to Secession' (2017) *19*(1) *Civil Wars* 26.

Dixon R, Levy R and Tushnet M, 'Theories and Practices of Federalism in Deeply Divided Societies' (2018) *46*(4) *Federal Law Review* 481.

Edou E, 'Implementation of Decentralisation in Cameroon: Problems, Challenges and Strategies' (Working Paper Presented by Minister Delegate at the Ministry of Territorial Administration and Decentralisation, in charge of Local Councils) 5 unpan1.un.org › intradoc › groups › public › documents › unpan030738 accessed 28 July 2018.

Edwards B and Yilmaz S 'Decentralisation as a Post-Conflict Stabilisation Tool: The Case of Sierra Leone' (2016) *36 Public Administration and Development* 347.

Enonchong N, 'Foreign State Assistance in Enforcing the Right to Self-Determination under the African Charter' (2002) *46*(2) *Journal of African Law* 246.

Freedom House, 'Freedom in the World 2019: Cameroon Country Report' https://freedomhouse.org/report/freedom-world/2019/cameroon accessed 10 September 2019.

Fröhlich S, 'Cameroon: Anglophone's Special Status – too little, too late?' (*Deutsche Welle*, 23 December 2019) dw.com/en/Cameroon-anglophones-special-status-too-little-too-late/a-51747683 accessed 7 January 2020.

Grandi F, 'Why Cameroon's Conflict Matters for Regional Security' (International Research Institute, 6 November 2018) https://www.iiss.org/blogs/analysis/2018/11/cameroon accessed 20 December 2019.

Gurr T, *Peoples versus States: Minorities at Risk in the New Century* (USIP 2000).

International Court of Justice, 'Accordance with International Law of the Unilateral Declaration of Independence in Respect of Kosovo: Advisory Opinion of 22 July 2010' https://www.icj-cij.org/files/case-related/141/141-20100722-ADV-01-00-EN.pdf≥ accessed 13 February 2019.

International Crisis Group, 'Cameroon Anglophone Crisis at the Crossroads' (2 August 2017, Africa Report No. 250) 9 https://d2071andvip0wj.cloudfront.net/250-cameroons-anglophone-crisis-at-the-crossroads_0.pdf accessed 24 June 2018.

Kathyola J and Job O (eds), *Decentralisation in Commonwealth Africa: Experiences from Botswana, Cameroon, Ghana, Mozambique and Tanzania* (Commonwealth Secretariat 2011).

Keil S, 'Federalism as a Tool of Conflict-Resolution: The Case of Bosnia and Herzegovina' (2012) *1*(363) *Centre International de Formation Européenne* 205.

Kimengsi JN and Gwan SA, 'Reflections on Decentralisation, Community Empowerment and Sustainable Development in Cameroon' (2017) *1*(2) *International Journal of Emerging Trends in the Social Sciences* 53.

Kindzeke ME, 'Cameroon MPs Approve Law Giving Special Status to English-Speaking Regions' (*Voice of Africa News*, 21 December 2019) https://www.voanews.com/africa/cameroon-mps-approve-law-giving-special-status-english-speaking-regions accessed 10 January 2020.

Kofele-Kale N, 'Local Governance under Cameroon's Decentralisation Regime: Is It All Sound and Fury Signifying Nothing?' (2011) *37*(3) *Commonwealth Law Bulletin* 513.

Konings P, 'The Anglophone Struggle for Federalism in Cameroon' in Lidija Basta and Jibrin Ibrahim (eds) *Federalism and Decentralisation in Africa: The Multicultural Challenge* (Fribourg: Institute of Federalism 1999).

Kouagheu J, 'Cameroon Grants Special Status to the Anglophone Regions' (*Reuters*, 20 December 2019) https://www.reuters.com/article/us-cameroon-separatists-lawmaking/cameroon-grants-special-status-to-anglophone-regions-idUSKBN1YO24S≥ accessed 5 January 2020.

Loh F, 'Ethnic Diversity and the Nation State: From Centralisation in the Age of Nationalism to Decentralisation Amidst Globalisation' (2017) *18*(3) *Inter-Asia Cultural Studies* 414.

Lunn J and Brooke-Holland L, 'The Anglophone Cameroon Crisis: April 2019 Update' (UK House of Commons Briefing Paper Number 8331, 17 April 2019) https://researchbriefings.parliament.uk/ResearchBriefing/Summary/CBP-8331#fullreport accessed 19 July 2019.

Lustick I, Miodownik D and Eidelson R, 'Secessionism in Multicultural States: Does Sharing Power Prevent or Encourage It?' (2004) *98*(2) *American Political Science Review* 209.

2019 'Major National Dialogue: Recommendations to Restore Peace, Stability and Development' (*Cameroon Tribune*, 7 October 2019) cameroon-tribune.cm/article.html/28306/en.html/major-national-dialogue-recommendations-restore-peace-stability accessed 24 October 2019.

Mbuagbo O, 'Cameroon: Flawed Decentralisation & the Politics of Identity in the Urban Space' (2012) *12*(11) *Global Journal of Human Social Science, Sociology, Economics & Political Science* 14.

McGibbon R, 'Secessionist Challenges in Aceh and Papua: Is Special Autonomy the Solution?' (2004) *10 Policy Studies* vii.

Miller MA, 'The Problem of Armed Separatism: Is Autonomy the Answer?' in Michelle Miller (ed) *Autonomy and Armed Separatism in South and Southeast Asia* (ISEAS Publishing 2012).

Muvunyi F, *'Cameroon's Stillborn Dialogue for Peace'* (*Deutsche Welle,* 30 September 2019) dw.com/en/opinion-cameroons-stillborn-dialogue-for-peace/a-50638224 accessed 12 December 2019.

National Commission on Human Rights and Freedoms (NCHRF), *'Report on the State of Human Rights in Cameroon in 2016'* (Ets Messie Printers and Publishers 2017).

Nauclér E, 'Autonomy and Multi-Level Governance: Experience in Nordic and Central European Cooperation' in Marc Weller and Stefan Wolff *Autonomy, Self-Governance and Conflict Resolution: Innovative Approaches to Institutional Design in Divided Societies* (Routledge 2005).

Ndi JF, *Press Release. Secretariat of the National Executive Committee of the Social Democratic Front*, Ref. 060/S2/SDF.NF/033 of 6 October 2019.

Nfobin N, 'The Francophone/Anglophone Split over Article 47 of the Constitution of the Federal Republic of Cameroon: An Abiding Malaise with an Explosive Charge' (2017) *25*(4) *African Journal of International and Comparative Law* 538.

Nfobin N and Minang NV, 'The Cameroon Anglophone Question in International Law' (2014) *22*(2) *African Journal of International and Comparative Law* 234.

Ngenge Y, 'Cameroon's Political Crisis: Why a Onetime Peace Haven Might Be Headed for the Unknown' (CONSTITUTIONNET, 24 November 2017) http://constitutionnet.org/news/cameroons-political-crisis-why-onetime-peace-haven-might-be-headed-unknown accessed 12 February 2018.

Nyamjoh F and Konings P, *Negotiating an Anglophone Identity: A Study of the Politics of Recognition and Representation in Cameroon* (Brill 2003).

'Office of the Prime Minister: Official Program of Consultations of the Prime Minister, Head of Government, in View of the National Dialogue' https://www.spm.gov.cm/site/sites/default/files/version_anglaise_planning_des_consultations_du_pmcg.pdf accessed 23 October 2019.

OHCHR, 'Opening Statement and Global Update of Human Rights Concerns by UN High Commissioner for Human Rights Zeid Ra'ad Al Hussein at 38th Session of the Human Rights Council' (18 June 2018) https://www.ohchr.org/EN/HRBodies/HRC/Pages/NewsDetail.aspx?NewsID=23206&LangID=E accessed 10 September 2019.

Okereke N, 'Analysing Cameroon's Anglophone Crisis' (2018) *10*(3) *Counter Terrorist Trends and Analyses* 8.

Olinga AD, 'La Question Anglophone dans le Cameroun d'aujourd'hui' (1994) *48*(3) *Revue Juridique et Politique, Indépendance et Coopération* 292.

O'Neill M, 'Re-Imagining Belgium: New Federalism and the Political Management of Cultural Diversity' 1998 *51*(2) *Parliamentary Affairs* 241.

Posner E and Vermuele A, 'Legislative Entrenchment: A Reappraisal' (2002) *111*(7) *Yale Law Journal* 1665.

Selassie BH, 'Comment: Self-Determination in Principle and Practice: The Ethiopian-Eritrean Experience' (1997) *29 Columbia Human Rights Law Review* 91.

Snyder J, *From Voting to Violence: Democratisation and Nationalist Conflict* (Norton: New York 2000).

Stark F, 'Federalism in Cameroon: The Shadow and the Reality' (1976) (10)*3 Canadian Journal of African Studies* 423.

The Aland Islands Question, *Report submitted to the Council of the League of Nations by the Commission of Rapporteurs.* Document du Conseil B7, 21/68/106, of 16 April 1921.

The Buea Declaration: *All Anglophone Conference, 2nd & 3rd April, 1993* (Nooremac Press 1993).

The Crux, 'Cardinal backs Federal Union to End Cameroon's Anglophone Crisis' (*The Crux*, 3 August 2019) https://cruxnow.com/church-in-africa/2019/08/03/cardinal-backs-federal-union-to-end-cameroons-anglophone-crisis/ accessed 12 September 2019.

Tiebout CM, 'A Pure Theory of Local Expenditures' (1957) *64 Journal of Political Economy* 416.

UNESCO, 'Cameroon: Joint Statement of UNICEF and UNESCO on Abduction of Education Personnel and Attacks Against Schools in the South-West Region of Cameroon' (1 June 2018) http://cm.one.un.org/content/unct/cameroon/en/home/presscenter/communiques-de-presse/cameroon–joint-statement-of-unicef-and-unesco-on-abduction- accessed 10 September 2019.

UNHCR, 'Cameroon Situation: Responding to the Needs of IDPs and Cameroonian Refugees in Nigeria' (1 March 2019) http://reporting.unhcr.org/sites/default/files/UNHCR%20Cameroon%202019%20Supplementary%20Appeal%20%28March%202019%29.pdf accessed 11 September 2019.

United Nations Department for the Coordination of Humanitarian Affairs, 'Cameroon: North-West and South-West Crisis, Situation Report N°8 as of 30 June 2019' https://www.humanitarianresponse.info/en/operations/cameroon/document/cameroon-north-west-and-south-west-crisis-situation-report-n%C2%B08–30-june accessed 9 September 2019.

US Department of State, '2018 Country Reports on Human Rights Practices: Cameroon' (13 March 2019) https://www.state.gov/wp-content/uploads/2019/03/Cameroon-2018.pdf accessed 10 September 2019.

Weller M, 'Settling Self-determination Conflicts: Recent Developments' (2009) *20*(1) *European Journal of International Law* 111.

Western Sahara, Advisory Opinion of 12 October 1975 (International Court of Justice) http://www.worldcourts.com/icj/eng/decisions/1975.10.16_western_sahara.htm accessed 15 February 2019.

7 The protection of human rights and fundamental freedoms

Introduction

The protection of human rights and fundamental freedoms (human rights) has always been on a negative trajectory in Cameroon. As far back as the Ahidjo regime, reports of massive violations of human rights, including torture and suppression of political freedoms, were not uncommon. Under President Biya, some efforts have been made at increasing the scope of human rights available to the population and improving on institutional protection mechanisms. This was the hallmark of the troubled 1990s when a number of laws, more widely known as the Liberty Laws, were promulgated to enhance the exercise of various freedoms[1] and to regulate the maintenance of law and order and a state of emergency.[2] The 1990s also witnessed a new addition to the human rights protection mechanism, in the institution of the National Commission on Human Rights and Freedoms to complement the role of the judiciary in the protection of human rights. Other initiatives have included the establishment of a Directorate of Human Rights in the Ministry of Justice with responsibilities in the protection and promotion of human rights. The state has also been adept at ratifying international human rights instruments – thus joining the community of states expressing an interest in enhancing human dignity.

There has, however, been a negative correlation between human rights commitments and their actual protection. Various independent international and domestic human rights organisations have noted Cameroon's poor human rights record, particularly in the civil and political rights category.[3] There are reports of pervasive human rights abuses such as extra-judicial executions, enforced disappearances, torture, arbitrary detention and suppression of political freedoms. The persecution of political opponents, journalists and human rights activists is a cause for concern.[4]

That's not to suggest that socio-economic rights receive more protection. In fact, the contrary is more likely the reality. In February 2019, Mr Rodrigo Uprimny, the Social and Economic Rights Committee Member and Country Rapporteur for Cameroon, noted with dissatisfaction that only 16% of public revenue was devoted to the protection of social, economic and cultural rights, a position even lower than the average in the African continent.[5]

The government's stated policy, however, is to treat all three generations of human rights with equality, reflecting the interdependent and interrelatedness of all human rights.

Against the backdrop of the government's commitment to human rights, why then has the country's record remained consistently poor? One important explanation is the problem of lack of judicial independence and judicial power, as we saw in Chapter 4. The judiciary is the main institutional protection mechanism and, as already discussed, it is seriously flawed, making it an unsuitable institution for the effective protection of human rights. That has been exacerbated by the limited mechanism for constitutional review and limited access to the Constitutional Council, which otherwise has the potential to safeguard human rights. In the proceeding sections, the role of the National Commission on Human Right and Freedoms and the Directorate for Human Rights will be examined to evaluate their contributions to the protection of human rights. That will be preceded by an examination of the constitutional foundations of human rights.

Part I. Overview of constitutional provisions

This section does not attempt to provide a detailed analysis of all the human rights provisions in the preamble. Nevertheless, a brief discussion of the justiciability of human rights and the substantive features of the constitutional provisions is provided in the following sections.

A. Justiciability of human rights

The Constitution is clear in its preamble on its attachment to international human rights. It states that, the people of Cameroon,

> Affirm our attachment to the fundamental freedoms enshrined in the Universal Declaration of Human Rights, the Charter of the United Nations, The African Charter on Human and Peoples' Rights and all duly ratified International Conventions relating thereto …

It states further that Cameroon endorses the principles espoused in those instruments and in that respect, enumerates some rights from the three generations of human rights, specifying that everyone is entitled to them. Doubts have often been expressed as to the justiciability of human rights, given that they appear in the preamble rather than the main text of the Constitution? In other words, what is the legal status of the preamble? The answer to that question may lie in an evaluation of the permutations of the preamble and human rights provisions in the different post-independence constitutions of Cameroon. The Federal Constitution of 1961, for instance, in its article 1(2), affirmed Cameroon's attachment to the fundamental liberties guaranteed in the Universal Declaration and the United Nations Charter. This was in the body of the Constitution, rather than in the preamble, incontrovertibly indicating that human rights were justiciable. The 1972 Constitution on its part listed a number of rights in the preamble, including affirmation of Cameroon's attachment to the United Nations Charter and the Universal Declaration. That was a retrogressive move from the perspective that the preamble of the 1972 Constitution was unenforceable.[6] It is that preamble that was re-enacted in the current 1996 Constitution, which now provides unequivocally in article 65 that the preamble is an integral part of the Constitution. The implication is that the preamble has been accorded an equivalent status to other constitutional provisions that are enforceable.

It has been argued that article 65 does not necessarily indicate that human rights in the constitution are justiciable because, on the one hand, there are no effective mechanisms to enforce them and, on the other, the preamble generally expresses aspirations of a people 'rather than state strictly enforceable legal rights and obligations'.[7] Having examined earlier the historical developments of the preamble and human rights in Cameroon, it is fair to assert that article 65 of the 1996 Constitution renders the preamble more effective than under the 1972 Constitution and, therefore, affirms the justiciability of the rights contained therein. In addition, the view that preambles merely express aspirations can no longer be supported. A more conventional view is that preambles perform various functions, depending on their status as provided by the constitution itself and the role ascribed to them by the judiciary.[8] In France, for instance, the justiciability of fundamental rights in the preamble was recognised by the *Conseil Constitutionnel*[9] in 1971[10] and has been affirmed in later decisions.[11] Similarly, in a landmark decision, the Indian Supreme Court ruled that the preamble was legally enforceable as an integral part of the Constitution.[12] In Cameroon, not only are human rights frequently referred to in court as guaranteed by the Constitution,[13] but also the Constitution itself makes clear in article 65 that the preamble is an integral part of it. The preamble can be considered as a substantive preamble which serves as an independent source of rights and obligations. In view of the political context surrounding the adoption of the 1996 Constitution, it may be that the constitutional revisions were influenced partly by the proposal from the Anglophone delegates to introduce a bill of rights. A compromise could have been arrived at by introducing article 65 in order to make human rights enforceable, dispensing with the need for a bill of rights. The problem with human rights in the Constitution may be more about the effectiveness of the enforcement mechanisms than the status of the preamble.

B. Substantive features of human rights provisions

I. Indivisibility of human rights

Despite the absence of a comprehensive bill of rights, the preamble to the Constitution contains a number of rights in the traditional three generations of rights. Although no overt statement is made as to their indivisibility, the inclusion of the three generations is a reflection of the relevance of the concept of indivisibility. Some of the rights in the first category (civil and political rights) include the right to equality, protection of minorities, liberty and security, privacy, fair trial, life, freedom of movement, freedom from torture, freedom of religion and democratic rights. In the second category (social, economic and cultural rights), the rights protected include the right to education, the right to work, social security guarantees and the right to property. Further, in terms of the third generation (collective-developmental rights), the preamble commendably includes the right to a healthy environment and the right to development. In the case of the environment, both citizens and the state have a duty to protect the environment, with the state given the additional obligation to ensure the 'improvement of the environment'.[14] The commitment to environmental protection is embedded in a 1996 law, which spells out the government's duties in that area.[15] With respect to development, it is the state that has the obligation to 'provide all its citizens with the conditions necessary for their development'. While the inclusion of third-generation rights is commendable, as is the case with these rights, enforceability is often problematic. Moreover, in Cameroon, there are no further constitutional provisions detailing the mechanisms by which these rights can be enforced. It may be argued that in view of the state of development in Cameroon and the environment, these collective-developmental rights may remain aspirational principles until the state makes specific provisions for their enforcement, especially in the area of accountability. It is necessary to establish some minimum standards or core obligations for the government to fulfil and a mechanism through which it can be held accountable for failure to discharge its obligations.

In terms of the spectrum of rights provided for in the preamble, there is no disaffirming the fact that the list is not comprehensive. Moreover, the rights provisions are very brief, lacking in significant details and sometimes vague. However, as we noted in Chapter 5, the African Charter on Human and Peoples' Rights (ACHPR) and other instruments ratified by Cameroon (including the International Covenant on Civil and Political Rights, the International Covenant on Economic Social and Cultural Rights, the Convention on the Rights of Persons with Disabilities and the Convention on the Rights of the Child) are directly enforceable in Cameroon. They complement domestic provisions on human rights.

II. The concept of 'duties'

The preamble displays further distinctiveness by adopting the concept of 'duties' introduced in the ACHPR.[16] In addition to the duty to protect the environment, paragraphs 22 to 24 impose such duties as the obligation to work, to pay taxes and contribute to 'the defence of the Fatherland'. The essence of these duties is broadly captured in the concept of the civic duty of the citizen, which is also aimed at promoting the right to development. The government has approached this partly by targeting the youths as the basis for developing and entrenching that culture of 'civic duty'. In 2005, a law was promulgated to that effect creating the National Civic Service for Participation in Development[17] with a complementary Agency established in 2010.[18] This service aims to contribute to harnessing efforts to meet the 'imperatives of the economic and social development of the country' and to promote in all citizens 'the national sentiment, a sense of discipline, tolerance, the general interest and dignity of work' and promoting 'a civic spirit and the culture of peace'.[19] While the initiative is laudable, at least in terms of its focus on educating the youths on environmental protection, development and human rights, one major criticism is that the model has been conflated with that of a 'youth service' without a specific focus on what the programme is meant to achieve.[20]

III. 'Claw-back' clauses

It is also worthy to mention the lack of normative clarity in the constitutional provisions due, in particular, to the distinctive inclusion of 'claw-back' clauses in some of the provisions on specific human rights, akin to the approach of the ACHPR.[21] In human rights, claw-back clauses are obnoxious as they effectively permit states to limit the scope of human rights by defining law very narrowly. The preamble adopts this approach to defining the scope of human rights. For instance, freedom of opinion is guaranteed 'subject to respect for public policy' and freedom of the press, communication, expression, assembly and association are guaranteed 'subject to respect for public policy'. The right to security is also made subject to the interest of other citizens and the 'the higher interests of the State'. The use of vague terms such as public policy in defining the contours within which rights should be exercised is problematic. Public policy, or 'ordre public', is not a concept that is particularly well defined under Cameroonian law. In the Anglophone regions where the common law is applied, the concept is understood to relate to 'natural justice, equity and good conscience'.[22] These are concepts that are supportive of human rights and, therefore, any exercise of human rights in that context is likely to be positive. However, the concept appears to suffer from ambiguity in the Francophone regions where the civil law applies. Maurice Kamto asserts that it can be subject to very broad interpretations and is sometimes conflated with the concept of the 'higher interest of the state'.[23] He argues that the two concepts (ordre public and 'higher interest of the state') are indeterminate, fluid and elusive and potentially obstructive to the protection of human rights. He notes further that subjecting the exercise of human rights to 'ordre public' or public policy puts the exercise of the rights in the hands of administrative authorities that can restrict them on the basis of the protection of public order, peace and security without judicial oversight.[24] In fact, it has become routine practice for administrative authorities to restrict the rights to freedom of association and assembly on the basis of 'ordre public'.[25] This is often the case where opposition parties and other critics of the government organise public gatherings or demonstrations.[26] The authorities often turn down request to organise such events on the basis that they constitute a threat to public order.[27] In other instances where public events (not organised by the government or the CPDM) are taking place, security forces tend to disperse populations attending the events, for same reasons. The National Commission on Human Rights and Freedoms, in its 2017 report on human rights, for instance, 'noted several cases where public demonstrations were prohibited simply on the basis that they threatened public order, but without specifying the elements constituting the threat'.[28]

IV. Institutional protection mechanisms

Besides the need for clarity in the normative provisions of human rights, their method of enforcement is equally important. The lack of clarity creates further difficulties for enforcement. In Chapters 4 and 5, we saw some of these difficulties in relation to the lack of independence of the judiciary and the limited scope of constitutional review performed by the Constitutional Council. The absence of judicial independence implies that the courts cannot often be assertive where the executive has infringed human rights. In cases where the courts assert their independence, as in *Nya Henry* and *Oyebowale*,[29] they are unable to compel the executive to respect orders from the courts. Moreover, the courts have been accused of complicity in perpetrating human rights violations, especially the rights of opposition political party leaders and human rights activists.[30] The Constitutional Council on its part has demonstrated weaknesses in protecting democratic rights and its limited mechanism for constitutional review restricts access to justice for ordinary citizens. In addition, it permits the application of provisions of the law, such as those with 'claw-back' clauses that implicitly undermine human rights.

In the following sections, the National Commission on Human Rights and Freedoms and the Directorate of Human Rights in the Ministry of Justice will be examined to assess their contribution to the protection of human rights.

Part II. Enforcement mechanisms

A. The National Commission on Human Rights and Freedoms

I. Background

Cameroon's national human rights institution has had a chequered history. It was originally created by presidential decree in 1990[31] and known as the National Commission on Human Rights and Freedoms (NCHRF). Its creation was shrouded in secrecy and did not comply with prevailing international standards, which, among other things, recommended that the process of establishing a national human rights institution should be consultative, inclusive and transparent.[32] The provisions of the decree were grossly inadequate in terms of guaranteeing the independence of the NCHRF and empowering it to undertake its responsibilities to protect and promote human rights. The Commission was accountable to the President of the Republic; it remained silent in the face of human rights violations and was largely unknown to the general public. In the light of these inadequacies and with the assistance of Cameroon's International Partners such as the Commonwealth Secretariat, a new statute was drafted. This was also to ensure compliance with international best practices in the establishment of human rights institutions. The Paris Principles, for instance, requires that the establishment of human rights institutions should preferably be incorporated into the constitution or the institution should be created by an act of parliament rather than an executive decree.[33] The 1990 decree was thus repealed by Law No. 2004/016 of 22 July 2004[34] adopted by parliament. More recently in 2019, parliament adopted a new law, which, among other things, repealed the 2004 law and changed the name of the institution to the Cameroon Human Rights Commission (CHRC).[35] As per section 67(1) of the new law, 'the CHRC shall ipso facto replace the NCHRF'. Although the government bill on the new law stated that the new law was intended, among other things, to be more compliant with the Paris Principles, that has not exactly been the case. The method of drafting the bill was again not inclusive of any civil society organisation or any other institution. It was not a national project eliciting broad-based participation or contributions from various sectors of the society. In assessing the structure and functioning of the Commission, amendments introduced by the new law will be highlighted.

II. Overview of the institutional structure and composition

The Commission is composed of a chair and vice chair appointed by presidential decree[36] and twenty-eight commissioners representing a broad spectrum of the professions and organisations in Cameroon and representatives from the judiciary, the legislature and the executive. They are all appointed by presidential decree following nominations from their relevant institutions or professional bodies.[37] The institutional structure also includes a permanent secretariat headed by a secretary-general, appointed by presidential decree (on the recommendation of the chair), and four working groups to assist the chair in monitoring the daily activities of the Commission.[38]

The composition of the Commission is comparably broad and has come under serious criticism as an unnecessary inflation and over-representation of the government.[39] The new law has attempted to address that criticism by reducing considerably the composition of the institution. Henceforth, it includes a chair and a vice-chair appointed by presidential decree and thirteen members (commissioners) appointed by presidential decree following nominations from the services or organisations they represent.[40] The law makes provisions for an office of the chairperson, a general assembly of commissioners, a permanent secretariat[41] headed by a permanent secretary, also appointed by presidential decree,[42] and three standing working sub-commissions.[43] The new law also makes progressive innovations to its membership, for instance, by having regard to the issue of linguistic, regional and gender balance.[44] It is prescriptive in its gender requirement provision, which states a mandatory 30% membership in favour of women.[45] There is also a distinct requirement for two members from organisations working on promoting the rights of certain categories of persons, one of whom must be a representative of persons with disabilities.[46]

Another welcomed modification is the apparent reduction of the overwhelming representation of the government and other administrative services.

There are nonetheless some shortcomings in the new law, which may perpetuate inadequacies witnessed under the 2004 law. For instance, even though there appears to be a reduction in the number of government representatives, the law provides that they shall serve in a permanent capacity, an attribute which deviates from the Paris Principles. The Paris Principles require that government representatives should only serve in an advisory capacity.[47] One of the criticism against the Commission is the overwhelming presence of the government and the fact that its representatives serve in a permanent capacity. Their presence is undesirable because it may inhibit effective participation, as members may feel unable to freely express their views on issues that may be sensitive to the government. It may also lead the public to believe that the institution is an extended arm of the government.

Under the 2004 Law, the appointment of the chair and vice-chair is left entirely in the hands of the President of the Republic,[48] with no broad participation of the civil society or parliament. Ironically, the law states that the chair shall be an independent personality but provides no definition of the term. That provision is too vague and it is unconvincing that the chair would be fully independent when their appointment is dependent solely on the President. This fact may constitute an inhibiting factor particularly in view of the fact that the tenure of the commissioners is fixed for five years and renewable once.[49] A life tenure is more likely to provide a more conducive context for better exercise of independence. The new law compounds the situation with uncertainty on the nominating authorities. It maintains the requirement that the commissioners, including the chair and vice-chair, shall be appointed by presidential decree following nominations by 'the services, associations and socio-professional bodies to which they belong'.[50]

III. Mandate

According to section 1(2) of the 2004 Law, the Commission shall be an independent institution for consultation, monitoring, evaluation, dialogue and concerted action in the promotion and protection of human rights. That mandate has been expanded under the new law, which makes the Commission also the national mechanism for the prevention of torture.[51] In essence, the Commission is 'responsible for the promotion and protection of human rights and freedoms'[52] and the 'prevention of torture in all places of detention'.[53]

As part of its responsibility to protect human rights, the Commission is mandated to receive 'all denunciations' relating to violations, conduct 'all enquiries' and carry out 'all necessary investigations' into alleged violations of human rights, and to study 'all matters' relating to the defense and promotion of human rights.[54] Remarkably, the Commission may carry out investigations on its own initiative.[55] It may also refer cases of violations of human rights and freedoms to the competent authorities and, when necessary, inspect penitentiary establishments, police stations and gendarmerie brigades, in the presence of the competent state counsel or his representative. In the latter case, it may be necessary to produce a report of its visits to the places of detention and to submit to the competent authorities. Its protection mandate is described in very broad terms with potential to permit it to carry out a wide range of activities with a view to protecting human rights. This broad approach to its mandate is in fact recommended by the Paris Principles[56] on the basis that a broad mandate provides scope for a greater protection of rights of all categories.[57] Nevertheless, the Commission seems restricted in terms of the extent to which it can influence the outcome of some of its investigative activities or the complaints received from the public. For instance, although it can submit reports to the competent authorities following visits to detention sites, it is not clear what the follow-up mechanism is, because the law is silent on the point. Moreover, following its inquiries and investigations into alleged violations, it is mandated to report to the President of the Republic.[58] The law is silent on subsequent action by the President. In 2017, when the Commission submitted its report of the Anglophone crisis to the President, it is not clear what action was taken as a direct response to that report.[59] It is worthy to note, however, that the new law dispenses with the requirement to report to the President.

With respect to its promotion role, the Commission has the responsibility of publicising instruments relating to human rights and to forge a culture of human rights through information and the holding of conferences and seminars.[60] To that end, it is expected to collect and disseminate international documentation on human rights[61] and liaise with non-governmental human rights organisations. Further, the Commission is required to maintain (where necessary) cooperation links with the United Nations, international organisations and foreign committees or associations that have the objective of promoting and protecting human rights in Cameroon and to inform the Minister of External Relations about such cooperation links.[62] The Commission has been active in its promotion role by organising sensitisation and education campaigns. For instance, it undertook a successful nationwide campaign from October to December 2010, during which public authorities and ordinary citizens were provided with basic human rights education and the procedures of the Commission.[63] It has also maintained productive cooperation links with regional and international human rights organisations. In 2018, with the assistance of the United Nations Centre for Democracy and Human Rights, it elaborated a plan of action comprising mainly of education and sensitisation, monitoring and reporting and support to victims of human rights violations. It was to be implemented as a pilot initiative from 2019.[64]

The new law goes further in terms of the promotion role by providing the legal basis for the Commission to contribute to human rights education in 'all training cycles and socio-professional environment'.[65] Further, through advocacy, the Commission can also make more useful contributions towards improving the legal and institutional framework for the promotion of human rights.[66] In that respect, it may advocate for the government and parliament to 'adhere to, sign and ratify' international and regional human rights instruments.[67] This is commendable because it is more focused and more specific in terms of its role in the ratification of international instruments. It provides a stronger legal basis than the terms used in the 2004 law which required very broadly that the Commission should 'propose to the public authorities, measures to be taken in the area of human rights and freedoms'.[68]

The Commission's third mandate, the prevention of torture introduced by the new law, is, strictly speaking, a consolidation of part of its duties relating to the protection of human rights. Under the 2004 law, the Commission had the duty to visit and investigate places of detention. However, as a state party to the Optional Protocol to the Convention Against Torture, Cameroon is required to establish a national mechanism for the prevention of torture. It opted to do so by specifically extending the competence of the Commission. The Commission is, therefore, responsible for conducting regular visits to all places of detention, including psychiatric institutions, engaging in constructive dialogue with the heads of the relevant institutions and conducting private and confidential interviews in the presence or absence of witnesses.[69] It may also make recommendations to the relevant authorities to improve on their conditions of detention. Additionally, the Commission is tasked with the duty to participate in monitoring the implementation of recommendations of the United Nations Committee Against Torture (CAT) and, at the request of the government, to provide an opinion on draft or existing legislation on torture.[70] As a torture-prevention mechanism, the remit of the Commission is very limited. Three observations are worth noting.

First, the visits to places of detention are limited to an examination of the conditions of detention. This may imply that the Commission is precluded from making observations on evidence of torture itself. Although it may assume such powers based on its broad protective mandate, that limitation is problematic as it may provide a basis for the relevant authorities to conceal information relating to torture. Second, the Commission may only participate in monitoring the implementation of recommendations. It is not clear what that means. For instance, can it compel the government to implement the recommendations of CAT or indeed its own recommendations? Third, the Commission cannot comment or make recommendations on existing or draft legislation and, in relation to torture, it can only do so on the invitation of the government. As per the Paris Principles, a human rights institution, such as the Commission, should be able to make such recommendations on its own initiative.[71] This should not be limited to legislation on torture but should cover all human rights and, in that respect, the views of the Commission should be mandatorily submitted.[72] By limiting the Commission in that way, the law prevents it from acting as an effective human rights institution and undermines its responsibility to contribute to the enhancement of the legal and institutional framework of human rights in the country.

IV. Powers

The Commission has been granted some powers to discharge its mandate discussed earlier. Under section 3 of the 2004 law, the Commission can summon a party or witness for a hearing, request the competent authority to carry out searches and require the production of documents and evidence. These provisions are important in that they may facilitate the role of the Commission in investigating complaints and acquiring evidence in support of allegations of violations. Anyone who fails to respond to the summons of the Commission is liable to penalties under section 28 of the Penal Code.[73] Moreover, the Commission can 'intervene in any case, to participate in upholding the interests of victims of human rights violations'. This is particularly important where proceedings have been instituted in court. The Commission can support a victim and the courts by providing an independent analysis of the relevant human rights principles and standards and facts on the state of human rights in the country that would be relevant to the case. In that way, it will provide an objective view of the human rights principles and statements of fact, which would be helpful for the courts to consider in deciding a particular case. The Commission may also refer any offence in matters falling within its remit to the Minister of Justice and in non-criminal matters, to use mediation and conciliation to resolve a dispute.

In spite of the powers described earlier, it is submitted that the powers to grant remedies and the powers of compulsion in particular are inadequate for the effective functioning of the Commission. For instance, the law is silent on what remedies the Commission may grant to the victim following the findings of an investigation. Its powers in that respect seem limited to making non-binding recommendations or referring the violation to the competent authority as per section 2 of the 2004 Law. This is, in fact, ineffective, as it cannot make any binding recommendations to the relevant authorities. In 2019, the Commission reported on a visit to a prison in Yoko, Garoua, carried out in 2016, where a group of prisoners have had their matter on appeal for thirty-one years.[74] In view of the serious breaches of human rights, in particular, the excessive and unlawful delay in the appeal process, the Commission was only able to report the matter to the Presidency of the Republic, the Minister of Justice and the president of the divisional High Court. The Commission recommended their immediate release as per section 584 of the Penal Code. It could not compel their release despite the gross violation of their right to personal liberty.

In terms of its powers of compulsion, despite the criminal sanctions for non-compliance with a summons, there is no sanction for authorities who fail to conduct searches or provide requested documentation or evidence. Thus, although the Commission can request assistance from the competent authorities, they are not under an obligation to cooperate. Section 4(2) also states that the Commission may request the competent authorities to conduct a study or draft a report on specific human rights issues relating to their duties, but does not provide any sanction for non-compliance. Rather, the Commission is required, under section 3, to refer offences falling within its remit to the Minister of Justice. This is objectionable in that it by-passes the prosecuting authorities, such as state counsels, who are in charge of public prosecution. Moreover, the law does not state what the Minister is required to do when offences are brought to his notice. It may be assumed that the Minister may use his discretion to instruct the state counsel to prosecute or not. This is undesirable because he is not obliged to respond to the Commission, and if he decides to act at all, he may instruct against prosecution even where a violation has been clearly established. The Commission's powers of compulsion should be complemented by a power to hold recalcitrant officials in contempt. The Minister should only be involved in so far as that intervention enhances the Commission's ability to sanction the contemptuous official.

Due in part to these weaknesses the Commission has faced difficulties in carrying out its duties, particularly in accessing places of detention. This was very problematic during its inaugural years, and an emblematic incident can demonstrate these difficulties. In 1992, the Commission attempted to investigate allegations of torture of protesters detained in the Yaoundé Central Prison. The protesters had been arrested in the North-West region during the National Youth Day celebrations. The commissioners were denied access to the prison and they were, themselves, detained for an hour and their operating materials were confiscated.[75] Although such overt hostilities to the Commission have lessened, commissioners still do not obtain the full cooperation of administrative authorities or security forces. More recently, on a number of occasions in 2018, the Commission was denied access to detention facilities.[76] Again, it encountered difficulties obtaining from judicial authorities, statistics of persons arrested in connection with the Anglophone crisis.[77] In its 2017 human rights report, the Commission explained in detail the obstructive practices of public authorities, notably at the level of the penitentiary services, actively preventing visits to detention cites or deliberately failing to cooperate.[78] Failure of cooperation is also common with judicial authorities. For instance, in 2017, a state counsel in the South-West region declined to join the team of officials who are required by law to accompany the Commission to detention sites. The visit had particular significance due to the large numbers of arbitrary arrests and detention of protesters in connection with the crisis in the Anglophone regions. The Commission regretted that the state counsel was uncooperative at a time when allegations of torture in the detention sites were rife and the presence of the state counsel was crucial to their investigations.[79]

The new law of 2019 does very little to address the weak powers of the Commission. Section 41 provides that the views and recommendations of the Commission contained in its special or thematic reports should be submitted to the relevant competent authorities for 'review and follow-up'. It states nothing about implementing the recommendations. Under section 7, the Commission may 'request the competent authorities to put an end to the human rights violations noted' and 'where necessary' request 'the assistance of the forces of law and order in the discharge of its duties'. There is still no mechanism to ensure compliance. Instead, section 43 'requires' the state, its agencies and any natural or legal person to 'help' the Commission to carry out its duties. The term 'help' is a very feeble expression of the obligation of the relevant authorities to assist the Commission. Stronger expressions such as 'compelled' and 'assist or cooperate' should be used and should be complemented by provisions forbidding any institutions or persons from obstructing or unlawfully interfering with the Commission in the performance of its duties.

V. Prospects and challenges

The Commission is an institution with potential to make significant contributions to the protection and promotion of human rights in Cameroon. Its broad mandate provides the opportunity to influence the respect for human rights. This can be gleaned from a number of areas as already discussed and also from its periodic visits to detention centres. The new law vests the Commission with powers to carry out regular, impromptu or announced visits to detention cites as part of the torture-prevention mechanism. Its visits in the past have registered modest successes as, for instance, in 2012 when it carried out a visit to a prison in Ebolowa, together with the state counsel. This culminated in the release of some persons who had been unlawfully detained, as the state counsel was in a position to provide that remedy.[80] On December 2016, the Commission was able to conduct an impromptu visit to the Secretary of State in Charge of the Gendarmerie in Yaoundé, following allegations of unlawful arrests of protesters in Bamenda early in December and a suspicion of their incommunicado detention. The Commission was able to locate some of the detainees and to communicate the information to their families. These successes could be consolidated, in particular where the Commission is given more powers to ensure that persons illegally detained are released and generally to instil that culture of respect for human rights among public authorities.

The Commission also makes significant contributions through its promotional activities. Among other things, it campaigns for improved health facilities and the provision of basic amenities like portable water, electricity and nutritious foods to deprived communities and to detention and education centres. Its work is, however, hampered by a number of factors, mainly the inability to make binding recommendations to the relevant authorities and the lack of sufficient funding. The Commission has persistently decried its lack of sufficient funding, which results in low levels of staffing and inevitably compromises its efficiency.[81] According to an international human rights organisation, the Commission's work is undermined by the lack of sufficient funding.[82] A number of international organisations, such as the United Nations Human Rights Committee and the Sub-Committee for the Prevention of Torture, have recommended an increase in the funding of the Commission.[83] In its 2017 report, the Commission acknowledged a slight increase in its 2017 budget which seemed insufficient as the Commission itself deplored the 'inadequate financial, material and human resources that should ensure the kind of deployment that would exert a higher impact on its activities'.[84] There was no increase in the budget for 2018 and the Commission confirmed the potential negative impact on certain activities in the crucial year of the highly contentious presidential elections.[85] The funding of national human rights institutions is pivotal to their success. The Paris Principles[86] emphasise the importance of adequate funding not only for the effectiveness of the institution but also to ensure independence from the government.

In spite of its challenges, the Commission appears to be achieving some modest results in the protection of human rights and freedoms. It has come a long way from its early days when it remained silent in the face of serious human rights abuses. These successes can be galvanised by genuine government support in the areas highlighted previously and further cooperation with civil society organisations and Cameroon's international partners.

B. The Directorate for Human Rights and International Cooperation

The Directorate for Human Rights and International Cooperation (DHRIC) is a department in the Ministry of Justice. It was created by a 2005 law[87] re-organising the Ministry of Justice in relation to the role of the Minister of Justice in the supervision of human rights enforcement. As discussed in the following section, it is vested with some duties in that respect.

I. Overview of the institutional structure

The Directorate consists of a Card Index and Filing Office and two sub-departments – the Sub-Directorate of Human Rights and the Sub-Directorate for International Cooperation, each headed by a sub-director. The overall head of department is the director to whom the sub-directors report.[88]

II. Mandate and powers

The Directorate is vested with three main supervisory duties[89]:

- To follow up human rights concerns, the prevention of torture and other cruel, inhuman and degrading treatment and cooperation with the Ministry's international partners, in collaboration with the relevant administrative services
- The implementation of human rights-related international conventions and bilateral agreements and those relating to the prevention of crime, the treatment of offenders, genocide and war crimes and all other crimes against humanity, in collaboration with the relevant administrative services and institutions
- To follow up the activities of the International Court of Justice, the International Criminal Court and the United Nations High

Commissioner for Human Rights in collaboration with the Ministry of External Relations
- To follow up the activities of the National Human Rights Commission

To discharge these broad duties, the two sub-departments have been assigned specific areas of competence. For instance, the Sub-Directorate for Human Rights is in charge of all the human rights enforcement-related duties outlined earlier.[90] Thus, it carries out assessments of the human rights situation in Cameroon, produces the Ministry's annual human rights reports, monitors and coordinates the activities of the Ministry on the enforcement of national and international standards of human rights and organises and coordinates the representation of the state before international jurisdictions. In addition, this sub-directorate engages with promotion and sensitisation campaigns on human rights at the level of state and non-state institutions and, in that respect, it acts in collaboration with the National Commission on Human Rights and Freedoms, the UN High Commissioner for Human Rights and all other national and international human rights organisations with an interest in human rights enforcement in Cameroon.

The Sub-Directorate for International Cooperation is essentially focused on cooperation between the Ministry of Justice and Cameroon's national and international partners in the area of human rights.[91] The duties include developing Cameroon's cooperation policy, following up cooperation projects and international negotiations and assessing the level of cooperation between the government and Cameroon's partners in human rights enforcement and in development.

III. Assessment of its role in the protection and promotion of human rights

One major area where the DHRIC has made a significant contribution to human rights is through the publication of the annual human rights reports. These reports provide the government's perspective on the state of human rights in the country and the measures adopted to address some of the human rights concerns. Moreover, the reports give visibility to the situation of human rights in the country to the national and international community. They also provide the opportunity for international jurisdictions to conduct a comparative examination of reports submitted by national and international NGOs. This is important because often discrepancies exist in these reports making it necessary for clarifications to be obtained through more credible processes, for instance, through the oral examination of a country's official reports by the UN Human Rights Committee. State officials are questioned on the basis of the reports of the state and other reports submitted by national and international institutions. The outcome of these sessions and the reports form the basis on which international jurisdictions make recommendations to the government of Cameroon on measures to improve on the human rights situation in the country.

The DHRIC has also contributed significantly to the drafting and adoption of the National Action Plan for the Protection and Promotion of Human Rights (2015–2019) by the Ministry of Justice.[92] This Plan elaborates on the government's objectives in regards to the realisation of human rights of all three generations within the specific period and the strategies to achieving the objectives. Some of the activities that have been successfully carried out include the training of security forces (in collaboration with the National Commission on Human Rights and Freedoms) on the implementation of human rights standards in their practices especially in the areas of personal liberty (detention) and the respect for prisoner's rights (especially freedom from torture and other inhuman and degrading treatment or punishment). These are principal areas where human rights standards have often fallen short and security forces are constantly accused of impunity.[93]

The work of the DHRIC is largely complementary and essentially supervisory. Due to its limited mandate, it does not make binding recommendations to the government on measures to enhance the enforcement of human rights. Moreover, it cannot act unilaterally to impose measures or sanctions on perpetrators of human rights violations. The independence and impartiality of the department is also doubtful, in particular in its assessment of the state of human rights in the country. This can be seen in its annual reports where, often, the state is not criticised for gross violations of human rights. A notable instance is the 2017 report, which, among other things, provides an analysis of the state of human rights in the North-West and South-West regions, which are in a state of crisis. In recounting the chronology of the crisis, the report failed to state that violent altercations were initiated by security forces, a fact which has been confirmed by multiple independent human rights organisations. According to the report, 'On 21 September 2017, activists attacked students on their way to school. The name "Ambazonia" was heard'.[94] The synopsis makes no mention of the abusive role of the security forces but instead appears apologetic to the government's human rights violations. For instance, it implicitly approves the shutting down of the internet and the arrest of the Consortium leaders and justifies it as a measure to prevent 'disinformation campaigns and dissemination of hate messages' against the state. The report states,

> In a bid to address the situation and restore public order, Government temporarily suspended the Internet in North West and South West Regions on 17 January 2017, dissolved the Cameroon Anglophone Civil Society Consortium and the Southern Cameroons National Council (SCNC) and initiated proceedings against several persons including Fontem Neba, Nkongho Agbor Bala, and Mancho Bibixy alias BBC.[95]

While derogation from certain human rights obligations may be permissible during exceptional periods such as a state of emergency, the situation in Cameroon was not officially proclaimed a state of emergency. Moreover, even where derogations may be permissible, certain international human rights standards must be adhered to.[96] This was not applied in Cameroon. It is submitted that the DHRIC must adopt an objective approach in assessing the state of human rights in its annual reports in order to ensure that more objective and credible information is provided to both the national and international community.

Moreover, its supervisory role makes it a feeble institution in terms of the protection of human rights. In addition, it should be an institution that cooperates with the national human rights institution rather than to 'follow up' its activities. The expression 'follow up' seems to suggest that the Ministry of Justice, through the DHRIC, supervises the Commission. That is inconsistent with its supposed independent status and is a factor that might serve to inhibit its effective performance. Both institutions can cooperate for the better protection and promotion of human rights. For instance, the department can be an effective mechanism through which the Commission's recommendations are channelled to the Minister for compulsory action.

Conclusion

The protection of human rights and fundamental freedoms remains a challenge in Cameroon. The constitution purports to respect and provide for these rights, indicating a certain commitment to their fulfilment. The mechanisms for their protection have limited the extent to which effective protection can be achieved. There is a nebulous relationship between legislative provisions on human rights on the one hand and their protection mechanisms on the other. The main challenge in this regard is to decrease the gap between the constitutional and legislative texts and the actual practice of human rights protection. This must commence with a genuine government commitment, backed by effective protection mechanisms.

The national human rights institution can make a significant contribution to the protection and promotion of human rights. There is need for a system of integrating its work into the general protection mechanism of the judiciary such that its work actually complements that of the judiciary, rather than being regarded as an impediment. The government needs to demonstrate its commitment to human rights by providing the Commission with a broad mandate, effective powers and sufficient resources. In addition, the DHRIC must perceive its functions not as the government's advocate but as an institution that reinforces the protection mechanism of the state. It needs to be more independent and objective in assessing the human rights needs of the country, without which it would be incapable of making useful recommendations to the executive.

Notes

1 Law No. 90/052 on the Freedom of Social Communication (FSC); Law No. 90/053 on Freedom of Association; Law No. 90/055 on Public Meetings and Processions; Law No. 90/056 on Political Parties, all promulgated on 19 December 1990.

2 Law No. 90/47 on the State of Emergency; Law No. 90/54 on the Maintenance of Law and Order.

3 See, for instance, Freedom House, 'Freedom in the World 2019: Cameroon Country Report' https://freedomhouse.org/report/freedom-world/2019/cameroon accessed 10 September 2019; US Department of State, '2018 Country Reports on Human Rights Practices: Cameroon' (13 March 2019) https://www.state.gov/wp-content/uploads/2019/03/Cameroon-2018.pdf accessed 10 September 2019.
4 ibid.
5 Office of the UN Commissioner for Human Rights, 'Committee on Economic, Social and Cultural Rights Reviews Cameroon's Report' (Geneva, 21 February 2019) https://www.ohchr.org/EN/NewsEvents/Pages/DisplayNews.aspx?NewsID=24189&LangID=E accessed 27 June 2019.
6 *Eitel Mouelle Kouala v République Fédéral du Cameroun*, Arrêt No. 178/CFJ/CAY of 29 March 1972, affirming that the preamble of the 1972 Constitution declares general principles of law and that it was not justiciable.
7 Charles Fombad, *Constitutional Law in Cameroon* (Wolters Kluwer 2012) 35.
8 Liav Orgad, 'The Preamble in Constitutional Interpretation' (2010) 8(1) *International Journal of Constitutional Law* 714–738.
9 France's Constitutional Court.
10 Decision CC No. 44–71 (1971).
11 Orgad, 'The Preamble in Constitutional Interpretation' (n 8) 714–738; Alec Stone Sweet, *The Birth of Judicial Politics in France: The Constitutional Council in Comparative Perspective* (OUP 1992) 40–44, 66–78.
12 *Kesavanda Baharati v State of Kerala* (1973) 4. SCC 225.
13 In *The People v Nya Henry & 4 Others* (2005) 1 CCLR, 61, the Court affirmed that the presumption of innocence was recognised by the Constitution of Cameroon and also protected under article 11 of the Universal Declaration of Human Rights, to which Cameroon affirms its attachment. It should be noted that the presumption of innocence appears in the preamble of the Constitution.
14 Preamble para 21.
15 Law No. 96/12 of 5 August 1996 on the Framework Law on Environmental Management.
16 For a discussion of the concept of 'duties' in the ACHPR, see Makau Mutua, 'The Banjul Charter and the African Cultural Fingerprint: An Evaluation of the Language of Duties' (1995) 35 *Virginia Journal of International Law* 339–380.
17 Decree No. 2007/003 of 13 July 2007 establishing the National Civic Service for Participation in Development (National Civic Service Decree).
18 Decree No. 2010/384 of 23 December 2010 on the creation, organisation and functioning of the National Civic Service Agency for Participation in Development.
19 National Civic Service Decree, s 2.
20 Decree No. 2012/086 of 9 March 2012 laying down the terms and conditions for participation, supervision and cooperation in the National Civic Service for Participation in Development. Section 2 focuses on conditions of participation and the issuance of certificates to acknowledge participation in the voluntary programme.
21 For a discussion of claw-back clauses in the ACHPR, see Loveness Mapuva, 'Negating the Promotion of Human Rights Through 'Claw-Back Clauses' in the African Charter on Human and Peoples Rights' (2016) 51 *International Affairs and Global Strategy* 1.
22 See Southern Cameroons High Court Law 1955, s 27(1). This concept has been discussed extensively in Nelson Enonchong, 'Public Order and Ordre Public: The Exclusion of Customary Law in Cameroon' (1993) 5 *African Journal of International and Comparative Law* 503.
23 Maurice Kamto, 'Actes de Gouvernement et Droits de L'homme au Cameroun' (UCAC 2000) 4 *Cahier Africain des Droits de L'homme* 135, 151.
24 See, for instance, Law No. 90/054 of 19 December 1990 on the Maintenance of Public Oder, s 2, which permits administrative authorities to detain persons for a

renewable period of fifteen days in order to fight banditry. This manifestly authorises arbitrary detention without judicial supervision in the guise of maintaining public order.

25 US Department of State, '2018 Country Reports on Human Rights Practices: Cameroon' (n 3) 20–22.

26 ibid.

27 ibid.

28 National Commission on Human Rights and Freedoms, 'Report on the State of Human Rights in Cameroon in 2017' 14 http://www.cndhl.cm/sites/default/files/NCHRF_EDH_%202017_0.pdf accessed 29 September 2019.

29 Discussed in Chapter 4.

30 Human Rights Watch, 'Cameroon: Separatist Leaders Appeal Conviction – Grave Questions about Fairness of Trial (3 September 2019) https://www.hrw.org/news/2019/09/03/cameroon-separatist-leaders-appeal-conviction accessed 10 September 2019; Lewis Mudge, 'Cameroon Cracks Down on Opponents: High Court Refuses to Release Opposition Figures' (7 March 2019) https://www.hrw.org/news/2019/03/07/cameroon-cracks-down-opponents accessed 10 September 2019. See also, Nelson Enonchong, 'Human Rights Violations by the Executive: Complicity of the Judiciary in Cameroon?' (2003) 47 *Journal of African Law* 265.

31 Decree No. 90/1459 of 8 November 1990 to set up the National Commission on Human Rights and Freedoms. For further details on the weaknesses of the Decree, see Laura-Stella Enonchong, 'Applying International Standards in Enforcing the Right to Personal Liberty in Cameroon: Prospects and Challenges' (2016) 60(3) *Journal of African Law* 389, 406.

32 For instance, the Commonwealth Secretariat, Legal and Constitutional Affairs Division. *National Human Rights Institutions Best Practice: Manual* (2001) (Commonwealth Best Practice) 9–10. The Commonwealth Best Practice was developed in 2001 by a group of experts convened by the Commonwealth Secretariat. The work of the group was designed to represent all the regions of the Commonwealth. It received assistance from the United Nations High Commission for Human Rights and the Asia Pacific Forum of National Human Rights Institutions.

33 Principles relating to the status and functioning of national institutions for the protection and promotion of human rights, Commission on Human Rights res 1992/54, 3 March 1992, annex: GA res 48/134 of 20 December 1993 (Paris Principles), para B(3). The Paris Principles are the most authoritative international statement on the role and structure of national human rights institutions.

34 Amended by Law No. 2010/4 of 13 April 2010 (the 2004 Law).

35 Law No. 2019/014 of 19 July 2019 relating to the Establishment, Organisation and Functioning of the Cameroon Human Rights Commission (Human Rights Commission Law).

36 The 2004 Law, ss 6 and 7.

37 The 2004 Law, ss 6 and 7.

38 The 2004 Law, ss 11 and 17.

39 Centre for Human Rights and Democracy in Africa, 'Concerns over the Bill to Establish a New Cameroon National Human Rights Commission' (Yaoundé, 3 July 2019) 1 https://www.chrda.org/wp-content/uploads/2019/07/CHRDA-Press-Release-Relating-to-National-HR-Commission-Bill.pdf accessed 11 October 2019.

40 Human Rights Commission Law, ss 12 and 13.

41 Human Rights Commission Law, s 22.

42 Human Rights Commission Law, ss 29 and 30.

43 Human Rights Commission Law, s 34(1).

44 Human Rights Commission Law, s 14(2).

45 Human Rights Commission Law, s 14(3).

46 Human Rights Commission Law, s 13.
47 The Paris Principles require that government representatives should serve only in an advisory capacity. See para B(1)(e).
48 The 2004 Law, s 6(1).
49 The 2004 Law, s 8(1).
50 Human Rights Commission Law, s 12(3).
51 Human Rights Commission Law, s 1(3).
52 2004 Law, s 2.
53 Human Rights Commission Law, s 3(1).
54 2004 Law, s 2.
55 2004 Law, s5.
56 Paris Principles, para A(2). See also, Commonwealth Best Practice, chapter III, section 3.1 at para 1.
57 Commonwealth Best Practice 19.
58 2004 Law, s 2.
59 National Commission on Human Rights and Freedoms, 'Report on the State of Human Rights in Cameroon' 134–135 http://www.cndhl.cm/sites/default/files/EDH%202017bon%20version%20anglaise_1.pdf accessed 29 September 2019.
60 2004 Law, s 2, line 7.
61 2004 Law, s 2, line 8.
62 Presumably, this is necessary for foreign relations and internal administrative purposes. The new law does not require the Commission to inform the Minister.
63 Mabelle Nforchu, 'Know Your Rights: Make a Difference!' N0.22, October–December 2010 *Born Free* (Magazine of the NCHRF) 22–23.
64 UN Centre for Democracy and Human Rights in Central Africa, 'Cameroon Human Rights Commission Adopts Action Plan on Business and Human Rights' (Yaoundé, 28 November 2018) https://unchrd.org/index.php?option=com_content&view=article&id=526%3Acameroon-national-human-rights-commission-adopts-action-plan-on-business-and-human-rights&Itemid=155 accessed 10 October 2019.
65 Human Rights Commission Law, s 5, line 2.
66 Human Rights Commission Law, s 4, line 5.
67 Human Rights Commission Law, s 5, line 6.
68 2004 Law, s 2, line 6.
69 Human Rights Commission Law, s 8; s 9, lines 1 and 2.
70 Human Rights Commission Law, s 9.
71 Paris Principles, para 3(a)(i).
72 These issues have also been raised by a number of domestic human rights organisations. See Centre for Human Rights and Democracy in Africa, 'Concerns over the Bill' 2.
73 Section 28 of the 2004 Law states that defaulters will be liable for penalties under s 370 of the Cameroon Penal Code. The penalties provided under this section of the Penal Code range from a fine of 4.000 CFA to 25.000 CFA (approximately £5–£35), imprisonment from five to ten days, or both imprisonment and fine. This sanctions are now incorporated into section 62 of the Human Rights Commission Law 2019.
74 Tige Gamba, 'Deux Sexagénaires en Attente de Jugement à la Prison Principale de Yoko: Dysfonctionnement Judiciaire ou Déni de Justice?' N0.044, March 2019 *Born Free* (Magazine of the NCHRF) 11–12.
75 Human Rights Watch, 'Government Human Rights Commissions in Africa-Activities' (2001) http://www.hrw.org/reports/2001/africa/cameroon/cameroon2.html accessed 20 June 2019. See also Enonchong, 'Applying International Standards' (n 31) 407.Human Rights Watch, 'Government Human Rights Commissions in Africa-Activities' (2001) http://www.hrw.org/reports/2001/africa/cameroon/cameroon2.html accessed 20 June 2019. See also Enonchong, 'Applying International Standards' (n 31) 407.

76 Victor Afoni, 'Situation in the North West and South West Regions: An Overview of the Crisis' N0.042, April 2018 *Born Free* (Magazine of the NCHRF) 6.
77 Afoni, 'Situation in the North West and South West' 6.
78 National Commission on Human Rights and Freedoms, 'Report on the State of Human Rights in Cameroon' (n 59) 15–16.
79 National Commission on Human Rights and Freedoms, '2017 Activity Report' 35–36, 50 http://www.cndhl.cm/sites/default/files/NCHRF_EDH_%202017_0.pdf accessed 29 September 2019.
80 Guy Essery A Zom, 'Pourquoi La Visite des Prisons?' N0.30, October–December 2012 *Born Free* (Magazine of the NCHRF) 4.
81 See The 2001 Annual Report of the NCHRF at pp 23 and 25, and 2001 Annual Report of the NCHRF at p 14.
82 Observatory for the Protection of Human Rights Defenders, 'Cameroon: Homophobia and Violence Against Defenders of the Rights of LGBT Persons' 14–15, (International Fact Finding Report – February 2015) https://www.fidh.org/IMG/pdf/report_cameroun_lgbti_eng_final.pdf accessed 10 October 2019.
83 National Commission on Human Rights and Freedoms, 'Report on the State of Human Rights in Cameroon' (n 59) 141; The 2001 Annual Report of the NCHRF at pp 14 and 15.
84 National Commission on Human Rights and Freedoms, 'Report on the State of Human Rights in Cameroon' (n 59) 144–145.
85 Serge Ngando Ntone, '23e Session Ordinaire de la CNDHL: Une Situation Financière Précaire' N0.042, April 2018 *Born Free* (Magazine of the NCHRF) 5.
86 Paris Principles, para 2.
87 Decree No. 2005/12 of 15 April 2005, repealed by Decree No. 2012/389 of 18 September 2012 to organise the Ministry of Justice (Ministry of Justice Decree), s 113.
88 Ministry of Justice Decree, s 41(2).
89 Ministry of Justice Decree, s 41(1).
90 Ministry of Justice Decree, s 42(1).
91 Ministry of Justice Decree, s 43(1).
92 Ministry of Justice, *National Action Plan for the Protection and Promotion of Human Rights (2015–2019)* (Cameroon News and Publishing Cooperation 2015).
93 Ministry of Justice, 'National Action Plan' 15–17.
94 Ministry of Justice, 'Report of the Ministry of Justice on Human Rights in Cameroon in 2017' (Yaoundé October 2018) 220 http://www.minjustice.gov.cm/components/com_flexicontent/uploads/rapport_minjustice_2017_en.pdf accessed 2 June 2019.
95 Ministry of Justice, 'Human Rights in Cameroon in 2017' 225.
96 See, for instance, ICCPR, art 4(2)(3).

References

Afoni V, 'Situation in the North West and South West Regions: An Overview of the Crisis' N0.042, April 2018 *Born Free* (Magazine of the NCHRF).

Centre for Human Rights and Democracy in Africa, 'Concerns Over the Bill to Establish a New Cameroon National Human Rights Commission' (Yaoundé, 3 July 2019) https://www.chrda.org/wp-content/uploads/2019/07/CHRDA-Press-Release-Relating-to-National-HR-Commission-Bill.pdf accessed 11 October 2019.

Commonwealth Secretariat, Legal and Constitutional Affairs Division. *National Human Rights Institutions Best Practice: Manual* (2001).

Enonchong N, 'Public Order and Ordre Public: The Exclusion of Customary Law in Cameroon' (1993) *5 African Journal of International and Comparative Law* 503.

Enonchong N, 'Human Rights Violations by the Executive: Complicity of the Judiciary in Cameroon?' (2003) *47 Journal of African Law* 265.

Enonchong L-S, 'Applying International Standards in Enforcing the Right to Personal Liberty in Cameroon: Prospects and Challenges' (2016) *60*(3) *Journal of African Law* 389.

Fombad C, *Constitutional Law in Cameroon* (Wolters Kluwer 2012).

Freedom House, '*Freedom in the World 2019: Cameroon Country Report*' https://freedomhouse.org/report/freedom-world/2019/cameroon accessed 10 September 2019.

Gamba T, *'Deux Sexagénaires en Attente de Jugement à la Prison Principale de Yoko: Dysfonctionnement Judiciaire ou Déni de Justice?'* N0.044, March 2019 *Born Free* (Magazine of the NCHRF).

Human Rights Watch, 'Government Human Rights Commissions in Africa-Activities' (2001) http://www.hrw.org/reports/2001/africa/cameroon/cameroon2.html accessed 20 June 2019.

Human Rights Watch, 'Cameroon: Separatist Leaders Appeal Conviction – Grave Questions about Fairness of Trial' (3 September 2019) https://www.hrw.org/news/2019/09/03/cameroon-separatist-leaders-appeal-conviction accessed 10 September 2019.

Kamto M, 'Actes de Gouvernement et Droits de L'homme au Cameroun' (UCAC 2000) *4 Cahier Africain des Droits de L'homme* 135.

Mapuva L, 'Negating the Promotion of Human Rights Through 'Claw-Back Clauses' in the African Charter on Human and Peoples Rights' (2016) *51 International Affairs and Global Strategy* 1.

Ministry of Justice, *National Action Plan for the Protection and Promotion of Human Rights (2015–2019)* (Cameroon News and Publishing Cooperation 2015).

Ministry of Justice, 'Report of the Ministry of Justice on Human Rights in Cameroon in 2017' (Yaoundé October 2018) 220 http://www.minjustice.gov.cm/components/com_flexicontent/uploads/rapport_minjustice_2017_en.pdf accessed 2 June 2019.

Mudge L, 'Cameroon Cracks Down on Opponents: High Court Refuses to Release Opposition Figures' (7 March 2019) https://www.hrw.org/news/201c9/03/07/cameroon-cracks-down-opponents accessed 10 September 2019.

Mutua M, 'The Banjul Charter and the African Cultural Fingerprint: An Evaluation of the Language of Duties' (1995) *35 Virginia Journal of International Law* 339.

National Commission on Human Rights and Freedoms, 'Report on the State of Human Rights in Cameroon in 2017' http://www.cndhl.cm/sites/default/files/EDH%202017bon%20version%20anglaise_1.pdf accessed 29 September 2019.

National Commission on Human Rights and Freedoms, '2017 Activity Report' http://www.cndhl.cm/sites/default/files/NCHRF_EDH_%202017_0.pdf accessed 29 September 2019.

Nforchu M, 'Know Your Rights: Make a Difference!' N0.22, October–December 2010 *Born Free* (Magazine of the NCHRF).

Ngando Ntone S, '23e Session Ordinaire de la CNDHL: Une Situation Financière Précaire' N0.042, April 2018 *Born Free* (Magazine of the NCHRF).

Observatory for the Protection of Human Rights Defenders, 'Cameroon: Homophobia and Violence Against Defenders of the Rights of LGBT Persons' 14–15 (International Fact Finding Report – February 2015) https://www.fidh.org/IMG/pdf/report_cameroun_lgbti_eng_final.pdf accessed 10 October 2019.

Office of the UN Commissioner for Human Rights, 'Committee on Economic, Social and Cultural Rights Reviews Cameroon's Report' (Geneva, 21 February 2019) https://www.ohchr.org/EN/NewsEvents/Pages/DisplayNews.aspx?NewsID=24189&LangID=E accessed 27 June 2019.

Orgad L, 'The Preamble in Constitutional Interpretation' (2010) *8*(1) *International Journal of Constitutional Law* 714.

Sweet AS, *The Birth of Judicial Politics in France: The Constitutional Council in Comparative Perspective* (OUP 1992).

UN Centre for Democracy and Human Rights in Central Africa, 'Cameroon Human Rights Commission Adopts Action Plan on Business and Human Rights' (Yaoundé, 28 November 2018) https://unchrd.org/index.php?option=com_content&view=article&id=526%3Acameroon-national-human-rights-commission-adopts-action-plan-on-business-and-human-rights&Itemid=155 accessed 10 October 2019.

US Department of State, '2018 Country Reports on Human Rights Practices: Cameroon' (13 March 2019) https://www.state.gov/wp-content/uploads/2019/03/Cameroon-2018.pdf accessed 10 September 2019.

Zom GE, *'Pourquoi La Visite des Prisons?'* N0.30, October–December 2012 *Born Free* (Magazine of the NCHRF).

Conclusion

This book has highlighted the relevance of the institutional structures and mechanisms in contemporary governance in Cameroon and the relevance of the Constitution and legislative texts in determining the extent of their effectiveness. It has also demonstrated the practical difficulties encountered by the institutions in carrying out their functions. A major theme that has featured throughout the discussion is the power imbalance that exists between the three arms of government. Chapter 2 has demonstrated that the Constitution provided for a semi-presidential system, which is purportedly intended to mitigate the overconcentration of powers in the President. However, that same Constitution undermines the advantage of semi-presidentialism by defining prime ministerial powers so narrowly that the executive power in effect rests solely with the President. This creates many problems because, as discussed in Chapters 3 and 4, respectively, both legislative power and judicial power are designed to depend largely on the President. In discussing the institutions and their operational mechanisms, it was clear that, to a large extent, the source of their authority and independence was the President. That applies to the judiciary, the legislature, the Constitutional Council, the National Electoral Commission and the National Commission on Human Rights and Freedoms. Such a system is a challenge to governance.

As the chapters have demonstrated, the issue of the dependence of the institutional structures contributes significantly to the difficulties in establishing democratic and accountable governance as neither parliament nor the judiciary or the Constitutional Council can exercise effective oversight of the government. It explains why the government is unresponsive to the disillusioned population, why it cannot deal effectively with issues like the Anglophone problem or address systematically its persistently poor human rights record. There has been a historical complacency in acknowledging those deficiencies in governance, but recent events demonstrate that there is a certain political awakening that has swept through the country. These events have caused the system of governance to be questioned. They have necessitated an investigation into the current normative framework regulating governance in the country.

In the preceding chapters, a number of recommendations were made with a view to addressing some of the weaknesses identified in the constitutional and legislative texts and in the practical operations of the institutions discussed.

These recommendations, if implemented, have potentials to address those weaknesses, at least in the short term. Nevertheless, this book has endeavoured to show that the current constitutional framework cannot provide scope for a solid foundation for democratic and accountable governance. Crucially, the ideological underpinnings of that Constitution limit the extent to which it can embrace modern features of democracy and accountability. As discussed in Chapter 1, the roots of that Constitution can be traced to the authoritarian Constitution of 1972, which laid down the foundations of a centralised governance system with an authoritarian presidency. The 1996 Constitution did not depart from that authoritarian philosophy. Consequently, the new institutions established under it did not have scope to develop robust accountability mechanisms. The Constitutional Council, for instance, has limited positive influence on democracy and constitutional justice because its powers are restricted inter alia, by mechanisms that depend to a large extent on the President and other politicians. Moreover, amendments made to existing institutions did not provide sufficient scope for these institutions to exercise their powers. For instance, although the judiciary's status was elevated to that of a power, it remains excessively dependent on the President. It is therefore, argued here that Cameroon needs a new constitution designed to create a new system of governance that can respond more effectively to contemporary challenges and represent the will of the people. Such a constitution should provide the necessary institutional mechanisms, processes and conditions that will make the government more democratic and accountable. For instance, if Anglophones demand more respect for their minority rights, how do they get the government to respond? If the electoral system disenfranchises a significant section of the population, how do they get parliament or the Constitutional Council to remedy it? If public authorities violate the rights of citizens, how do they get the judiciary to provide effective remedies? A new constitution should be able to provide satisfactory answers to these questions. The idea is not to paralyse government decision making, but to enable the government to function in a responsive and accountable way.

Some African countries have adopted new constitutions that have set their path of governance on a progressive trajectory. Kenya and Ghana are contemporary examples of countries where a completely new dispensation was engineered by more progressive and popularly adopted constitutions.[1] The argument is not that a 'good' constitution would resolve all the governance challenges that Cameroon is facing. There may be other social or economic factors that have not been addressed in this book and may well contribute to these challenges. Nevertheless, it is contended that the constitution sets the tone and the framework to establish the relevant robust governance institutions, processes and mechanisms.

Constitutional engineering

Pursuant to the preceding argument, a pertinent issue to consider is the method of constitutional engineering. The process of making a new constitution has great significance for the outcome.[2] Considering the 'process' through which the 1996 Constitution was adopted and the trajectory of governance since then, it may be argued that a new dispensation requires a novel approach to constitutional engineering. One method advocated here is a participatory approach to constitution making. This requires that the public is included in the process of constitution making, such that it would be the people acting as constituent power in formulating that foundational document which signifies a new dispensation.[3] Public participation is ubiquitous in recent constitution-making processes and it has received wide support.[4] That approach is advocated for a number of reasons. First, it fosters ownership of the process and the outcome.[5] Second, it lends legitimacy to the document and the governance system that eventually results from it.[6] Third, it is seen as an educational exercise in democracy and a means of promoting the development of a democratic culture.[7] Fourth, it gives a voice to those who would be governed by the constitution, to address past grievances and inequalities, to define their rights and aspirations and how they wish these rights and aspirations to be provided and protected by the government. In Cameroon, the public has largely been relegated to the background of political activity. The government is very centralised and far removed from the populations. A participatory process will allow the populations to contribute to developing a progressive governance system.

Of course, public participation is not a panacea. There is also the possibility that a poorly designed process might undermine the positive dimensions of public participation and instead perpetuate regressive democratic practices. Moreover, the very idea of public participation may indeed be seen as counterproductive in some sections of the population. Yet, comparative examples around the world demonstrate that it is an approach worth pursuing.[8] Recent and ongoing events in Cameroon indicate that, like the turbulent 1990s, a constitutional moment has arrived and, this time, things need to be done correctly.

Notes

1 See Rose Macharia and Yash Ghai, 'The Role of Participation in the Two Kenyan Constitution Building Processes of 2000–2005 and 2010' in Tania Abbiate, Markus Bockenforde and Veronica Federico (eds) *Public Participation in African Constitutionalism* (Routledge 2018) 86–99.

2 See generally Tom Ginsburg, Zachary Elkins and Justin Blount, 'Does the Process of Constitution-Making Matter?' (2009) 5(5) *American Review of Law and Society* 201; Jon Elster, 'Forces and Mechanisms in Constitution-Making' (1995) 45 *Duke Law Review* 364.

3 Tania Abbiate, Markus Bockenforde and Veronica Federico (eds), *Public Participation in African Constitutionalism* (Routledge 2018) 1–2.

4 ibid. See also Jonathan Wheatley and Fernando Mendez (eds), *Patterns of Constitutional Design: The Role of Citizens and Elites in Constitution Making* (Ashgate 2013); Vivien Hart, 'Constitution Making and the Right to Take Part in a Public Affair' in Laurel E Miller (ed) *Framing the State in Times of Transition: Case Studies in Constitution Making* (USIP 2010) 20–56; Joanne Wallis, 'How Important is Participatory Constitution-making? Lessons from Timor-Leste and Bougainville' (2016) 54(3) *Commonwealth and Comparative Politics* 362.

5 Tania Abbiate et al (eds), *Public Participation in African Constitutionalism* (n 3) 1–2.

6 ibid.
7 ibid. See also Macharia and Ghai, 'The Role of Participation in the Two Kenyan Constitution Building Processes' (n 1) 97–98.
8 For an account of the processes and stages in public participation, see Jennifer Widner, 'Constitution Writing in Post-Conflict Settings: An Overview' (2008) 49(4) *William and Mary Law Review* 1513.

References

Abbiate T, Bockenforde M and Federico F (eds), *Public Participation in African Constitutionalism* (Routledge 2018).
Elster J, 'Forces and Mechanisms in Constitution-Making' (1995) *45 Duke Law Review* 364.
Ginsburg T, Elkins Z and Blount J, 'Does the Process of Constitution-Making Matter?' (2009) *5*(5) *American Review of Law and Society* 201.
Hart V, 'Constitution Making and the Right to Take Part in a Public Affair' in Laurel E Miller (ed) *Framing the State in Times of Transition: Case Studies in Constitution Making* (USIP 2010).
Macharia R and Ghai Y, 'The Role of Participation in the Two Kenyan Constitution Building Processes of 2000–2005 and 2010' in Tania Abbiate, Markus Bockenforde and Veronica Federico (eds) *Public Participation in African Constitutionalism* (Routledge 2018).
Wheatley J and Mendez F (eds), *Patterns of Constitutional Design: The Role of Citizens and Elites in Constitution Making* (Ashgate 2013).
Widner J, 'Constitution Writing in Post-Conflict Settings: An Overview' (2008) *49*(4) *William and Mary Law Review* 1513.

Index

www.ingramcontent.com/pod-product-compliance
Ingram Content Group UK Ltd.
Pitfield, Milton Keynes, MK11 3LW, UK
UKHW010959180926
475701UK00004B/452
9780367627324